Beyond the Developmental State

Political Economy and Development

Published in association with the International Initiative for Promoting Political Economy (IIPPE)

Edited by
Ben Fine (SOAS, University of London)
Dimitris Milonakis (University of Crete)

Political economy and the theory of economic and social development have long been fellow travellers, sharing an interdisciplinary and multidimensional character. Over the last 50 years, mainstream economics has become totally formalistic, attaching itself to increasingly narrow methods and techniques at the expense of other approaches. Despite this narrowness, neoclassical economics has expanded its domain of application to other social sciences, but has shown itself incapable of addressing social phenomena and coming to terms with current developments in the world economy.

With world financial crises no longer a distant memory, and neoliberalism and postmodernism in retreat, prospects for political economy have strengthened. It allows constructive liaison between the dismal and other social sciences and rich potential in charting and explaining combined and uneven development.

The objective of this series is to support the revival and renewal of political economy, both in itself and in dialogue with other social sciences. Drawing on rich traditions, we invite contributions that constructively engage with heterodox economics, critically assess mainstream economics, address contemporary developments, and offer alternative policy prescriptions.

Also available

The Political Economy of Development:
The World Bank, Neoliberalism and Development Research
Edited by Kate Bayliss, Ben Fine and Elisa Van Waeyenberge

Theories of Social Capital:
Researchers Behaving Badly
Ben Fine

Dot.compradors:
Crisis and Corruption in the Indian Software Industry
Jyoti Saraswati

BEYOND THE DEVELOPMENTAL STATE

Industrial Policy into the Twenty-First Century

Edited by Ben Fine, Jyoti Saraswati and Daniela Tavasci

www.plutobooks.com

First published 2013 by Pluto Press
345 Archway Road, London N6 5AA

www.plutobooks.com

Distributed in the United States of America exclusively by
Palgrave Macmillan, a division of St Martin's Press LLC,
175 Fifth Avenue, New York, NY 10010

Copyright © Ben Fine, Jyoti Saraswati and Daniela Tavasci 2013

The right of the individual contributors to be identified as the authors of this work has been asserted by them in accordance with the Copyright, Designs and Patents Act 1988.

British Library Cataloguing in Publication Data
A catalogue record for this book is available from the British Library

ISBN	978 0 7453 3317 5	Hardback
ISBN	978 0 7453 3166 9	Paperback
ISBN	978 1 8496 4900 1	PDF eBook
ISBN	978 1 8496 4902 5	Kindle eBook
ISBN	978 1 8496 4901 8	EPUB eBook

Library of Congress Cataloging in Publication Data applied for

This book is printed on paper suitable for recycling and made from fully managed and sustained forest sources. Logging, pulping and manufacturing processes are expected to conform to the environmental standards of the country of origin.

10 9 8 7 6 5 4 3 2 1

Typeset from disk by Stanford DTP Services, Northampton, England
Simultaneously printed digitally by CPI Antony Rowe, Chippenham, UK and Edwards Bros in the United States of America

Contents

Acronyms and Abbreviations   vi

1. Beyond the Developmental State: An Introduction   1
   Ben Fine
2. The Rise and Fall of the Developmental State? The Case of the Japanese and South Korean Steel Industries   33
   Hajime Sato
3. An Alternative Perspective on Industrial Policy: The Case of the South Korean Car Industry   61
   Kwon-Hyung Lee
4. Labour and the 'Developmental State': A Critique of the Developmental State Theory of Labour   85
   Dae-oup Chang
5. What of the Developmental State beyond Catching Up? The Case of the South Korean Microelectronics Industry   110
   Humam Al-Jazaeri
6. Globalisation and the Decline of the Developmental State   146
   Iain Pirie
7. The IT Industry and Interventionist Policy in India   169
   Jyoti Saraswati
8. Lessons for Nigeria from Developmental States: The Role of Agriculture in Structural Transformation   187
   Eka Ikpe
9. Finance and the Developmental State: The Case of Argentina   216
   Daniela Tavasci
10. Systems of Accumulation and the Evolving South African MEC   245
    Sam Ashman, Ben Fine and Susan Newman

References   268
Contributors   297
Index   299

Acronyms and Abbreviations

AAC	Anglo American Corporation
ADP	Agricultural Development Project
ADR	American Depositary Receipt
ANC	African National Congress
ASEAN	Association of Southeast Asian Nations
BOF	Basic Oxygen Furnace
BEE	Black Economic Empowerment
CDMA	Code Division Multiple Access
CKD	Complete Knock-Down Kit
CKTU	Korean Trade Unions
DEP	Department of Economic Policy
DMIU	Digital Monolithic Integrated Unit
DoE	Department of Electronics
DRAM	Dynamic Random-Access Memory
DRI	Directly Reduced Iron
DS	Developmental State
DSP	Developmental State Paradigm
EAF	Electric Arc Furnace
ECIL	Electronics Corporation of India Limited
EDSP	Enhanced Developmental State Paradigm
EIAK	Electronics Industries Association of Korea
EOI	Export-Oriented Industrialisation
EPZ	Economic Processing Zones
FAO	Food and Agriculture Organisation
FDI	Foreign Direct Investment
FLACSO	Facultad Latinoamericana de Ciencias Sociales (Latin American School of Social Sciences)
GDP	Gross Domestic Product
GEAR	Growth, Employment and Redistribution
GM	General Motor
GNP	Gross National Product
HCI	Heavy and Chemical Industry
HSRC	Human Sciences Research Council
IC	Integrated Circuit
IFI	International Financial Institution
INDEC	Instituto Nacional de Estadística y Censos (National Institute of Statistics and Censuses)

IPAP	Industrial Policy Action Plan
IRDP	Integrated Rural Development Project
ISI	Import-Substitution Industrialisation
IT	Information Technology
KD	Knock-Down
KMT	Kuomintang: The Chinese National Party
KTCU	Korean Confederation of Trade Unions
M&As	Mergers and Acquisitions
MAIT	Manufacturers' Association of Information Technology
MEC	Minerals–Energy Complex
MERG	Macro Economic Research Group
MITI	Ministry of International Trade and Industry
MNC	Multinational Corporation
NASSCOM	Association for Software and Service Companies
NEITI	Nigerian Extractive Industries Transparency Initiative
NFC	National Finance Corporation
NGP	New Growth Path
NIC	Newly Industrialised Country
NIE	Newly Industrialising Economies
NIPF	National Industrial Policy Framework
OBM	Own Brand Manufacturing
ODM	Original Design Manufacturing
OEM	Original Equipment Manufacturing
OHF	Open Hearth Furnace
PRSP	Poverty Reduction Strategy Paper
RCA	Revealed Comparative Advantage
R&D	Research and Development
RDP	Reconstruction and Development Programme
SACP	South African Communist Party
SKD	Simple Knock-Down Kit
SMEs	Small- and Medium-Sized Enterprises
STP	Software Technology Park
UNESCO	United Nations Educational, Scientific and Cultural Organisation
VLSI	Very-Large-Scale Integration
WTO	World Trade Organisation
YPF	Yacimientos Petrolíferos Fiscales

1
Beyond the Developmental State: An Introduction[1]

Ben Fine

1.1 INTRODUCTION

In their edited collection entitled *Deconstructing Development Discourse: Buzzwords and Fuzzwords*, Cornwall and Eade (2010) range over 30 or so entries that critically unpick the more prominent concepts that have been deployed in the study and practice of development. These include poverty reduction, social protection, globalisation, participation, citizenship, empowerment, social capital, gender, sustainability, rights, NGOs, social movements, country ownership, transparency, accountability, corruption, governance, fragile states, knowledge, and so on. 'Developmental state' is notably absent. Indeed, 'state' itself only appears as a heading within one entry: 'fragile state'. This is not an oversight or error on the part of the editors, but a genuine reflection of the nature and extent to which the (developmental) state has been written in and out of development discourse by 30 years of neoliberalism. To put it crudely, the term 'developmental state' could not have been expected to become prominent, given that it is a point of critical departure from orthodoxy, and so unlikely to have been adopted, let alone promoted, by the World Bank.

Yet, whilst development and the state are everywhere in the Bank's activities, the developmental state is nowhere. The contrast for the entry in the collection on 'social capital' (Fine 2010e) is striking, not least because of that concept's heavy promotion by the World Bank at the close of the millennium and its use as a device to outflank and marginalise the adoption of the developmental state in the shift from the Washington Consensus to the post-Washington Consensus (Fine 1999, 2001). In the event, containing any potential radical content and implications of the post-Washington Consensus needed at most to draw only temporarily on the notion of social capital and, within the new millennium, it has been as rapidly abandoned as it was previously promoted by the World Bank (see Fine 2010a and 2011 for a full account and Bayliss, Fine and Van Waeyenberge 2011 for the trajectory of World Bank research more generally).

The limited influence of the developmental state paradigm (DSP, as we shall refer to it throughout this volume) is all the more unfortunate in light of the responses to the global crisis that broke from 2007. It might have been expected that one of the consequences of the crisis would have been to have shattered the confidence in neoliberal policymaking in general and for finance in particular, especially given the huge support given by 'neoliberal' states to private finance, which had been promoted so strenuously and had benefited from the liberalisation of financial markets. But, despite the role of the state in rescuing finance, reconsideration of its interventions on a grander scale across the economy has been extremely limited. Indeed, orthodox prescriptions of austerity have been adopted for all but the bankers.

Thus, despite the desperate need for alternatives, for developing and developed countries alike, these have not emerged; and, by the same token, the DSP has not prospered as buzz, fuzz or otherwise – something that might have been anticipated in the wake of the crisis, with the need to get the state and development, and not just finance, back on track. This is not to suggest that the DSP has remained stuck in a time warp of its own making, and of establishment neglect, arising out of the earlier experiences of success from the East Asian NICs. Indeed, the DSP has continued to evolve, as will be charted in this book. But how and with what influence are highly dependent on more general material and intellectual developments.

One thing in particular is notable: so successful has been the neoliberal project that, even in its crisis of legitimacy, the developmental state has with few exceptions failed to emerge as a prominent alternative as a response to, or in anticipation of, the crisis. The purpose of this book is less to explain why the developmental state should have failed in this way than to examine its strengths and weaknesses as an approach to development (without simply presuming that the approach has remained unpopular because of its weaknesses and despite its strengths – its failure has had much more to do with the stranglehold that neoliberalism has exerted over this field of study).

In this light, this Introduction proceeds in the next section by providing an overview of the DSP, pointing to two broad strands in the literature, known as the economic and political schools. This is followed in Section 1.3 by an account of, and explanation for, the extent to which the developmental state approach has been self-limiting. It has been unduly preoccupied with East Asian NICs, taking the Washington Consensus as point of departure; heavily confined to an inductive methodology, focusing upon development as a particular phase of industrialisation; and, within that, drawn to a narrow notion of industrial policy itself (especially, if not exclusively, of trade policy and directed finance). To some extent, the DSP cuts across the 'flying geese' paradigm, the more so as late latecomer developers insert themselves, or are inserted, into a global division of labour. The flying geese paradigm is critically assessed in Section 1.4, immediately followed in Section 1.5 by a discussion of the relationship between the potential for development and the impact of China both as exemplar (of a developmental state) and as a threat or opportunity to those who aspire to be a developmental state. That China is increasingly seen as a developmental state is indicative of the buzzword character of the DSP; this is more generally reflected in the most recent literature and discussed in Section 1.6. Further, the broader the DSP's scope of application, the more both its previous limited scope of application and its limitations are exposed. Section 1.7 outlines an alternative approach to the DSP that draws critically, in part, upon the DSP literature as point of departure, offering a broader framework for the case studies that follow and the comparative lessons that can be drawn from them. And the final section concludes by pointing to the dilution and marginalisation of the DSP over the past 20 years, as reflected in the less than spirited response to the latest postures of the World Bank on approaches to development.

1.2 TWIXT ECONOMIC AND POLITICAL SCHOOLS

What is it that characterises a developmental state, and what makes it so? Answers to these apparently simple questions are elusive. This is not just because of denial of the potential for, or desirability of, the developmental state in deference to the market, in accordance with the Washington Consensus. For nor does the developmental state paradigm itself offer satisfactory responses. One reason for this is the tension between the *universal* applicability of the DSP (its analytical framework should apply everywhere, in principle, explaining, as required, both success and *failure*) and its frequent confinement in practice to examples of success.

This tension, and the way in which it has been resolved, is brought out by acknowledging that the DSP readily, if roughly, divides into two separate schools (as highlighted in successive surveys of the DSP literature: Fine and Stoneman 1996; Fine and Rustomjee 1996; Fine 2005, 2006, 2007, 2010b, 2010c; Ashman, Fine and Newman 2010a); each of these schools emphasises a different explanation of how successful development has been (or might be) achieved, this being the goal of the developmental state literature.[2]

For the first of these, the economic school, the focus is on those policies that are necessary for an economy to achieve development. Drawing primarily on the idea that markets do not work perfectly and, correspondingly, upon economics as a discipline, the state is required to accrue, for example, the economies of scale and scope, to coordinate investments within and across sectors, to harness positive and eliminate negative externalities, and so on. For the economic school, then, it is a matter of identifying the appropriate policies, with the presumption that they will, or might, be implemented by a developmental state because they ought to be.

By contrast, and completely complementarily, the political school, with its own disciplinary origins predominantly from within political science (and certainly separate from economics), is remarkably aloof from consideration of the economy itself and the nature of the policies required to bring about development. Rather, the political school is concerned with the nature of the state itself and whether it has the potential in general, and the independence in particular, to adopt the necessary developmental policies more or less irrespective of what these might be. Here emphasis is placed upon the necessity for the developmental state to be free of capture by particular interests, and so to be able to implement appropriate policies.

Taken together, the economic and political schools address what policies are to be adopted and what allows them to be adopted. Nevertheless, merging the two schools together does not lead to a satisfactory analytical framework, for reasons that will emerge below. However, successful cases of development in practice can be interpreted through this dual prism, and such is a major methodological thrust of both schools. For each has been highly inductive in practice, examining the role of economic policy in bringing about development and the nature of the states adopting such policies. This is not to suggest, however, that the developmental state literature has been without theory or analytical content. The economic school, for example, strongly emphasises the significance of market imperfections and the role of a developmental state in addressing (if not necessarily correcting) them. In highlighting the departure from neoliberalism, Amsden (1989) famously declared that it was a matter of 'getting relative prices wrong', of not conforming to the dictates of the market.[3] In principle, the economic school could have drawn upon orthodox economics and its deductive methods, especially in its emphasis upon market imperfections. In practice, though, as indicated, it has been drawn towards more inductive case study methods, and it has generally been characterised by a mutual suspicion of orthodoxy even when the latter is itself based on market imperfections.[4]

Similarly, the political school has tried to identify empirically what characterises the nature of the states, and the societies containing them, in which development has proved possible. Posing this in terms of the independence of the state from economic and other interests has itself presumed an analytical approach in which society is structured along the lines of the state as opposed to the market, with the addition of civil society to fill out the remaining economic, political and ideological space. In this way, not only is the (developmental) state seen as potentially independent (the term favoured is 'autonomous'); it is also perceived to evolve interests, an ethos, or practices of its own that prevail over those of the market and civil society, especially where these conflict with developmentalism. This approach of the political school is admirably captured in the notion of 'bringing the state back in' as an agent of development in its own right (Evans, Rueschemeyer and Skocpol 1985).[5]

Across both economic and political schools, then, there is a predilection to set up an opposition between state and market. For the economic school, the state overrules the market and so is able to improve upon it. For the political school, the state needs to stand aloof from the market, and the economic interests found within it. The result has been to downplay the role of class in the analysis (Radice 2008). With the economic school, considerations of class do not tend to appear at all; it is simply a matter of identifying the right policies, not whether they have sufficient support to be implemented, or on whose behalf, or to whose benefit. On the other hand, matters are not so simple for the political school. It is not that class interests are absent; but it is important that the state has the capacity to neutralise if not to override them. And, of overwhelming importance even if so much is taken for granted as to remain more or less unstated, there is a total preoccupation with the nation state and its capacity to bring about development irrespective of the impact of international or global factors.[6] This does not mean that the global is absent; only that it needs to be incorporated as an influence on the policies to be adopted or the attainment of independence in policymaking that is either positive (availability of catch-up technology, for example) or negative (competition from imports).[7]

Such are the general characteristics of the economic and political schools; but the developmental state literature has a rhythm of greater or lesser prominence and a more detailed content that are in conformity with more general events and intellectual trends. Early traces of the economic school are to be found in the protectionism associated with Friedrich List in the nineteenth century; for the political school, developmentalism is associated with nation building through industrial and military strength.[8] Latin American import substitution industrialisation from the 1930s until the 1980s is seen as successful (economic school), until radical populism placed undue burdens upon the state (political school).[9] But the developmental state comes of age with the rise of the East Asian NICs in the post-war period. The classic case study derives from Johnson (1982) from within the political school, and emphasises the role played by the Japanese trade and industry ministry, MITI. Significantly, Johnson (2006), a former CIA analyst, admitted that this study had been motivated by support for the USA in its Cold War aspirations; he advised that, judging from the experience of Japan, the unrealistic and abstract propositions derived from neoliberalism would not bring about capitalist development and would make Soviet prescriptions more attractive (Johnson is particularly scathing of the propositions derived from mainstream economics).

But, although still acknowledged as a classic contribution that is unique in modern times in its message of the need for a powerful state agent to underpin industrialisation (and with a case study giving a close account of Japan as a latecomer), the ensuing literature on the developmental state focused its critical attention entirely upon the target of neoliberalism in general and the Washington Consensus in particular, whose own version of neoliberalism could only scarcely have been anticipated by Johnson just a few years before. By contrast, by the mid-1980s, inspired by the developmental successes of the East Asian NICs and the unremitting hostility to state intervention being displayed by both the World Bank and the IMF, the DSP became one of the two leading strands of criticism of the conditions being attached to these organisations' offers of aid.[10] Apart from Amsden's (1989) study of South Korea's industrialisation, Wade's (1990) account of Taiwan's, offering the mantra of 'governing the market', also rapidly became a classic.

The growing intellectual momentum of the DSP in the wake of the success of the East Asian NICs, and the incontrovertible evidence of extensive state intervention in these countries, was complemented by the growing sense of failure, indeed a crisis of legitimacy, of the Washington Consensus as the 1980s was appropriately seen as a lost decade as far as development elsewhere in the world was concerned. In the early 1990s, the Japanese funded a study to reassess the role of the state in the East Asian NICs. It had three good reasons to do so. First, the Washington Consensus denied the historical reality of its own latecomer success. Second, it was on the point of becoming the leading donor to developing countries. And, third, most important of all, its own industrial strategy, of contracting out less technology-intensive production to countries within the Asia–Pacific Rim, required for success that this be supported by appropriate local industrial policies. Japan could hardly be expected to continue to pay for policies that it knew both to be based on falsehood and to be against its own interests![11]

In the event, the World Bank's (1993) report on the East Asian NICs proved a remarkable piece of intellectual acrobatics. It did not deny that the state had intervened extensively, but suggested that it had done so in a way that was 'market-conforming', doing what the market would have done had it been working perfectly. It further suggested that the conditions which had allowed for this were not to be found replicated elsewhere. Essentially, the relevance of the East Asian NICs as a model or models for development was discounted, except to confirm the rule of following, or conforming to, the market.[12]

Whether such a contorted logic could have prevailed for long is a moot point, especially given the shifting contradictory relationship between the scholarship, rhetoric, policy and representation of reality that emanates from the World Bank (Bayliss, Fine and Van Waeyenberge 2011). But the logic did not persist in any case, though this was for reasons that witnessed, not the triumph of the developmental state paradigm, but its demise from the middle of the 1990s. First and foremost, the Asian financial crises of 1997/8 cast a long shadow over the region's economic miracle, some economists even denying that it had ever occurred and arguing that it had simply reflected the heavy accumulation of resources as opposed to disproportionate increases in productivity.[13] Second, though, the second half of the 1990s also witnessed the shift in the World Bank from the Washington to the post-Washington Consensus, inspired and launched by Joe Stiglitz in 1997 as chief economist at the Bank. Underpinning this shift within the neoliberal paradigm is the idea of market and institutional imperfections as the source of failing economic performance, and for policy to be addressed at correcting these in a piecemeal fashion. In addition to a more favourable stance in principle towards the state, the Bank also placed emphasis upon good governance, the elimination of corruption, empowerment and democracy, all elements that were supposed to enable the state to act developmentally.

As a result, if in its own way, and at a microeconomic as opposed to a systemic level as far as the economics is concerned, the concerns of the developmental state had been at least partially addressed by the new Bank orthodoxy, but in a way that meant that the term never had to be used. The 'market versus state' agenda set by the World Bank gave way to one of 'market plus state'. Symbolically, the person who continues to be seen as leading proponent of the developmental state, Ha-Joon Chang, both tends not to use the term himself and aligned himself with the post-Washington Consensus, at least to the extent of editing a volume of Stiglitz's contributions on his new paradigm (Chang 2001).[14]

In addition, the constraining influence of the Washington Consensus on the DSP has been felt through the division of labour that emerged in critique of that consensus, with the parallel assault of the 'Adjustment with a Human Face' approach. On the one hand, this occupied the subject matter of what might have helped to contribute a more rounded approach to industrialisation, let alone development, instead of assigning it to another stream of endeavour around poverty alleviation that could also be picked off separately in the post-Washington Consensus, ultimately leading to PRSPs. On the other hand, considerations of welfare posed difficulties for the developmental state approach, not least because of a conventional wisdom that it had been sacrificed in the interests of industrialisation and that this, once wedded to authoritarianism, offered a less glowing account of achievement. For the developmental state paradigm, it was both sufficient and more appealing for it to limit itself to industrialisation and a narrow conception of industrial policy, at the expense of a broader notion of development, and to contest only parts of the analytical and policy terrain addressed by the Washington Consensus, primarily through an inductive methodology accepting a market-imperfections view of the world, whether through a systemic approach or otherwise.

And possibly most important from an academic point of view, the terrain and appeal commanded by the DSP was severely constrained by broader intellectual developments across the social sciences as a whole and in addressing development in particular.

Over its short life, the inductive (and more informal) approach of the economic school has been contemptuously dismissed by the axiomatic deductivism and econometric methods associated with mainstream economics, especially the new development economics, which has displayed total intolerance for any approach other than its own (Fine 2009a; 2010d). And the political school, again with a heavy dose of inductive realism around what makes for embedded relative autonomy, has tended to fall foul of postmodernist trends within development studies. On either side, the developmental state approach has tended to find itself shunned by both orthodoxy and more radical heterodoxy. And this has only been compounded by the rise of what has been the most significant concept across the social sciences in the last two decades, globalisation. For this concept has allowed for the nature and salience of the state in promoting development (or not) in the contemporary world to be addressed in ways that are more general, more wide-ranging and have, as a result, sidelined notions of the developmental state.

For a decade or so following the Asian crisis, then, the DSP went into decline. But it is important to recognise that doubts about its continuing relevance had already been sown amongst its own practitioners before the crisis struck, particularly as far as South Korea in particular is concerned. The South Korean model of the developmental state eventually involved a focus on what might be termed the Giants of Asia's 'Next Giant', to be found within the conglomerate chaebol system. Even before the financial crisis of 1997, it was being argued that the developmental state had become a victim of its own success, possibly as the result of a general rule. For, in South Korea, for example, it had spawned the chaebol and, hence, a powerful class of capitalists who were now in a position to challenge and, ultimately, to prevail over the state.[15] In addition, the working class also becomes more numerous, organised and powerful with development (as industrialisation), and demands for democratisation challenged the authoritarian origins of the state's autonomy.[16]

Indeed, such insights inevitably informed the eruption of diagnoses over the causes of the crisis that emerged so rapidly, despite their failure to anticipate its occurrence. In crudest form, they placed emphasis on corruption and rent-seeking at the expense of the state and of coordinated industrial policy; more subtle was the idea of the demise of powers of the state over the chaebol as these pursued the state's favour through diversified profitable outlets in industry as well as property, financial and international markets; as already mentioned, there were those prepared to deny there had ever been a miracle; and yet others who emphasised the failure of the state to be able to hold off any longer the interventions of international capital as it sought, not without willing domestic partners, both to deregulate the state's control of finance and to open the economy's productive basis and markets to foreign multinationals.[17] In short, following the crisis, the DSP suffered for a decade or so from being outflanked by the new post-Washington Consensus orthodoxy at the Bank and, paradoxically, by a pincer movement of being caught between the consequences of developmental success (capitalists emerging to challenge autonomy) and a revisionist interpretation of failure in the wake of the Asian financial crisis.

1.3 ON TARGET BUT LIMITED?

Yet, one of the unnoticed and essential features of the original DSP literature, which persisted with minor exception up to the new millennium, is the extent to which it has been extraordinarily self-limiting, especially the economic school. From the review given above, it is instructive to examine this in some detail. First and foremost, based on its inductive method of identifying developmental states, and explaining them in terms of the policies adopted and the capacity to adopt them, case studies within the developmental state literature have been self-selecting. Elsewhere, this has been parodied as a law of economics (Fine 2010c), that wherever there is developmental success (or not), the developmental state paradigm will be more or less casually applied and will prosper.[18] Of course, this is a process of self-limitation in practice rather than in principle. For, from a logical point of view, failed developmental states – those economies that did not adopt the right policies (if for unexplained reasons) or were unable to do so (because of insufficient autonomy of the right type) – should also fall within the paradigm as case studies.

In the event, this latter logic has not been followed other than cursorily. Rather, the literature has proceeded primarily, but not exclusively, by providing a cumulative basket of successful case studies, with East Asia to the fore, and a few bright spots elsewhere such as Botswana, Mauritius, and the Republic of Ireland (see Maundeni 2002 and Robinson 2009, Meisenhelder 1997, and O'Hearn 2000 and Riain 2000, respectively). For the economic school, this has commendably led to the conclusion that there is no single model for the developmental state: the different East Asian economies have little in common. In a sense, this is all illustrated by the thrust of Chang's (2002, 2007) work and message: that the developmental states of the past (the developed countries of today) did experience a wide variety of conditions and causes but these were all quite different from the recommendations for both economic and non-economic policies that they currently offer to the developing world (especially as regards neoliberalism and the premature burdens of democracy and modernisation). In this way, the failures of developmental states (or, more exactly, of development) are explained, if only implicitly, as being due to divergence from one or other developmental state model, rather than being closely examined from within the broader application of the DSP itself.

The political school avoids this single-minded preoccupation with those developmental states that have succeeded, instead attempting to tease out the surrounding conditions explaining why appropriate policies could be adopted rather than being subverted by special (non-developmental) interests derived, normally, from the economy but also potentially from civil society. Recall that the rationale underlying the examination of ever more case studies is to identify conditions under which the state is able to act independently or even to have a (developmental) interest of its own. Indeed, initially, the presence of a developmental state (through MITI for Japan for example) was taken as sufficient evidence of the required state autonomy. But, obviously, this does not probe very deeply into the social, political, cultural and ideological circumstances that both create such preconditions and allow them to prevail over other causal factors and interests. The search was mounted, again within an inductive framework, for the sources of what became somewhat inconsistently known as relative, or embedded, autonomy – a growing recognition for the paradigm that the state had to be both independent of, and yet responsive to and controlling of, other structures, processes and agents 'in thick social relationships with various institutions of society' (Khondker 2008, p.36). This seems to be a matter of bringing back in what has been left out of the state when bringing back in the state as an autonomous agent!

Not surprisingly, as the number of case studies of relative, embedded autonomy grew, the conditions found to be of relevance became more numerous and refined. The literature has offered attention to consensus, institutions, political participation, authoritarianism, inclusion and exclusion, the international environment, bureaucratic cohesion, depoliticisation, weakness and strength, efficacy, adaptability, networks, politics in all of its forms (leadership choice, regime maintenance, and interaction between economic performance and coalition formation), and social structure, comprising class, gender, ethnicity, culture and religion.[19] In this respect, at least for the political school, the paradox is that limitation to political capacity to deliver developmental policy has led to unlimited scope for case studies to incorporate both successes and failures.

The difference with the economic school, with the latter's tendency to shy away from failure, is explained, despite a common inductive methodology, by the extent to which much state failure in economic policy cannot in and of itself be readily distinguished from the instances of success from within the economic school. For both success and failure of intervention breach with the dogma of relying exclusively upon the market – where (especially for pro-market orthodoxy) does developmentalism end and rent-seeking and corruption take over? By contrast, because it does not look at the economy as such, and takes the distinction between successful developmental states and unsuccessful states as its starting point, the political school can round up the evidence across as many states and as many variables as it chooses, and seek to discover empirical regularities in the determination of success or failure. In this, it has some sort of advantage over the economic school, which can only, for example, insist that some degree of protection is essential for developmental success, but cannot guarantee it. On the other hand, the results of the political school are far from solid and are unable to offer simple nostrums around the relationship between authoritarianism, say, and developmentalism. There are also too many variables that can be added to the unpicking of relative, embedded autonomy, and there seem to be no fixed interactions between them, although the results swing towards democracy and against authoritarianism as we move forward in time (in line with more progressive stances that consider equality to be good for growth, etc.). But, by being more rounded than the economic school in addressing state success *and* failure, the political school becomes vulnerable to being outflanked by a literature that addresses the same issue whilst totally ignoring the DSP, precisely as good governance, institutional analysis, etc., come to the fore, not least with the desire to identify and explain the African dummy for poor performance, for example (Jerven 2011).

The limitation to successful developmental states, most notably for the economic school (other than in critique of the rest as relying too heavily upon neoliberal prescriptions, something that need not arise for the political school more concerned with internal politics and external influences), has inevitably involved a self-limitation with a regional bias towards East Asia as the preferred area of application of the DSP. Africa, for example, is notable for the relative absence of corresponding case studies (Mkandawire 2001). But, surely, if adoption of the right interventionist policies is able to explain success in East Asian NICs, it ought equally to be possible to explain failure elsewhere by their lack of adoption, or by the adoption of the wrong policies. The point here, and it will recur across other issues around the self-limiting scope of the developmental state approach, is to question what it is that the approach applies to, how wide is its explanation, whether it explains success as well as failure, and whether or not this is a matter of self-confinement in its causal principles or analytical framework. Simple propositions concerning the necessity of state intervention, given that markets do not work perfectly, seem to be extremely wide in application, more or less without limit, as opposed to being confined to developmental success alone (and within a particular region of the globe). And, by the same token, the concerns of the political school around the conditions which allow for efficacy in state intervention (whatever that might be in practice) are also not confined to accounts of developmental success in particular parts of the world, or for particular phases of development. This is especially the case for large-scale statistical cross-country exercises, as opposed to more informal individual case studies, where the choice of success over failure often continues to loom large even for the political school.

Precisely because of the narrow geographical confines of the developmental state approach, this book has included case studies on a much wider terrain, especially from Africa (Chapters 8 and 10, taking in Nigeria and South Africa). India is also covered, not least because its supposedly miraculous development over the recent period defies the DSP by being putatively associated with attachment to neoliberal policies, especially for services associated with new technology (Chapter 7).[20] In this way, the approach is both stretched in its application and critically assessed for the extent to which its more general propositions stand up to scrutiny in a wider context. Much the same interrogation of the self-imposed limits of the DSP is salient across issues other than its geographical scope. The literature, for example, has been almost exclusively concerned with development as the phase of industrialisation associated with catch-up by latecomers. But development also depends upon an earlier phase of transition from an agrarian economy, raising the role of the developmental state in this phase (Chapter 8), quite apart from those economies that might draw on natural resource exports as a source of surplus for industrialisation. Has the developmental state literature nothing to say, as seems to be the case, on the resource-curse thesis – the idea that ready export earnings discourage development? Even leaving this aside, how do we explain how successful developmental states, whether across time or across sectors, do also experience failure, as illustrated in Chapter 3 for the South Korean car industry and Chapter 2 for the Japanese and Korean steel industries at various times? Of course, the answer is that the state was not developmental at those times! And, further, what of the developmental state once it has caught up? – can it maintain its place at the frontier or even forge the way towards being a leader (Chapter 5)? Such issues are found to be of significance for the continuing performance of the East Asian NICs and range beyond the normal limits of the DSP.

Not surprisingly, given its emphasis on East Asian NICs, and the particular phase in the process of development attached to latecomer, catch-up industrialisation, the DSP has been drawn into assessing industrial policy at the expense of other policy and aspects of the process of development and even of other stages of development, including those of industrialisation itself except for latecomer catch-up. Most obviously absent is the role of agriculture, in and of itself, and as a crucial catalyst to industrialisation in providing a source of surplus for investment, thereby alleviating savings constraints, labour for industrial employment, demand for domestically produced industrial goods, and measures to enhance productivity of agriculture itself. The same applies to the role of other primary products in development, not least oil (see Chapter 8). It is, of course, not accidental that such considerations derive from seeking to extend and strain the DSP to incorporate the classic concerns of the old development economics. And, by the same token, whilst there are extensive literatures on both agriculture and development (not least for the successful developmental states), these tend not to have been incorporated into the DSP itself.

1.4 FROM FLYING GEESE …

And much the same is true of closer consideration of different stages of industrial development themselves other than that of latecomer catch-up. The exception in this respect is the 'flying geese' approach.

This has two aspects. On the one hand are the dynamic linkages from one sector to another, with potentially increasing degree of technical sophistication and value added as we move through the flock. Here, once again, limitations have arisen through taking the Washington Consensus as point of departure. For the neoliberal reliance upon getting the prices right, perceiving the state as a source of corruption and rent-seeking, and denying its capacity to pick and promote winners, induced corresponding counterclaims around these factors alone. Consequently, the result again was not only to focus upon industrial policy, but also to frame it in a narrow way, straying little beyond trade policy, preferential access to finance, and coordination and promotion of investment within and across sectors. But this tends to leave a number of vital elements of industrial policy (or factors within industrial policy) out of the picture – such as skills and the labour market, the role of the financial system more generally than directed finance, and technology policy.[21] It seems more or less to have been assumed that these will fall into place by virtue of other policies as prime movers.

On the other hand, the idea of a 'flying geese' strategy serves to highlight the shifting international division of labour between, or across, national economies, as those at lower levels of development and wages and skills take on the relocated manufacturing roles of those already upgrading or upgraded to higher stages of industrialisation. The classic case is Japan's investment strategy into the Asia–Pacific Rim in the last decades of the twentieth century, although China currently presents a more complex picture as it both leads the geese of follower nations and competes with them. This and a closer examination of historical experience in terms of (and increasingly at the expense of) the metaphor adopted suggest questioning whether geese fly in a two-dimensional V-shaped pattern or formation alone, and whether other birds or creatures might not either join the flock or even challenge the hierarchy within it. A failure to consider such questions results in a limited form of technological determinism that strains both the evidence and the potential for policies that breach with, or progress beyond, confinement to latecomer catch-up that preserves the existing order in the international division of labour, a confinement that has indeed been broken by the East Asian NICs in the past, with China possibly ready to repeat the exercise in its own fashion.[22]

Thus, certainly, labour-intensive industries in the first instance can then form the basis for a 'flying geese' pattern of upgrading into linked higher value, skilled and more capital-intensive production

(Shafaeddin 2005, p.1153; Haque 2007, p.6).[23] What will mark the (success of the) earlier stages of such processes is the extent and sustainability of markets against volatility and competition. This means a premium both on export markets and on domestic production for domestic markets deploying domestic resources. The latter can neatly dovetail with the provision of a number of basic needs. But it remains essential to acknowledge that such stylised forms of progress may not be the only ones, and must be subjected to investigation as such, even if they are the only options available, in order to identify shifting potential in light of technological imperatives and domestic and global market and other economic and social conditions.

This is also, however, to raise the issue of global factors, both logically and analytically. Not every latecomer can catch up, otherwise there would never be leaders, despite the pressures on economies to gain and sustain technological advance. Indeed, much of the DSP's latecomer catch-up perspective neglects not only the earlier stages of industrialisation, but also the later stage of being on the frontier itself (as if, once the finishing line has been reached, the story is over). That staying at the front is neither simple nor automatic is evidenced by Japan's industrial travails over the past two decades, whilst the record of the East Asian NICs more generally of getting beyond the frontier remains mixed, contingent on the nature of the technologies, consumer products and the strategies of incumbents (the original geese).[24]

1.5 ... TO THE CHINA SYNDROME

And as mentioned, the closely studied impact of China is also relevant in suggesting wider origins and destinations for foreign direct investment. Thus, the increasing spread of sources of foreign direct investment is indicative both of enhanced opportunities (availability of, and competition between, sources) and of the erosion of potential for national developmental strategies insofar as there is dependence on global value chains or networks.

On the lessons to be learned in assessing the impact of China itself, there are burgeoning literatures. Here, a few simple assertions are offered from this literature.[25] First, in the past, Chinese economic development has been primarily based on rapidly expanding *domestic* markets. This has been accompanied by relatively rapid growth in labour productivity, contingent upon very high levels of investment, and has given rise to increasing real wages and even to the emergence of shortages for skilled labour.

Second, export growth has more recently been of increasing importance, with a corresponding widening of China's trade surplus; but this has been associated with relatively lower levels of wages for employment in sectors attached to foreign direct investment, particularly those geared towards the processing trade. Whilst this growth has been large enough at least to account for China's total trade surplus, its contribution to value added is no more than 5 per cent of Chinese GDP, more or less conforming to an enclave-type economy typically found across multinational corporation activity across the world within export-processing zones, etc. But this should not be taken as being typical of, nor predominant in, the Chinese economy and its success.

Third, the dependence of China upon banks for finance for industrial investment is staggering. As Carney (2009) reveals, bank investment is proportionately roughly four times higher than for the United States, and at least double that of most other countries. This is, however, indicative of the *limited* extent of financialisation of the Chinese economy, since finance has derived primarily from state-owned banks that have been policy driven. Of course, this does not guarantee developmental success in the absence of other conditions; but such conditions are precisely what have been present in China, where, nonetheless, development is fraught with the tensions associated with sustaining international competitiveness and domestic economic and social stability.

Fourth, this is indicative of China's totally breaking away from Washington Consensus policies in general, and in particular from those prescribed for transition economies (where the outcomes by comparison with Eastern Europe are salient).[26] Significantly, for a short period, China did succumb to Washington Consensus-style policies in the mid-1990s but, as a matter of pragmatism in the wake of the crisis this induced, it immediately abandoned them for policies of Keynesian expansionism led by welfare provision, a renewal of the role of the state sector, and reversal of foreign sector liberalisation.

Fifth, in this light, it is hardly surprising that a very wide spectrum of opinion from across different positions regarding the sources of China's success and its responsibility (if any) for prompting, aggravating or ameliorating the current crisis is in substantial agreement on how it should proceed – by expanding domestic production to serve both higher wages and higher levels of social provision, and reducing the overall level of domestic investment as a proportion of GDP. Indeed, such postures are in line with those actually being adopted by China.[27]

Nonetheless, sixth, myths do prevail concerning China and its role in the world economy. These tend to originate from an ethos of blame, which incorrectly specifies the factors involved (or the causal roles they play) and (often falsely) associates China with responsibility for these factors. These factors include the idea of a global savings glut, unreasonable trade surplus and competitiveness from too low an exchange rate, and China's export growth at the expense of domestic consumption. In contrast, it should be emphasised that China's success or impact in these areas, properly interpreted, can only be of considerable benefit to the world economy (as well as its own), although the incidence of such benefits is uneven and possibly negative for some. Failure to realise these benefits is no fault of China; and that they do not accrue (for other, unrelated reasons – financialisation elsewhere is clearly culpable) is no reason to displace blame onto China.

More specifically, insofar as China might serve as an enabling factor in the promotion of developmental states elsewhere, its size and diversity give rise to a complex mix of complementary opportunities and sources of competition. Inevitably, these are variously spread across different countries, at different stages of development, across different sectors, technological capabilities and levels of value-added, and corresponding position within global value chains and networks (Kaplinsky 2008), in sub-Saharan Africa for example. Across the literature more generally, the level of uncertainty and unevenness involved is conducive to metaphor, with China variously being described in terms such as 'Engine, Conduit, or Steamroller?' (Haltmaier et al. 2007), or as a perpetrator of 'Flying Geese or Sitting Ducks' (Ahearne et al. 2006). For Haltmaier et al. (2007) in particular, China offers large, growing and varied markets (including its own growing foreign tourism), as well as competition in its own domestic market and in third-party markets in other countries. And it is a conduit for regional manufacture and assembling of goods across internationally fragmented production processes and markets (p.25):

> As China has moved up the value chain in recent years, increasing its presence in electronic high-tech exports in particular, there have also been shifts in the pattern of production in the other economies in the region. For instance, Japan and Korea have

further increased their presence in the medium-tech automotive industry and Singapore has developed its biomedical sector. At the same time, the Philippines has increased its revealed comparative advantage in exports of electronic high-tech products, a large proportion of which are parts and components. However, our analysis of product displacement suggests that China's increasing export share has not reduced export growth for the other countries in the high-tech industries, although it has had a negative effect in the medium-tech and low-tech industries.

Further, though, the following implications are drawn, with the first proposition no doubt being tested much earlier than could have been anticipated:[28]

First, although China's rise as an economic powerhouse is undisputed, at this point it is unlikely that emerging Asia could weather a significant slowdown in the U.S. economy, for example, without being noticeably affected. Second, our results on displacement of exports and changes in product mix of exports suggest that for some countries the rising trade in parts and components may be an endogenous response to competition from China, as these countries try to find areas of complementarity with China rather than compete head-to-head. Third, China's impact on the economies of the region is not uniform.

And they continue, 'Finally it should be emphasized that the debate on these issues is still evolving (the present paper included) and is difficult to settle. Additional research is needed'.

Similarly, Ahearne et al. (2006, pp.2–3) point to the variety of manners in which global production is organised, possibly allowing for complementary patterns of growth:

As an example of how vertical integration might make export growth rates similar, take the example of a small electronic device like a DVD player. The manufacturing of some components – e.g., motherboards, memory, etc. – might be handled in one or several of the ASEAN economies or the NIEs. Those components are then exported to, say, China, where they are assembled into the DVD player. The DVD player is then shipped out to its final destination. Several economies in the region might thus provide value-added to a single device. Hence, as demand for

DVD players fluctuates, one would expect export growth to be positively correlated across economies.

However, they add (p.14):

> When one looks at the sectoral data on U.S. imports from Asia, there is no doubt that China is displacing other Asian economies across a wide spectrum of markets. Not all of this displacement is symptomatic of competition. First, a significant portion of the final assembly of Asian-made products takes place in China.

And, further complicating matters, they observe that 'to some extent the changes in trade shares reflect a longer-term trend of China moving into the product space vacated by the Asian NIEs as they move to higher value-added products' (p.14); but they also quote McKinnon and Schnabl (2006), who suggest yet another role around intra- and inter-regional assembly, in which 'China is merely the face of a worldwide export surge into American consumer markets' (p.15).

Here, given the diverse and shifting roles to be played by China, it is necessary to be mindful of the most recent lessons to be drawn from the Japanese experience. Prior to the emergence of China, Japan was seen as driving the Asian region and, with it, the potential for developmental states to emerge (see Chia 2007, for example). Its own malaise over the past two decades, and its turn towards a new 'industrial policy' based on infrastructure and social welfare, possibly to be reinforced by the tragic consequences of the 2011 earthquake and tsunami, is a telling testimony not only to the need for continuing research in and of itself, but also to how rapidly circumstances can change. And as a result, as Haltmaier et al. (2007, pp.25–6) suggest, 'In particular, acquiring a more detailed understanding of the country-specific responses to the rapid emergence of China would be a fruitful line of further inquiry.'

1.6 THE DSP AS BUZZ AND FUZZ

Over the most recent period, the case of China has, as an example in itself, but also as a potential prompt to other economies, offered the chance for a limited revival of the DSP. This might best be seen in terms of a failed buzzword. The main reason for failure, as already indicated, is that within development discourse, success almost inevitably depends upon adoption by the World Bank. Here, as observed, the DSP has been notably absent. Yet, the corresponding lack of prominence apart, the DSP has exhibited what might be taken to be a number of buzzword characteristics. First, especially but not exclusively through the South Korean experience, the DSP has attracted renewed attention. One reason for this has been the need to examine whether the developmental states of the East Asian NICs have, indeed, suffered a demise, not least through more considered attention to the causes of the 1997/8 crisis, and the consequences for aftermath in terms of the nature and depth of the recession and the speed and extent of recovery. Possibly, some have argued, reports of the death of the developmental states of the East Asian NICs have been exaggerated.[29]

Second, not least because this deeper and broader attention to the crisis has revealed some strengthening of welfare provision by way of response to the crisis, as opposed to the anticipated neoliberal reductions, the developmental state literature also began to broaden its scope of analysis beyond attention to industrialisation as such and industrial policy, as well as questioning the extent to which welfarism, and other forms of intervention, were absent during the classic phase of catch-up (Kwon 2005; Ku and Finer 2007; and especially Kasza 2006). This has even given rise to the notion of a developmental *welfare* state (as discussed in Fine 2009b and c; but see especially works derived from the UNRISD social policy programme book series, such as Riesco (2007)). Such widening of the scope of the approach is also unsurprising, as those who are attached to it (old adherents as well as new) seek to find new avenues for their research. Mok (2007), Green (2007) and Gopinathan (2007) are concerned with the developmental state and (higher) education as East Asian NICs have responded to crisis; Neo (2007) with the environment; and Fritz and Menocal (2007), Sindzingre (2007), and Randall (2007) with aid, taxation and political parties, respectively. And industrial policy also benefits from a broader perspective, as Park (2007) examines the treatment of SMEs, Lazonick (2008) is mindful of entrepreneurship, Lee and Tee (2009) take on cluster analysis for bio-medicine in Singapore, and Bowen (2007) weds global production networks to aircraft manufacture in the Asia–Pacific Rim.

Different but continuing state intervention – of different types, in different circumstances, and under different influences – tends to lead the DSP to be invoked once more on a wide terrain. After all, both state and development are involved, and so more or less casually constructed descriptors are deployed to resurrect the developmental state. Thus, for Chu (2009, p.291), there is a 'reconfigured developmental state', geared towards the knowledge economy, in which

> Korea remains inclined towards development and does so by serving as a leader and an arbitrator of interests. In seeking to attain its development goals, the Korean state articulates visions and deploys public resources to structure the market and shape innovation.

(See also Lim 2010 and Lee 2009a, and Lee and Kwak 2009 for a comparative account of South Korea and Japan.) Further afield, Kuriyan and Ray (2009), in an account of ICT industries in India, perceive public–private partnerships as a form of developmental state; and, in a sophisticated analysis of the Tema port in Ghana, Chalfin (2010, p.580, emphasis added) concludes:

> The result is a port dominated by what can be described as a *neo(-liberal)* developmental state maintaining select features of an earlier statism rooted in the expansion of bureaucratic oversight and the protection of national interests and market share, now repurposed in line with a neoliberal agenda focused on trade facilitation, multinational corporate advantage, and financial speculation.

The counterposing of neoliberal with developmental state is striking; it raises the question of just how far the two can be accommodated with one another, conceptually and in practice.

This all relates to the second aspect of the buzz in the DSP; not only its limited revival and continuing life, but, as indicated, its extended scope of application. From being previously confined to a large extent to the developmental role of the state in latecomer, catch-up industrialisation, 'developmental state paradigm' now serves as a blanket buzz term for any circumstance in which there is state involvement and some aspect of development (just as 'globalisation' is attached to anything that is international and 'social capital' to anything that is in civil society, etc.). This also allows a certain promiscuity in forging relations between the DSP and other paradigms. For Yeung (2009), the development state is situated in relation to global production networks and regional integration; Gomez (2009) incorporates firm organisation by appeal to Chandler; Kwon and Yi (2009) and Kwon (2009) address poverty reduction and international policy transfer, respectively; Eimer and Lütz (2010) offer a comparative study of HIV/AIDS drugs policy across India and Brazil; Aiyede (2009) questions whether federalism can overcome predatory fragmentation; and de Haan (2010) is concerned with corruption, clientelism, patronage, resource curse, and rent-seeking (p.109):

> So neo-patrimonial states do not have to democratize, liberalize and outlaw corruption before they can become developmental states. But their political–administrative elites *do* have to feel a need – because of political pressure from society – to engage in a social contract for economic growth with their population instead of just engaging in a redistribution system of state revenues based on patronage and a fat bank account abroad.

Interestingly, such a prognosis within the political school is entirely without roots within particular economic activities at whatever stage of development. The DSP is, in principle, and to some degree in practice, of universal applicability.

Further, as in the past, if now as buzz and fuzz, newly emerging developmental states provide the raw material for further contributions, not least with China's economic miracle to the fore.[30] What is more novel is the goal of identifying developmental states in the making. This is true of the hopes placed for a new developmental state on more progressive governments in Latin America (Moudud and Botchway 2008; Caldentey 2008), as well as on Africa (Matlosa 2007; Moudud and Botchway 2007). Barbara (2008, p.311) views post-conflict states as potentially developmental, since '[t]he economic environments of failed states provide extreme examples of market failure'. And, in a bizarre way, developmental state optimism takes an extreme form with the self-declaration of post-apartheid South Africa, after a decade or more of neoliberalism, as a prospective candidate, all evidence to the contrary (Chapter 10). This is ironic given that most developmental states were, at least initially, blissfully unaware of their status as such whilst experiencing (let alone anticipating) it! They needed western academics to tell them what they were after they had already been it.

1.7 TOWARDS AN ALTERNATIVE

There is a further irony in the sudden prominence of South Africa within the developmental state literature. This is that the critically constructive approach to the paradigm, which underpins the contributions to this book, was first aired 20 years ago in seeking to explain both the nature and the dynamic of the South African economy, and to explore its potential with the demise of apartheid (see Fine 2008 for a retrospective account; also Fine and Rustomjee 1996). Initially, the DSP was fitted within the more general typology derived from linkages and agencies, or 'linkagencies', in which the linkages were covered within the economic school and the agencies within the political school (Fine 1992, 1993). Whilst the linkagency approach is methodologically and, to a large degree, substantively neutral,[31] it has the potential merit of drawing attention to the processes and structures through which the dynamic of development does, or does not, evolve.

This was important for understanding the nature of the South African apartheid economy, particularly in light of the 'class versus race' debate that had marked previous historiography. And it drew attention to the unique features of the economy, especially the extent to which it had been centred on what was termed the 'minerals–energy complex' (MEC), the conglomerate ownership of a core set of sectors that had extended its reach far beyond this core, through finance, into each key area of economic and social control (Chapter 10). Through continuing interrogation of both the developmental state approach and its alter egos in the Washington Consensus and post-Washington Consensus, an alternative approach was posited that could be deployed more generally as well as in tracing the dynamic of the post-apartheid economy.

It has the following elements that have, subsequently, been refined and that have informed the other studies gathered here. First and foremost is the rejection of 'state versus market' as an analytical starting point, with the presumption that developmental prospects depend upon the relative, embedded autonomy of the state (if, given the acceptance of a significant role for the state, this can be anything more than a tautology). It is not simply that the state and the market can be complementary, and that development depends upon access (and the terms of access) to the market – a factor in which the state can play a major role, as has now been recognised by the post-Washington Consensus in seeking to promote the market (and globalisation) through the interventions of the state. Indeed, this continues to take the dichotomy between state and market as basic if not necessarily conflictual. Rather, both the state and the market, and their interaction, are themselves determined by, if not reduced to, the economic, political and ideological interests which act upon them. These have to be identified prior to an account of the (potential) role of the state. The lesson is obvious for the economic school, given its neglect of why ideal policies would or would not be adopted in practice. But it is equally important for the political school, which seeks an autonomous state with its own interests; though it also recognises as decisive, through appeal to relative embeddedness, the impossibility of achieving such a state. This is not to reduce the role of the state mechanically to the interests that act upon it without regard, for example, to the evolution of institutions within and around the state apparatus. For underlying economic, political and ideological interests cannot be taken for granted; they themselves need to be formed in the practices of the state, market and civil society (including the military, the corrupt and the illegal).

Second, it is insufficient to talk about underlying economic, political and ideological interests in the abstract (and the same applies to the state and the market). The societies under consideration are capitalist, certainly embroiled within global capitalism, and are subject to the interests defined by capital and labour, but also by other (fractions of) classes attached to particular sectors (finance, trading, etc.) and activities (agriculture, health, education and welfare), and not necessarily irreducibly governed by the imperatives of short- or long-term capitalist profitability, whatever the direct or indirect influences these may exert. Further, such interests are themselves engaged in specific material practices, structures and relations that define the economy and society under consideration, and its evolving dynamic – including the formation of new or transformed classes and underlying interests themselves.

For, as strikingly revealed in Chapter 9 on the Argentinean debt crisis of 2001, there is no simple or fixed relationship between underlying economic interests and their representation through the market–state dualism. Nor is it helpful, then, to see developmentalism along a market–state spectrum, with neoliberalism promoting one at the expense of the other. For traditional divisions, across financial and industrial, and national and international fractions of capital, overlook how such dualities are in any case both far from sharply defined and fluid in their mix. And, over the course of the Argentinean crisis, the state intervened extensively to promote conglomerate interests through privatisation, financial and industrial restructuring, and dealings in foreign currency, which ultimately led both to the default itself and to much of the way in which it was resolved.

Third, then, the approach seeks to identify at a more specific level what might be termed the systems of accumulation associated with particular economies (Chapters 3, 7 and 10). Such a system involves both the underlying interests and the structure and dynamic of the economy through which these interests are formed and expressed. It might, for example, be the chaebol system for South Korea (Chapter 3), the Indian IT industry (Chapter 7) or the MEC for South Africa (Chapter 10). All this provides the basis for comparative analysis: both a common framework and the space for contextual difference.[32]

Last, and by no means least, such an approach offers the possibility of identifying alternative policies that support and promote the interests of progressive movements. In this respect, at least, there is much to commend the DSP, particularly as it has increasingly been identified with progressive economic policies and political perspectives. The goal is to identify what might be done, who might do it, and how; but the realisation of such aims in practice depends upon a shift in the balance of class forces and the ways in which these are resolved. The extent to which this can be realised in the context of global capitalism in or out of crisis is yet to be tested and depends upon how the crisis of neoliberalism is addressed at both global and national (and other) levels.[33] Certainly, the DSP might paint too rosy a picture of what will be attempted, and what can be achieved at the national level. For Hayashi (2010), this means that neoliberal globalisation has not undermined the potential for developmental states.[34] Indeed, far from being outdated, they are necessary in order to be integrated into the world economy, rather than being protected from it (p.62):

> the developmental state is a model of state-led industrialization for developing countries, where the market mechanism is underdeveloped or the market itself does not exist. The underdevelopment (or nonexistence) of the market means that the market does not signal which industries should grow or disappear. Under the circumstances, the government should be more proactive than just leaving any economic activity to the market: the government should identify which industries should be targeted and actually promote such industries. However, the means to promote particular industries do not have to equate to trade protectionism. Southeast Asian countries have implemented state-led industrialization by utilizing MNCs, and have been successfully upgrading their economic structure through FDI.

Their experience provides an important insight when considering future strategies that today's developing countries could pursue.

This stands in sharp contrast to developmental state agnostics, not least a contributor to our own volume (Chapter 6). Here Pirie argues that the prospects for successful industrial policy on a broad and national front are limited by virtue of the first-comer advantages of competitors and the scale of domestic markets that would need to be available to be able to compete even if protection were a viable policy option. The alternative is offered of national promotion of social provision as some insulation from global dominance. Yet the burden of these arguments surely depends upon the nature of the sectors concerned, how they are or can be organised and integrated nationally and internationally, and how domestic and international interests are forged and realised. This suggests the need to finesse a number of (false) dualisms – reformism versus revolution, nation state versus globalisation, state versus market, democracy versus authoritarianism, and so on – each of which can only fit uncomfortably within the DSP itself. Even so the attempt to realise the goals of the DSP can potentially make a major contribution to the progressive transformation within (if not of) global capitalism, if only as a stepping stone (or should that be 'impediment'?) that must be surpassed both analytically and strategically. For the moment, at least, as neoliberal scholarship, ideology and policy in practice remain severely unchallenged in the alternatives being offered in the wake of global crisis, the DSP is worthy of critical attention as opposed to deliberate and far from benign neglect.

1.8 ONE QUESTIONABLE STEP FORWARD: TWENTY YEARS BACK

For the current financial crisis has raised more prominently the role of the state in contemporary capitalism. At the very least, there is a renewal of interest in mild forms of Keynesianism: how to get the economy moving again, or at least, how to prevent it from collapsing further, by lowering interest rates, raising liquidity, rescuing firms in difficulties and possibly stimulating demand through tax cuts and infrastructural spending. These measures remain dominated in numerical terms by the extent of support being offered to the financial system itself through the nationalisation of failing financial institutions and corresponding toxic assets. In such circumstances, of a crisis of legitimacy, at least to some degree, of the neoliberal ideology of non-interventionism, in light of the extensive (financial) interventions in practice, it is hardly surprising that there should be some adjustment, disarray even, in the postures of erstwhile leading neoliberal institutions such as the World Bank and the IMF, and some comfort, self-satisfaction even, amongst those who have sustained criticism of them (see Grabel 2011, for example).

For our purposes, though, what is striking is how little this has been associated with the resurrection of the DSP (and developmental policies in practice) as opposed to a hardening up of the conflicting rhetoric and scholarship of the Washington Consensus. This is most marked in the initiative being taken by Justin Lin, chief economist at the World Bank, and (almost in a parody of the launch of the post-Washington Consensus by Joe Stiglitz in 1998) proponent of his newly invented 'new structural economics' (Lin 2011b). This has a number of features: it is explicitly based on neoclassical economics; it disassociates itself from the 'old' structural economics; it favours the market over the state; but it sees a role for the state in promoting 'latent' comparative advantage. By the latter term Lin means that countries should prepare themselves for market participation in what will be appropriate sectors a decade or so into the future. This is spelled out a little more in a later contribution (Lin 2011a). Here developing countries are perceived as having the opportunity, in 'flying geese' fashion, of taking over the low-wage, labour-intensive, low-technology activities that become available as China moves up the value chain. In section 1.4, this posture has already been shown to be deficient in terms of both the inapplicability of the metaphor of flying geese to the process of (industrial) development (under current conditions), and the likelihood that China will continue to engage in low-wage production into the foreseeable future, even if it also moves up the value chain.[35]

In addition, it has been argued elsewhere that Lin's new structural economics is little more than a tautology – countries that have developed will be seen as having adopted policies sequentially favouring their latent comparative advantage, even if, miraculously, this only becomes apparent in retrospect (Fine 2012). In this respect, there is a striking parallel with the World Bank's 'East Asian miracle' of 20 years ago, in which extensive state intervention was accepted as having been successful only if it had been 'market conforming', i.e. doing what the market would have done had it been working perfectly (see above).

In short, Lin's new structural economics is a new way of presenting a pro-business, low-wage strategy, grounded in neoclassical orthodoxy, and yet presenting itself as favourable to state intervention (to promote latent comparative advantage). Despite this, it has been warmly if critically received, not least by erstwhile champions of the DSP.[36] Surely we are not surprised to find that Lin steers clear of mentioning the DSP; but the same is true amongst those who debate with him, with the honourable exception of Wade.[37]

This is indicative of four things. First is how much the DSP has been marginalised, even by its own proponents. It is, as indicated previously, a failed buzzword and has, accordingly, become widely applied, in scope of application if not in weight of influence – especially in so far as systemic developmental transformation (its initial object) is concerned. This limits the substance of the critical engagement with the new structural economics, let alone the capacity to go beyond both it and the DSP itself. Second is how far neoliberalism has gained hold of scholarship and ideology, so much so that even marginal shifts towards interventionism are welcomed as progress or opportunity. Third, the most striking feature of Lin's contributions is that they live in their own world, completely detached from the world of Bank policy, hardened on the Washington Consensus (albeit in changed circumstances in which postures of non-intervention are no longer defensible). Will we see Lin being forced to resign, like Stiglitz his predecessor, for taking his scholarly stance into the real world of policy? And fourth is to observe how in practice, if not necessarily in principle, the DSP has been diluted, eroded and induced to be complicit with the new structural economics – in part, if not fully, because of its own self-limitations of focus upon state–industry relations as the source of a healthy balance between state and market, in the context of latecomer, catch-up industrialisation. This dovetails with the dominance of the World Bank in developmental discourse, readily inducing critics to sacrifice analytical principles and postures in order to be able to engage. The hope is that this volume can provide a corrective of sterner stuff by moving beyond, rather than retreating from, the staging post previously offered by the BDS.

NOTES

1. Thanks to fellow editors for comments on earlier drafts.
2. These earlier contributions offer extensive surveys of the evolving literature; this introduction focuses on more recent contributions.
3. In an interview, in response to the question, 'What made your work on industrialization and on Korea so influential?', she replied, 'Showing that Korea developed by getting the prices "wrong"' (van der Hoeven 2008, p.1093).

4. Significantly, the leading orthodox proponent of the consequences of increasing returns to scale, Paul Krugman, has advised against drawing policy conclusions from his deductive theory, even though they clearly offer a rationale for state intervention, on the grounds that policy is liable to be captured by special interests (something he, paradoxically, ignores in developing his theory of uneven development). See Fine and Milonakis (2009) and Fine (2010d) for a discussion.
5. See Stubbs (2009) for this point amongst others in a useful retrospective on the developmental state. But note that he manages to avoid discussion of class altogether, with the exception of one reference to the middle class! See also Beeson (2009) for an overview of East Asian developmental states.
6. Note that for Yazid (2007, p.39), 'the success of a developmental state requires external support from external powers'. Does this apply to China?
7. See Pirie (2009), and also Radice (2008), for a strong statement of the constraints imposed on prospective developmental states by the impact of globalisation and neoliberalism; but also Khondker (2008) and Pereira (2008) for continuing possibilities in the case of Singapore. See also below.
8. For the past, see Blecher (2008, p.171) for the view that 'Bonapartism was not just a forerunner of modern authoritarianism, but also of the capitalist developmental state'. And, for the present, see Lange (2009) for the potential for crises to prompt nation-building developmental states, drawing upon Botswana and Malaysia as case studies, and also Barbara (2008) for post-conflict economies as potential developmental states. See also Kim (2009) for the importance of the historical origins of contemporary developmental states, de Haan (2010) and Di John (2010) for developmental state building, and Berger and Ghosh (2010, p.586) for the interesting proposition that the end of the Cold War has witnessed 'an important shift from developmental nationalisms to cultural nationalisms', with correspondingly negative implications for developmental states, as 'the nation-state system itself is sliding deeper into crisis against the backdrop of the global framework of "genuinely existing" liberal capitalism'.
9. The Latin American experience raises the question of whether a developmental state can survive without being authoritarian, confronting the demands both for democracy and from an organised labour movement the more it is successful. Note, though, that for Draibe and Riesco (2007, p.1), the Latin American developmental welfare state (LADWS) is a crucial factor for success, not a disintegrating cause derived from radical populism: 'The core argument ... is that LADWS was the original historical form that drove forward social and economic development in the particular conditions of the region during the twentieth century.' See below on bringing welfare back into the developmental state paradigm.
10. The other was the social costs of the policies, adjustment without a human face, on which see below. For critical presentation of the Washington Consensus and its aftermath as the post-Washington Consensus, see Fine, Lapavitsas and Pincus (2001), Jomo and Fine (2006) and Bayliss, Fine and Van Waeyenberge (2011).
11. See Wade (1996).
12. For continuing but long-established recognition of variety of models across developmental states, see Bardhan (2010). He contrasts India and China with one another and with east Asian NICs – politically, regionally, by relations between public and private sectors, sources of finance, role of conglomerates and foreign capital, and role of state officials.

13. See Young (1994, 1995) and Krugman (1994), although a simple visit to factories throughout the region might have offered a contrary view about the progress made in the adoption of new technologies (as opposed to simply accumulating on the basis of the old).
14. See Pirie (2009) for an exposure of the ambiguities in Chang's analytical stance.
15. But see Hundt (2009) for this in the context of a continuing if shifting developmental alliance between the state and capital in South Korea.
16. See Pereira (2008) for a clear statement of the 'developmental state death' hypothesis using Singapore as a counterexample of a case where the capitalist class remains relatively marginal and the working class is incorporated, thereby allowing the state to continue to be developmental.
17. See Phelps (2008) for a discussion of the role of, and need for, the developmental state in forging developmental clusters out of multinational corporate investment. Note that, primarily within the economic school, this involves a 'state versus market' approach, in which MNCs are a proxy for the market. See also Cherry (2007) on the South Korean developmental state in light of crisis, neoliberalism and foreign direct investment.
18. For two arbitrarily and unfairly selected examples, see Kumar (2008) for India and Xia (2008) for China.
19. See especially White (1998), Chan, Clark and Lam (1998) and Leftwich (2000).
20. See also Salter (2009) for the role of the state in promoting knowledge-based medicines against global competition in China and India. See Greene (2008) for science and technology policy in Taiwan and its complex rhythm in relation to the developmental state.
21. For a recent exception for considering technology policy, see Lee (2009a).
22. Thus, Masina (2010) deploys the common metaphor from global network approaches of Vietnam's recent successes being dependent upon its position in relation to manufacturing hubs, with corresponding constraints on moving through higher stages of industrial upgrading and on retaining independence over industrial policy given its reliance on foreign direct investment and technologies.
23. But see Hart-Landsberg and Burkett (1998) for an early critical review of the potential of 'flying geese' strategies for development.
24. See Ohno (2009), both for his five stages of catching-up industrialisation (numbered zero to four) – which may or may not (be intended to) have affinities with Rostovian stages – and for the suggestion that there is the prospect of a middle-income trap, or 'invisible "glass ceiling"', between his Stage 2 ('have supporting industries, but still under foreign guidance') and Stage 3 ('management and technology mastered, can produce high quality goods') (p.28). The transition between these two stages is seen as depending upon the capability for 'technology absorption', with that between Stage 3 and (the final) Stage 4 ('full capability in innovation and product design as global leader') depending on 'creativity'. Various countries are distributed across these stages as well as across the different characteristics within specific stages. See also Al-Jazaeri (2008) and Chapter 5 for the problems of getting beyond catch-up.
25. What follows draws heavily on Lo and Zhang (2011) and Lo (2010).
26. As well as, for example, for Vietnam (see Masina 2010).
27. See, for example, Lippit et al. (2011), Zhu and Kotz (2011), Hart-Landsberg (2011) and Piovani and Li (2011) in a special issue of *Review of Radical Political Economics*, vol.43, no.1.

28. See also Zebregs (2004) for a detailed discussion of the rise of intra-regional trade in Asia, who is quoted by Ahearne et al. (2006, p.15) to the effect that 'the rise in intraregional trade is largely driven by rapidly growing intra-industry trade, which is a reflection of greater vertical specialization and the dispersion of production processes across borders. This has led to a sharp rise in trade in intermediate goods ... but the EU, Japan and the United States remain the main export markets for final goods.'
29. See Lee (2008); also Kalinowski (2008), who supports Weiss (1999) and Thurbon and Weiss (2006) against Pirie (2005, 2006, 2008), to the effect that the development state has not succumbed to neoliberalism in the wake of the crisis, although it does, for him, seem to be in its last death throes! Note that Bae and Sellers (2007) find for South Korea that democratisation can strengthen the developmental state in urban policy as technocracy is married with middle-class interests as opposed to individualised pursuit of profitability.
30. For accounts which place some emphasis on provincial or local developmental states and their relations with the centre, see Liu (2008) and Thun (2006); also Ferdinand (2007), for whom Russia has become a developmental state alongside (if later and less effective than) China. Note that Cao (2009) examines the role of urban property in China in identifying the presence (or absence) of (local) developmental states. See also Blecher (2008) for the ubiquitous emphasis on contradictions between local and central states across planning and the promotion of private capital. For a contrary view around the retrenchment to the centre for major investment projects, see Kun-Chin (2007).
31. Thus, mainstream neoclassical economics deploys the individual as agent and the market as linkage, with institutions added as their consequence and continuing causal factor in the case of market imperfections.
32. For a critique, by reference to the Malaysian model, of the limited notion of context incorporated into the pluralist developmental model of the post-Washington Consensus, see Maseland and Peil (2008).
33. See Gray (2008) for the suggestion for South Korea, and possibly of wider relevance, that more prominent labour movements and democratic participation can be associated with incorporation into more favourable negotiating of neoliberal globalisation.
34. See also Rock et al. (2009) for discussion of the developmental state, technological change and environmental sustainability in the context of globalisation.
35. See also Ozawa (2009) for a rounded account of Akamatsu's original 'flying geese' framework, together with misperceptions that in many respects have been fully embraced by Lin. These include the failure to take account of the fact that China itself is far from being the leading goose (so situating follower countries far behind those that do lead and neglecting the opportunities that they also offer) and that China is itself subject to the vagaries of global (and internal) forces and so not guaranteed to be a secure flying goose. And there are complex patterns of leader–follower, both along vertical chains of production (from simple consumption through to complex capital goods), from low to high quality, and from domestic consumption to export market. As argued above in terms of the modern world of global production networks, this is not so much refinement as the undermining of 'flying geese' perspectives.
36. See Lin and Chang (2009) and contributions to the debate between Lin and Monga (2011a) and Lin and Monga (2011b).
37. See Wade (2010, 2011) in debate with Lin (2010).

2
The Rise and Fall of the Developmental State? The Case of the Japanese and South Korean Steel Industries

Hajime Sato

2.1 INTRODUCTION

The Japanese and South Korean steel industries have typically been addressed as successful examples of state-led catch-up industrialisation and of the 'developmental state' (e.g. Amsden 1989; Shin 1996). It is undeniable that industrial policy in the broadest sense towards the industries in both countries had contributed to their rapid growth and modernisation. However, crude steel production in Japan has been stagnating since the mid-1970s, and the South Korean steel industry has suffered heavily from the East Asian crisis in the late 1990s. Do these experiences confirm the views of the developmental state paradigm (DSP) that the 'developmental state' is limited to a certain phase of industrialisation and that it ceases to exist as an economy matures?[1] In addition, even within the successful periods, the effects and outcomes of industrial policies that have the same features to some extent differ in outcomes across countries and over time. How can their experiences be generalised as the 'developmental state'? Is the DSP appropriate for examining the role of the state in development and development itself?

On surveying the literature, it also becomes evident that the DSP tends to have shied away from addressing 'failed' industrial policy within the successful periods of the Japanese and South Korean steel industries, on the one hand, and the restructuring and transformation of the industries around the long recession in Japan and the crisis in South Korea, on the other. Thus, it has not offered a coherent and systemic explanation for the changing performance of the industries across periods and across countries (and sectors). In other words, the DSP has not fully succeeded in understanding in a consistent way the role of the state in the accumulation and restructuring of the industries and in relating to the totality of empirical evidence.

Also, as emphasised throughout this volume, a weakness of the DSP is to take the dichotomy between market and state as analytical starting point, whether examining the role of technological change or state intervention. However, the ideological and theoretical framework of 'market versus state' or 'market plus state' is problematic. The dichotomy reduces the agenda of development into a framework for finding the appropriate level of state intervention in the market for 'optimal' resource allocation. Consequently, various factors are obscured.

Instead, this chapter adopts an approach that sees both market and state as being 'the consequence of or form taken by underlying political and economic relations and interests' (Fine 2006, p.114). Specifically, first, the chapter suggests that it is the underlying time and country-specific political and economic relations and interests in and surrounding the steel industry that forge and implement policy, rather than economic justification such as market failures. Second, the chapter argues that the outcome of such policy depends upon history-specific, country-specific and industry-specific factors, so that it is no less important to analyse the structural and other changes in and surrounding the industry than to observe its output performance. Third, the chapter shows that sectoral development, in turn, affects underlying political and economic relations and interests in and surrounding the industry, which then feed into new and different policy. As this spiral interaction continues over time, the chapter insists that it is misleading to understand that the role of the state lessens as the economy matures.

In a nutshell, a major purpose of the chapter is to critically examine the DSP, through the restructuring of capital in the Japanese and South Korean steel industries.[2] Situating political and economic relations and interests as a basic layer of analysis, it highlights certain aspects of the accumulation and restructuring of the industries which have been overlooked by the DSP. In doing so, it attempts to understand the role of the state in the experience of the industries in the context of the workings of contemporary capitalism, rather than in terms of the 'developmental state'.

The next section briefly reviews selective literature on the steel industry and argues the limitations of the approaches taken. The following two sections delineate some aspects of the underlying political and economic relations and interests which have been driving the accumulation and restructuring of the industries in Japan and South Korea; Section 2.3 analyses periods of rapid growth and Section 2.4 those of stagnation and crisis. The last section offers some implications for industrial and sectoral studies, based on the findings of the preceding sections.

2.2 THE JAPANESE AND SOUTH KOREAN STEEL INDUSTRIES AND THE DSP

The steel industry is a key sector with regard to the industrialisation of an economy. First, the linkages between the steel industry and the other manufacturing industries are extremely important. Hirschman (1958), who presented the concept of backward and forward linkages, pointed out that the steel industry scored highest in these effects. However, he also conceived that it was unrealistic for developing countries to adopt a policy to push forward the industry. Hirschman (1958, p.108) observes: 'It is interesting to note that the industry with the highest combined linkage score is iron and steel. Perhaps the underdeveloped countries are not so foolish and so exclusively prestige-motivated in attributing prime importance to this industry!' Despite his perspective, some underdeveloped countries such as South Korea have made an attempt to develop the industry and have deployed various policies towards the steel industry in order to introduce state-of-the-art technology to steel production and to establish the coordination of backward and forward linkages between the steel industry and others.

Second, the role of the state has been extremely important in developing the steel industry. It has often been designated as a national strategic industry and given preferential treatment (Howell et al. 1988). Indeed, as suggested by the well-known saying 'Steel is the nation', the industry has often occupied a central position in the industrialisation process of a nation state. As such, its development has often been a crucial task for governments, not only economically but also politically.

However, there is much less literature studying the steel industry than focusing on other manufacturing sectors, such as electronics and automobiles, as pointed out by Kawabata (2005). For, in the debate about the East Asian development experience, the literature tends to pick up on those industries whose development was associated with foreign direct investment (FDI) and export-oriented policy, neither of which has been prominent in the steel industry. Even so, the integrated steel firms of Japan and South Korea have been studied relatively widely because of their impressive success.

In observing this success, although neoclassical economics tends to undervalue the role played by the state and industrial policy, the steel industry has been an exception.[3] Case studies of the steel industry are also provided by the DSP (e.g. Amsden 1989; Shin 1996; D'Costa 1999). To put it differently, steel industries, not least those of Japan and South Korea, have been studied as providing a case for industrial policy and state intervention. As the facility investment needed for establishing a modern integrated plant is massive, developing countries launching steel projects are confronted by a high barrier. And when such projects are successful, as in Japan and South Korea, latecomer's advantage is often stressed and, in realising this advantage, the role and capability of government are highlighted.

The DSP can be divided into two schools, the political and the economic (Fine 2006). The political school focuses upon whether the state has autonomy in forming and implementing industrial policy independent of various interests in the market (Evans 1995). However, the concept of the developmental state has increasingly been diluted to accommodate new case studies that tend to add various factors such as international regime, culture and ideology in attempting to measure the levels of autonomy. Thus the dichotomy between market and state has ironically been undermined. This indicates that the dichotomy as analytical starting point generates various theoretical and empirical problems in understanding economic development, for policies and their effects always reflect 'the balance of class forces and not their absence' (Fine 2006, p.114). In addition, the political school does not examine what type of industrial policy is developmental, leaving this issue to the economic school.

In contrast, the economic school focuses upon the content of industrial policy. Theoretically, as the steel industry is characterised by significant economies of scale, various externalities and market imperfections, industrial policy is often justified through drawing upon traditional market-failure arguments. Also, infant-industry protection has provided a theoretical basis for state intervention in bringing dynamic comparative advantage for the industry. Furthermore, Chang (2006), arguing that 'there are more theoretical justifications for industrial policy than is normally acknowledged' (p.9), offers various examples of industrial policy that can be justified by economic theory.[4] In short, the economic school has pointed out that state interventions went beyond remedying cases of market failure, as exemplified by the well-known phrases, 'getting the relative price wrong' (Amsden 1989) and 'governing the market' (Wade 1990). Thus, an implication of this school is that in the catching-up phase, there is plenty of room for the state to push economic development in general, and the steel industry in particular, through trade, industrial, and technological policies.

However, theoretical (ahistorical and universal) 'justification' for industrial policy cannot explain why and how such policy materialises (or fails to materialise) in certain countries at certain times, bringing different results, and as such, throws this problem back to the political school. As Fine (2006, p.106) puts it, 'the economic schools arrive where the political school begins'. In addition, 'justifying' industrial policy in this manner presumes a state and market dichotomy; a problem with this framework is that the 'success' or 'failure' of industrial policy is readily interpreted in terms of the dichotomy. For, as noted earlier, the dichotomy in itself lures the interpretations of the experience into identifying appropriate levels of state intervention to address market imperfections. Consequently, as Fine (2006) points out, this approach can be and has indeed been absorbed and outflanked by the information-theoretic approach, which 'justifies' wider state intervention in developing rather than in developed countries, based on the existence of pervasive market imperfections in the former.

One implication that can be drawn from this brief literature survey is that the dichotomy between market and state conceals the simple fact that economic development is a complex amalgam of processes and outcomes derived from capital accumulation, where state and market, and their interaction, are themselves attached to the economic and political relations and interests which act upon them. From this viewpoint, the steel industries of Japan and South Korea as the successful examples of the developmental state need to be re-examined and the scrutiny must include the periods of 'failure' of the industries in addition to those of 'success'.

2.3 MIRACULOUS DEVELOPMENT: THE RISE OF THE DEVELOPMENTAL STATE?

The Japanese steel industry showed rapid development from 1946 to the early 1970s. Crude steel production increased from 0.6 million tonnes in 1946 to 119.3 million tonnes in 1973, even exceeding that of the USA.[5] Japan established the most efficient steel-making industry in the world in the late 1950s, building integrated steel works with mammoth blast furnaces, basic oxygen furnaces

(BOFs), and hot strip mills sited at deep-water ports. Competition among the six private integrated firms realised economies of scale throughout the 1960s and 1970s.[6] In the case of South Korea, crude steel production increased from almost zero in 1970 to 23.1 million tonnes in 1990. The main agency in this process was the sole integrated firm, POSCO, a state-owned firm.

As noted above, various studies have attributed the development of the steel industries of Japan and South Korea to wise industrial policy in selecting state-of-the-art technology and successfully raising finance for this, on the one hand, and the autonomy of the government, the non-existence of a strong economic class, and the capability of bureaucrats and institutions in formulating and implementing policies, on the other (e.g. Amsden 1989; Shin 1996; D'Costa 1999). Needless to say, these arguments by the DSP have raised a number of important points which cast doubt on the dominant neoclassical view that tends to stress the importance of free markets and free trade in the East Asian development experience. These points are now discussed one by one.

2.3.1 The Japanese Model of the Developmental State?

From the end of the Second World War to the early 1970s, the development of the Japanese industry is characterised by rapid growth in production and by the installation of integrated steelworks in coastal areas, with blast furnaces becoming larger and larger and open-hearth furnaces (OHFs) being replaced by BOFs. In other words, accumulation in this period primarily took the form of fierce competition in installing integrated steelworks across private integrated firms, responding to rapid growth in demand.

The economic school of the developmental state approach has praised the role of government. D'Costa (1999, p.80), analysing policies relating to the steel industry, argues that these 'not only mobilised finance through its national banking system but also assisted domestic firms to secure modern technologies from abroad'. Shin (1996, p.101), in addition to credit allocation and technological transfer, points to the protection measures of domestic steel markets, suggesting the significant contribution of import-substituting policies. Thus each stresses the importance of the role of the government for latecomers in steel production. For D'Costa (1999, p.80), the state has played the critical role in placing the Japanese steel industry 'on a higher technological trajectory'.[7] Political questions therefore arise as to why and how the government was able to adopt and implement these policies, how they arose, and how they resulted in contributing to the industry's rapid development.

The political school of the development state has tried to identify the political and institutional conditions which enabled the policy success of this period. Johnson (1982), depicting in detail the close relationship between the government, not least the Ministry of International Trade and Industry (MITI), and industries, including steel, in the late industrialisation of Japan,[8] argues that Japan had been a developmental state in nature. This meant that economic development enjoyed first priority, and that there was continuity of policy tools as well as of the people who formulated and exercised industrial policy before and after the Second World War. As a 'Japanese model', he delineated four elements of the Japanese developmental state (Johnson 1982, 1999).[9] These elements were, first, a small and excellent bureaucracy capable of formulating policy and guiding the economy; second, a political system that allowed the bureaucracy to do this; third, market-conforming methods of state intervention; and fourth, an organisation commanding the powers necessary for implementation, such as MITI. Shin (1996) strengthens this argument by adding that with one-party rule and the absence of the armed forces, the bureaucracy enjoyed autonomy, which enabled strong economic intervention.

These arguments of the political school presume that there was wide room and sufficient power for the Japanese government to manoeuvre various policies for industries and to discipline firms, since it enjoyed autonomy, or embedded autonomy, free from the interests of various classes. Indeed, Aoki, Murdock and Okuno-Fujiwara (1997, p.25) argue that Japan enjoyed 'a unique initial condition of economic development', that there was no dominant economic class. This enabled the state to act developmentally in relative freedom from any economic and political interests. However, whether this holds true for specific industries has not been examined; and, indeed, it is misleading in the case of the steel industry.

First, for the 'initial conditions', the government was heavily affected by internal and external interests and by the inherited capital surrounding the industry. On the one hand, many things, such as facilities, technologies, and knowledge and experience, had been inherited from before 1945, and these formed the basis of the 'initial conditions'.[10] On the other hand, the international environment was an important factor, not least the strategies for Far-East Asia of the US government.

US policy towards the steel industry changed from paying no interest in rebuilding it, to providing financial and other forms of support to stabilise the vulnerable Japanese economy and, ultimately, to requesting the reconstruction of the industry (Nihon Tekkō Renmei 1959; Ichikawa 1974; Yonekura 1994). D'Costa (1999, p.68) points out that the basis of the Japanese domestic competitive market was 'bequeathed by the US'; the creation in 1950 of Fuji and Yawata by dividing Japan Steel resulted in 'an industry structure with five or six large firms of roughly equal size'. It is right to point out that during the US occupation (1945–52) the role of the US government was extremely important. However, the content and effect of the US policies and their interactions with the underlying political and economic relations and interests of the industry were not confined to effecting the market structure. In the provision of technologies, finance, raw materials and steel demand, in addition to the formulation of market structure, US policy played a critical role. The interaction between the changes in the policies of the US Occupation Force and the response to these policies by the industry, as well as by the government, eventually led to the rehabilitation of the industry and brought about the basis for the pattern of capital accumulation in this period. Also, 'it was nothing more than superb luck' (Yonekura 1994, p.197) that steel demand increased owing to the outbreak of the Korean War in 1950. Even after independence in 1952, the industry continued to be heavily dependent upon the United States for technologies, finance, raw materials and export markets.

Second, in looking at the steel industry, the DSP pays attention to the relationship between only the integrated firms and the state, tending to put aside the restructuring of other steel companies. In other words, the focus is on the relations among the government, integrated firms and the financial sector in achieving the introduction and diffusion of technology, and neglects changes in the steel industry as a whole.

Within the Japanese steel industry, the impressive development in production and exports of this period coincided with the massive restructuring of OHF and electric arc furnace (EAF) companies as well as of the workforce. In Japan, OHF and EAF companies producing ordinary steel competed with integrated firms from the very start and, in the 1950s, the number of such small steel firms was significantly greater than in either the USA or any European country, resulting in acute conflict of interests among the integrated firms and OHF and EAF steel firms (Iida, Ohashi and Kuroiwa

1969). Before long, most OHF and EAF companies came under the control of the integrated companies (Ichikawa 1974).

Industrial policy tended to be deployed in favour of large firms at the expense of small- to medium-sized firms, reflecting the changing power balance among various steel firms and other agencies. For example, by permitting a cartel for steel scrap in 1955, MITI allocated the amount of scrap to companies and decided prices for it. In this system, the integrated companies received preferential treatment, which indirectly forced other OHF and EAF companies to be restructured (Nihon Tekkō Renmei 1969; Ichikawa 1974). In addition, MITI formed the OHF–EAF subcommittee of its Industrial Structure Council in 1965, when OHF and EAF companies were suffering severely from recession (Nihon Tekkō Renmei 1969; Noble 1998). The subcommittee advised that the number of OHF and EAF companies should be significantly reduced through becoming affiliates of the integrated firms and by cooperating on their own for purchasing raw materials, adjusting production and marketing. In this way, the process of centralisation and concentration of capital into the six integrated firms was intensified, strengthening the oligopolistic structure of the industry.

Third, the involvement of the government was extensive and identifiable in every aspect of the production and exchange spheres, such as coordinating with steel users, facilitating finance, importing technology, stabilising prices, changing industrial structure and securing raw materials. However, the formation and impact of these policies depended upon the shifting underlying political and economic relations and interests.

For example, in 1958, on the initiative of MITI, the open-sales price system was adopted; this placed a high priority on the stability of the price of steel, for the benefit of the Japanese economy as a whole (Iida, Ohashi and Kuroiwa 1969; Nihon Tekkō Renmei 1969; Ichikawa 1974; Yonekura 1994). In fact, MITI's intervention 'was not the cause of aggressive investment but rather the result of it' (Yonekura 1994, p.230). The open-sales price system was effectively a cartel of 31 major ordinary steel-producing companies, coordinated by MITI through administrative guidance, shrewdly avoiding the anti-trust laws.[11] However, by 1962 this price system had collapsed. The competition between integrated firms was the immediate cause of the breakdown, as evidenced by the fact that products over which integrated firms had strong market power were the first to breach the open-sales price system.[12]

In sum, major factors of the developmental state induced from the successful Japanese experience turn out to be too abstract and misleading. The government was far from enjoying autonomy in formulating and implementing policies towards the steel industry, even in the period of rapid growth. Reflecting changes in underlying economic and political relations and interests, policies towards the industry were frequently modified; their outcomes also depended upon these changing relations and interests.

2.3.2 The South Korean Model of the Developmental State?

In contrast to the Japanese case, which was largely characterised by the oligopolistic competition among the six private integrated firms, the establishment and expansion of the state-owned firm POSCO was the core aspect of the system of accumulation in the South Korean steel industry in the period of miraculous growth in the 1970s and 1980s. As a result, the development of POSCO has been the main subject of study, and the DSP has attributed this to the same factors as those for the Japanese steel industry, i.e. to wise industrial policy, on the one hand, and the autonomy of the government, the absence of a strong economic class, and the capability of bureaucrats and institutions in formulating and implementing industrial policy, on the other (Enos and Park 1988; Amsden 1989; Juhn 1990; D'Costa 1994; Stern et al. 1995; Shin 1996).[13] According to D'Costa (1999, p.117), 'the autonomy of the state, which was also extended to POSCO, definitely played a role in capturing the benefits of changing technologies'. Needless to say, it is extremely important to examine the developmental process of POSCO. However, the preceding literature tends to neglect the many different aspects of the industry other than the remarkable technological achievement by POSCO.

First, before the establishment of POSCO, as the steel rolling-mill sector grew in the 1960s, there appeared an acute imbalance between the upstream and downstream processes in the industry, necessitating a 'big-push' policy for upstream processes (Nihon Tekkō Renmei 1968). The import substitution in the rolling sector rapidly proceeded in the 1960s, as the development of private EAF and rolling firms had been undertaken by various groups of firms or conglomerates. It was mainly the increase in domestic demand that brought about the development of the steel industry up to around 1970. Indeed, steel demand reached a level (1 million tonnes) that would allow for large-scale integrated steel production by the early 1970s. In addition, from the early 1960s, the development depended upon imports of steel scrap, semi-finished products and hot-rolled coils (Tekkō Kaigai Sijō Chōsa Iinkai 1966). Thus, the import substitution of iron-making and steel-making processes became an important task, politically and economically, because the underdevelopment of these processes often became disadvantageous for the rolling sector and steel users in terms of stable procurement of inputs and cost competitiveness, and also contributed to worsening the balance of payments. These underlying relations and interests were the basis of the steel project of the government during this period and forged the state policy of introducing an integrated steel works.

Second, the effort of the government to raise funds for its steel project was significantly affected by the changing wider political and economic relations and interests of the time. In the 1950s and 1960s, the development of the South Korean economy in general, and the steel industry in particular, was heavily influenced by US policies. As South Korea had been facing a reduction in US aid and mounting military and political pressure from North Korea, and as the international competitiveness of light manufacturing industries such as textiles was eroding, the steel project was given top priority for laying the foundations for heavy industrialisation. As described by various studies (Amsden 1989; Fukagawa 1989; D'Costa 1994), when the World Bank rejected South Korea's request for a loan, concluding that its economy was too immature to allow it to have integrated steel production, the finance and technology was arranged by the government, mainly through the Japan–Korea Normalisation Treaty of 1965. In short, the government went through significant struggles before POSCO was established as a state-owned company.

Third, the rapid growth of POSCO as well as the manufacturing sector brought about changes in political and economic relations and interests in and around the steel industry. Entry regulation introduced in 1970 led to a structure which gave POSCO a monopolistic position during the period of rapid growth from the 1970s to the mid-1980s, with other EAF and rolling firms playing subsidiary roles (Abe 2008). For example, the construction and operation of the second integrated steelworks was allocated to POSCO. The government had considered building a second integrated steelworks as early as the mid-1970s, in view of the rapid increase in domestic steel demand arising from the development of the heavy and chemical industries (POSCO 1998). Responding to this idea, POSCO and other large private business groups, such as the Hyundai Group, submitted their plans for building an integrated steelworks to the government (Amsden 1989). Innace and Abby (1992, p.141) report:

> In fact, this impending battle became one of the country's leading news stories. The government was split into two fractions. One backed POSCO, with the other supporting Hyundai. And the question of where to build the second mill was at the center of the storm.

Finally, the government gave POSCO the licence in 1978, and Kwangyang was selected as the location in 1981. The reason for the selection of POSCO rather than Hyundai remains a matter of debate.[14] What is important is that this decision that the second integrated steelworks should be owned and operated by POSCO had the effect of maintaining POSCO's monopolistic position over the production of both pig iron and steel from BOFs. In other words, the government regulated new entry so that POSCO could enjoy a monopolistic position in the upstream processes. Consequently, other EAF and rolling firms grew, depending upon this monopolistic industrial structure, and, in so doing, forged the structure. As a result of this division of labour, by the late 1970s the industry had resolved the problem of the imbalance among the processes as well as expanding production, an aspect of the underlying political and economic relations and interests that prompted policy changes in the 1980s, to be discussed in the next section.

In short, it is misleading to assume that the South Korean government was free from political and economic relations and interests in launching its massive steel project and deploying its policy towards the industry. The DSP, defined either in terms of autonomy from the market or in terms of the content of policy, misses out various factors and mechanisms specific to the pattern of capital accumulation of the industry, even in the periods of 'success'.

2.4 STAGNATION AND CRISIS: THE FALL OF THE DEVELOPMENTAL STATE?

Since the early 1970s, crude steel production of the Japanese steel industry has been stagnating. As a result, the role of the government in the restructuring of the industry during this period has attracted less attention than it did during the earlier period. Also, changes in the South Korean industry in the 1990s and the way in which its growth led to, and was punctuated by, the East Asian crisis have not been sufficiently studied. Even so, in general, it is often conceived by the DSP that the role of the government had become limited in these countries and that industrial policy had shifted towards liberalisation. In other words, the argument is that there is a demise in the role of developmental industrial policies as the economy matures, since it becomes difficult for the government to formulate and implement industrial policy.[15] However, various relations and interests continue to flourish and work through governments and other institutions, whatever the stage of development of a country. For the formation, implementation, effect and repeal of industrial policy depend on, and are attached to, the political and economic context, which is always changing. In addition, liberalisation should be understood as another type of state intervention. As Pirie (2005, p.27) points out, market disciplines 'depend on the existence of strong legal institutions (systems of market-based financial regulation, strong bankruptcy and accountancy laws, and statutory corporate governance standards) if they are to function properly'. Indeed, this section argues that state intervention shows no demise at all, even in the era of neoliberal liberalisation.

2.4.1 Restructuring in Japan

Since the early 1970s, production of steel in Japan has been fluctuating at around 100 million tonnes, only once, in 2006, exceeding the level achieved in 1973. Because of overcapacity, the production capacity of the integrated firms was reduced, particularly in the mid-1980s. At the same time, the established integrated steel-making model was strengthened by the introduction of various energy- and cost-saving technologies, such as continuous casting machines and automation.

Generally, for the DSP, sectoral studies of the Japanese steel industry for this period do not focus upon the role played by government. For example, D'Costa (1999, p.80) observes that

> the restructuring process has been largely self-led. Except for small subsidies from the government to meet certain costs associated with industry adjustment, much of the disciplining of the industry to coordinate investment and production is carried out by the industry itself.

Instead, the continuing international competitiveness of the Japanese integrated firms has been the subject of study. Itami (1997) shows how the integrated firms maintained their competitiveness even in the era of stagnant production, and Yonekura (1994) describes how the industry has 'overcome the problems associated with the oil crisis and the yen's rapid appreciation' (p.238). These contributions tend to add appeal to the 'Japanese management' argument, praising such factors as the seniority wage system, company-based trade unions, lifelong employment, and the system that inspires workers' initiatives to improve productivity. Although these studies show various important aspects of change in the industry, a major problem is that the changing pattern of capital accumulation and the role of the state in it are not appropriately captured.

It is true that Japan clearly entered the era of neoliberalism around 1980 (Itoh 2000). The government, following the United States and the United Kingdom, began to stress a balanced budget, privatisation of state-owned firms and deregulation across industries. The propaganda put forward was one of 'a small government', meaning reduction in its role and size, criticising not only Keynesian policies for effective demand, but also industrial policy relating to the supply side. However, in reality, the budget of the government has never been balanced, and its fiscal debts have been constantly increasing (Itoh 2000).

Thus a crucial question is whether the role of the state has been reduced, rather than merely being transformed, during this period? Upon surveying the empirical evidence, the role of the state cannot be said to have decreased, even though the contents, effects and forms of intervention have changed under a more neoliberal regime. In short, it is important to reveal the driving forces of neoliberal policy and its effects on the steel industry, and in doing so, to deny 'the neoliberal myth of the non-interventionist state' (Kiely 2007, p.179). Three crucial aspects in the restructuring of the steel industry are discussed in turn.

First, with regard to the integrated steel firms, the Japanese government has frequently attempted to mitigate their competition for facility investment and to facilitate their restructuring. For example, it promoted a merger between the largest two. The merger took place in 1970 to form Nippon Steel, but the fierce investment competition amongst the integrated firms was neither stopped nor coordinated by this measure, even in the face of stagnating demand after the first oil shock. Thus, through the 1970s, the integrated firms continued investment competition, but mainly by increasing their exports, which resulted in intensified trade frictions with the United States. Finally, after the second oil shock, as the overcapacity problems became severe, radical restructuring of the sector began.

As well as these trade frictions, the Japanese integrated firms were increasingly faced with price competition from EAF firms and growing foreign firms such as POSCO. In addition, it is important to note that in forming their rationalisation plans, the integrated firms exchanged information with one another and with the government. They promulgated these plans one after another between 1986 and 1987, basing them on the common assumption of an annual crude steel production in Japan of 90 million tonnes and an exchange rate of 150 yen/dollar (Kawabata 1998). In the background, the Plaza Accord of 1985, by which the yen appreciated from 255 yen/dollar in 1984 to 125 yen/dollar in 1988, was crucially important. The government quickly responded to this rationalisation. For example, MITI published a report in 1987 titled 'Towards the New Generation of the Steel Industry', which discussed the direction of the industry and measures to facilitate the changes (Tsūshō Sangyō Shō 1987). The Act on Temporary Measures for Transformation of the Industrial Structure was enacted in 1987. One purpose of the Act was to ease social conflicts in the regions where blast furnaces were pulled down by offering the regions some preferential measures in tax and finance. In addition, the supplementary budget of public works of the fiscal year 1986 was preferentially allocated to these regions (Tsūshō Sangyō Shō 1987; Nihon Tekkō Renmei 1988).

Furthermore, the government has continuously decreased corporate tax from 42 per cent to 30 per cent over the last 20 years, which assists firms in raising finance internally.[16] Since the early 1990s the integrated firms have raised finance by selling land freed up by rationalising their production. The government and regional governments have often been involved in planning the new utilisation of such land – building theme parks, shopping centres with cinema complexes, and football stadiums, for example.[17] In the late 1990s, after experiencing the long recession and in the face of external and internal pressures, the government abolished the ban on establishing holding companies by amending the Anti-Trust Act.[18] This and other factors, such as massive international restructuring in the automobile and mining sectors, prompted the reorganisation of the five integrated firms into two groups in 2002. NKK and Kawasaki Steel formed JFE Holdings in 2002; one of the affiliates of the holding company is JFE Steel, which merged the steel businesses of the two companies. Nippon Steel, Sumitomo Metal Industries and Kobe Steel came to an agreement to hold shares in one another (capital tie-up) in the same year.

Second, in contrast, the restructuring of the EAF sector became apparent as early as the mid-1970s, and governmental coordination took the form of formal measures that allowed the sector to create a recession cartel and control capacity. These measures were requested by the industry and lasted until the late 1980s, which considerably affected not only the EAF sector but also the industry as a whole, not least in terms of the speed and rhythm of restructuring.

EAF firms sought policy measures to coordinate falling prices of their products after the first oil shock in a situation of low capacity utilisation, rapidly increasing wages and electricity prices, and rising import prices of steel scrap. The government allowed a recession cartel for some long products (e.g. bars, rods and sections) in 1977, based on the Act on the Organization of Small- and Medium-Sized Enterprise Association, and implemented a structural improvement programme to abolish excess capacity of 3.9 million tonnes in 1978, designating the EAF sector as the 'structural recession sector', through enacting the Act on Temporary Measures to Stabilise Designated Depressed Industries (Nihon Tekkō Renmei 1981). The latter policy also regulated new establishment and renovation of EAFs, and promoted mergers and acquisitions. MITI enforced its policy via soft measures, for the Act did not give it the authority of compulsion. As such, it requested financial institutions to help EAF firms cut their production in line with MITI directives. As Noble (1998, p.54) puts it, 'to ensure rigorous implementation of capacity reduction schemes, MITI mobilized its network of agents throughout the country to monitor individual firms'. Even so, some firms tried to resist this policy and began to compete with the integrated firms in some relatively high-value-added long products in the early 1980s, undermining the price leadership of the integrated firms (Yonekura 1994; Kawabata 2005).

As the economic boom in the late 1980s increased steel demand, various firms, including the integrated firms, invested in the EAF method and pushed for deregulation of the EAF sector. Due to the recession that followed the appreciation of the yen by the Plaza Accord, the government lowered the bank rate to extremely low levels from 1987 to 1989, triggering an economic bubble. As a result, the regulation of the establishment and renovation of EAFs lapsed in 1988. Consequently, there was an investment boom on building EAFs as domestic steel demand surged. EAF capacity began to increase from 1988 and reached over 50 million tonnes in 1994.[19] This again gave rise to an overcapacity problem as the economy entered the long recession of the 1990s. After the bursting of the bubble, the government was forced to cut its budget on public works. Major industry groups in the EAF sector repeatedly requested the government to implement legal measures to protect the sector, which was significantly dependent upon public construction (Nihon Tekkō Renmei 2008). The government partially picked up the requests in the Act on Special Measures for Industrial Revitalisation of 1999, which provided tax and financial preference for the reconstruction of business, diversification, etc., and steel companies have been restructured utilising these measures.[20]

Third, the government was involved in assisting the integrated firms to strengthen their international network of steel production. The Japanese steel industry made significant FDI in the USA in the 1980s, especially for rolling plants, for which mother steels (slabs and hot-rolled coils) were provided locally (Sakuma 1994; Yonekura 1994; Nihon Tekkō Renmei 1999). FDI by the Japanese integrated firms in the USA was prompted by US trade policy, which restrained steel imports from Japan, and by the request of steel users, especially the Japanese automobile industry, which had earlier made FDI in the USA.

In addition, since the 1990s, the Japanese integrated steel firms have increasingly invested in downstream processes (such as cold rolling and galvanising) in Asian countries (Sakuma 1994; Nihon Tekkō Renmei 1999; Kawabata 2005). This is partly to meet the demands of the Japanese automobile and electronics sectors, which had invested in these countries a little earlier. So in providing mother products (e.g. slabs and hot-rolled coils) to their affiliated firms abroad, the integrated firms have increasingly begun to depend upon exports to Asia.

Apart from FDI, other types of internationalisation have proceeded since the 1990s. The Japanese integrated firms also have been making efforts to cooperate with foreign firms (Kawabata 2005). For example, in 2000 Nippon Steel and POSCO agreed to hold shares in one another and to cooperate in research and development for some steel products, and in securing raw materials provision. The steel-making process of Sumitomo's Wakayama works has been co-owned by Sumitomo and China Steel of Taiwan through a joint holding company since 2003, providing slabs to China Steel.

These developments suggest that the international division of labour in steel production has been changing. The integrated firms initiated cooperation in the steel markets, not least in Asia, and the government is supporting this trend by various measures, such as free trade agreements and the deregulation of international mergers and acquisitions and tie-ups (Nihon Tekkō Renmei 2008).

To sum up, the government has always been involved in mediating interests. It has continued to provide assistance for the rationalisation of the integrated firms and the EAF sector, in addition to supporting local regions and the workforce adversely affected by the rationalisation. In the struggle with the long recession of the 1990s, the move from industry-specific policies to (neoliberal) functional measures accelerated. The government enacted and amended various laws: for example, to allow the establishment of holding companies, which had been banned for nearly half a century; to ease (international) mergers and acquisitions; to deregulate labour markets, not least for the manufacturing sector; to provide rehabilitating schemes for rationalisation and diversification of business; and to reduce corporate tax. These had been requested by ailing industries, including steel, and facilitated the restructuring of the industries, in order to sustain international competitiveness. However, though these measures were not specific to the steel industry, the industry played an important role in requesting and utilising them. Furthermore, macroeconomic policy, such as the exchange rate (the Nixon shock and the Plaza Accord), the bank rate and fiscal policy towards public construction, interacted with the changing underlying political and economic relations and interests of the Japanese economy as a whole, and had a significant impact on the industry.

Chang (2006, p.254) argues:

> The Japanese corporations had already become very powerful and internationally mobile during the 1970s and 1980s, but Japan had great success with industrial policy during that period, because these firms accepted the legitimacy of industrial policy and cooperated with the government for its success.

However, steel firms were not concerned with the 'legitimacy' of industrial policy, but lobbied for, and responded to, various policies, based on the political and economic relations and interests specific to each period in which they operated. In short, first, the government has been, and continues to be, far from non-interventionist. Second, although the development of the Japanese steel industry may be divided into catch-up and mature phases, it is misleading to characterise the former as a time when industrial policy had a significant role to play, and the latter as a time when its role was insignificant.

2.4.2 Restructuring before and after the Crisis in South Korea

While the experience of the South Korean steel industry up to the late 1980s has been widely studied as a successful example of latecomer advantages and of state-led industrialisation, few studies have addressed the development and restructuring of the South Korean steel industry from the late 1980s to the early 2000s.[21] In terms of its output performance, crude steel production had recorded even faster growth from the late 1980s to the East Asian crisis of 1997 than from the early 1970s to the late 1980s. In addition, since the crisis, crude steel production has again increased steadily, exceeding the level achieved before the crisis (42.5 million tonnes in 1997), and reaching 50 million tonnes in 2007, although the pace of growth has slackened. The point is that this performance cannot be explained by focusing only upon POSCO, or by pointing to the demise of industrial policy. There is a need to offer an industry-specific study of what had been taking place prior to the crisis as well as what happened after it.

The second oil crisis triggered the economic crisis of 1979–80 and punctuated the economic growth of South Korea. The country was forced to borrow stand-by credit and thus had to follow the conditionality imposed by the international financial institutions (Fukagawa 1999; Kim and Cho 1999). Consequently, economic liberalisation became a policy task, even though the conditionality focused more on macroeconomic than on industry-specific policy. Furthermore, in the mid-1980s, as the yen appreciated sharply after the Plaza Accord of 1985, the export of South Korean manufactured goods, mainly automobiles and electronic products, surged, not least towards US markets. As a result, trade friction with the USA became acute. Therefore, external pressure for economic liberalisation became even stronger. In addition to external pressure, the government came under rising internal pressure to liberalise its economy (Fukagawa 1999; Kim and Cho 1999). As the economy grew rapidly in recovering from the recession, the private sector increasingly demanded a liberalised regime, calling for deregulation of new entry and capacity expansion to allow entry into successful sectors and to raise corporate external finance for facility investment. In this way, policy changes such as the liberalisation of entry and the partial privatisation of POSCO were pushed forward and finally materialised in the late 1980s. These triggered fierce facility investment competition, which was further facilitated and fed by financial liberalisation. Three points are worth highlighting.

First, responding to liberalisation and increasing demand from the late 1980s, various groups of firms, including POSCO, aggressively entered in the downstream processes of steel production (Abe 2008). POSCO invested, for example, in cold rolling, since privatisation forced POSCO to invest in high-return projects as well as to try to match the development of the Korean automobile and electronics industries. This created intense competition in the flat-product markets (e.g. coils, sheets and plates) among existing EAF and rolling companies, and they too began to invest in new facilities, with the involvement of conglomerates. In addition, from the late 1980s the government implemented various policies to boost a boom in home ownership. This contributed to increasing the demand for long products and, in turn, stimulated private companies to build new EAFs in the 1990s. Even POSCO built an EAF in 1993.

Second, the intensified investment competition in the steel and other industries further pushed forward deregulation, not least of finance. As financial liberalisation finally took hold in the mid-1990s, it fuelled investment competition. This took the form of competition between various groups of companies. Many investments would not have been possible for a single firm, for a steel facility necessitates significant investment (Mizuno 1999). Further, the investment competition depended upon external finance, and optimistic expectations over such investment based on the long boom (Kim and Cho 1999).[22] In other words, the intensified competition between conglomerates across the industries exerted internal pressure on the government to deregulate further, not least in finance, and in turn investment was driven by financial liberalisation.[23]

Third, even though the government was losing its coordinating authority through the licence system because of deregulation policies, it tried to keep the monopoly of POSCO in the upstream process in the 1990s (Suzuki 2003; Abe 2008). In 1995 the Hyundai Group announced installation of a new integrated steelworks, with blast furnaces. The government, fearing excess capacity, decided not to accept Hyundai's (or any other such) plan by resorting to its remaining regulatory authority.[24] Also, seeing the rise of new mini-mill technology (utilising an EAF with thin-slab continuous casting machines and a compact hot strip mill), not least in the USA, the idea had been gaining momentum in the mid-1990s that steel production using the BOF method had become obsolete (e.g.

Crandall 1996). With regard to this government decision, Chang (2006, p.216) argues that the government

> supported what many, if not all, people regarded as an over-ambitious steel venture by Hanbo, a medium-sized chaebol with a dubious track record in manufacturing. The decision was emphatically not taken as a part of any coherent industrial policy, and looked particularly strange when the government had already refused to endorse the largest conglomerate Hyundai's entry into the steel industry.

This might be misleading in two senses. The government, on the one hand, liberalised investment and entry, and the Hyundai Group did enter into the steel business in the downstream sector (EAFs and rolling processes). On the other hand, the government tried to maintain the monopoly of POSCO in the upstream process (blast furnaces and BOFs). The technology that Hanbo chose (EAF-based integrated production) did not conflict with this policy towards the steel industry. Thus, it may be the case that the decision to approve Hanbo's plan and reject Hyundai's was part of a coherent industrial policy.[25]

This pattern of capital accumulation resulted in a renewal of increasing imbalance among the processes of iron-making, steel-making and rolling. On one hand, POSCO's monopolistic position in steel-making had been weakened. The share of POSCO in such capacity decreased from 68.9 per cent in 1990 to 59.4 per cent in 1999, due to the massive investment of other firms in EAFs. On the other hand, POSCO maintained its monopoly over iron-making. A result was an emerging imbalance of capacity amongst iron-making, steel-making and rolling: the iron-making capacity of the South Korean steel industry as a whole became significantly too small compared to the rapidly increased size of rolling and steel-making. As a result, steel firms other than POSCO had to procure mother products such as slabs and hot-rolled coils from abroad.

Finally, when the steel-using export-oriented industries showed signs of a downturn, excessive investment in the steel industry became a burden. From 1996, the Korean economy faced the depreciation of the yen and the fall in price of semiconductors, two factors damaging the export-oriented industries (Mitarai 2000). Accordingly, domestic demand for steel products plummeted and so did steel prices (Kawai 1997). This severely hit steel makers, not least the firms that had aggressively made facility investment. The steel industry entails significant investment, and the gestation period of building plants is long, so that it is vulnerable to cyclical demand, not least when the facility investment depends on loans. Indeed, the first three companies whose collapse triggered the crisis in Korea in 1997 were steel companies. Hanbo Iron and Steel, which was the most aggressive company in facility investment, was the first to become insolvent, followed by Sammi Special Steel and Kia Special Steel (Mizuno 1999). Afterwards, Kwangwon Industries and Korea Iron and Steel in the EAF sector went into bankruptcy (Park and Tcha 2003).

The government, following the conditionalities imposed by the IMF, implemented various measures (Kim and Cho 1999); indeed, neoliberal policies were further promoted (Chang 2006). For corporate restructuring, it laid down a bankruptcy scheme and debt-decreasing guidelines, and the privatisation of state-owned companies became a main issue. The government also deregulated labour markets as well as foreign investment, in order to facilitate restructuring (Honjo 2000). The post-crisis restructuring of the steel industry took place in this further liberalised policy regime. This restructuring process was driven by conflicting interests in the industry, which had their basis in the imbalance among the steel processes discussed above.

First, the Hyundai Motor Group enhanced its presence significantly in the steel industry (Park and Tcha 2003). The group started buying bankrupted steel makers. Inchon Steel, a firm belonging to the group, absorbed Kwangwon Industries in 2000, and took over Sammi Special Steel, altering its name to BNG Steel. Inchon Steel became INI steel in 2001 (now Hyundai Steel) and, in 2004, INI Steel bought the Dangjin plant of Hanbo Iron and Steel.

Second, POSCO was completely privatised in 2000 (Lim 2003). The government announced its privatisation policy for state-owned companies in 1998, and POSCO was given top priority for privatisation, since it was competitive and the government considered that privatisation would enhance its competitiveness. The remaining shares held by governmental institutions were to be phased out in steps from 1998 to 2000, so that even POSCO could in principle be acquired at any time by domestic or foreign firms or investors. In this way, the crisis triggered a restructuring. The monopolistic position of POSCO was on the decline; however, crude steel production as a whole became concentrated into the hands of a small number of groups of firms, namely the POSCO

Group, the Hyundai Motor Group and the Dongkuk Steel Group (Mizuno 2000).

Third, the conflict of interest between the fully privatised POSCO and the Hyundai Motor Group, based on the continuing imbalance among processes, was an important factor driving the restructuring of the industry after the crisis. In 1999, Hyundai Pipe requested POSCO to supply hot-rolled coils for cold rolling (Suzuki 2003; Abe 2008). However POSCO rejected the request, insisting that it did not have sufficient capacity. Hyundai Pipe managed to procure hot-rolled coils from Japanese integrated firms and began operation of cold-rolling lines.[26]

The government attempted to coordinate the conflicts between POSCO and the Hyundai Motor Group. However, due to the further liberalisation of its regulatory power after the crisis by the repealing or amendment of the Industry Development Act and other acts (Honjo 2000), it no longer had the measures to make these companies follow its instruction. Instead, the government intervened by way of competition laws (Abe 2008). The Fair Trade Commission (FTC) adjudicated that POSCO's refusal to supply hot-rolled coils to Hyundai Pipe was an abuse of its monopolistic position. POSCO appealed this adjudication of the FTC to the High Court. Finally, in 2003, POSCO decided to supply hot-rolled coils to Hyundai Hysco (the renamed Hyundai Pipe), thus bringing the conflict to an end, at least temporarily.

Later, the Hyundai Motor Group announced the building of a new integrated steelworks and started construction in 2006. If completed, the Hyundai Motor Group will have an integrated steel works with an annual capacity of 12 million tonnes in addition to EAF plants, and will become a strong competitor to POSCO. The government no longer had any powers to stop the group and also had no reason to oppose the plan (Abe 2008). For the world steel industry showed an upward trend from 2002, mainly because of the miraculous increase in demand from China. In addition, at this stage, the idea that mini-mill technology would be the next generation technology and would replace steel production using the BOF method had lost momentum in the world steel industry after the East Asian crisis.

Seeing the strategy of the Hyundai Motor Group, POSCO is now trying to find a new strategy of its own (POSCO 2006). It has been making efforts to develop export markets for high-value-added steel products. For the Hyundai Motor Group is POSCO's biggest domestic customer, and it will have its own integrated steel firms. POSCO is therefore seeking to find new customers who will purchase its steel product for automobile manufacture (Abe 2008). POSCO has established many coil centres abroad, especially in Asian countries, and has launched a steel project in India to build an integrated steelworks (Park 2008).[27] Further, POSCO perceives Vietnam as a priority country in which to allocate its resources (Kawabata 2007). As a background to this, in 2003 the government announced a policy of promoting free-trade agreements (Okuda 2007).

In sum, investment competition materialised and intensified, based on liberalisation which was itself prompted partly by the 'successful' economic growth of the economy, and this finally led to the crisis. On the one hand, it is misleading to understand the neoliberal reform as encompassing a non-interventionist state. On the other hand, it is also misleading to presume that the reform necessarily harmed the investment dynamism of the South Korean economy, although there are certainly a number of serious problems with neoliberalism. As shown above, the neoliberal policy reform reflects the changing pattern of capital accumulation, and its effect depends on changing political and economic relations and interests.

2.5 CONCLUDING REMARKS

This chapter's limited overview reveals that policy is continuously formulated and implemented, and brings about various results and changes, reflecting changing political and economic relations and interests. The study of the Japanese and South Korean steel industries shows that the role of the state has not been decreasing at all, even though the contents and methods of state intervention are certainly changing towards neoliberal policy. Therefore, it should be conceived that what has eroded in Japan and South Korea is a certain type of state intervention, or more precisely, a certain type of state–capital–labour relations, rather than industrial policy per se.

In addition, it becomes clear that each industrial and other sector within an economy has its own pattern of capital accumulation, and the diversity among them is obscured by the dichotomy between market and state. For the dichotomy depends on unduly abstract concepts, not least 'market'. In other words, the dichotomy as such inherently has the tendency of neglecting and concealing various political and economic (class) interests which are always exerted upon the formation and implementation of policy and affect its outcome.

Thus, the findings of this chapter cast doubt on the DSP as an appropriate and effective framework for examining the role of the state in development and for studying development itself. Further, this chapter demonstrates the strong need to situate state intervention in the context of political and economic relations and interests, rejecting the dichotomy of state and market as an analytical starting point.

In other words, there are alternatives to the DSP. The task of understanding development

> depends upon rediscovery, and not peremptory dismissal, of the political economy of the past and its careful attachment to an understanding of the restructuring of capital through the movement of the different forms of capital and their association with class, interests and the state. (Fine, Petropoulos and Sato 2005, p.62)

This study is such an attempt, and will need to be extended in the future.

NOTES

1. See Chapter 1 of this volume for a critical overview of the DSP.
2. The restructuring of capital is a concept 'drawing upon Marx's notion of centralisation (and concentration) of capital and its implications through production, distribution and exchange. The approach argues that the restructuring of capital materialises in production but can be levered (or not) through corporations directly, the state (industrial policy in the broadest sense), exchange (access to markets and competition), finance (the role of banks in funding and/or directing investment) and labour (through its workplace and political struggle)' (Fine, Petropoulos and Sato, 2005, p.45).
3. For example, even Balassa (1988), in denying the role of strategic state intervention in South Korea during its rapid economic growth, accepted the importance, or at least the existence, of industrial policy for the South Korean steel industry.
4. The categories of industrial policy listed by Chang can be summarised as follows: first, the state coordination for complementary investments in the presence of scale economies and capital-market imperfections ('big push', industrial plans); second, the coordination of investments for competing projects (managed or excessive competition), recession cartels and M&As for decreasing social costs; third, industrial policy for ensuring cost competitiveness (industrial licensing, government procurement, export requirements, and subsidies) and the maximum possible scale in production (luxury consumption control) in the presence of scale economies; and fourth, protective industrial policy offering social insurance for the short run (recession cartels) and promoting structural change in the long run (cartels for the structurally depressed industries).

5. Figures of steel production in this chapter are derived from International Iron and Steel Institute (now World Steel Association), *Steel Statistical Yearbook* (Brussels), various issues, Japan Iron and Steel Federation, *Handbook for Iron and Steel Statistics* (Tokyo), various issues, and Korea Iron and Steel Association, *Steel Statistical Yearbook* (Seoul), various issues, unless otherwise indicated.
6. The process of steel production basically consists of three steps, iron-making, steel-making and rolling. In iron-making, pig iron is made from iron ore, cokes, and limestone by using blast furnaces. In steel-making, in the indirect method, pig iron is turned into molten steel in open-hearth furnaces (OHFs) or basic oxygen furnaces (BOFs). In the direct method, scrap or directly reduced iron (DRI) is cast in electric arc furnaces (EAFs). This process decides the quality or type of steel, such as mild (carbon) steel, various alloy steel and stainless steel, which are distinguished by the amount of alloying metals and carbon included. The molten steel is then transformed into semi-finished steel products (blooms, billets or slabs). In rolling, by using various mills, finished products are made from the semi-finished products, yielding flat products (coils, sheets and plates) or long products (bars, rods, sections). Integrated firms or plants are involved in all three processes, while mini-mills or EAF companies produce steel in EAF and rolling processes.
7. In addition to industrial policies in the broadest sense, institutions have attracted attention. D'Costa (1999, p.80) emphasises the importance of the 'institutional arrangement between the state, business, and the banking sector'. Yonekura (1994, pp.207–9) focuses on the birth and innovation of entrepreneurs, such as Nishiyama's model of integrated steelworks sited at deep-water ports, and on the oligopolistic competition between the private integrated firms in the development of the industry. Hasegawa (1996, ch.6) sheds light on the internal relations of the integrated steel firms, i.e. management and labour, not least the so-called dual workforce system, in enabling 'the labour flexibility required' (p.97) for introducing and upgrading technologies.
8. For example, Johnson (1982, pp.255–6) describes in detail how a high-ranked bureaucrat of MITI was cordial towards Yawata and Fuji, the largest steel firms, which had been a single government enterprise up to 1951.
9. Note that Johnson formulated this model with a caveat that 'analytically speaking, the issue still remains that it is hard to abstract a "model" from historical reality' (Johnson 1999 p.43).
10. Before the Second World War, as the steel industry became extremely important for the country's interests in terms of military necessity, it was strongly promoted, supported and controlled by various governmental policies. Reflecting the power relations between the government and the private sector, some private firms remained outside the creation of Japan Steel, into which the government attempted to concentrate steel production. Damage by the war to the production facilities was small, even though production was not sustained due to the consecutive defeats in the final stages of the war. The collapse of the steel industry mainly derived from the loss of ships which delivered raw materials from abroad. For the development of the Japanese steel industry before the Second World War, see Iida, Ohashi and Kuroiwa (1969), for example.
11. It is important to note that this system also included the 'adjustment' of operations, controlling quantity of production, not least for OHF production, and this policy too promoted a shift of technology to BOFs from OHFs.

12. Integrated companies began to penetrate into one another's steel products from the late 1950s, not least in strip-mill products, when demand for these products, mainly from the shipbuilding and automobile industries, began to increase. At this stage, there was huge pressure from interest payments, for the integrated firms had taken out huge loans externally.
13. Note that it has been argued that South Korea's strategy to create the steel industry was functionally and technologically an imitation of Japan's, but institutionally different (Shin 1996, ch.7; Kipping 1997). For, due to the size of the economy and the difference in political regime, in addition to the non-existence of integrated steel production before the Second World War, state intervention in South Korea had been much more direct than in Japan.
14. POSCO argued that the steel industry had a public content, so that even the second integrated steelworks should not be delegated to the private sector and that it was an international trend for steel firms to become larger. In contrast, the Hyundai Group insisted that the steel industry should be brought under a competitive structure and that the Group could forge backward and forward linkages with the construction, shipbuilding and other industries, where it had significant presence. See Innace and Abby (1992, ch.17).
15. For the political school of the developmental state approach, once industrialisation is achieved, the scope and effect of industrial policy will fade away; thus the developmental state has a limited life. The autonomy of the state will be damaged by the strong economic class that appears as industrialisation proceeds (Moon 1999; Minns 2001). In contrast, the economic school argues that various liberalisation measures resulted in the demise of industrial polices and that the liberalised regime for foreign capital exposed the economies to an inherently unstable international capital market (Chang, Palma and Whittaker 1998; Wade 1998). Therefore, the literature characterises this stage as reflecting the decline, or even demise, of industrial policy, thus of the developmental state.
16. Corporate tax was reduced from 42.0 per cent to 40.0 per cent in 1989, to 37.5 per cent in 1990, to 34.5 per cent in 1998 and to 30.0 per cent in 1999. Also, in the 1990s the government deregulated requirements for issuing shares and bonds by amending relevant laws. See Nihon Tekkō Renmei (1981, pp.363–72; 1988, pp.294–304). In contrast to the reductions in corporate tax, in 1989 the government introduced a consumer tax, increasing the rate from 3 per cent to 5 per cent in 1997. See Itoh (2000, p.103).
17. This also involved deregulation in laws that regulated land usage (Nihon Tekkō Renmei 2008, pp.158–66).
18. The ban on establishing holding companies was introduced by the US Occupation Force, to repress the revival of Japanese conglomerates.
19. At least eleven EAF units were newly installed between 1988 and 1994 (Nihon Tekkō Renmei 1999, p.62)
20. The Act was twice amended, in 2003 and 2007, in order to widen the scope of its application. In addition to EAF firms such as Toyo Seiko and Kunimitsu Seiko, the integrated firms have also utilised the scheme of the Act; by 2007, 28 applications from steel firms had been approved by the government (Nihon Tekkō Renmei 2008, pp.181–2).
21. Indeed, the continuous growth of POSCO has been the only aspect in focus even in these studies (Shin 1996, ch.7; D'Costa 1999, ch.4), which chart how POSCO constructed the second integrated steelworks (the Kwangyang works) between 1985 and 1992.

22. For the steel industry, the share of internal finance was significantly lower in the 1990s, compared to the 1980s. It was 59.6 per cent during 1981–85, while it decreased to 40.1 per cent during 1991–95 and to 32.4 per cent during 1996–2000.
23. Needless to say, the financial deregulation was also promoted through external pressure.
24. Although the government had liberalised entry regulation, it still retained some measures to control entry. For example, it was able to influence entry and expansion by designating a sector as the object of rationalisation or by not allowing the import of a particular technology if this had already been imported by other companies. See Chang (2006, ch.2) and Honjo (2000, pp.24–5).
25. Be that as it may, it has been claimed that corruption affected the government's support for Hanbo (Nozoe 1999).
26. The Japanese integrated firms were suffering from the long recession with low operating rates, so that Hyundai Pipe was able to procure hot-rolled coils at a low price, not least from Kawasaki. Hyundai Pipe made a comprehensive technological agreement with Kawasaki (now JFE Steel) in 2000, including hot-rolled coil procurement and technological cooperation.
27. By 2016, it plans to expand capacity to 12 million tonnes. However, it has been facing significant difficulties in land acquisition.

3
An Alternative Perspective on Industrial Policy: The Case of the South Korean Car Industry

Kwon-Hyung Lee

3.1 INTRODUCTION

Over the past four decades a wide variety of literature on industrial policy has inspired numerous wide-ranging practical and theoretical issues. Much of this has focused on the successful role of industrial policy in post-war East Asian economies, such as Japan and NICs (newly industrialising countries) including South Korea, favourably comparing an 'East Asian model' with Latin American ISI (import-substitution industrialisation) (Amsden 1989; Wade 1990). East Asian industrial successes were also contrasted with the deindustrialisation of the Anglo-American economies in the 1970s. This brought about heated industrial policy debate in the 1980s, producing controversial arguments for reindustrialisation (Stout 1979; Zysman and Tyson 1983; Johnson 1984). From the 1990s, however, industrial policy was increasingly considered old-fashioned and inefficient, with such changes reflecting a retreat from the developmental state. Industrial policy was often regarded as an influential factor in the Japanese economic recession and the Asian financial crisis of the late 1990s (Porter and Takeuchi 1999; Crafts 1999). Specifically, in South Korea, deregulation was strengthened as an IMF austerity programme was implemented. Most recently, though, the role of industrial policy is being re-examined in the wake of the global financial crisis. According to European commentators, industrial policy is back as a strategy for economic recovery and industrial sustainability (Bailey, Lenihan and Arauzo-Carod 2011).

The stance towards industrial policy, then, displays a rhythm in line with industrial performance, correspondingly (dis)favouring state and market in opposition to one another. But it often does so without sufficient regard to the deeper contexts of specific countries and sectors. Successful industrial-policy-practising countries are often regarded as big corporations, as reflected in expressions like 'Japan, Inc.', 'Korea, Inc.', without reference to the complex peculiarities of each industry and country. This shows that existing arguments over industrial policy have placed emphasis on the roles of state and market.

Moreover, it should also be noted that the typical question of why industrial policy has been so successful in the East Asian economies, if only temporarily, tends to presuppose a regional dichotomy. However, many cases of inefficient and ineffective performance of industrial policy can be found alongside successes in the same region. Also, even the same kinds of policy in the same sector can bring about different outcomes across countries. For example, according to Jenkins's (1995) comparative study of some NICs' car industries, Taiwan's automobile sector is less successful than those of Latin American NICs such as Brazil and Mexico. The outcomes of industrial policy practices of the same kind can be different at different times even in the same country. In effect, South Korea's various regulatory policies implemented in the car sector were not effective until the early 1970s, because they failed to remove a vicious circle of small scale of production, high production costs and narrow domestic demand. In contrast, industrial policy practices from the mid-1970s to the late 1980s recorded a remarkable performance in production and exports of cars. In particular, the Long-Term Promotion Plan for the Motor Industry of 1973–74 played an important role in setting a particular industrial strategy of local development and exports of 'Korean-type' cars and, thereby, reshaping the economic relations in the sector. These cases demonstrate that it is meaningless to link a certain type of industrial policy directly to success or failure without analysis of the concrete contexts in which industrial policy is exercised. To some extent, such lack of realism in established perspectives on industrial policy arises from the ways in which such policy is defined and its objectives understood, only relying on stylised and selected economy-level characteristics of those countries perceived as economically successful. These considerations reinforce the imperative of paying attention to specific and shifting contexts as well as avoiding self-selected evidence across economies deemed to be successful.

Once heterogeneity in policy and outcome is recognised, different kinds of research questions present themselves in order to avoid misleading judgements and to broaden perspectives on industrial policy itself. Firstly, the economic forces that promote industrial policy should be examined in each case. Conventionally, the necessity of industrial policy has been explained by the presence of market or coordination failures. It is argued that the government directs industrial policy at correcting those failures or reducing the economic costs caused by them. Moreover, it is suggested that investments across sectors should be coordinated by the state with the aim of industrialisation of the economy, as shown, for example, in the debate between balanced and unbalanced growth or the 'strategic industry' argument.[1] As Grant (1982) points out, it is understood that industrial policy is motivated by government measures to influence the investment decisions of individual enterprises. That is, from a policymaking point of view, there is a need for coordination to preclude excessive competition through too many entrants, which may give rise to unnecessary price wars and overinvestment (Okimoto 1989; Chang 1994).

Arguments of this kind, however, do not explain why some countries use industrial policy in certain sectors while others do not. Nor do they explain different outcomes when the same policies are adopted. In contrast, it is suggested here that underlying economic and political interests in capital accumulation are unavoidable factors in forging and implementing industrial policy. Thus, the way in which underlying economic agents with different economic interests are linked to each other needs to be at the heart of any analysis of industrial policy.

The second question is how industrial policy affects industrial performance. Outcomes are often seen in aggregate industrial figures such as production or exports. However, these are not a sufficient indicator, not least because they fluctuate significantly, regardless of changes in policy. Why this should be so needs to be explained; and reference needs to be made to underlying economic relations as the reasons for, and effects of, industrial policy. For such relations are relatively stable and a major influence on the profitability of manufacturing, say, motor vehicles. In other words, it is assumed here that the effects of industrial policy lie in providing new conditions for capital accumulation by readjusting economic relations, although the latter in themselves cannot guarantee specific linkage effects. As far as the car sector is concerned, an oligopolistic structure, assembler–supplier relations, and local assembler–multinationals relations are the most significant factors determining the context in which cars are built and automobile capital accumulates. However, as emphasised, the effects of industrial policy are diverse as a result of the different conditions obtaining in different countries.

The third question is why industrial policy has been eroded if it contributed to industrial development earlier. Existing literature has explained the 'life cycle' of industrial policy in two different ways. One is that it is necessary only at the initial (sunrise) and senile (sunset) stages of industrial development in view of the 'industry ageing' hypothesis (Okimoto 1989). The other is that the emerging strength and organisation of both capitalists and workers come to limit state autonomy (Evans 1995). Interestingly, although they explore different aspects, the economic and the political, both views lead to the same implication: when the industry matures, the state shrinks. However, in the case of South Korea in the early 1980s, market-oriented policy reforms, including market liberalisation and deregulation, were promoted less by a weak state than by a strong one with the capacity to act in line with global trends towards neoliberal policies. In addition, they occurred even before national strategic industries had matured. Seen in this vein, the erosion of industrial policy in South Korea can be interpreted as a different form of state intervention unconnected with the degree of state strength and industrial maturity.

By examining these research questions in more detail, this chapter attempts to provide an alternative perspective on industrial policy, focusing on South Korea's car manufacturing sector, which has been touted as one of the most impressive industrial successes across the NICs. Section 3.2 mainly deals with the first and second questions, suggesting an alternative research framework on industrial policy to identify economic realities and rationales underlying government intervention. Then, by way of illustration, Section 3.3 shows the characteristics of various relations between local assemblers, suppliers, and multinationals in the South Korean car sector. Section 3.4 explores the third question and the South Korean case in the 1990s. The final section summarises the major points of this chapter and offers some concluding remarks.

3.2 THE ECONOMIC IMPERATIVES AND EFFECTS OF INDUSTRIAL POLICY

Much of the existing literature has suggested that the economic rationale for state intervention in industry involves market or coordination failures, a view that gives rise to some analytical problems. Most significantly, state intervention is understood as being opposed to economic activities undertaken by the private sector. This view implies that non-market institutions such as the state have different economic aims, visions and interests from industrialists, or market forces. Accordingly, it is assumed that the state should 'regulate' and 'coordinate' private interests for the sake of public interests. It should be noted, however, that industrial policy promoting public or national interests cannot be an appropriate analytical starting point because of the following points.

First, the criteria for the division between public and private interests regarding the conduct of a certain industrial policy are not well-defined. For example, regulatory measures such as import bans and entry licensing are understood as aimed at the establishment of a local industry, which can be interpreted as government decision based on a national interest. In effect, however, these measures primarily favour the economic interests of local producers and incumbents against importers and prospective entrants, respectively. In addition, the promotion plans for strategic industries are regarded as necessary for nationally coordinated investment in the public interest.[2] It cannot be denied, however, that they come to protect selected private interests through a wide variety of fiscal and financial incentives.

Second, the dichotomy between public and private interests tends to neglect the need to explore what specific forms industrial policy takes across different sectors and circumstances. In reality, although their broad aims are similar across countries and sectors, industrial policies in practice have been formulated differently, depending on socio-economic and sectoral structures, with various levels of competition prevailing between industrialists – local assemblers, component and part manufacturers and multinationals, in the case of the car sector. This structure-specific nature of industrial policy cannot be analysed simply by identifying public as opposed to private interests.

Third, the argument favouring public interests against private interests tends to suggest that policy successes or failures are attributed to non-economic factors, such as policymakers' capabilities to design policies and state autonomy to implement them, rather than to socio-economic or sectoral structures. In effect, even if designed appropriately and implemented firmly, industrial policies in themselves cannot guarantee their assumed effects without structural changes in industry.

In contrast, the alternative perspective on industrial policy adopted here suggests that economic imperatives to make and implement industrial policy can be derived from the exigencies of capital accumulation. Large-scale capital and the state may forge a common interest in sustaining accumulation of capital. However, the relations between capital and the state are neither a direct economic relation, apart possibly from state-owned corporations, nor a result of simple political negotiations. Rather, it is assumed that large-scale capital has various economic relations with other economic agents, such as Small- and Medium-Sized enterprises, foreign multinationals and the like, in the process of capital accumulation. The economic interests of large-scale capital against those of other economic agents have an influence on the conduct of industrial policy, although other economic interests may be protected in disproportionate ways. Thus, without an analysis of concrete economic relations, it is almost impossible to uncover the imperatives of industrial policy in a specific conjuncture.

With respect to identification of economic interests, three points should be made. First, economic interests should be distinguished from 'self-interest', based on the methodological individualism which mainstream economics regards as a starting point. As Adam Smith (1986, pp.118–19) observes:

> Whoever offers to another a bargain of any kind, proposes to do this. Give me that which I want, and you shall have this which you want, is the meaning of every such offer ... It is not from the benevolence of the butcher, the brewer, or the baker that we expect our dinner, but from their regard to their own interest.

Such a notion of self-interest may expand to a national economy, creating a notion of 'national interest'. The latter has dual meanings. On the one hand, it indicates public or impartial interests against private interests. On the other hand, it is used in the context of international competition between nation states. A national economy is, within this perspective, treated as an individual participating in global competition. In contrast, in this chapter, underlying economic relations making a socio-economic structure are the basis on which competing economic interests are constructed. For example, profitability in manufacturing cars, in which assemblers' economic interests are primarily expressed, relies heavily not only on industrial relations but also on assembler–supplier relations, market structure, international linkage with multinationals, and so on. In turn, differing levels of profitability are the basis of continuous competition between economic agents. In this respect, the analysis of economic interests should not be confined to either microeconomic scope or interest-group politics. Rather, it should embrace both economic structure and complex patterns of competition between economic agents located in broader contexts.

Second, it is assumed here that changes in industrial policy reflect changing or emerging economic interests of socially dominant economic agents. For example, an emphasis placed on export promotion cannot be sustained without the support of large-scale exporters.[3] Not surprisingly, it is accompanied by new legislation and institutions making large-scale export possible.

Third, providing large-scale capital with institutional incentives and promoting an industry in a specific way involve political decision making of high-ranking policymakers intertwined with economic agents' political lobbying, including the resistance from those agents or companies discriminated against by the policy. This is the basis of political interests that have an influence on the making of industrial policy along with economic interests. Although creating considerable conflicts at times, the interaction of economic and political interests results in concrete policies, pursuing a common goal of capital accumulation. It is of great importance, therefore, to 'unravel the formation and representation of economic and political interests through both the state and the market' (Fine 1997b, p.125).

Conversely, though, how can industrial policy affect underlying interests? Conventionally, the effectiveness of industrial policy is evaluated by industrial performance, such as production and exports. However, as long as the effects of industrial policy are examined superficially by performance of 'nationally picked' players, the question is not properly grounded. For such figures as production or exports fluctuate massively according to international economic conditions apart from policy changes. For example, rapid increase in production and exports of South Korean cars in the mid-to-late 1980s is to some extent attributed to improvements in international terms of trade (Green 1992).[4] Without consideration of the latter, the efficacy of industrial policies implemented in the early 1980s might be overestimated.

Unlike much of the literature, it is assumed here that the effect of industrial policy is to provide specific conditions for sustainable capital accumulation by coordinating economic and political interests based on economic relations in a sector. While industrial policy is driven by economic and political interests, as explained earlier, its effect is to coordinate them. It should be noted, however, that the term coordination here is understood in a broader context than in usual arguments. According to these, coordination is narrowly applied to inter- or intra-industry investments as targeted in strategic trade policy and industrial-structure-upgrading arguments. In other arguments, the significance of coordination is confined to political negotiation between government and business, ignoring the presence of socio-economic structure. In contrast, it is suggested here that coordinating economic and political interests involves changes of various levels of economic relations underlying an industry, which themselves determine a pattern of capital accumulation. For economic relations are the basis on which economic and political interests are constructed and, furthermore, on which the structure of profitability primarily relies. More specifically, changing economic relations as an effect of industrial policy signify industrial restructuring or structural (re-)adjustment in a sector, which might exploit further economies of scale and external economies. So the concrete analysis of changing economic relations is necessary for identification of the effects of industrial policy; in other words, the latter cannot be analysed appropriately just with indications of some stylised linkage effects between industrial policy and performance, whether economic or political.

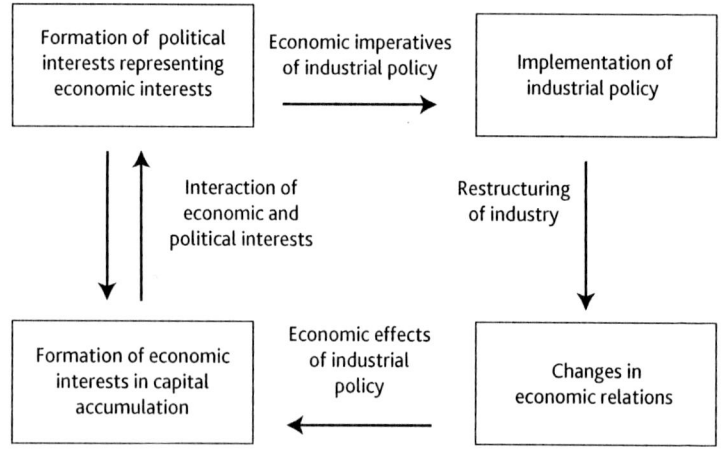

Figure 3.1 An Alternative Research Framework for Industrial Policy

Nevertheless, it should be noted that acknowledging the importance of the representation of business interests does not necessarily entail a passive role for the state. The success of industrial policy depends on the ability of the state to forge a new set of economic and political interests where previously these did not exist (Fine 1997a). For example, when a state attempts to initiate industrialisation or upgrade industrial structure, economic interests to back the structural shift need be formed and, thus, the process cannot be assumed to be automatic (see Figure 3.1).

3.3 THE CASE OF THE SOUTH KOREAN CAR SECTOR

This section considers the case of the car manufacturing industry in South Korea, focusing on the three levels of economic relations in the sector.

3.3.1 Inter-Assembler Competition

Issues regarding inter-assembler competition have dominated policy discussions among South Korean policymakers since the early 1960s. More specifically, although there are many factors influencing the form of competition between large-scale assemblers, limiting the number of final assemblers has been the most significant policy tool.[5] In view of narrow and uncultivated car demand, concern about excessive competition and overinvestment was prevalent, leading to a policy consensus to limit the number of assemblers to between one and three until the end of the 1980s.

As a result, as shown in Table 3.1, the number of car assemblers did not exceed three until the early 1990s. In particular, the early promotion period of the sector from 1962 to 1967 witnessed only a single assembler, endorsed by legislation and national planning. More significantly, control of the number of assemblers involved coercive exit from the sector in the process of state-led restructuring. In the mid-1970s, Asia Motors, then one of the three existing car makers, was deprived of a licence to produce cars on the grounds that its investment plan fell far below government guidelines. Then Kia, a truck and motorbike assembler, was allowed to produce passenger cars. The company, however, was again forced to leave the car sector in the aftermath of the economic and political crisis of 1979–80, although it was exclusively allowed to produce light commercial vehicles.

This successful application of entry regulation in South Korea has been regarded as distinct from other NICs (Wade 1990). Above all, such monopolistic or oligopolistic market structure has an economic rationale for reaping scale economies, which are crucial for the development of the sector.[6] In other words, tough entry regulation was conducive to hindering fragmentation of the final assembly sector. In addition, allowing only a small number of car makers was advantageous to policy communication between government and business (Chang 1994).

Table 3.1 Number of Passenger Car Assemblers in South Korea

Number	1962–63 1	1964–67 1	1968–73 3	1974–80 3	1981–86 2
Companies	Saenara	Shinjin	Shinjin/GMK Hyundai Asia	GMK/Saehan Hyundai Kia	Saehan/Daewoo Hyundai

Number	1987–92 3	1993 4	1994–97 5	1998 3	1999–present 4
Companies	Daewoo Hyundai Kia	Daewoo Hyundai Kia Ssangyong	Daewoo Hyundai Kia Ssangyong Samsung	Daewoo–Ssangyong Hyundai–Kia Samsung	GM-Daewoo Hyundai–Kia Renault-Samsung Ssangyong

Notes
1. Assemblers that produce Jeeps or SUVs are excluded.
2. Owing to changes in capital ownership and management, Shinjin was renamed GM Korea in 1972, Saehan in 1976, and Daewoo in 1983.
3. Ssangyong and Samsung were allowed to produce passenger cars in 1993 and 1994, respectively.
4. In 1998 Ssangyong and Kia were taken over by Daewoo and Hyundai, respectively.
5. In 1999 Daewoo went bankrupt; thus Ssangyong was separated from the company.
6. Samsung was taken over by Renault of France in 2000, Daewoo by GM of the United States in 2001.
7. Ssangyong was taken over by Shanghai Automotive Industry Corporation (SAIC) of China in 2004. SAIC gave up its management of Ssangyong in 2010, and Mahindra & Mahindra of India took over the Korean company in 2011.
8. GM–Daewoo was renamed GM Korea in 2011.

With the help of a neoliberal policy perspective, the practice of entry regulation was scrapped in 1989. There were two beneficiaries of this deregulation. Ssangyong, a utility vehicle maker, was allowed to produce sedan-type passenger cars in 1993. More significantly, the Samsung Group, the largest chaebol in South Korea, entered into the motor industry for the first time in its business history, by attaining a licence to produce commercial vehicles in 1992, and passenger cars in 1994. In the aftermath of the 1997 financial crisis, however, they could not grow successfully because of their highly leveraged capacity investment and stagnating demand for cars. Ssangyong was taken over by Daewoo in 1998, and Samsung by

Renault of France in 2000. In addition, even existing firms such as Kia and Daewoo, the second- and third-largest car makers, were unable to avoid the sectoral problems, including excess capacity and financial difficulties; this is explained in more detail in Section 3.4. Consequently, Kia was taken over in 1998 by Hyundai, the largest car maker in South Korea, while Daewoo was taken over in 2001 by General Motors (GM) of the United States.

Based on this phenomenon of chain bankruptcy in the sector following the 1997 crisis, there is an argument that relaxation of entry regulation – for example, Samsung's new entry in 1994 – resulted in a policy failure that led to excess capacity and excessive competition (Chang, Park and Yoo 1998). It should be noted, however, that this argument needs to be complemented with a broader and more concrete analysis of the peculiarity of inter-assembler competition in the South Korean car sector. First, the measure of the abolition of entry regulation stimulated the existing car makers' massive investments to consolidate their market share and pre-empt the entrants' challenges. The Big Three – Hyundai, Kia, and Daewoo – each planned to expand its production capacity to 2 million units, which was regarded as the firm-level minimum efficient scale at that time. In addition, each company attempted to establish a full line-up of models, from mini-sized cars to luxurious cars. This is because, for domestic assemblers at the time, economies of scale and scope were the most significant factor in reducing production costs and improving market share, contributing to massive exports of cars. Second, the three local car makers tightened the exclusive and hierarchical transactions with their subcontracting component manufacturers in order to make it difficult for new entrants to procure parts and components from the existing component makers.[7] This peculiar practice hindered the stable market penetration of the new entrants as well as the self-reliant and profitable growth of the component sector, giving rise to accelerated erosion of competitiveness of the South Korean car manufacturing sector.

3.3.2 Assembler–Supplier Relations

Given that car manufacturers purchase more than half the total inputs from outside components makers, the importance of establishing cooperative assembler–supplier relations is obvious.[8] However, the South Korean policymakers at the initial stages of automobile industrialisation do not seem to have considered this. They ignored the presence of the local component sector, which, in effect, was one of the most active manufacturing sectors in the 1950s and 1960s, since it had a nationwide association which made policy recommendations to the government.[9] Not surprisingly, the new car assembly company, Saenara, established under the auspices of the military regime that took power in the early 1960s, provoked serious resistance from the component sector, since it relied heavily on imports of knock-down (KD) kits from Japan, ignoring the presence of local production facilities. As a result, industrial policies in the 1960s were not able to coordinate the competing economic and political interests between the traditional component sector and the new assembly sector. Thus, policies were ineffective; for example, those directed towards a high degree of local content could not attain their aims because of the absence of productive relations between the assemblers and component manufacturers.

From the 1970s the government substantially promoted the subcontracting system, following Japanese practices in its car sector. It encouraged the horizontal type of subcontracting system, in which a component manufacturer could supply its specialised product to every assembler (see Figure 3.2). This was initially intended to improve economies of scale and product quality in the component sector, along with the promotion of small and medium-sized enterprises (SMEs). However, this policy stance was not fruitful. Many suppliers were unable to meet the volume and the quality demanded by assemblers at that time. In contrast, assemblers preferred in-house manufacturing of the most functional and profitable components, such as engines and transmission, with non-profitable or bulky components supplied more cheaply by the SMEs. In such a context, because of export imperatives applied to the heavy industries from the mid-1970s, the government could no longer favour component makers over assemblers; from the late 1970s it allowed assemblers not only to manufacture their own functional components in-house but also to manage their own pool of component makers. This is called the vertical subcontracting system, the main feature of which is exclusive transactions between assemblers and suppliers (see Figure 3.3). Not surprisingly, the system made the component sector more fragmented and dependent on large-scale assembler capital.

Nonetheless, the South Korean car industry developed remarkably, especially from the mid-1980s. As far as assembler–supplier relations are concerned, paradoxically, the exclusive relations between the two sectors played an important role in industrial success. First, considerable externalities were involved, although these were limited

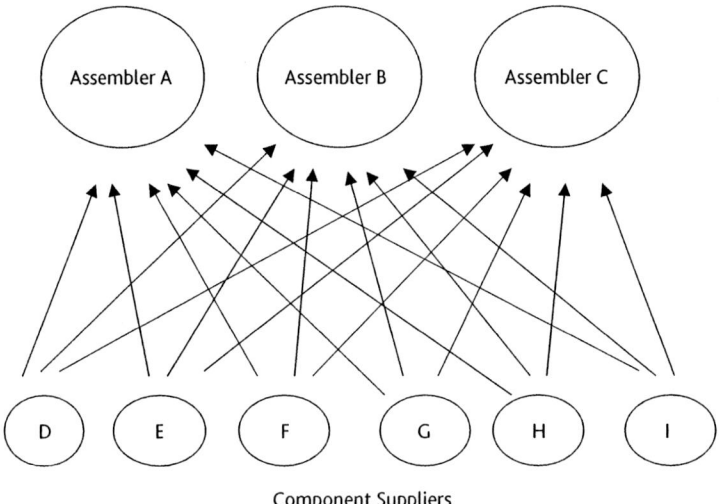

Figure 3.2 The Horizontal Subcontracting System

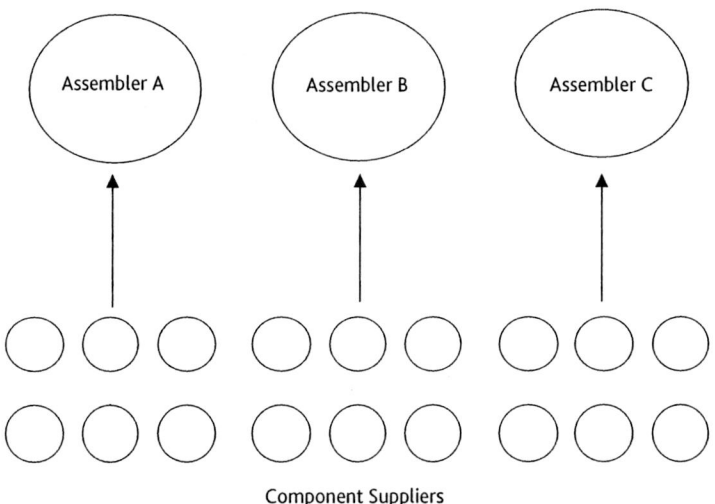

Figure 3.3 The Vertical Subcontracting System

to an assembler's exclusive subcontracting system. For example, assemblers channelled their imported and imitated technology to their affiliates and suppliers at reduced prices. Second, rapid increase in domestic and foreign demand for cars since the mid-1980s was conducive to overcoming to some extent the fragmentation in the component sector. By and large, these two reasons made component makers prefer being under the umbrella of an assembler to being independent. Third, more component-sector-oriented policies were implemented in the 1980s, reflecting the criticism that automobile policies in the 1970s had overemphasised the large-scale assembly sector compared to the component sector. As a result, there were some improvements both in productivity and in the quality of components, which no doubt improved the standard of cars in the final assembly line, to the benefit of exports.

3.3.3 Local Assembler–Multinationals Relations

The low involvement of foreign direct investment (FDI) has been regarded as one of the most conspicuous characteristics of the South Korean car sector. There had been no car assemblers in which foreign stakes surpassed 50 per cent until 2000, when Samsung Motors was sold to Renault in the aftermath of the Asian financial crisis of the late 1990s. Before that, during the 1980s, Hyundai and Kia had minority foreign shares. Hyundai sold 15 per cent of its shares to Mitsubishi of Japan; Kia sold 10 per cent to Ford of the United States and 10 per cent to Mazda of Japan. Daewoo ended its joint venture with GM in 1992, GM having acquired 50 per cent of Shinjin shares in 1972.[10] So local car makers pursued a self-reliant growth strategy without managerial interference from multinationals. This feature is in contrast with other countries which were late in developing an automobile industry, such as Brazil, Mexico, Taiwan, etc., where multinational assemblers occupied a significant market share in the automobile sector.

It should be noted, however, that the government did not discourage foreign companies from investing in the local market, although there was a regulation prohibiting more than 50 per cent foreign ownership. In effect, it preferred joint ventures with multinationals, on both economic and political grounds.[11] In the event, multinationals were not interested in the South Korean car market because of its low demand and political instability, at least until the 1970s. These factors show that the limited involvement of foreign direct investment cannot be explained only as an effect of the 'nationalist' industrial policy. Rather, it was an outcome of conflicts of economic and political interest between local companies and multinationals, as is demonstrated in the three rounds of joint venture negotiations that took place in the early 1970s following government recommendations.[12] One was between Shinjin and Toyota of Japan, Shinjin's technical partner.

Both companies obtained a licence for a joint venture with Toyota's capital participation of 70 per cent.[13] Suddenly, though, Toyota decided to pull out of the South Korean market. This was simply because it preferred the Chinese market, taking advantage of the mood of détente which existed at the time. Another joint venture was attempted between Hyundai and Ford. But Hyundai adhered single-mindedly to its own corporate interests and subsequently failed to agree a new business as a joint venture. Instead, it decided to develop its own cars, in line with the new government policy in support of companies' own independent strategies. The third joint venture was negotiated between Shinjin and GM in 1972. Unlike Hyundai, Shinjin was experiencing financial problems, and the shock of the failed negotiations with Toyota allowed excessively generous conditions to the US negotiating partner. As a result, the company went bankrupt four years after the establishment of the joint venture and handed over its shares to the Korea Development Bank, the state-run industrial lender.

Relations between local assemblers and multinationals in the 1980s were different from those of the previous period. In the aftermath of the economic and political crisis of 1979–80, the domestic companies pursued a strategy of mass export to the US market as a means of survival. The local market was repressed, with disposable incomes too low for people to be able to afford cars. Two key conditions were required to promote the export strategy. First, higher safety and environmental standards had to be met for the US market. Second, sales networks needed to be established in the export market. Although concrete solutions to these problems were different for each company, local companies attempted to rely on the multinationals' advanced technology and sales networks. In the process, multinationals wanted only minority shares to reduce the risk to their investments. Thus seen, the smaller involvement of foreign direct investment in the 1980s should be understood as reflecting the economic interests of local companies and multinationals.

To a considerable extent, the low presence of multinationals in the local market made government policies more effective. For local companies are more submissive than foreign ones in accepting government recommendations, such as local content requirements, export obligations and the development of indigenous cars. For example, if Hyundai (or Kia) and GM Korea are compared in terms of their reaction to government policies for developing a 'Korean-type' car in the mid-1970s, their differing attitudes and strategies can easily be identified: while Hyundai succeeded in developing and exporting a new indigenous model, the Pony, in spite of a financial loss, GM Korea merely adapted GM's unsuccessful models to the local market without any new technological development.

3.4 THE EROSION OF INDUSTRIAL POLICY

The existing literature has too readily concluded that state intervention is only effective at the initial stages of industrial development, regardless of the degree of state commitment to economic development. Most arguments have assumed that state intervention shrinks as an economy develops, providing the idea of the 'rise and fall' of state intervention. Some analysts argue that if prices are set right, or market coordination works well, the state has no need to intervene in economic activities. Others consider that if industrialists or workers grow strong enough to challenge state autonomy, the effectiveness of state intervention will be diminished. Those arguments might eventually prove the superiority of the market over the state as a single regulator of the world economy as well as the singularity of the industrialisation model rather than its plurality.

More specifically, the 'industry ageing' argument (also known as the retardation thesis) justifies a U-curve view of the level of state intervention in accordance with industrial development (Norton 1986).[14] Okimoto (1989) suggests that Japan's Ministry of International Trade and Industry (MITI) used 'the concept of industrial life cycle as a basis for determining what might be considered an appropriate level and form of state intervention'. Such intervention 'tends to follow a curvilinear trajectory' which he neatly summarises as

> extensive involvement during the early stages of an industry's life cycle when market demand is still small, falling off significantly as the industry reaches full maturity and demand reaches its peak, and rising again as industry loses comparative advantage and faces the problems of senescence – saturated markets, the loss of market share, and excess capacity (Okimoto 1989, p.50).

Arguments of this kind are combined not only with the analogy of 'flying geese', which points out the development pattern of leading sectors in the sequence of imports, import substitution, and exports, but also with product cycle theory, which assumes that 'the less-developed countries may offer competitive advantages as a production location' (Vernon 1966, p.202) at the standardisation stage of some products.[15] Accordingly, the practice of sectoral targeting becomes a necessary policy tool for effective industrial upgrading by promoting specific growth industries or rationalising retarding industries. This argument can be extended to the situation of deindustrialisation and the promotion of knowledge-intensive industries in developed countries. Seen in this vein, the role of industrial policy can be generalised as dealing with the ageing process of traditional industries and the promotion of new growth industries on the basis of the law of industrial growth and decline that encompasses both the developing and developed countries.

South Korean policymakers in the 1980s drew on this logic when they promoted policy reform in the aftermath of the economic and political crisis of 1979–80.[16] New legislation in the form of the Industrial Development Act of 1986 assumed that the sectors, if any, in which the government should intervene were emerging growth industries and declining industries. The car manufacturing industry was included in the former category, for instance, enjoying temporary government support until 1989. Also, the government's stance on industrial policy shifted from the promotion of specific industries and large-scale capital to the functional promotion of technological development and small and medium-sized enterprises.

However, the notion of the erosion of industrial policy, corresponding to an industrial life cycle, is oversimplified. For example, as far as car manufacturing is concerned, the notion of the rise and decline of industrial policy is difficult to apply. First, the 'industry ageing' argument does not fit the industry. Although it began in the form of mass production in the early twentieth century, the industry has been regarded up to the present as a growth or strategic industry, by advanced economies as well as developing countries. The South Korean case is no exception. The automobile sector still accounts for a significant proportion of national production, exports and employment, even beyond the late 1990s (see Table 3.2).

Second, the 'flying geese' hypothesis does not readily fit with developments in the car sector. And as Jenkins (1987, p.248–9) suggests, since the sources of main technological change have been advanced countries and the effects of economies of scale and managerial cost recovery have diluted price competitiveness of the NICs, relocation of the car industry has not automatically taken place.

Table 3.2 Economic Significance of the Motor Industry in South Korea

		1980	1990	2000	2009
Production	Amount (₩b)	1,201	16,239	53,889	113,028
	Share in the manufacturing sector (%)	3.31	9.16	9.54	10.07
Value added	Amount (₩b)	294	5,839	20,575	35,223
	Share in the manufacturing sector (%)	2.48	8.23	9.38	9.41
Employment	Number of workers	62,889	186,288	203,952	250,069
	Share in the manufacturing sector (%)	3.12	6.17	7.69	10.19
Exports	Amount ($m)	88	2,369	15,343	37,122
	Share in the whole economy (%)	0.50	3.64	8.91	10.21

Source: Korea Automobile Manufacturers Association, 2011, http://www.kama.or.kr/board/Board?master_id=Reports

Third, as a result, policymakers in many countries have implemented a wide variety of measures, not only to improve the international competitiveness of their national car sectors, but also to provide critical assistance to troubled car makers. For instance, the US government bailed out Chrysler in the early 1980s and played a significant role in creating an industry-wide consortium for developing next-generation cars in the 1990s. Leading European car makers such as Volkswagen and Renault would not exist without state involvement. Moreover, various governments introduced measures to protect their own automobile industries and enhance competitiveness of their car companies in the aftermath of the global financial crisis of 2008. In particular, a bailout fund was provided again for GM and Chrysler.

Thus seen, the mode of division of industries such as emerging and declining ones is too superficial to show specific industrial realities of different industries. The simple analogy of industry to a biological entity (with a life cycle) also worsens the understanding of industrial realities, because it neglects to explore the peculiar patterns of competition between the economic agents concerned as well as of the underlying economic relations in production. As has been shown in the case of the car industry, the degree of state intervention relies on neither industrial maturity nor exclusive compliance with 'strong' class interests. Instead, from the perspective of industrial policy being an integral element of a specific pattern of capital accumulation, it is argued here that the apparent disintegration of industrial policy is regarded as a change in the form and content taken by the state in representing and coordinating economic and political interests. In other words, it shows a change to a different pattern of capital accumulation.

In effect, in South Korea, industrial policies from the late 1980s became more politicised, fragmented and uncoordinated than those of previous periods. As shown earlier, lack of strategic policy perspective on industrial promotion coupled with implementation of deregulation policies in the sector contributed to exposing the peculiar pattern of competition between local assemblers and uncoordinated changes of relational structure between local assemblers, suppliers and multinationals in the sector.

The following two events strengthened the peculiarities of competition between local assemblers. First, a massive labour struggle developed in the car sector from July 1987 in the aftermath of the democracy movement.[17] As a response, local car makers made a concerted effort to bring costly automation into production facilities as a way of minimising the impact of the emergence of labour struggles, trade unions and wage increases. In addition, the advantages of the hierarchical subcontracting system exploited until the mid-1980s began to erode as industrial relations were destabilised from the 1980s. After experiencing halts in their assembly lines due to stoppages at their subcontractors, the assemblers attempted to avoid an overdependence on one supplier for a certain component. They began to prefer to make contracts with several suppliers for the same component (Mihn and Oh 1993; Oh and Cho 1997).[18]

Second, exports of locally processed cars to the United States, which contributed to the growth of the South Korean car sector, diminished rapidly from 1989. Apart from such reasons as unfavourable trade conditions, the low quality of South Korean cars and increasing wage levels,[19] local car makers also attributed export decrease to the export methods of OEMs through the US companies' sales network. In effect, US car makers began to change their small car procurement strategy from importing cheaper South Korean products rather than Japanese ones to themselves producing small cars in-house. As a response, local car makers tried to attain more autonomy in their alliance relations with multinationals in terms of exports strategy. Hyundai was the forerunner in the direction of 'self-reliant' strategy, becoming less dependent on multinationals by establishing its own export models and sales network in the United States. Both Kia and Daewoo began to emulate Hyundai's strategy. For example, Kia attempted to establish its own sales network in the US market to sell its indigenous models, with the aim of reducing its reliance on Ford, its strategic partner. Daewoo also attributed its own poor performance in domestic sales and exports to its unfair relations with GM. Accordingly, much conflict occurred between Daewoo and GM regarding product development and exports strategy. In 1992, Daewoo finally ended its two-decade-long 50:50 joint venture relation with GM. Since then, Daewoo has attempted to expand its export markets into South American and Eastern European countries, and also to establish its own sales network in the United States.

In short, the South Korean Big Three have established a costly and over-leveraged production capacity without proportionate development at the technological level and in the face of an insufficient market demand for cars. Economies of scale have also deteriorated due to model proliferation and market fragmentation. Such peculiarities in the pattern of both corporate investment and inter-chaebol competition in the car sector, in conjunction with the stagnating demand for cars, resulted in most car manufacturers suffering from low or negative profitability during the 1990s (Table 3.4). As a result, in 1997 local car makers had to suspend operation of some production lines, with the capacity utilisation rate in the car sector decreasing to under 70 per cent (Table 3.3).

Table 3.3 Capacity Utilisation Ratio in the Car Sector (1993–2002)

	1993	1994	1995	1996	1997	1998	1999	2000	2001	2002
Production capacity (A) (thousand units)	1,985	2,265	2,605	2,735	3,300	3,330	3,547	3,542	3,590	3,893
Production (B) (thousand units)	1,593	1,806	2,003	2,265	2,308	1,625	2,362	2,602	2,471	2,651
B/A (%)	80.3	79.7	76.9	82.8	69.9	48.8	66.6	73.5	68.9	68.1

Source: Korea Automobile Manufacturers Association, 1999 and 2003, http://www.kama.or.kr/board/Board?master_id=Reports

Table 3.4 Selected Financial Indicators in the Car Sector (1993–98) (%)

	1993	1994	1995	1996	1997	1998
Growth rate of turnover	20.0	26.0	18.0	15.5	3.8	−25.5
Debt-to-equity ratio	415.8	460.5	460.6	530.4	857.8	655
Financial expenses-to-turnover ratio	6.72	6.43	6.37	6.32	7.98	17.88
Profit rate to total assets	−0.37	−0.07	0.2	−0.44	−2.64	−27.42

Source: Korea Automobile Manufacturers Association, 2009, http://www.kama.or.kr/board/Board?master_id=Reports

Moreover, they had to offer loss-making sales promotions, such as interest-free three-year instalment financing, with the aim of disposing of the increasing inventories in 1997. More significantly, all the indigenous car manufacturers except Hyundai went bankrupt in the course of 1997–99.

3.5 CONCLUDING REMARKS

This chapter has attempted to establish an alternative research framework on industrial policy with reference to the South Korean car industry, avoiding the analytical dichotomy between the state and the market as well as the regional divide between East Asia and Latin America. Three research questions were posed to do this: what economic forces promote industrial policy; how industrial policy affects industrial performance; and why industrial policy has been eroded if it contributed to industrial development earlier. In addition, some industrial policy practices implemented in the South Korean automobile sector were examined in terms of various economic relations, such as inter-assembler competition, assembler–supplier relations, and local assembler–multinationals relations. According to the findings from this chapter, the economic imperatives and effectiveness of industrial policy rely on underlying economic interests and the peculiar pattern of competition conditioned by those economic relations in the sector, rather than depending on either state autonomy or policy efficiency by themselves. In other words, successful industrial policies in the South Korean automobile sector hinged on the changing content of inter-assembler competition and the erosion of the uncoordinated structure between assemblers and component manufacturers as well as on the nature of multinational car makers' involvement in local production. Also, the apparent erosion of industrial policy in the 1990s reflected not the decreasing role of the developmental state but the varying economic interests of large-scale capital and its changing relations with its subcontracting firms and foreign partners. From this perspective, accordingly, identification of economic interests in accordance with changes in economic relations in a sector is of great significance in understanding the dynamic of industrial policy.

In retrospect, there has been no industrial policy solution that fits all places and all times. As mentioned in the introductory section, although most developing countries have practised similar policies for the protection and promotion of their local industries, their performance, in terms of measures such as production and exports, has varied substantially (Jenkins 1995). Specifically, the effects of export promotion policies in the South Korean car sector are different from those in the Brazilian sector, since the economic circumstances of exporters are different from one another. Moreover, state intervention occurs in the specific contexts in which the underlying economic agents' interests are formed and (mis)represented alongside and through the market. As a result, the form of state intervention in industry varies, depending on the demands of economic agents and differing economic structures. This implies that the effects of industrial policy cannot be generalised without considering the specific conditions that each economic agent faces and attempts to challenge.

NOTES

1. In effect, the idea that private investments should be coordinated by the state has been formulated since the 1940s. Rosenstein-Rodan (1943) favours a large-scale planned industrialisation comprising a simultaneous promotion of several complementary industries, on the grounds of the presence of external economies. His argument for 'balanced growth' or 'big push' is followed by Nurkse (1953), Scitovsky (1954), Fleming (1955) and Murphy, Shleifer and Vishny (1989). In contrast, Hirschman (1958: ch.3) criticises the 'balanced growth' argument. According to him, the underdeveloped countries lack the initial resources and capabilities for simultaneous and balanced expansion across industry. He also argued that centralised investment decisions may be biased against innovations. Instead, he suggests an unbalanced growth pattern in which sectorally sequential development is used to promote industrialisation. However, the final outcome of the industrialisation process in his argument does not differ from the balanced growth model since the unbalanced growth strategy also ultimately pursues a balance between industries (Hirschman 1992).
2. Industrial structure upgrading can be seen as a specific pattern of investment coordination, which has been a major theme for policymakers in South Korea and Japan (Chang 1994). In effect, the heavy and chemical industrialisation promoted in those countries was to upgrade industrial structure from light to heavy industries along the lines of the 'Hoffmann ratio' (O 1996). The latter indicates the ratio of the net output (value added) of the consumer goods industries to that of the capital goods industries, which it is argued continually declines throughout the process of industrialisation as a general pattern of development of manufacturing industry (Hoffmann 1958). As a rule, a Hoffmann ratio between 0.5 and 1.5 indicates that the country is industrialised to some extent.
3. Most large-scale exporters in South Korea in the 1970s began to wield economic power as part of business groups or chaebols.
4. In addition, competition between the USA and Japan in the global car industry favoured South Korean assemblers by creating new low-end niche markets with the help of the rapid appreciation of the yen.

5. Even after the recent financial crisis in South Korea, reducing the number of assemblers was again one of the most important policy issues.
6. In the 1960s and 1970s, policymakers had to control the number of assemblers and models produced given the small local market, although they did not know the minimum efficient scale for the sector.
7. Moreover, antagonism between the incumbents and the entrant, based on inter-chaebol competition, made it harder for Samsung to procure components from the existing companies.
8. According to Mihn and Oh (1993), the outsourcing ratio of the South Korean assemblers in the early 1990s was about 65 per cent, while that of the Japanese assemblers in the mid-1980s reached around 70 per cent. In South Korea, engine, transmission and large pressed parts are normally made in-house.
9. The component manufacturing sector first appeared in the late 1930s with the specific aim of supplying automobile components to the Japanese army in Korea, while the car assembly business began in the early 1960s.
10. Shinjin was the leading car assembler until the mid-1970s and formed a 50:50 joint venture, called GM Korea, with GM in 1972.
11. From the late 1960s to the early 1970s the government faced both an economic decline and a military crisis with North Korea. It was thought that the intervention of a multinational in the local market might relieve both difficulties at the same time.
12. This feature contrasts sharply with the cases of Latin American NICs, where the bargaining process between the state and multinationals is regarded as the most significant factor in their motor industries (Bennett and Sharpe 1985; Shapiro 1994).
13. Original negotiations suggested an 80 per cent Toyota share, but, in line with the government's insistence on reducing the foreign share, this was revised to 70 per cent.
14. The argument is also associated with an assumption that industrial improvements are achieved slowly at first, then accelerate and finally slow down again (S-shaped pattern). This path is claimed to rest on the so-called Wolff's law of diminishing returns to innovative efforts or investment in incremental innovations (Perez and Soete 1988).
15. The combination of these two arguments provides an explanation of regional patterns of industrial diffusion from Japan to the East Asian NICs (see Cumings 1987). For a critical position on this explanation, see Bernard and Ravenhill (1995).
16. In effect, the crisis raised doubts about the positive effects of industrial policies adopted in the mid-1970s, in particular, those relating to the heavy and chemical industries (HCIs). Above all, overinvestment in the heavy and chemical sectors was regarded as an inevitable outcome of government-led HCI projects. As Sakong (1993) points out, the fiscal crisis in the government and the mismanagement of the financial industry, which were attributed to massive policy loans, worsened the crisis. In such contexts, the newly established military regime of 1980 promoted an economic reform, including privatisation of banks, import liberalisation, competition policy and so on, in accordance with the policy recommendations of the international financial institutions such as the IMF and the World Bank. In the process, the government placed an emphasis on the creative role of the private sector in economic development, although its authoritarian rule remained intact.

17. Until the mid-1980s, labour movements had been effectively suppressed by the government, so that car makers made little effort to establish cooperative industrial relations. For example, it was only in September 1987 that Hyundai's trade union was established. For a brief introduction of industrial relations in the auto sector see Oh and Cho (1997).
18. This practice is called multi-sourcing.
19. Three 'lows' – a weak won (South Korean currency), relatively cheap oil and low interest rates – in the mid-1980s changed to three 'highs' – the rising cost of labour and oil and the appreciation of the won – in the late 1980s, which led to the erosion of the cost advantage of South Korean products.

4
Labour and the 'Developmental State': A Critique of the Developmental State Theory of Labour

Dae-oup Chang

4.1 INTRODUCTION

As suggested in the introduction to this volume, the predilection to set up an opposition between state and market has resulted in 'downplaying the role of class' in analysing development. This chapter aims to take this critique a step further by looking in detail at the impact of this on development discourse around 'labour'. I argue that the problem of the developmental state theories is not so much a lack of apparent emphasis on individual classes but the de facto dissolution of the concept of class through the distancing of 'classes' from class relations and, in particular, the contradictory concept of labour whose subordination to capital is both the basis of capitalist development and a major driving force for social change. I suggest that the concept of the developmental state can be derived only with a particular understanding of labour that is disempowered and depoliticised. Statist development policies are essentially anti-labour in that they 'fetishise' or mystify the state as if it exists apart from social relations in 'facilitating' development.

This posture constitutes an effective barrier in the attempt to assign the labouring population a role in bringing about alternative social relations and more democratic processes of development, quite apart from writing them out of developmental states historically, other than at most as some sort of potential obstacle to developmentalism as opposed to some ex post target of benefit. Section 4.2 shows how developmental state theories have mystified the state in the developmental process by taking a one-dimensional approach to state–society relations. Section 4.3 then addresses how this particular setting of state–society relations detaches classes from class relations, reducing class to a group of owners of a particular source of revenue or, at best, a sociological agent. Instead, the form of the capitalist state in capitalist development needs to be addressed in bringing labour back into the analysis of development and the state. Sections 4.4 and 4.5 develop a historical critique of existing expositions of East Asian development, with a particular focus on the internal and external dynamics in which capitalist states in Japan, South Korea and Taiwan have taken a particular form that provides the basis for the myth of the developmental state. The concluding section draws out the implication that the future prospects of the East Asian NICs are not best approached in terms of whether the developmental state survives or not, to what extent and in what form, but by focusing on the continuing evolution of the state in the context of both capital–labour relations and a heavily influential external environment.

4.2 ONE DIMENSIONAL STATE–SOCIETY RELATIONS IN DEVELOPMENTAL STATE THEORIES

In development discourse, developmental state theories enjoy popularity for being the only realistic alternative to free-market development. Contemporary accounts of the developmental state rely largely on empirical studies of East Asian states, focusing on the conditions of successful state promotion for capitalist development. In doing so, those studies address *state–society relations* of these East Asian countries. However, it is important to recognise that state–society relations analysed in developmental state theories have a distinctive emphasis in how the composition of state–society relations is analytically and empirically constructed. For the quintessential flaw in developmental state theories is that they define the form of capitalist states mostly, if not exclusively, on an utterly *partial* basis, through preoccupation with the relations between 'private business' and 'government' (Amsden 1989; Johnson 1982; Evans 1995; Wade 1990; Chang 2006), effectively reducing state–society relations to state–capital relations and reducing this itself to government–business relations. The essence of developmental state theories lies in this subsequent reduction process.

For the developmental state paradigm (DSP), the dominance of the state over capital is the single most important condition for successful industrial policies that are in turn the most important evidence for the existence and legitimacy of developmental states. This particular state–capital relation is supported with plentiful empirical evidence. This includes state control over banks and other financial institutions, strategic and selective allocation of financial and other resources through governmental agencies, the effectiveness of macroeconomic policies, and individual success stories of industrial policy at firm and sectoral levels. As far as this relation is concerned, the developmental state is a strong and disciplinary state that can regulate and guide private capital, drawing its strength from the 'unusual degree of bureaucratic autonomy' (Önis 1991, p.114). This political autonomy from the private sector makes it possible for the state to 'avoid becoming the captive of its major clients' (Johnson 1985, p.81).

Here, an 'authoritarian' political regime that can exercise strong state power against other societal forces is a necessary but not a sufficient condition for a developmental state. Statists maintain that the particular state–capital relation featuring in developmental states is not exclusively a one-way coercive relation. Defining the developmental state only in terms of coercive power is considered misleading. For developmental states not only exercise disciplinary power against private capital, but also know how to work with private capital. Statists argue that instead of exercising its power excessively, the developmental state demonstrates an 'unusual degree of public–private cooperation' and therefore 'the coexistence of two conditions: the autonomous bureaucracy and co-operation between private sectors and the state' (Önis 1991, p.114). Involved, therefore, is a 'specific kind' of governmental autonomy vis-à-vis private capital. This particular autonomy has been theorised by Peter Evans (1995) in terms of the *embedded autonomy* of the developmental state. This is 'an autonomy embedded in a concrete set of social ties that bind the state to society and provide institutionalised channels for the continual negotiation and renegotiation of goals and policies' (p.59).

As Evans (1992, p.154) notices, the co-existence of the autonomous state with the tightly networked relations between business and bureaucracy is a 'contradictory combination' – how can the state both be autonomous from private capital while working closely with it? Statists answer this question by attributing it to the relative strength of the state bureaucrats over other social actors, and the strong determination of the state to promote national development, for which they have to work with private capital. Statists then proceed to identify specific conditions that are favourable to this stance and to the relative strength of state bureaucrats. The Cold War world order, for example, is said to have legitimated government leadership, leaving it with no choice but the pursuit of market-based development (Johnson 1985; Evans 1992). Japanese colonisation, on the other hand, gave East Asian states an interventionist character. Similarly, the land reform deprived the traditional landlord class of power within or against the state (Amsden 1989; Evans 1992; Wade 1990); whereas a labour movement that could possibly have prevented state autonomy was absent (Wade 1988). Amsden (1989, p. vi) also points to the 'hyperactive student movement', whose participants 'mobilize popular support to keep the government honest'.

However, these *other* dimensions of state–society relations are introduced mostly to highlight the different *environments* that are conducive, or not, to the sort of autonomy that can be formed and used by state bureaucrats. One dimension of state–society relations conditioning such autonomy is the *state–labour relation*, which can be called the developmental regime of labour relations (D.-O. Chang 2009). Thus Amsden (1989, p.147) briefly describes 'weak labour' as a condition for state domination over society. Johnson (1985, p.75) also does not forget to point out how 'weak labour' was socially engineered by the government as a condition for successful state domination. Weiss and Hobson (1995, p.164) as well as Leftwich (2000, pp.163–5) point to weak 'civil society' forces, including labour, as a historical condition for developmental states. So although statist literature appears to cover dimensions of state–society relations other than state–capital relations, these are brought to bear only to explain the capacity of state bureaucrats and the state's determination to promote fast economic development.

As a consequence, the developmental state is based on a *one-dimensional* analysis of state–society relations which looks into labour–capital relations and the state's relation to them only through the prism of the effect on autonomy. Worse still, the particular nature of state–society relations is often attributed to the internal characteristics of the state itself (bureaucracy, ethos, competence, corruption, etc.) and its corresponding capacity for the right sort of autonomy. In the DSP, state officials appear to provide 'a vision' and pursue 'institution building' that 'gives an institutional reality to the vision' by 'shaping the emergent coordination structure' (Chang 2003, p.57). All other societal conditions are implicitly reduced in significance to mere *events*, without which the developmental elite's 'vision could not be implemented' (Amsden 1989, p.52). In effect, the statist argument derives the autonomy of the state from internal and organisational features of the state or even from characteristics of elite bureaucrats and individual rulers, such as Park Chung-hee of

South Korea or Chiang Kai-shek of Taiwan. The ability to negotiate policies with private groups, either formally or informally, without subordination to particular interest groups, appears here to be a quality of the bright bureaucrats selected through a 'rigorous system of recruitment' (Weiss and Hobson 1995, p.165). For some statists, it is not the quality of the state bureaucrats but 'calculated political moves' and 'institutional innovations' pursued by the top political leaders, who were 'no fan[s] of the free market', but much committed to 'industrial upgrading' and able to mobilise capitalists, farmers and millions of workers, i.e. the entire population to work harder and faster for the renaissance of the nation (Chang 2006, pp.95–102). So, despite statists' claims for a theory of the state addressing its socially-embedded characteristics, the success of the developmental state is often reduced to 'the best and the brightest' personnel (Evans 1995, p.51), whilst the outer relations with society in general and labour in particular are landscaped – with the exception of those with business.

Worse still, statists tend to identify business–government relations with those between 'the state and capital'. Because capital is understood in its most vulgar form as *'individual owners of a source of revenue'* rather than as *a social relation*, it is understood *without regard to labour*. The consequence is that the organisational relations between government and business are presented as if they are exclusively state–capital relations. With neglect of other dimensions of state–society relations, those between government and private business are presented as all-inclusive, with a corresponding absence of capital–labour relations. Strikingly, capital–labour relations as such do not even appear unless mediated by the state, having no existence apart from and through the state (an ex post imposition of developmental state autonomy on labour and capital–labour relations).

This has a serious implication for the concept of class in statist analyses of the state. Statist attempts to theorise state autonomy in the development process appear to integrate social classes and use 'class analyses' as a part of its analytical framework. However, it is important to notice that the statist concept of class differs significantly from that of existing class-based analyses of the state in the developing world. Although class-based theories tend to define class relations primarily as economic relations of exploitation, and theorise the state largely through a dichotomy between the economic and the political, such theories do take into account the relation between such class relations and the nature of the state and, in doing so, attempt to derive the nature of the state from more comprehensive state–society relations. Neocolonial state monopoly capitalism theory, for instance, emphasises the class nature of the state based on the ways in which the ruling class extends its power into the state. The state's authoritarian nature is strengthened by its dependent form of capitalist development. Neocolonial capitalist development is then driven by monopoly capital and supplemented by the state largely for the interest of the core imperialist countries and ruling elites in developing countries. The *authoritarian state* is the superstructure of dependent capitalist development.

On the other hand, the theory of bureaucratic authoritarianism, such as O'Donnell's (1988), offers a more sophisticated basis for the capitalist state in dependent economic development: the state is not a guarantor of an immediate interest of the ruling elites, but a guarantor of the ensemble of social relations that establish the elites as the dominant class. In other words, the state takes care of the environment of capitalist domination rather than purely the interests of capitalists or other elites directly. From this perspective, East Asian states can be identified as bureaucratic–authoritarian, as they act to maintain an international order in which local elites can reproduce their dominance over the societies by deactivating and excluding previously active or popular movements. Rather than critically engaging with the existing class-based theories of the state, developmental state theories established themselves by engaging with the neoclassical market theory of development in East Asia and *inherited* the market–state dichotomy approach from its counterpart, with the imperative of 'bringing the state back in' as a prime mover (Evans, Rueschemeyer and Skocpol 1985) (see below). The consequence is that developmental state theories tend to strengthen the market–state dichotomy of existing state theories rather than overcome it. And, whilst class relations appear to occupy an important place, they are conceptualised in a manner very different from previous class-based theories of the state that are its determinant rather than vice-versa.

4.3 ABSTRACTION OF CLASSES FROM CLASS RELATIONS

While statists address the relations of the state to different 'classes' (capital and labour), they do not deal with the engagement of the state in capital–labour class relations (hereafter 'capital relations'). So 'classes' in developmental state theories are not 'classes' in a relational sense but 'social groups' with different economic functions.

The methodological and theoretical ground of this approach derives from the monumental work of Evans, Rueschemeyer and Skocpol (1985) that put the state as an independent agent at the centre of analysis. It began with a critique of 'relative autonomy', itself a critical departure from vulgar Marxian theory, such as the 'state monopoly capitalism' approach, in which the state figured as an immediate extension of class relations. Significantly, the neo-Marxist theory of relative autonomy sees the state as enjoying a degree of independence from the economy because of its location in the autonomous sphere of politics; but this does not render the state independent of classes which influence the economy through the state. Thus, both approaches agree on the relative autonomy of the state (of politics from economics or of the state from classes), but from different structural perspectives, thereby misrepresenting or downplaying the dependence of the state upon, or its derivation from, capital (or other class) relations (see Clarke 1991 for a critique).

According to Skocpol (1985), relative autonomy is not a general feature of the state as not all capitalist states have the same generic form. As each capitalist state acts differently, the reason for this needs to be explained. Skocpol does so by looking, not into the ways in which capital relations assume different political forms, but into the *organisational features* of a given state. State autonomy is to be understood 'only in truly historical studies that are sensitive to structural variations and conjunctural changes within given polities', because 'state autonomy is not a fixed structural feature of any governmental system' (p.14). State autonomy is then understood as a potential, contingent on the *organisational features* of the state. The state can even act in its own interest, as opposed to the national interest or the interest of particular social groups.

Autonomy of a state is then presented as a 'choice' rather than a result of interactions within conflict-ridden capital relations. The theory emphasises the 'particularity' of individual states. However, it rests on a universalist argument in that the state, any state, has the inherent potential to have 'organisational' autonomy as 'a set of organisations through which collectivities of officials may be able to formulate and implement distinctive strategies or policies' (pp.20–1). In doing so, it effectively gives the state a transhistorical nature without regard to the social relations in and through which it comes into being. The state is not a relatively autonomous superstructure as in Poulantzas (1969, 1973), but may be so on the basis of 'bureaucratic strength' and coherence – therefore not necessarily subjected to the ruling class all the time. What matters is not the relation between the 'state' and 'class relations', but the relation between the state and other groups of collective individuals. All social categories are 'abstracted' from capitalist social relations to become 'independent actors'. By making the state, workers and capitalists into individual actors and highlighting the state as a supreme social organisation, Skocpol's formula effectively *released the state from capital relations*.

This does not mean statist theories ignore *individual* 'classes'. They do investigate the state's relations to workers, on the one hand, and its relations to capitalists, on the other. For instance, Rueschemeyer and Evans (1985) seek a general theory of the capitalist state by addressing state autonomy in a way that allows for but is not reduced to the neo-Marxist approach and, in so doing, deal with classes more substantively. State autonomy is understood in principle as autonomy from the 'dominant class', with *contradictory* tensions between gaining or losing this in reality. The state can be an instrument of domination of a certain segment of the capitalist class or the guardian of the universal interest, depending on the degree of autonomy from the dominant class. The degree of state autonomy depends on cohesiveness and coordination within state structures, the relative strengths of social forces and the state itself, and the channels through which the state works with the social structure of interests. In his later work on East Asian developmental states, Evans (1992, 1995) ultimately discovers the ideal prototype of maximal autonomy, provided by the East Asian developmental states and based most of all on the 'extraordinary' leadership of the state in promoting capital accumulation.

But the limitation of Evans's seemingly class-based approach is that the nature of the state is derived from its relations to individual 'classes' rather than to 'class relations'. It is through this particular understanding of the relations between the state and classes that the state's leadership vis-à-vis the capitalist class appears to be sufficient evidence for the idea that the state exists above class relations, without regard to its relations to the production and reproduction of class relations. Consequently, individual *classes* are divorced from class relations and become 'social groups'. Classes can be then discussed as individual social actors without reference to the class relations, structures and processes to which they are attached. Labour and capital as classes are treated separately as such social groups and only meaningfully addressed in relation to one another through the state. By drawing on the East Asian experience in particular, the presumption is that the developmental state is the conduit through which all significant class relations must be filtered, and those that exist outside that filter must be either insignificant or dysfunctional for development.

Furthermore, the pluralist understanding of class relations induces two further mutually contradictory stances. One is to allow class relations to be just *one* of the potentially significant social relations between different groups of social actors. Class is one of many other social groupings that relate to each other and to the state. In this respect, there is no difference between classes and other social groupings or other factors such as culture, nationalism, etc. Consequently, although the relations between individual classes and the state may be analysed, the relations between the 'state' and 'class relations', which was the major focus for traditional state debates, are no longer central. This ultimately allows class relations to be bypassed in identifying forms of capitalist states. On the other hand, whilst any social factor is significant in defining the state as developmental in principle, the focus in practice has been on state–business relations in particular, with obvious advantages for empirical case studies where success, or failure, can be read off from the corresponding contextual contingencies (bureaucracies, leaders, ethos, etc.).

Significantly, this version of state theory was designed to overcome crude forms of economic basis and superstructure approaches to the state, such as the 'state monopoly capitalism' approach. In its place, it offers a displacement of the 'capitalist class relation' as the totality of social relations in capitalist society by pluralist relations between actors of different sociological groups. With, in addition, the state itself understood as a sociological actor in and of itself, no account is taken of the state as the political form adopted by the totality of class relations. Instead, this pluralist sociology of the developmental state allows for reduction of capital to business, institutions to actors, class relations to individual group interests, and the totality of social formations to the selectively segmented forms that they adopt. As a result, the question of the relations between the state and class relations is mangled rather than resolved.

4.4 MYSTIFIED STATE AND MARGINALISED LABOUR

By attributing the power and capacity of the state to the state itself rather than to capitalist social relations behind the political form, the statist theory of the autonomous state mystifies the state. The particular characteristics of the state are interpreted as if given by nature and pertaining to the state as an innate possibility. Consequently, the state, historically established by interactions with unequal class relations, now appears to be class neutral and therefore appears as if it represents technically equal social relations.[1]

Just like the mystified notion of the market, which, in neoliberalism, is endowed with the ultimate power and legitimacy to promote development by those who rule the market, the mystification of the state in developmental state theories offers the same to those who rule the state. This marginalises labour in development and creates the basis of legitimacy for authoritarian development. As indicated, the consequences in practice in the DSP of the dissolution of class relations into sociological actors and groups are much more severe for 'workers' than for 'capitalists'. Labour, like technology, trade or finance, simply becomes a factor in productive success and appears to be most of all a mere input for production. Its role as an active social force, other than as one that is potentially disruptive, is denied, and it is otherwise depoliticised and disempowered. Indeed, 'only scattered attention has been given to the crucial role of labour in explaining the NICs' rapid economic growth' (Deyo, Haggard and Koo 1987, p.42). Having reduced labour to a productive input, however, it is subsequently endowed with a separate but secondary identity corresponding to the market–state dualism as soon as it also serves as a social actor. For, once labour manifests itself politically, it becomes something other than labour in the market. Instead, social struggles in which the working population takes a central role are seen as actions taken by a group motivated by something other than being labour in conflict with capital. And any causal relations between these struggles, development and the state are overlooked unless in some way dysfunctional.

Not surprisingly, this is a recipe more for overlooking the role of labour in the DSP than for locating it properly analytically. This allows authoritarianism in relation to labour and more generally to be glossed over or reluctantly accepted as the price that must be paid for development and for the state to achieve it. The contrast with capital is striking as it has much to gain (and most of it has little to lose) as long as it cooperates with developmentalism. On the contrary, the labouring population needs to endure an extraordinary intensity of exploitation in the industrial catch-up development process and to wait for the promised link between economic growth and the general welfare and democratic rights that accrue with modernisation. The more or less implicitly designated role for labour is to work really hard under the guidance of the state until a certain level of development has been achieved and then, while still working hard, participate with restrained enthusiasm in social activities to 'remind' the state of its ethos and deliver on its responsibilities of sharing the fruits of national development.

Of course, to acknowledge that the developmental state can depend on brutally authoritarian regimes is not to accept this as inevitable, since the state only needs autonomy to implement the right economic policies. Therefore, statists such as Ha-Joon Chang (2003, 2009) and Chalmers Johnson (1999) argue that there is not necessarily a connection between authoritarianism and the developmental state. For Chang, the correlation is peculiar to the East Asian NICs. Johnson also distinguishes 'true developmental states' from mere authoritarian regimes. These attempts to disconnect authoritarianism from developmental states are motivated by the wish to make the developmental state into a more acceptable developmental model. Chang and Johnson suggest that there can be, and are, many non-authoritarian developmental states (in Scandinavia for example).[2] In this way, the developmental state ranges over the bits and pieces of the history of capitalist development that can be deemed to have been successful in outcome and acceptable in process. But the relationship between democracy and development remains unresolved, improperly addressed, if labour's conflict with capital must be subordinated to the latter's imperatives through state developmentalism (or should that be authoritarianism).

This is not to suggest that development must be authoritarian and repressive of labour, only that the DSP precludes proper consideration of such issues, especially in reducing the analysis to state–society relations, and focusing on and treating these as state–business relations. In fact, the role of labour in forming the state is itself of significance. Emerging discontent from labour and its disruptive potential, alone or in combination with other forms of social unrest, was a key factor in East Asia that prompted individual capitals at an early stage to concede to state coordination in exchange for its tight control over collective labour. This caused the politicised formation and reproduction of capital–labour class relations. Indeed, the strength and characteristics of the East Asian states, and the illusion of their autonomy, are a consequence of the isolation and suppression of workers and social movements.

Further, these internal contradictions dovetailed with the external and the political. The Cold War established a political geography for East Asian capitalist development. Japan's recovery from the war was based upon the newly emerging Cold War order over the Pacific. First, the mini-boom during the Korean War jump-started Japan's economy. Special procurement from the US government for war supplies greatly contributed to quick recovery of Japan's industrial capacity to the pre-war level – accounting for 60 and 70 per cent of total exports in 1952 and 1953, respectively. The USA 'secured' provision of oil and food for Japan while maintaining a large military presence there. Japan's industrial capacity grew rapidly as it became major producer of light goods and machinery for the Asian market. Later it moved to automobiles, electronics, shipbuilding and other capital-intensive industrial goods, more for the US and European markets.

Meanwhile, Taiwan and South Korea faced great difficulties in initiating development after civil wars against communists. South Korea faced total destruction of infrastructure and productive capacity from the three-year Korean War, while Taiwan suffered from severe inflation as well as a massive influx of 1.5 million mainlanders, while also contending with the end of Japanese rule that left behind abandoned productive facilities. Lacking financial resources to rebuild economies, they had to rely on capital inflow from outside – largely the influx of foreign aid from the USA that enabled them to overcome post-civil war difficulties. Between 1945 and 1978, Taiwan received economic and military aid from the USA that totalled US$ 5.6 billion. During the same period, South Korea also received aid from the USA, a total of US$13 billion. This aid from the USA in turn guaranteed US influence over both countries (Cumings 1987, p.67). Indeed, only US East Asia achieved the so-called economic miracle through a USA–Japan–Asia triangular regime of accumulation primarily under the auspices of the USA. This offered preferential access to US markets, official loans and financial aid. Ultimately, Japan played a secondary but essential role of providing Taiwan and South Korea with machinery and other means of production, technology, loans and direct investment that in turn contributed to its own trade surplus.

While the Cold War established a political geography for the USA's construction of Asia, the post-war boom promoted a new international division of labour conducive to a particular trajectory of capital accumulation in the area. However these external conditions were not *sufficient* for fast economic development but yet were taken advantage of by East Asian countries. Taiwan, Korea and Japan were able to take advantage of different aspects of these external conditions on the basis of the particular articulation of capital relations that had been formed through particular world historical events and class struggles, a partial picture of which has been captured by 'developmental state' theories. It is through this historical process that the states in East Asia took a particular form. Overcoming developmental state theories requires us to review this historical process with a particular focus on labour. A thorough reconstruction of this history is beyond the scope of this article. However, it is important for us to see some historical moments in which labour was pushing the state and capital into a constant move in search for different modes of the articulation of capital relations. A critique of East Asian states needs to trace the historical development of capital relations as a whole, through which the social domination of capital could appear in the form of an autonomous state, attempting by any means to represent itself as the guarantor of the general interest of citizens. This historical critique can penetrate into the mystified forms by looking at the ways in which those social categories are constructed and reconstructed as moments of the formation of capital relations.

4.5 BRINGING LABOUR BACK IN: THE LABOUR HISTORY OF THE DEVELOPMENTAL STATE

It is against both the logical and historical nature of state developmentalism that it is possible to examine the secret, at least as far as the DSP is concerned, history of labour in the East Asian NICs. In the case of Japan, there is a myth that the entire trajectory of development was moulded by the state after the Meiji restoration. However, the restoration, the form of the post-Meiji Japanese state, and post-Tokugawa reforms were not entirely based on a decision taken by the brilliant state bureaucrats. It was a 'response' of a segment of the ruling elites to the deconstruction of the Tokugawa system caused by the increasing external pressure from western empires, spreading capitalist commercial and industrial activities, and the impoverishment of the rural population and subsequent emergence of discontent from the lower strata of society. The state, established by a revolution from above, was never free from capitalist class relations from then on. Early capitalist development in Japan was led by the desire of state bureaucrats to transform Japan into an Eastern empire in response to imperialist pressure from the west and by large individual capitals who wanted to be capitalist masters by expanding their capital accumulated through commercial activities from the late Tokugawa era. Early *zaibatsus* were engaged as much in politics as the state was involved in capitalist development, and a close relation was firmly established between them. At the beginning of this new capitalist drive, the state and capital did not face strong challenges either from new workers or from the farming population in rural areas. However, as early as the 1880s, they began to face collective protests from labouring people, both workers and peasants, to confront and change the way in which their labour power and products were socially mobilised, utilised, consumed and appropriated (Garon 1987). Workers often escaped from extreme exploitation by simply returning to their hometowns or organising unnoticed walkouts (Garon 1987; Gordon 2003).

The state began in 1900 to intervene in capital–labour relations with heavy-handed methods, introducing the Police Security Act, which rendered trade unions illegal. A more organised form of labour movement emerged in the meantime. The Rodo Kumiai Kiseikai (Association for Encouragement and Formation of Trade Unions) was created in 1897 and supported union organising with reformist ideals. Another attempt to mobilise workers materialised in 1912 with the establishment of the Yuaikai (Friendly Society), which in 1919 developed into the first real confederation of unions, Sodomei (the Greater Japan Federation of Labour). Although the early labour-movement organisations had moderate reformist orientation, labour disputes steadily increased in the early twentieth century, particularly in the metal, mining and textile industries, participated in by both male and female workers. In Tokyo alone, there were 151 labour disputes between 1887 and 1917. This was a steep increase in comparison with the 15 labour disputes between 1870 and 1896 (Gordon 2003). Labour disputes reached a peak in 1919, with 497 solidarity strikes and 1,892 other labour disputes not involving strike action (p.152). Despite the non-legal status of unions, workers' aspiration to change the status quo was high enough to organise 8 per cent of the Japanese workforce by 1931. On top of the struggles of manufacturing workers, the state faced protests from the peasant population, which suffered from both traditional tenancy relations with landlords and the emerging capitalist market economy that was radically reorganising traditional ways of living in rural Japan. Thousands of tenant disputes on various scales were reported between 1923 and 1931. Those movements developed hand-in-hand with the more politically oriented movements that engaged an increasing number of the working-class population. The democratisation and people's rights movements emerged during the 1870s and 1880s and pursued constitutional democracy. In response to these developments, the Meiji government introduced constitutional monarchy.[3] In 1897, the Universal Suffrage League (Futsu Senkyo Kisei Domeikai) was created. Students, intellectuals, journalists and labour unions, influenced by democratic, socialist, communist, anarchist and other western schools of thought, mobilised large-scale demonstrations in 1919 and 1920. The communist movement also gathered support with the creation of the Japanese Communist Party in 1922. Interestingly, by the 1920s – the year Johnson (1999, p.37) identifies as the starting point for the developmental state – social tension reached a peak, so that the reproduction of the early capital relation in Japan was only possible either by more democratisation or more radical reorganisation of society based on an extreme form of nationalism. The Taisho democracy[4] and the ensuing relaxation of political control reflected the former, while the latter is demonstrated by Japan's turn to the war effort and imperial expansion from the 1930s. Although popular protests were reshaping early capitalist development in Japan, they were not strong enough to prevent the general population from being pulled towards, and controlled by, ultra-nationalist movements and the right-wing military. The 1930s was dominated by right-wing violence and a coup. In 1940 all unions were replaced by the war-effort association 'Labour Front', and other forms of resistance to the rulers of modern Japan died out.

However, Japan's defeat in the Second World War and the subsequent American occupation reopened space for the Japanese working population to challenge the ways in which capitalist development had been organised in the early twentieth century. Initial occupation policies of the US military government focused on punishing war criminals and introducing liberal democratic institutions. The military and big businesses were the major targets to be tamed. *Zaibatsus* were to be broken into small corporations through the 1947 Act for Elimination of Excessive Concentration of Economic Power. A radical land reform also dramatically decreased the number of tenant farmers. The government encouraged unions as a method of taming the huge *zaibatsus*. Union membership reached a record high of 4,890,000 in December 1946. The unionisation rate reached 58.8 per cent in 1949 with an organising campaign by Sanbetsu Kaigi (The Congress of Industrial Organization, communist, the biggest), Sodomei (The Japan Confederation of Labour, socialist), and Nichiro Kaigi (the Japan Congress of Trade Unions).

However, the occupying regime took 'the reverse course' as communism gained ground in China, Korea, Japan, Vietnam and many other countries (Cumings 1987), and began to suppress labour activism, cracking down on the general strike in Japan in 1947. Focus of the reconstruction policy changed from democratisation to economic growth and building Japan as a bulwark against spreading communism. No further breaking up of the *zaibatsus* was enforced, thus allowing them to regroup. Trade unions were no longer encouraged. However, this did not immediately put Japanese capitalist development back on track. After the *zaibatsus* and state bureaucrats were back in business and office, they had to deal with what they had destroyed during the war period – strong unions such as the socialist Sohyo, massively organised workforces, the anti-American peace movement, the student and women's movements, and the radical political parties taking advantage of the liberalised political space. Unions utilised nationally coordinated strategies such as *shunto* (spring offensive). Protests against post-war arrangements for Japan to resume as a rapidly developing capitalist country reached their peak in 1960 when the Japanese state faced waves of strikes and street protests against the US–Japan Security Treaty. In a desperate attempt to pacify these struggles, Japanese capital and the state needed to take a different path. More egalitarian development, with better wealth redistribution, began to be regarded as desirable, and a particular set of relations between capital, state and labour began to take shape. The pursuit of more balanced development, one of the supporting arguments for the so-called Japanese developmental state, was, as Gordon (2003, p.279) pointed out, a part of a political strategy that 'had been worked out beneath the turbulent political surface for about a decade' after the war.

The new strategy left the reproduction of Japanese capital relations to be politically mediated. However, this was approached differently from the earlier period of development and also from the western counterpart of the welfare state. The Japanese state, rather than focusing on welfare provision, focused on securing and yielding favourable conditions for capital accumulation, while Japanese individual capitals, particularly the *zaibatsus*, distributed wealth through higher wages, corporate welfare and what is usually called the Japanese employment system. This proved to be an important moment for Japanese labour, as it allowed male workers in the core industries to enjoy the so-called Japanese-style labour relations, while hierarchical subcontracting chains left more vulnerable workers under harsh working conditions and low pay. This functioned to decompose the Japanese working class from above, proving very effective for Japan in achieving the economic miracle of the 1960s and 1970s. This development in the 1960s, and the earlier configuration of the state that Johnson describes as a developmental state, were both products of class struggles in the particular global context of Japanese capitalist development, rather than exclusively an invention, or intervention, of the state (through one section of the Japanese trade and industry ministry, MITI).

Based on a quasi-consensus between capital and labour, the politicised capital relations in Japan were much less overtly suppressive than in South Korea and Taiwan, where capital had neither the will nor the resources to share profits with workers. Early capital relations in Korea and Taiwan were articulated on the basis of a well-equipped authoritarian state apparatus, internalised Cold War sentiment legitimating rule by supra-constitutional measures, a politically decomposed working class that allowed unilateral relations at the workplaces, and weakened power of the traditional landed class. In the 1950s, the social domination of capital in South Korea and Taiwan was not fully established, although aid-based economic development witnessed emerging local capital that was represented by either traditional landlords who survived post-war land reform or new industrialists taking the opportunity in aid-dependent product processing in Korea; whereas, in Taiwan, it was largely businesses owned by KMT (Kuomintang: the Chinese National Party) that benefited from aid-based development. It was the state which then played an important role in jump-starting capitalist development in both countries. State-led capitalist development in Korea and Taiwan was initiated in the early twentieth century when imperial Japan 'implanted' colonial states in both societies. During Japanese colonisation, early capital relations in Korea and Taiwan took shape by separating the means of production and subsistence from peasants, turning traditional landownership to capitalist private property rights and, most of all, commodifying labour and popular consumption.

While Japanese colonisation initiated serious capitalist development in Korea, it also experienced specific colonial features. Integration of the mass of the population into capitalist wage relations was so limited that the vast majority of the population still lived in rural areas, not as wage workers employed in commercial farming, but as a surplus population earning their living within tenant–landlord relations. Labour relations in manufacturing sectors in many cases also featured feudal-like labour contracts, backed by surveillance and violence by police and security unions. This colonial development also determined the immature development of the Korean capitalist class, due to the lack of accumulation in their hands during the colonial period. On the other hand, colonial development precipitated a strong anti-colonial labour movement. The first labour organisation was Joseon Nodong Gongjaehoe (the Korean Labourers' Mutual Aid Association) established in 1920, which later led to the birth of the Joseon General Federation of Labour in 1924 – the first organisation agitating class struggles against Japanese capitalists and imperialism. Later it developed into two separate organisations for workers (Joseon Nodong Chong Yeonmaeng: The General Federation of Labour) and peasants (Joseon Nongmin Chong Yeonmaeng: The Korean Peasants' Union). Marxist activists organised the Joseon Communist Party in 1925, which was small but influential in anti-Japanese struggles. In some specific sectors and industrial areas in which Japanese capital invested intensely, regional and industrial levels of struggle also developed throughout the 1920s. The strong legacy of the communist-driven labour movement was sustained until the liberation. In its aftermath, Geongukjunbiwiwonhoe (The Committee for the Preparation of Korean Independence) was quickly organised and declared the 'People's Republic of Korea' in September 1945. Its attempt to put the previously Japanese-owned factories and land under their committees' control was prevented by the US occupation government. The labour movement continued to develop under the US occupation regime by organising Jeonpyeong (the Korean National Council of Trade Unions) with 16 industrial unions and approximately 500,000 members.

However, those trade unions suffered suppression and were soon made illegal by the US military regime. Furthermore, the strong basis of the radical labour and peasant movements was completely destroyed during the war by regimes in both the South and the North and the working class was decomposed. As Cho (2000) points out, after the war South Korea was an anti-communist regimented society, in which anti-communism became the most important basis for legitimate individual and collective behaviour. The post-war period then witnessed a particular class composition which consisted of the decomposed workers' movement, critically declining power of landlords, and an immediate alliance between the state and a few capitalists. The 1950s marked the beginning of the politicised formation and the reproduction of capital relations, through which the state regulated individual capitals and workers. However, the early politicisation of the formation of capital relations could not move beyond the immediate alliance through which a few capitalists funded Rhee Syng-man's Liberal Party and, in return, enjoyed highly exclusive allocation of raw materials from US aid. After the Korean War, capitalist development was soon challenged by the student movement and growing social unrest, which achieved formal democratic reforms against the 'corrupt' government in 1960.

The development of this specific articulation of capital–labour class relations culminated with the Park regime (1961–79). This tightened the state's control over collective labour through emergency decrees, nullifying all existing workers' rights by super-constitutional measures. Under the auspices of the state, individual capitals exercised unlimited authority at the workplace. The new military regime excluded from politics the capitalists who had been allied with Rhee Syng-man's government and put all individual capitalists under more 'institutionalised' control by nationalised banks and financial institutions. A new government agency, the Economic Planning Board, was set up as the institutional basis for the selective promotion of industrial investment, in which the state allocated foreign loans to specific individual capitalists satisfying the government-planned developmental strategy. As a result, capitalist social relations in South Korea were arranged so that 'the political' regulated individual capital as well as labour.

Taiwan underwent a similar experience of colonisation by Japan, experiencing industrialisation and early trade union movement under colonial rule. However, there were significant differences from Korea. First, the state created by the KMT after the return of Taiwan to the Republic of China was not a native national state. It was as alien to the local Taiwanese as the Japanese colonial state had been, since it derived from the KMT's military migration from mainland China. This implanted nature played an important part in shaping state–society relations in Taiwan, together with the class composition left by Japanese colonial rule and class struggles in the mainland. The extreme authoritarian nature of the KMT rule was legitimated and reproduced on the basis of Taiwan's unfinished war against communists in the mainland. The state confiscated the means of production left by the Japanese, even if previously owned by Taiwanese capitalists, and utilised them for KMT-controlled state enterprises. The KMT introduced land reform, finally resolving the land problem that had haunted the KMT throughout the civil war.

It was possible because the implanted KMT state had no tie with Taiwanese landlords, and the KMT secured absolute domination over the Taiwanese population as a result of its externally imposed and massive military presence. This allowed the KMT state to dispense with concerns over an alliance with existing Taiwanese elites.

But, equally, there was significant inheritance from organised social movements under Japanese rule that might have posed a challenge to the implanted KMT state. Although not as strong as in Korea, labour and peasant movements grew out of Japanese-controlled manufacturing industries and sugar-cane farming. There were also political groups such as the Popular Party and Cultural Association that supported those emerging struggles of the colonial labour force and, in doing so, sought either autonomy for Taiwan or complete entitlement of Taiwanese to the civil rights the Japanese population enjoyed (Chen 1972). However, most political activism was rooted out by the KMT even before it began to consider Taiwan as a base for recapturing the mainland. The notorious 28 February Incident, in which between 18,000 and 28,000 Taiwanese were killed, eradicated most leading figures of the Taiwan people's movement (Minns and Tierny 2003). Even so, having fled from the peasant-driven revolution in the mainland, the KMT feared class struggles and any sort of social unrest so much that it introduced the 'Temporary Provisions Effective During the Period of Communist Rebellion in 1948'. Martial law was promulgated in 1949, outlawing political activities as well as industrial action. It remained effective until 1987. On top of this, the KMT state introduced 'labour-demobilised laws' in an attempt to contain communist efforts to organise workers in the mainland during the civil war period (Hsu 1989; Hsiao 1992). Trade unions were not forbidden; but the KMT had to ensure that union leadership at every level was under the control of KMT party cadres. The subversive power of labour was directly controlled by cadres infiltrating trade unions of public enterprises. In the private sector, dominated by small-scale Taiwanese individual capitals, workers remained largely unorganised. As a result, capitals were not encouraged to expand, enterprises typically remaining of small or medium size with very limited numbers of employees. In such factories, workers had personal bonds with the Taiwanese employers, and the possibility of upward mobility into managerial positions or ownership of their own businesses (Deyo, Haggard and Koo 1987). In addition, the unique social division between mainlanders and Taiwanese made it difficult for Taiwanese workers to express their grievances through collective action against Taiwanese capitalists.

On this basis, both Taiwan and South Korea could respond to the opportunities offered by the evolving international division of labour as manufacturers of low-value-added goods that were mostly exported to the US market. Korea and Taiwan moved to export-oriented development from the 1960s onward. After this, capital relations in Taiwan and South Korea were articulated so that 'the political' regulated individual capitals through nationalising banks and financial institutions and allocating foreign loans, either (in South Korea) to large-scale family-owned conglomerates, following the state's industrial policies, or (in Taiwan) to enterprises under the control of the KMT. The state, both in South Korea and Taiwan, also exercised strong power over labour through anti-communism-based control at the level of the immediate production process, by the use of police and intelligence agents and a government-directed union federation. This particular arrangement of capitalist social relations provided developmental leadership of the state over individual capitals, suppressive labour relations at the workplace, and coercive control over the collective power of the working class, allowing for the 'miraculous' economic development of the 1960s and 1970s in the context of the regional division of labour. Experiencing remarkable average annual GDP growth rates of 9.2 and 9.5 per cent in South Korea and Taiwan, respectively, between 1961 and 1980, industrialisation was successfully transformed from ISI (import-substitution industrialisation) to EOI (export-oriented industrialisation). Despite extreme suppression of labour, the class characteristic of the state did *not* appear directly in the form of the subordination of the state to capitalists, but rather in the form of the subordination of individual capitalists to the state, creating the image of a state independent from the dominant class.

In these circumstances, workers suffered extremely long working hours and low wages. Nonetheless, individualised struggles against such extreme forms of exploitation continued to emerge and, ultimately, began to take more collective forms in the late 1970s and early 1980s. Growing independent trade unionism as well as the dynamic democratisation movement, with workers' involvement, contributed to the increasing aspiration for electoral democracy in both countries. The continual development of class struggle in the face of military governments and conservative regimes shows that the state, while succeeding in leading the reproduction of capitalist social relations in South Korea and Taiwan, could not resolve the contradictions inherent in capitalist development. When the state could not regulate the re-emerging class struggles, individual capitals also no longer willingly followed the state strategy of development. The decade from 1987 was marked by the resurrection of the working-class movement and the declining efficacy of the authoritarian state in directing capitalist development.

Over the 1960s and 1970s, the working-class movement in South Korea transformed from scattered spontaneous resistance into an organised movement in the form of 'democratic trade unionism'. In the 1970s, the development of the democratic trade union movement was led by women workers in export industries, as represented by the intense struggles in the Dongil Textile Company in the mid-1970s and the YH workers' struggle in 1979. The violent suppression of the YH workers' struggle precipitated a nationwide political campaign that finally led to the overthrow of President Park. South Korea's capitalist development faced the explosive emergence of new independent trade unionism in the summer of 1987, during which 1,300 new democratic trade unions were organised and recognised (Chang 2002). Between 1977 and 1986, the average number of disputes per year was 174, while in the period from 1987 to 1996 the number was 846 per year (Koo 2000). Democratic trade unions engaging in these industrial disputes changed the nature of labour relations on the shop floor by encroaching into the managerial decision-making process. Furthermore, the Council of Korean Trade Unions (CKTU), a national centre for newly created independent unions, was established in January 1990. Later, in 1995, the CKTU developed into the first nationwide independent national confederation, the Korean Confederation of Trade Unions (KCTU).

In Taiwan, although new labour activism did not emerge as explosively as in South Korea, labour's discontent surfaced from the 1970s. First of all, a genuinely independent union movement re-emerged (Minns and Tierny 2003). The workers in Far East Textile, for example, showed dissatisfaction with the KMT-controlled pro-management unions and wanted to build an independent union movement. Workers' discontent also took the form of political activism through participation in the democratisation movement. A dramatic sign of this was the Chungli incident, in which local people, mostly workers, organised a street demonstration and stormed a police station to protest against suspected local election fraud by the KMT. The number of labour disputes steadily increased throughout the 1970s as well. This trend accelerated in the 1980s, particularly after martial law was lifted. Between 1981 and 1988, there were

10,441 disputes with a total of 106,147 workers involved (Hsiao 1992). In 1987 alone, 3,000 labour disputes were reported, calling for wage increases and the implementation of labour law (Burkett and Hart-Lansberg 2000). The 1980s also witnessed more organised forms of the labour movement with emerging new associations and federations of the newly established independent unions, such as the Brotherhood Union (1987), the Kaoshiung Workers' Alliance (1988), and the National Alliance of Autonomous Unions (1988) (Hsiao 1992). Labour support organisations, such as the Taiwan Labour Movement Assistance Association, were organised and worker activists and radical intellectuals formed political parties aiming to defend workers' interests. This re-emerging labour activism was a result of both the expansion of capital relations and changes in their configuration. Taiwan witnessed the declining political domination of the KMT. Indeed, this political liberalisation 'did not come about naturally'; it was shaped by 'mobilised civil society' and the response of the KMT to the emerging pressure (Hsiao 1992).

4.6 CONCLUSION

The evidence from Japan, South Korea and Taiwan reveals a complex and shifting relationship between capital, labour and the state. These are not independent agents from one another, and cannot be understood independently from one another. The celebrated autonomy (whether relative, embedded or something else) of the developmental state from business is nothing of the sort, but a complex consequence of the form taken by the state in response not only to the industrial policy needs of capital but also to the form and content of class struggle itself across both the political and the economic arenas.

But the relations between the developmental state and business have also been heavily influenced by external conditions, as starkly revealed by the simultaneous confrontation of the miracle economies with strengthening demands by labour and social movements and increasing competitive pressure in global markets from the late 1980s. With limited options, the state and capital accelerated financial liberalisation, enabling, at least temporarily, individual capitals to introduce new means of production through massive expansion of short-term credit. This ultimately eroded capital allocation by the state, an important element of the earlier success. And individual capitals sought for more flexible and disposable labour to secure profitable bases for their businesses within and beyond their territories. The continuing transformation of East Asian states can be best understood in this context. The putative death of the developmental states, especially from the Asian crisis of 1997/8 onwards, requires a proper understanding of what these living creatures were in the first place. Indeed, as I have shown, recent developments need to be wedded to a fuller and proper reconsideration of the past – one in which the myth of the developmental state as such is fully exposed for its inadequate understanding of the state, capital and capital–labour relations, quite apart from the correspondingly skewed focus on state–business relations alone. For, if there is one thing that can be said of a myth, it is that it only exists in the imagination, and that is where it must also die.

NOTES

1. Divorcing the state from capitalist social relations is based on and reproduces what might be termed 'state fetishism'. In parallel with commodity fetishism, where the commodity appears to attain the characteristic of being exchangeable by virtue of its own inner nature, the state appears to attain the characteristic of a powerful social institution on its own account. According to Marx (1990), the specific mutual relations between commodity producers, in which they do not appear to mediate the relation between products but products appear to mediate the relation between producers, create the 'fetishism of the world of commodities'. The commodities' property of being exchangeable appears to be a consequence of their physical properties (as use values) not as the result of the organisation of producers within specific social relations. In other words, although 'it is nothing but the definite social relation between men themselves which assumes here, for them, the fantastic form of a relation between things', the social relations between producers disappear behind, and are veiled by, the social relations between things, and do not appear immediately as such (Marx 1990). As Marx observed, however, fetishism is not a false idea, but a reflection of real processes that both convey and conceal the reality of power, reproducing the social domination of capital by continuously presenting capitalist social relations as natural and technical relations. The state also presents itself and is understood as if 'the state has always existed since man is "by nature a creature of the state", or else the state is indispensable for social (i.e. bourgeois) life, or again it was established consciously by social contract' (Müller and Neusüss 1978, p.36). In doing so, it creates itself and is understood as an independent social entity whose power is *inherent* in its institutional form, without regard to specific social relations giving birth to its illusory image as well as its real power. To avoid being captured by state fetishism, according to Bonefeld (2008, p.65), it is important to see markets and the state 'as forms of capitalist social relations' rather than emphasising 'either state over markets or markets over state'. Markets and the state are arenas through which the same capitalist social relations are expressed. But they are expressed differently in these arenas, and that is why the state appears to be separated from markets. Through the state form, capitalist social

relations appear, at least potentially, to be politically equal relations between citizens who share universal citizenship without any formal clue being given of class difference, just as, through markets, capitalist social relations appear to be economically equal relations between owners of different commodities. State fetishism resonates with neoliberal market-fetishism in many senses. For, once the market is abstracted from class relations, and money is regarded as mediating economic relations neutrally between rational individuals, so the market as a mechanism accrues enormous social power, ceding that power to those who rule the market whilst, where possible, claiming otherwise. Many statist arguments, by merely accepting the independent social institutions and arenas as they are, suffer from a lack of understanding of these social entities as distinctive forms of capital relations. A critique of the capitalist state needs to look into the ways in which the state acquires power rather than merely recognising the existence of that power. This can be done, as Holloway (1995) argues, by understanding the areas and categories of social interconnection, including the state, as forms of the totality, modes of existence of capitalist social relations that are not merely economic relations, but social relations of political, economic and social struggle. (For a Marxian critique of the theoretical framework of the developmental state, see D.-O. Chang 2009).

2. Although Ha-Joon Chang (2006) has a nuanced argument that authoritarianism is not an essential part of the developmental state, he also presents militarism as an acceptable option, as long as it invokes development. This is indeed highly problematic and dangerously legitimating of authoritarianism (Berger 2004).

3. In 1889 the Meiji government drafted a constitution based on the Prussian constitution and arranged for it to be given by the Emperor to the people. One per cent of the population could vote for the Imperial Parliament, whose decisions were then censored by the upper house, composed of the imperial family and other elites. Elected Diet members were mostly landlords, businessmen, professionals and former samurais.

4. The Taisho democracy introduced universal suffrage from the 1928 election. About 20 per cent of the population could vote.

5
What of the Developmental State beyond Catching Up? The Case of the South Korean Microelectronics Industry

Humam Al-Jazaeri

5.1 INTRODUCTION

There is a favourite term for late industrial catch-up development – the 'developmental state'. It was coined by Chalmers Johnson, who in 1982 explained the Japanese industrial 'miracle' through MITI, the government's 'developmental' arm. This term was used, subsequently, for explaining industrial catch-up (or the lack of it) in East and South-East Asia. Then it was carried over across wider international borders. However, the developmental state's enthusiasts have missed out on one thing: development does not end with 'catching up'; it has to go beyond it.

The developmental state approach was constituted on the view that development is the phase of industrialisation associated with catch-up by latecomers. First, latecomers are seen to have peculiar properties that require peculiar measures. This is drawn primarily, if not exclusively, from the idea that the markets of latecomers do not work perfectly and, as a result, the state is required to 'govern' the market with some 'optimal mix' of incentives and disincentives in policy intervention. Secondly, and more critically, the developmental state approach has, overwhelmingly, occupied itself with the phase of catching up. What of the developmental state beyond catching up? Can the latecomer firm or industry maintain its place at the frontier or even move towards becoming a leader?

In this chapter, a distinction is drawn between catching up with the technological frontier and advancing that frontier forward and, most importantly, how the two relate to one another, both amongst competitors on and off the frontier and as a competitor seeks to make the transition beyond catch-up. This is crucial, since it cannot be presumed that the factors that allow for catch-up, including the state's involvement, automatically allow for innovation beyond the frontier. The processes involved in approaching the frontier do not necessarily offer advantage once upon it. There are elements, or indeed missing elements, that obstruct further progress. This simple insight is applied to, and confirmed by, the case study of South Korea, focusing primarily on the microelectronics industry.

In our case study, we go beyond tracing the history of the catching-up process of a latecomer. We ask, how was knowledge accumulation and technological progress sustained, and why could it not be sustained further? Why is technological progress suspended beyond particular thresholds? The most critical challenge facing the South Korean electronics firms is their low and stagnant industrial ranking in the technology architecture of microelectronics. This is shown in the wide and continuing profitability gap between themselves and the firms at the frontier. It is also shown in their dependency on foreign supplies of core components, equipment and designs. What denies the South Korean firms the capacity to improve or upgrade their rank in the industry? Why is it hard for them to break into the making of microprocessors or the manufacturing of their own equipment?

Our argument is twofold. First, contrary to the dominant view of the role of the developmental state in South Korea, the government was not of great help in reducing the dependency of South Korean producers on foreign sources of technology, not even in the semiconductor business – the core electronics component in the South Korean electronics industry. At the start, the government was reluctant to get itself into the semiconductor business, and after it got itself into it, it did little, and did not last long. Secondly, the government's role, though critical for development, remains questionable since government policies may actually play against the principle of innovation and technological deepening.

Section 5.2 defines the terms upon which latecomers from East and South-East Asia have entered the electronics industry. Section 5.3 assesses the experience of Samsung. It demonstrates the limits and potential of a successful latecomer. The section addresses how learning can be dissociated from doing and how sometimes the path of development is driven into blind alleys. Section 5.4 evaluates the rank of the latecomer in the technological architecture of the industry. It seeks to illustrate why it is so hard for the latecomer to move towards the frontier of the industry. In Section 5.5, the role of the government is taken more explicitly and assessed critically in the context of the continuous lack of technological depth by the latecomer and the government's failure to bridge it.

5.2 LATECOMERS WERE INSERTED INTO THE SEMICONDUCTOR INDUSTRY RATHER THAN INSERTING THEMSELVES

5.2.1 Defining the Terms of Entry for Latecomers: Rivalry at the Frontier of the Microelectronics Industry and the Technology Architecture

Before the arrival and proliferation of electronics manufacturing in Asia, changes on the global stage were conducive for Asian latecomers to move into the industry and become important players. Their entry, however, was conditional. When South Korean firms, along with other latecomers from East and South-East Asia, entered the microelectronics industry, they created a new dynamic that led to profound effects on how the industry conducts itself.

At first, the Asian latecomers played at tempering the balance of market power between US companies and their Japanese counterparts. By the end of the 1960s, large US corporations in consumer electronics were beginning to lose out to their Japanese counterparts. During the 1970s, Matsushita, Sony, Sanyo and Sharp were rapidly taking over American and European markets (Chandler 1997, 2001; Levy 1981). The Japanese were systematically targeting one sector after another. After establishing a strong position in consumer electronics, the Japanese moved into microelectronics. Gradually, Japan had overtaken the United States in the key areas of semiconductor technology and had become the number one producer of semiconductors. In 1985, Japanese firms had already captured the DRAM (dynamic random-access memory) market, crossing a critical threshold to the frontier of microelectronics technology (Ferguson 1985).[1] In 1986, the Japanese share of the world semiconductor market reached 46 per cent, overtaking, for the first time, the United States, which was left with 42.4 per cent. At its peak in 1988, Japan controlled over 51 per cent of the global microchip market, leaving the United States with 37.3 per cent (see Figure 5.1).[2]

Against these developments, the entry of the Asian latecomers into the electronics industry created a default dilution in the control of production capacity that was established by the Japanese in the 1980s. Gradually and methodically, however, they played to

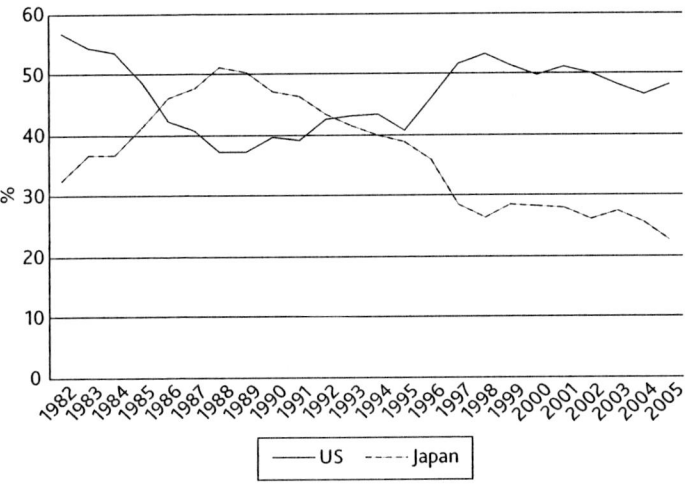

Figure 5.1 World Market Share of US and Japanese Semiconductors (1982–88)

Source: Semiconductor Industry Association, http://www.sia-online.org/galleries/press_release_files/shares.pdf, last accessed 2008

the emergence of a dual organisation within the industry, most notably, in facilitating the blossoming of design-only ('fabless') firms at the frontier. While firms at the frontier moved systematically into consolidating their market position through marketing and specialising in the higher ranks of the technology architecture (e.g. designs of logic chips and microprocessors, as well as specialised tools and equipment), latecomers took on the burden of the factory and formed the manufacturing powerhouse of the industry.

Most critically, these changes at industry and market levels were triggered by changes in the technology itself. Most obviously, the rapid growth of the computer industry, following IBM's System 360, transformed the production of microchips from custom-designed into standardised, volume-produced devices (see Chandler 2001; Langlois and Robertson 1992; Langlois 1997; Baldwin and Clark 1997, 2000). Gordon Moore (1996), one of the founders of Intel and research director at Fairchild Semiconductor, wrote that 'the new microcomputer, powered by the microprocessor, created a new sector overnight' and eventually caused 'the Japanese challenge to fade away'. The prime source of demand for microchips was shifting from consumer electronics to personal computers (PCs). Initially, the Japanese did not have any substantial advantage in this market. Japanese semiconductor firms largely depended on the demand generated by consumer electronics applications (demand for computer applications was limited).

However, at a more fundamental level, these radical changes in the technology architecture constituted the grounds for one of the most dramatic industrial restructurings in the history of the industry. To put this into perspective, the new architecture developed from the IBM System 360 introduced two radical splits into the process of computer making.[3] The first was that between software and hardware. In the new architecture, each can be developed separately, as long as they are compatible. In the software business, Microsoft quickly dominated, and eventually established a de facto monopoly in both PC operating systems and software applications. But with regard to hardware, it was the second split that was essential in defining market positions and industry leadership.

The second split took place in the technology of microchip making. The production of logic chips (microprocessors) now became technically separable from the production of memory chips.[4] The implications are far-reaching. The microprocessor, by design, functions as the central processing unit (CPU) of the computer system. It processes system data and controls the other devices in the system. It is described as the 'computer-on-a-chip' in Langlois (1992), Moore (1996) and Chandler (2001). Its maker becomes the de facto performance leader in essentially all categories of computing; it *defines* the entire semiconductor industry – the size of the chip, its speed and how it is made.

Gradually and consistently, the split at the technological level constituted a more radical split at the industry level. Having acquired the technological control over microprocessors, Intel, together with other US chip makers such as AMD, Texas Instruments and Motorola, could choose to abandon the memory business altogether.[5] The microelectronics industry is now divided into those companies that specialise in the memory chip and those that specialise in the higher-ranking microprocessor. Market leadership no longer lies in the semiconductor chip-making business. Instead, the semiconductor chip maker has to *follow* the design and architecture drawn by the microprocessor maker.

Soon, these developments paved the way for the rise of the 'foundry–fabless' business model. The semiconductor industry is now divided between those manufacturing the chip (the 'foundries') and those designing it ('fabless' firms, or design houses without factories).[6] The new model was enabled through clean interfaces

– both in technical and business terms – between foundries and fabless firms (Ernst 2003). A company's competitive position in the production of memory chips depends primarily on its manufacturing capabilities, i.e. its ability to produce the chip *cheaply* and *fast*, according to a specific design developed elsewhere (by a fabless firm). This largely price-based competition, even if accompanied with the persistent need for process innovation (to keep costs down and increase speed-to-volume production), is precisely what has occupied the research and investment efforts of the Asian latecomers ever since they entered the industry. By contrast, the competitive position of a company making logic chips (microprocessors) depends more on its design-intensive skills; the competition is product (and process) innovation-based. This segment was quickly dominated by US design-only (fabless) companies such as Altera, Qualcomm, Broadcomm, SanDisk, and NVIDIA Corporation.

The uneven distribution of the burdens and benefits of the industry is inherent within the very nature of the technology. Delegating the burden of manufacturing (i.e. the heavy investment and sunk costs associated with semiconductor plants) to latecomers has enabled firms at the frontier progressively to specialise in high-end segments and advancing technology. In the following section, we show how the terms upon which the South Korean companies entered the electronics business determined, from the outset, their industrial potential as well as their limitations.

5.2.2 Fuelling the Take-off of the South Korean Industry: Foreign Direct Investment and Foreign Borrowing

It is widely known that the South Korean industrial catch-up was brought about by its own 'developmental' state and business conglomerates, the chaebols (Amsden 1989, 2001; Kim 1991, 1993, 1997b; Johnson 1985; Chang and Grabel 2004; Fitzgerald and Kim 2004; Evans 1995; Wade 1990). The way in which the semiconductor industry began, however, offers a slightly different picture. In South Korean semiconductors, the catalyst for initial development was the US and Japanese companies. Foreign direct investments and joint ventures were never more decisive and critical for South Korean industrial development than in semiconductors in the 1960s and 1970s.[7]

Compared with local firms, foreign firms operating in the electronics industry were fewer in number but larger in terms of amount of equity investment and number of employees (Cyhn 2002). By 1968, foreign companies (primarily from the United

States) were already responsible for more than 71 per cent of South Korea's electronics exports. Over 97 per cent of South Korea's exports of integrated circuits (ICs) and transistors were produced by Fairchild, Motorola Korea, Komy, Signetics or International Micro Electronic.[8] By 1969 semiconductors represented around 46 per cent of total manufacturing production (by value) in South Korea and over 80 per cent of that of the electronics industry. In most cases, the United States was the recipient country. US firms were first to arrive on the South Korean shores and had a preference for wholly-owned subsidiaries. Soon, the Japanese followed, but relied more on joint ventures. Together, foreign and joint-venture investments made 64.4 per cent of the total investment in South Korean electronics in 1969 (see Table 5.1).

Table 5.1 Composition of Electronics Firms in South Korea (by Ownership Structure) (1969)

	Number of firms	Equity
Total	145 firms	$33.6m
Domestic	86.20%	35.60%
Foreign	8.30%	36.60%
Joint-venture	5.50%	27.80%

Source: Korea Development Bank, 1970, in Cyhn (2002, Table 3.3, p.82)

The 1970s saw more local firms (e.g. Korea Semiconductor Company,[9] Keumsung (Goldstar) Semiconductor Company, and Korea Electronics Company) and joint-venture companies assisting in the take-off stages of electronics (see Jun and Simon 1995 for a detailed study of the Hitachi–Goldstar alliance). From 1972, foreign firms more and more became buyers of microchips and suppliers of design, equipment and core components. South Korean production increased from $45.9 million in 1968 to $3.3 billion in 1979; exports grew rapidly from a mere $20 million to $1.8 billion during the same period (Hobday 1995, p.59). Electronics was gradually becoming the centrepiece of the economy's industrialisation (Hobday 2000). Nonetheless, large domestic firms remained reluctant to enter into semiconductor production until the mid-to-late 1970s. They were busy developing electronic devices such as the microwave oven and the VCR.

Foreign aid and cheap loans provided by the Americans and the Japanese were large next to the private capital that helped fuel the catch-up 'miracle' (Woo-Cumings 1991; Hart-Landsberg

1993; Chang and Park 2004; Chung 2007). Whilst stressing his reservations about explaining Asian latecomers' development on the basis of initial conditions (e.g. human resource endowments, physical and social infrastructure, previous industrial experiences under colonial periods, etc.), Chang (2006, pp.145–74) admits the exceptional role of foreign aid in the take-off phase of South Korean industrialisation.[10]

From 1945 to 1965, South Korea obtained $12 billion in US aid. During the 1950s, the amount of aid was equal to the total budget of the South Korean government (Woo-Cumings 1991, p.44–6). From 1966, South Korea relied increasingly on foreign loans to fill the gap between domestic savings and investment needs. Between 1962 and 1967, the value of foreign long-term loans reached an amount roughly equal to that of domestic bank loans. Foreign loans increased to $541.4 million in 1971. Between 1966 and 1974 they amounted to 6.2 per cent of GDP, and 35.4 per cent of all investment in the country. During the same period, foreign assistance constituted about 4.5 per cent of GNP[11] and about 20 per cent of all investment. In 1979, long-term foreign loans peaked at $2.1 billion (Chung 2007).

Foreign public loans were used to finance large industrial projects such as the construction of production facilities for the HCIs, and import capital goods (Amsden 1989; Choi and Lee 1990). Of the $960 million devoted to HCIs between 1972 and 1981, $580 million came from foreign loans (Chung 2007, p.331). More than 83.5 per cent of the public loans were used to acquire capital goods. The Import–Export Bank of the United States was the major source of financing for equipment purchases abroad. Chang and Park (2004, p.39) estimate South Korean investments that were financed from internal funds between 1970 and 1989 at only 29 per cent.

Meanwhile, foreign commercial borrowing represented a prime source of finance for private businesses. Commercial loans reached $1 billion in 1976 and $1.93 billion in 1978. They were offered at a lower interest rate than that of the state-run South Korean banks. Foreign loans came at an average price of 6.5 per cent, compared with the 11 per cent applied on South Korean bank loans. The government responded to the influx of foreign loans by providing loan repayment guarantees to private businesses[12] (Amsden 1989; Kim 1997a). South Korean state-run commercial banks guaranteed a high 50.2 per cent of total foreign loans in 1986 (Chung 2007; Chang and Park 2004).[13]

In this respect, the government role was merely a predictable extension of developments at the global (industrial) stage. It should not be seen as the distinctive industrial policy of a sophisticated developmental state. Evidently, it was the United States (and Japan) that directly promoted the rapid entry and growth of the South Korean (among other Asian) latecomers. In extending credit facilities, offering market access, and directly investing in plants and facilities, the forerunners were lifting up the latecomer. Harrison and Prestowitz (1998) report that the tacit collusion between the United States and the Asian latecomers has been a central feature of the pattern of direct and indirect US subsidies that has accelerated Asian economic expansion.[14]

5.3 THE SEMICONDUCTOR CHIP LEADS THE PERFORMANCE OF THE ELECTRONICS INDUSTRY

It was not until 1983 that South Korea began the big push towards establishing a local microchip-making industry. In 1983, the three largest chaebols, Samsung, Hyundai and Goldstar, entered the mass production of VLSI (very-large-scale integration) chips (Amsden and Kim 1985; Kim, Lee and Lee 1987). The crossing of this threshold marked a significant upgrading from simple assembly to the more sophisticated wafer-fabricating production. The semiconductor business soon affirmed its position as a critical and strategic part of the electronics industry. South Korean firms achieved remarkable growth in both output and new-product development. The entry into the semiconductor business proved a turning point in the performance of South Korean electronics firms (Mathews 1995; Kim 1997b). In 1988, South Korean production of semiconductors surpassed that of consumer electronics (Suarez-Villa and Han 1990, p.273).

In 1984 South Korea produced just over $1.2 billion worth of semiconductors. By 1992, this had risen to $7.8 billion in value – a more than sixfold increase. Meanwhile, wafer fabrication production increased rapidly from the late 1980s, reaching $3.3 billion in value in 1992. By then, South Korea was satisfying around 10 per cent of the world market for semiconductors (see Table 5.2).

Annual capital spending increased from $800 million in 1987 to an estimated $1.8 billion in 1993, amounting to more than 20 per cent of the world's total semiconductor facility investment in that year (Ernst 2000a, p.6). Whilst the world market was growing on average at 25 per cent per annum, production in South Korea was growing at more than double that rate (61 per cent). In 1990, the world market was growing at 8 per cent but South Korean production was growing at an unprecedented 66 per cent.

Table 5.2 The Take-off of South Korea's Semiconductor Industry ($m)

	1984	1986	1988	1990	1992
Production	1,268	1,469	3,066	5,104	7,800
Wafer fabrication	109	303	1,389	2,441	3,300
Exports	1,250	1,397	3,179	4,538	6,804
World's market	29,087	30,642	54,017	58,200	65,300
Market share (%)	4	5	6	8	10

Source: Electronics Industries Association of Korea, 1995, http://www.gokea.org/neweiak/eng

Remarkably, semiconductors represented more than 55 per cent of electronics exports in 1984, earning more than $1.2 billion in revenues (Suarez-Villa and Han 1990). Between 1984 and 1992, annual semiconductor production was increasing on average at more than 25 per cent (two and a half times the world's average of 10.6 per cent).[15] Exports were increasing annually by around 24 per cent (about three times the average growth of all South Korean manufacturers). In 1994, a total of $10 billion worth of semiconductors was exported, of which $4 billion was attributable to Samsung alone. By the end of the 1990s, the dynamic random-access memory (DRAM) chip had become the biggest money-spinner of the entire industry. It not only dominated the South Korean semiconductor business, but also South Korean electronics as a whole. In 2000, South Korean semiconductors, centred on DRAM chips, accounted for 15 per cent of total South Korean exports – most coming from DRAM (Samsung Electronic Research Institute, 'Economic Report', 2001, http://seriworld.org). In 2006, the South Korean IT industry represented 34.8 per cent of total exports (at $113.3 billion) (Korea Association for Information and Telecommunication, 2007, http://www.kait.or.kr/eng).

5.3.1 Crossing towards the Frontier of Technology Development

IT integrated the value chain of the DRAM technology from assembly process to process development and then to wafer fabrication and inspection. In 1983, Samsung developed the 64K DRAM, making South Korea the third country in the business, after the United States and Japan.[16] It began mass production four years behind the forerunner firms. By late 1989, it was only six months behind in the development and mass production of 4M DRAM. In 1991, it was able to produce 16M DRAM concurrently with Japan and started supplying major companies, including IBM. In 1992, South Korea's leading semiconductor company, Samsung, held a 13.6 per cent share of the world DRAM market.

Samsung's dependence on foreign technology in the production of 64K and 256K DRAMs was reversed in later chips. The latecomer was increasingly becoming self-dependent in design and development.[17] Samsung introduced its own 1M DRAM only one year after the Japanese pioneer. Developing the 4M DRAM meant competing head-on with Japanese and US companies in reaching the frontier of DRAM technology. The 64M DRAM and then the 256M DRAM were introduced ahead of any others in 1992 and 1994 (see Table 5.3). Samsung was the world's first supplier of commercial samples of 64M and then 256M DRAM, to users such as HP, IBM and Sun. It had rapidly assumed the leading role in the industry (Hong 1992; Kim 1997b; Pecht et al. 1997), becoming the number one producer of DRAMs. It had moved from being a follower (in the 1980s) to becoming a leading contender in the memory chip business.

Table 5.3 Samsung's Timeline in DRAM Development (1984–94)

	Mass production	Gap with forerunners
64K DRAM	1984	4 years
256 DRAM	1986	2 years
1M DRAM	1987	1 year
4M DRAM	1988	6 months
64M DRAM	1992	Ahead
256M DRAM	1994	Ahead

Source: Company reports (various years)

Much of Samsung's catching up was accompanied, and induced, by intensive and conscious technological learning and knowledge accumulation. Substantial qualitative gains in memory chip production were accompanied by significant qualitative improvement in design and product technology. The accumulated learning and experience gained in developing the processes of earlier chips (64K and 256K DRAM) had allowed Samsung to direct resources and efforts towards learning more about the *design* of the next generation of chips.[18] The period of rapid technological development witnessed intensified R&D efforts. For instance, research investment increased from $8.5 million in 1980 to $891.6 million in 1994. The ratio of R&D to total sales also increased from 2.1 per cent to 6.2 per cent (Kim 1997a, p.94).

Ironically, the state did not come on board with any substantial support until the early adventures had proved successful.[19] Only when Samsung managed to narrow the time-lag with the forerunners did the state intervene. In contrast to the conventional model of the developmental state (Johnson 1982; Wade 1990; Amsden 1989; Kim 1997a), the South Korean 'developmental' state did *not* initially 'pick up' a 'winning' semiconductor industry. The government did not see the potential of the semiconductor business.[20] Samsung did; and the state *followed* with critical support in R&D, financing, production, marketing and training.[21] In semiconductors, the chaebols (particularly Samsung) acted independently of government intervention, only then becoming the major stimulus to the government's policy and implementation process, not the other way round.[22]

However, as the government came onboard, it played a considerable role in building up in-house technological development. Its research institutes took a critical role in the development of chips, particularly the 4M DRAM. The government stepped up its R&D support and made the development of the 4M DRAM a national project in October 1986 (Kim 1997b). The Korean Electronics and Telecommunications Research Institute (ETRI) led a private–public collaboration project (including three chip makers, Samsung, LG and Hyundai, along with six universities) under which the 4M DRAM was developed (Lee et al. 2004).[23] The government participated by contributing 57 per cent of the total R&D expenses ($110 million), a disproportionately large share in comparison with any other national project (Kim 1997a, p.95).

Together, government support, intensive research and product development, as well as successful innovation (new DRAM designs) brought great rewards to South Korean electronics and national chaebols.[24] Samsung, along with other South Korean semiconductor firms (LG and Hyundai), made enormous profits in 1993. South Korea became the world's number two producer of DRAM, with its local conglomerates (Samsung, LG, and Hyundai) holding 24.3 per cent of the world DRAM market. The semiconductor unit of LG merged with that of Hyundai in 1999 and formed Hynix. Among the top 15 semiconductor vendors by revenue, Samsung is ranked second only to Intel, the world's leader (Table 5.4).

Table 5.4 Top 15 Semiconductor Vendors by Revenue, Worldwide (2006)

Rank	Company	Revenue ($b)	Market share (%)
1	Intel	30.437	11.6
2	Samsung Electronics	20.138	7.7
3	Texas Instruments	11.984	4.6
4	Infineon Technologies	10.533	4.0
5	STMicroelectronics	9.854	3.8
6	Toshiba	9.783	3.7
7	Hynix	8.007	3.0
8	Renesas technology	7.900	3.0
9	Advanced Micro Devices	7.434	2.8
10	Freescale Semiconductor	6.046	2.3
11	NXP	5.874	2.2
12	NEC Electronics	5.680	2.2
13	Micron technology	5.027	1.9
14	Qualcomm	4.528	1.7
15	Sony	4.434	1.7
	Total market	262.690	100.0

Source: Gartner Dataquest, March 2007, http://www.gartner.com

In DRAMs, Samsung today continues to sit comfortably at the top of the list of the world's suppliers, having leapt there in the early 1990s. According to iSuppli Corporation (http://www.isuppli.com), Samsung was the number one supplier of DRAM chips in 2007 in all of the five product categories – chips for PCs, servers, graphics, mobile and consumer applications. In the biggest market segment (chips for PCs), Samsung and its local rival Hynix Semiconductor Inc. together covered 44 per cent of the global DRAM supply in the same year (Table 5.5). Samsung also produces the world's most advanced static read-only memory (SRAM), NAND flash memory and display driver integrated circuits (DDI).

Table 5.5 World Market Share in DRAMs for PCs, (2007)

Rank	Company	Revenues ($b)	Market share (%)
1	Samsung Electronics (South Korea)	3.65	22.7
2	Hynix Semiconductor Inc. (South Korea)	3.43	21.3
3	Qimonda* (Germany)	1.56	9.7
4	Elpida (Japan)	1.42	8.8
5	Micron Technology (U.S.)	1.24	7.7

*Qimonda: a memory unit spanned off from Infineon in 2006

Sources: iSuppli Corporation, http://www.isuppli.com; Korea Herald (30 March 2008)

5.4 THE LATECOMER'S RANK IN THE TECHNOLOGY ARCHITECTURE

The rank of a latecomer in the technology architecture expresses itself in two ways. First, and more obvious, is in the profitability gap between latecomers and firms at the frontier. On a more fundamental level, the rank of the latecomer is defined by its reliance on firms at the frontier for core technologies, design and equipment. In this section we argue that the real source of trouble for Samsung and, indeed, other latecomer chip makers, lies in their industrial specialisation, their *rank* in the technology architecture.

5.4.1 The Profitability Gap between Industry Leaders and Followers

Although Samsung appears second in the list of the top 15 semiconductor vendors in terms of revenues (Table 5.4), it nevertheless diverges considerably from many of these firms in rate of profitability.[25] Samsung not only lags in profitability with the industry leader, Intel, but also with other firms lower in the list. The largest gap in profitability appears with fabless firms such as Qualcomm.

We showed above that in the early 1990s, the South Korean latecomer Samsung was increasingly becoming self-dependent in the design and development of new chips. Unlike the making of earlier chips, Samsung went ahead on its own in designing and commercialising the 64M DRAM (in 1992) and the 256M DRAM (in 1994), ahead of Japanese and US companies. It was at the frontier of product innovation. Who says adoption, adaptation or imitation of new technologies wins the battle of competition? Only the *creation* of new technologies does this.

In 1994, Samsung was making over $3.3 billion in profits from $14.6 billion in sales, a staggering 23 per cent profitability rate. In 1995, sales jumped by more than 43 per cent to $20.9 billion. Profits increased over 66 per cent to $5.5 billion. Profitability rate reached a record level, 26 per cent. Samsung was not far behind Intel, the industry leader. In 1994, Intel was making $3.38 billion in profits out of $11.5 billion in revenues (a profitability rate of 29 per cent). In 1995, its profitability rate was 32 per cent ($5.25 billion in profits from $16.2 billion sales).

From 1996, things took a different shape. While Samsung profits were going down, Intel enjoyed healthy returns. In the period between 1996 and 2006, Samsung's profitability rate was about 14 per cent on average. Intel's rate, however, was almost 30 per cent. Both companies recorded a low profitability rate of 8 per cent in 2001, owing to the radical fall in semiconductor prices and the market stagnation in the world's IT industry. Otherwise, the profitability gap between the two was wide (see Figure 5.2).

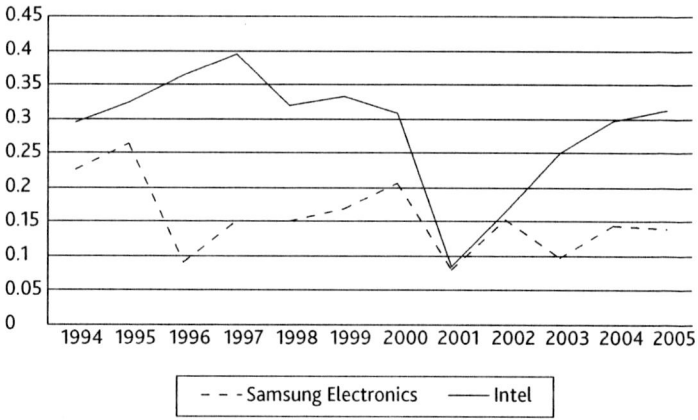

Figure 5.2 Share of Operating Profits in Total Sales (Samsung vs. Intel) (1994–2005)

Source: Calculated by the author, based on company reports (various years)

Interestingly, while Samsung's profitability rates were 14 per cent and 12 per cent in the years 2005 and 2006 respectively, the rates of Texas Instruments (which comes third on the list) were over 21 per cent and 24 per cent respectively (company annual reports). A larger gap appears when Samsung is compared with fabless companies. For instance, the rates achieved by Qualcomm (a chip designer and chipset supplier specialising in telecommunications chips, particularly those related to CDMA (code division multiple access)) were 41 per cent in 2005 and 64 per cent in 2006. In 2006, Qualcomm made a remarkable $4.8 billion in profits without having a 'fab' (a production facility) of its own.[26]

Notably, the profitability gap with fabless firms is not a South Korean peculiarity. Brown and Linden (2005, p.17) report that over the period 1995–2005, fabless revenues have been growing fast. The compound annual growth rate (CAGR: the year-over-year growth rate) in revenues recorded 20 per cent in fabless business, whilst remaining at an average of 7 per cent for the semiconductor industry as a whole.

Significantly, while Samsung lags in profitability rates, its R&D expenditure has been bold and consistent throughout the period, particularly since 2000 (Figure 5.3). In 2006, Samsung overtook

Intel in R&D expenditure; it invested $6.1 billion in R&D (9.6 per cent of total sales).

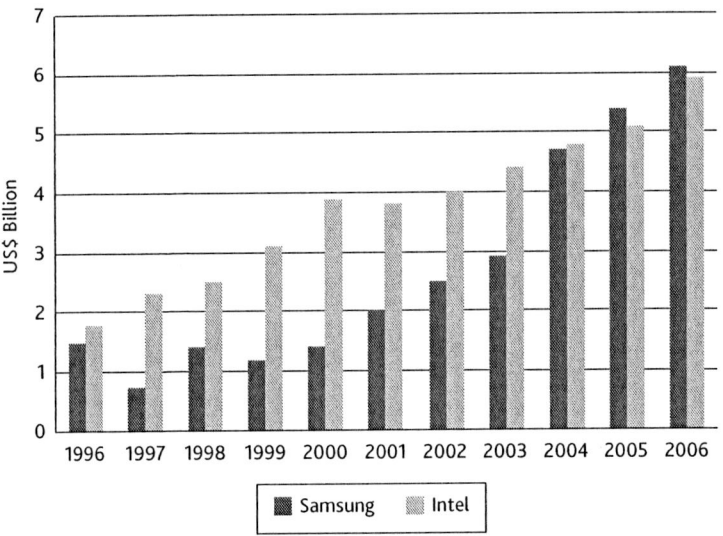

Figure 5.3 R&D Expenditure (Samsung vs. Intel) (1996–2006)

Source: Company reports (various years)

The latecomer has further developed an extensive R&D network across the globe.[27] It has six research centres located in South Korea, and ten overseas (in China, India, Israel, Japan, the Russian Federation, the United Kingdom and the United States) (UNCTAD 2006; company annual reports (various years)). Its core research institute, Samsung Advanced Institute of Technology (SAIT), already has four liaison offices (in San Jose, Yokohama, Beijing and Moscow). In 2006, the *Financial Times* ranked Samsung Electronics ninth in R&D investment among 1,250 companies around the world. The newspaper reported that over the period 2003–06, Samsung's massive investment in R&D had a great impact on the electronics industry. In 2005, it registered 1,641 patents in the United States (see Table 5.6). In the following year, it jumped to second position among the top seven electronics firms filing for US patents, with 2,453 patents of its own.

Recently, Samsung managed to enter into Interbrand's annual rankings of the world's top 100 brands, as published by *BusinessWeek* magazine, breaking into the top 25 by 2005, with an estimated brand value of $14.95 billion (in 2003, Samsung made it to the top 25 with an estimated value of $10.85 billion).[28]

Table 5.6 US Patent Filed by Top Seven Electronics Firms in 2005

Rank	Company	Number of patents
1	IBM	2,941
2	Canon	1,828
3	HP	1,797
4	Matsushita Electric	1,688
5	Samsung Electronics	1,641
6	Micron	1,561
7	Intel	1,546

Source: USPTO database, 2005, http://www.uspto.go

But why is it that Samsung's strong investments in R&D have not been reflected in its profits? Why was Samsung not able to close the gap in profitability with others? Texas Instruments has less production capacity than Samsung and comes behind in terms of revenues. Qualcomm has no production lines of its own. Economic theory often relies on R&D spending and patent registration in accounting for growth and predicting potential. But evidence at the corporate level exposes serious problems in relying on such measures to analyse innovative capability, or the lack of it. Also, while the industry continues to rely on increasing scale of production, Samsung's position as a large producer of chips seems to have had little bearing on its profitability.

We argue that Samsung was prompted by others in a particular direction and magnitude of investment. After Samsung briefly reached the frontier of product innovation (the making of the 64M and 256M DRAMs), it was gradually locked into a backward position in technology development. Product innovation has drifted away from the core of the company's business model. Everything has come to be about manufacturing. Samsung spends the bulk of its money and research efforts on expanding production facilities and fast-tracking the production of chips.

The industry is characterised by high costs, such as those related to facility construction and equipment. These are costs that are either fixed or hard to reduce in the short term. According to OECD (1985), the requirements were about $100,000 in 1954, $500,000 in 1967, $5 million in 1976, $10 million in 1978 and $60 million in 1982. By the end of the 1980s, South Korean chip makers, including Samsung Electronics, Hyundai Electronics and LG Semicon, had spent more than $4 billion on production equipment (Ernst 2000a).[29] The cost of constructing a semiconductor fab in 1966 was about $14 million. As chip making scaled up both in size and complexity and became more automated, the tools and equipment needed became increasingly critical and complex. In the 1980s, the cost tag reached $50 million. It rose even more rapidly in the 1990s – reaching about $2 billion by 1996. By 2005, constructing a new factory already cost over $3 billion (Brown and Linden 2005; Dicken 2003; Mazurek 1999; Jun and Simon 1995).

The increase in capital intensity and capital requirements is the result of the ever increasing density of IC chips. The increasing complexity of the IC designs and processes has required more precise, automated manufacturing and testing equipment.[30] The continued increase in the cost of such equipment and other plant facilities has continued to push upward the capital requirements. Furthermore, most semiconductor equipment has to be replaced every three to five years with increasingly advanced equipment – obsolescence rates are determined by technological requirements and not by the physical status of the equipment. Efficient production of semiconductor products requires continuous utilisation of advanced semiconductor manufacturing techniques.

In turn, continued increase in capital spending in order to boost capacity is crucial to maintaining competitiveness and sustaining the growth of the firm as the capital-to-sales ratio increases. These forces drive the firms in the industry to aggressive capital spending. Factories must now integrate an even larger number of new and different equipment types and software applications to meet complex market objectives and customer requirements (Dicken 2003; Brown and Linden 2005). This can be seen in the rising capital cost of constructing semiconductor fabs (Figure 5.4).

Meanwhile, Intel (the industry leader) has directed its R&D expenditure towards strengthening its learning and knowledge base in higher-premium segments such as design and product innovation (microprocessor and microchip architectures). The different paths of investment and development between the latecomer and the industry leader both reflect and emphasise a deeper and more profound split at the technology level. In this regard, understanding the nature of technology and technological specialisation at some depth is essential. The following section illustrates (with particular regard to Samsung) how South Korean firms have remained highly dependent on foreign sources of core technologies. Not much 'learning by doing' seems to have taken place.

128 BEYOND THE DEVELOPMENTAL STATE

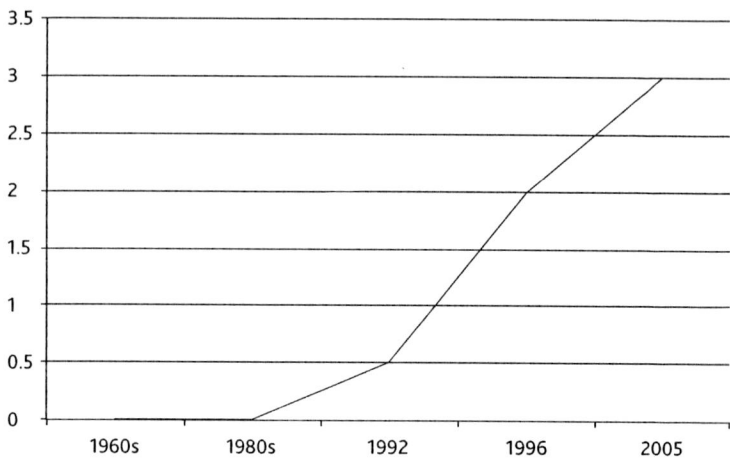

Figure 5.4 Capital Cost of Constructing Semiconductor Fabs (1960s–2005) ($b)

Sources: Brown and Linden (2005, p. 24); Dicken (2003, p. 364); Mazurek (1999); Jun and Simon (1997).

5.4.2 Continuous Dependence on Foreign Designs, Equipment, and Core Components

5.4.2.1 *The Latecomer's Dependency on Core Technologies and Designs*

In the 1970s and 1980s, South Korean firms were already making steady progress in reserving higher shares in world markets for a number of products. One in three microwave ovens sold in the US market in the late 1980s was built in South Korea; one in five was made by Samsung (Magaziner and Patinkin 1989). Samsung, along with LG, Daewoo and Hyundai Electronics, were producing colour television sets, computer monitors, printers, DVDs players, video cassette recorders, and many other electronics products. In 1994, South Korea became the fourth largest electronics producer, after the United States, Japan and Germany (Kim 1997a, p.131). The 1990s also witnessed the arrival of mobile phones and LCD display panels. The South Koreans quickly caught up with the high output of the world's largest producers.

However, while they were pushing ahead in expanding their product mix and increasing their production volume, they lacked technological *depth*. Core technologies and components were coming from abroad, primarily through licensing. For example, in the development of television sets and VCRs, Samsung had to rely on Thomson Multimedia, Toshiba and Sanyo for core technological components (Cyhn 2002). When the technology moved towards the production of DVD players, Samsung followed, but continued relying on foreign suppliers of core components. Samsung also relies on Cisco Systems for the cable modems it uses in the telecommunications business; and on Sun Microsystems for Java software and home networking. It relies on Microsoft for mobile phones and PDA software and on Siemens for smart card ICs. Significantly, the telecommunication and networks business of Samsung (and other South Korean companies) relies, almost entirely, on a sole technology provider, Qualcomm of the United States, for the core chips and chipsets in their CDMA network system (adopted as a national standard in 1991).

A more dramatic case appears in the semiconductor business. While Samsung had designed the 64M DRAM and 256M DRAM on its own in 1992 and 1994 respectively, soon the position was reversed and it is now forced to license foreign designs for almost every chip it makes. In its flash memories, Samsung relies heavily on Toshiba of Japan, which invented the NAND flash memory (Samsung entered the flash memory business in April 1995 in a tie-up with Toshiba). With mobile and portable electronics devices occupying an increasing share of the world market, flash memories gain greater significance. NAND flash memories have increasingly become a prime source for Samsung's revenues. Samsung, along with its native rival Hynix, has to license the technology design from Toshiba.[31]

5.4.2.2 *The Latecomer's Dependence on Equipment*

South Korean microchip makers probably have the world's best manufacturing technology for memory production and the largest production capacities for chips, but they remain highly dependent on equipment and core components made by others (primarily Japan, but also the United States). Ultimately, 'the dependence lent catching up its distinctive norms' (Amsden 2001, p.2; see also Lee et al. 2004; Ernst 2000a, 2003). Samsung did not make chips from scratch. Equipment and components as well as plant design came from the United States and Japan. It entered an industry where the market was already established and supply was running short of rising demand; it did not need to be a 'good salesman'. Its rapid catch-up was constituted solely on the ground of a rapid scale-up of output.

The latecomers continue to be incapable of manufacturing high-performance equipment that is cost effective and compatible with state-of-the-art applications. Core components continue to occupy a good share of imports to South Korea. These important weaknesses make South Korean chipmakers particularly vulnerable (Pecht et al. 1997); they are locked into an indefinite position of catching-up in the technology, in both equipment and materials.

In the global semiconductor equipment industry, we observe only a small number of manufacturers, with only two or three companies for each type of equipment. Since the beginning of the industry, semiconductor equipment manufacturing has been highly concentrated. Some original players continue to lead in these industrial segments. Applied Materials, Novellus, Tokyo Electron, Advantest, Canon and others have been at the frontier of the industry for many years, some for over five decades. According to VLSI Research Inc., Japanese suppliers claimed five positions in the top-ten list for 2007, accounting for 38 per cent of total sales – slightly down from 42 per cent in 2004. Four US companies claimed nearly 48 per cent of the total, up from 47 per cent in 2004. Together US and Japanese firms account for over 85 per cent of the top-ten sales in 2007, with only one European firm in the list, accounting for just under 15 per cent. In 1996, Japanese companies occupied six positions and accounted for over 58 per cent of top-ten sales (Table 5.7). Both Applied Materials and Tokyo Electron have maintained their first and second positions since 1992.

Table 5.7   Top Ten IC Equipment Manufacturers Suppliers by Revenues (1996, 2004 and 2007) ($b)

Rank	Company	2007	2004	1996	Headquarters
1	Applied Materials	8.400	7.500	4.000	United States
2	Tokyo Electron	5.100	4.700	3.300	Japan
3	ASML	4.500	3.000	0.778	Europe
4	KLA-Tencor	2.400	1.800	(not included)	Japan
5	Lam Research Corporation	2.200	1.300	1.200	United States
6	Advantest	1.900	3.000	1.200	Japan
7	Nikon	1.900	1.400	2.100	United States
8	Novellus	1.600	1.300	(not included)	United States
9	Dainippon	1.300	Hitachi at 1.300	0.815	Japan
				Hitachi at 0.867	
10	Canon	1.300	1.200	1.200	Japan

Source: VLSI Research Inc., 2005 and 2008, http://www.vlsiresearch.com

The top ten equipment suppliers accounted for over 71 per cent of worldwide sales of semiconductor manufacturing equipment in 2007, which reached $42.77 billion. According to SEMI, the global industry association for companies that supply manufacturing technology and materials to the world's chip makers, the South Korean market accounted for about 17 per cent of world sales, with over $7.35 billion spent on equipment. The Taiwanese market, however, accounted for a staggering 24.8 per cent, spending over $10.64 billion. Together South Korea and Taiwan accounted for over 42 per cent of the world market in 2007. Meanwhile, the Japanese market accounted for above 21 per cent of total equipment sales (at $9.3 billion) (Semiconductor Equipment and Materials International, http://www.semi.org; Semiconductor Equipment Association of Japan, http://www.seaj.or.jp/English).

South Korea led world market growth in semiconductor equipment in 2003 with a 91 per cent expansion in equipment spending ($3.1 billion). It subsequently increased its spending by an additional 45 per cent in 2004 to reach $4.6 billion. The Taiwanese market began a strong upward turn in 2004, rising by 166 per cent to $7.8 billion, compared to $2.9 billion in 2003.

It is important to note that not all of these top ten equipment suppliers produce the same products. On the contrary, each is specialised in a particular segment of the industry; they are rarely in competition with each other. Semiconductor equipment manufacturing is divided into three categories: wafer processing equipment; testing, material-handling and process diagnostics equipment; and assembly equipment. Wafer processing equipment occupies a central position, accounting for three quarters of the entire manufacturing equipment market. For instance, Nikon, Canon and ASML of the Netherlands manufacture wafer-processing equipment such as steppers, while Tokyo Electron (with a 90 per cent share of the market) and Dainippon Screen make coat/develop track equipment, and Tokyo Electron, Hitachi Kokusai Electric and Lam Research Corporation (which has a relatively large market share) make CVD (chemical vapour disposition) equipment. With regard to testing equipment, the leading maker is Advantest, with a 70 per cent share of the market (information derived from SEMI and VLSI Research Inc.).

The established dominance of this small number of US and Japanese companies in the business goes back to their established position in the machinery and equipment industry. Their early involvement with the semiconductor industry proved critical in enabling them to establish a dominant position. Technological skills and knowledge gained at the early stages of semiconductor development were indispensable for developing the tools and specialised equipment for making chips.

By the time latecomers entered the industry, chip design and manufacturing had already gone through significant stages of development. The industry has transformed from human-embedded to machine-embedded technological knowledge. Unlike 'old generation' chip makers, the knowledge base of latecomer chip makers did not go much beyond production lines. As described by Ernst (2000a; 2003), their successful catch-up was based on limited and achievable technological learning of mature technologies that were easy to replicate. Tool and equipment making were different and more complex matters. In order to build the machines and make the necessary tools, latecomers would need to know a great deal about the inner workings of the overall product or process. Partial knowledge was not enough.

In discussing the terms upon which latecomers have entered microelectronics, we have observed how the split in the semiconductor industry between designers of chip architecture, chip makers and tool and equipment suppliers has systematically suspended technological learning at the production lines of chip makers. Intensive learning as well as skills and knowledge formation are shuttled out to the frontier of chip design and equipment making.[32] Accordingly, it was US and Japanese firms which occupied the frontier of the industry.[33] Latecomer chipmakers were left out of the most advanced and sophisticated product segments in the industry, and they continue to find it extremely hard to catch up.

It is not surprising, then, that a critical characteristic of South Korean electronics is its continuing reliance on imported equipment and core technological components. South Korea has made very little progress in reducing its dependence on imported equipment and materials, primarily from the United States and Japan.[34] According to the South Korean Semiconductor Association (KSIA), domestic chip makers in 1994 relied on foreign suppliers for 84 per cent of equipment and 52 per cent of materials. By 2000, not much had changed; chip makers relied on foreign suppliers for over 88 per cent of equipment, 48 per cent of devices, and 40 per cent of materials.

South Korea continues to import integrated circuits, such as digital and non-digital monolithic integrated units (DMIUs and non-DMIUs), which are amongst the building blocks for computers, telecommunications equipment, electric and electronic instruments, and transportation equipment. Together these accounted, on average, over 1998–2006, for around 10 per cent of South Korea's total imports (around 21 per cent of their imports from the United States and 8 per cent of those from Japan). During the period 1991–2006, South Korea spent $188.45 billion on imports of these devices. Since 2004, South Korea has imported over $20 billion a year ($21.08 billion in 2006).

We have calculated the rates of growth in IT exports and those on the imports of the two devices (DMIUs and non-DMIUs) from 1991 to 2002. The two are highly correlated throughout the period (Figure 5.5). While South Korean companies were producing almost a full set of IT products, they showed no tendency towards reducing their dependence on the expensive core devices. They did not show any sign of learning by doing in this respect.

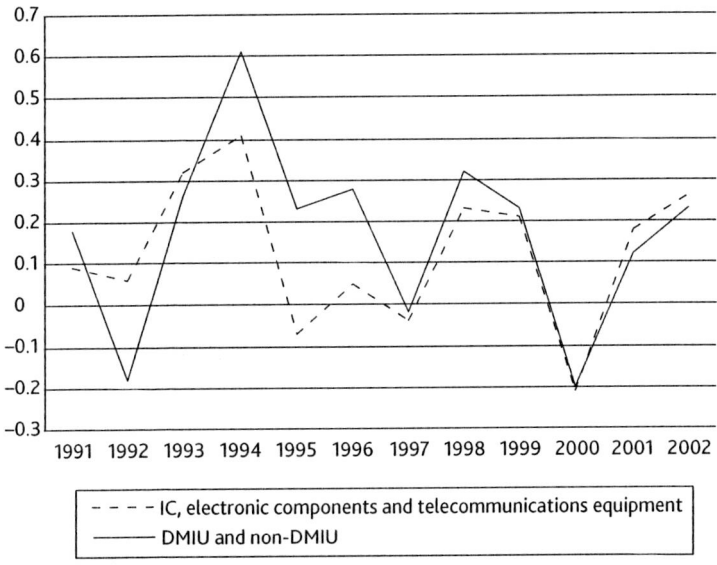

Figure 5.5 The Association between IT Exports and DMIU and Non-DMIU Imports: Rates of Growth (1991–2002)

Source: Data collected from WTO database (various years) and calculated by the author

South Korea's weakness in parts and components is also captured by the World Bank's RCA index of component production, as reflected in 2001 export statistics (WTO database, various years).[35] South Korea has an RCA (revealed comparative advantage) in only nine component product groups out of 60, compared with 40 for the United States and 34 for Japan. Component product groups with RCA exceeding unity for South Korea electronics include telecommunications equipment (2.70) and electronic components (1.58).

The South Korean low ranking in the technology architecture and its continuing reliance on foreign sources for core technologies, components and equipment is recognised in many studies of latecomer economies, and of South Korea in particular (Amsden 2001; Amsden and Chu 2003; Ernst 2000a, 2000b; Kim 2003; Lall 2000). For instance, Ernst (2000a) argues that catching up has focused on expanding capacity and international market share for homogeneous, mass-produced products, such as television sets, monitors, DRAM and displays. He further observes that very little upgrading has occurred into higher-end and rapidly growing market segments for differentiated products and services, such as design-intensive ICs and computer products, software and internet services. Ernst concludes that South Korea's unprecedented speed of entry into high-risk and very demanding manufacturing, such as DRAM and displays, may signal the limits of what is possible.

Although Samsung has moved consistently and actively to diversify its business portfolio, the semiconductor chip continues to dominate much of what it does. In 2000, it accounted for over 81 per cent of total profits. All other segments, including telecommunication networks, digital media and home appliances, suffer from low profitability. In 2006, the contribution of the semiconductor business in total operating profits was tempered, but remained, nonetheless, significantly high at over 56 per cent (Samsung Electronic Research Institute Economic Report 2008, http://www.seriworld.org).

5.5 THE GOVERNMENT'S ROLE AND THE LACK OF TECHNOLOGICAL DEPTH

For some, dependence on external sources of technology, including design and equipment, was a convenient and appropriate strategy for catching up. In this regard, Lall (2003, p.21; 2000), for instance, claims that reliance on foreign sources of technology can shorten the industrialisation period. It also provides access to state-of-the-art technologies along with entry into global markets. In fact, this view does not depart much from the neoclassical orthodoxy, in which the 'rational' choice is determined by the cheaper, the faster and the best practice. We argue that reliance on foreign sources of technology (including design and equipment) was often forced upon the latecomer. This dependence, ultimately, rendered the latecomer in a perpetual status of catching up and consistently kept it away from the frontier of the industry.

Others, however, explain the lack of technological depth of latecomers in the context of the government's role and policies, ranging from export-led strategies to cronyism. Krugman (1998), for example, stresses that crony capitalism, personal connections and political patronage (often mixed up with government policies), rather than entrepreneurial abilities, determined who got access to credit and subsidies and on what terms.[36] Amsden and Hikino (1994, p.114) temper the argument for cronyism and argue that the appeal to South Korean chaebols of excessive product diversification (with little upgrading in a particular segment) corresponded to an 'opportunistic' behaviour by the South Korean firms to benefit from government support. In some respects, it represented a desperate move to capitalise on mass production (Ernst, Ganiatsos and Mytelka 1998; Amsden and Chu 2003).

Since South Korean firms typically relied heavily on debt to finance their diversified expansion, it seems reasonable to explain their aggressive product diversification in the context of government export-led policy. In order to qualify for the government's preferential treatment (most notably in forms of credit allocation and tax subsidies), South Korean firms had to increase their exports. Accordingly, they placed more emphasis on output growth than on profitability and technological integration.

In one respect, the government's policies were, indeed, playing *against* the principle of innovation and technological deepening. When institutional arrangements offer greater rewards for an increased volume of exports than they offer for technological deepening and in-house development, we can expect firms' efforts to be allocated away from the more critical activities. From the beginning, the priority for South Korean firms rested upon how many products they were able to export and in what quantities. The government's export-led policy was effectively a policy that associated every benefit with the volume of exports. A firm might be allowed to borrow money from banks at far below the normal borrowing rate on the basis of the total amount exported.

In lacking domestic technological capabilities (and the incentive to make them), it was more convenient to rely on OEM contracts and to import equipment and components, quickly installing them and getting them up and running. Imports of capital goods (equipment and machinery) and licensing of new technologies and designs replaced extensive investment in developing often highly expensive in-house technologies. Samsung and the other South Korean chaebols had no choice but to give export performance the highest priority, regardless of how the product was made.

What further intensified the trouble was the gradual evaporation of government support.[37] Contrary to the dominant account of the role of the developmental state in South Korea, the government was not – at any rate in the semiconductor business – of great help in reducing the dependency of South Korean producers on foreign sources of technology. The government had been reluctant to get into the semiconductor business in the first place; it did little, and its involvement did not last long.[38] From the mid-1980s the government's active role in R&D went into decline (Chang 1994; Chang and Shin 2003; Kim and Kim 2006).[39] According to Chang (1994, 2006), until the mid-1980s the country had practised one of the most comprehensive and systematic industrial policies in the world. However, slowly from the late 1980s, but very rapidly from 1993 (the year that marks the official end of the three-decade old five-year plans), the South Korean government dismantled its active developmental policy.[40]

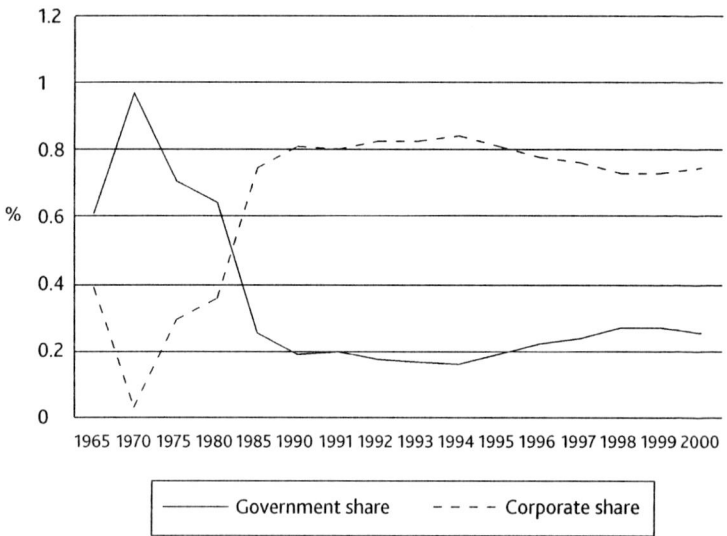

Figure 5.6 Government and Corporate Contributions to R&D Expenditure (1965–98)

Source: Ministry of Science and Technology (MOST), Seoul, South Korea (2001)

The retreat of the public share of R&D expenditure (see Figure 5.6) has systematically pushed South Korean firms into the hands of foreign firms. Money for R&D expenditure has been increasingly raised through joint research with foreign companies and institutes. Foreign firms have become increasingly influential in determining the direction of R&D in local firms. Significantly, the remaining share of the public sector in the total R&D budget has itself changed course; instead of venturing (or leading) in new, risky investments, it has played more of a complementary role (Cyhn 2002).[41]

In this chapter, we have tried to show that the government's role, though critical, does not say it all in explaining development (or the lack of it), certainly not beyond catching up. Instead, beyond the 'developmental state' lies in what is possible and not possible for a latecomer.[42] The latecomers were unable to 'pick the right asset'. The *rank* of the latecomer in the 'technology architecture' was, and still is, subject to a disciplinary mechanism.

The word 'discipline' should not be taken too literally. It should be seen as being the outcome of external and internal forces that have kept the path of development (and learning) of the latecomer in check. At one level, as the technology (of producing the chip) has developed, it gradually became possible to individualise the architecture of production into separate units which were immediately brought together to exploit economies of scale and scope. At another level, firms involved in reciprocal obligations and exercising asymmetrical activities became at the same time hierarchically – related in technological terms.

In 1996, Samsung was presented with a rare chance to acquire the rights to produce a microprocessor of its own, the Alpha microprocessor. Following the acquisition of the rights from Digital Equipment Corporation (DEC), in 1996, Samsung Electronics, introduced its microprocessor, the 633 MHz Alpha 21264 design. According to the contract, Samsung was to contribute the production process technology and manufacturing capacity, while DEC was to contribute the basic architecture technology of Alpha.

To some extent, the Alpha processor represented a divergence from the conventional operating systems running under Microsoft dominance. Alpha supported open-source operating systems, notably Linux and Unix, and hence presented Samsung with a chance to leapfrog. Compaq, a significant PC maker, bought DEC, the technology architecture designer (for $9.6 billion) and retained the arrangements with Samsung. Compaq found it tempting to rely on its own systems and not those of Microsoft.[43] Samsung now had on board an important player in the industry to drive the technology. In June 1998, a new entity, Alpha Processor Inc. was set up jointly between Samsung (with a stake of 87.5 per cent) and Compaq (12.5 per cent), with a commitment of $500 million to support the Alpha architecture.

Alpha was short-lived. Leaping into microprocessors is technologically difficult enough, even without Intel's firm grip on the market. Following the development phases, Samsung was able to export the first Alpha chips to America and Japan – a total of 4,000 533MHz chips. However, in 2001, when Samsung was just beginning to manufacture the Alpha EV68A in quantity, Compaq (which by then had merged with Hewlett-Packard) announced that Alpha would be phased out by 2004 in favour of Intel's processors.[44] Compaq was giving up the fight with Intel; after all, its desktops, notebooks, workstations and servers had long been based on Intel's processors.[45] Accordingly, in June 2001, Intel bought Alpha Processor Inc. and terminated the project. Samsung could not wage the fight on its own. After all, while AMD and Compaq had been working on the design of Alpha, Samsung had been busy learning how to produce it. Its capabilities were focused on manufacturing and the production process, not on design and product innovation. Alpha immediately ceased to exist.

The example of the Alpha microprocessor shows that the development of the technology was beyond the control and influence of the latecomer. It remains technologically infeasible for the South Korean latecomers to break into the business of microprocessors or chipsets. Their knowledge and learning base is insufficient for them to leap forward into this more lucrative business. Moreover, once the firms at the frontier of technology had established their lead, they moved consistently to tie their customers (e.g. PC makers) into their own technologies. Their positions in determining the direction of the industry reflected the critical role of their product (the microprocessor) in computing and the electronics industry at large.

The influence of Intel, for example, in determining the technology cycle of microprocessors and memory chips (for PCs) has manifested itself most dramatically in setting its chips as the de facto standards and in establishing a pace of its own. Accordingly, latecomer chip makers were not only disbarred technologically, i.e. in terms of their learning and knowledge base, from breaking into the microprocessor business, but were also subject to the use (or abuse) of the leading firms in setting industrial standards and the boundaries and conditions of entry into the business.

5.6 CONCLUSION

Proponents of the developmental state model, whilst appealing for a more rounded treatment of industrial development, have taken the view that what happens to latecomers after they have caught up with the industrial and technological frontier is more or less unproblematic. Crossing towards the technological frontier or going beyond it remains outside the scope of the developmental state model. This is an extraordinarily crude and oversimplified view of the nature of technology and technological change. Latecomers' development is reduced to the understanding that industrial structure moves from the simple to the more complex in a steady predictable way, subject (solely) to learning and 'self-discovery' (Hausmann and Rodrik 2003). The role of the state is then to facilitate the accumulation of this learning and the promotion of this discovery process. The latecomer closes the gap with forerunners as it evolves along the route of organic and cumulative learning.

This is misleading. First, and above all, one should decipher in the discovery process as such, a network of relations, constantly in tension. This is in contrast with the argument put forward by the developmental state model, where the state or the entrepreneur occupies a privileged position and makes the 'right' choice or 'picks the right asset'. On occasion, industrial development is not driven by a process of self-discovery, but by external influences that determine the path of learning. Without understanding the technology in some depth and defining the specificity of the technological architecture upon which particular industries are organised, that tension cannot be made explicit, and the policy implications are equally questionable. For instance, at an obvious level, different rankings in the technology architecture, or differences in industrial specialisation, naturally constitute different paths. Such divergence has not usually favoured bringing latecomers closer to the frontier, let alone taking them beyond it. This, immediately, provokes the question: what is possible and what is not possible for a latecomer? Latecomers have often been denied entry to particular industrial segments or precluded from moving towards certain technological ranks.

Second, following this last point, the efforts involved in catching up with those at the frontier, including learning and investments (of various kinds), do not necessarily offer advantages once the frontier has been reached, nor do they allow automatically for innovation beyond it. The limits as well as the potential for industrial development for latecomers are defined primarily and fundamentally at the frontier of the industry. Latecomers' inherent capabilities, as well as their industrial policies and institutional structures, may influence how things can be done *within* those specific limits, but not beyond them.

NOTES

1. In 1980, Hewlett-Packard sounded the alarm for the US industry by announcing that the Japanese 16K DRAMs were of far higher quality than those made in the United States (Moore 1996). From a chip trade surplus with Japan in 1980, the United States ran up a trade deficit of $800 million in 1984 (Forester 1993).
2. Forester (1993) estimated the Japanese share at 67 per cent in 1988.
3. The new design of IBM System 360 allowed PC makers, for the first time, to adopt a 'plug-in' manufacturing system. According to this system, parts and components can be produced separately (potentially by different suppliers), according to specific standards and compatibility measures, and subsequently brought together to make the computer (the final product). This division within the architecture of PC manufacturing led to new specialisation streams at the industry level, with various companies (in different locations) specialising in the manufacturing of specific components. Meanwhile, IBM and the manufacturers of IBM clones (Compaq, Dell, etc.) have effectively become PC marketers rather than PC makers; they specialise in the design and marketing of the new PC, rather than in the making of its parts and components.
4. In contrast to all other hardware devices, chips are more central and often they are integrated to system-level complexity on account of their size and compatibility. They fall into two categories: memory chips, which are basically, data storage devices; and logic chips, which effectively process system data and *control* other devices in the system. Peripherals and desktops [Computers themselves and their peripherals] are less complex and more standardised. A complete product specification can be codified and accordingly handed for development and production to an OEM or ODM manufacturer.
5. All but two American merchant companies (Texas Instrument, which kept its production facility in Japan, and Micron Electronics) withdrew from DRAM production after the mid-1980s (Howell, Bartlett and Davis 1992). Motorola moved into new electronic products, including modems and telecommunications equipment, and maintained a competitive position in microprocessors. Apple bought the logic chips for its Macintosh from Motorola.
6. A 'fab' is defined according to the Semiconductor Industry Association as the manufacturing plant that makes semiconductor devices. It originated from 'fabrication', the process used to create chips.
7. Similarly, the entry of Taiwan into the semiconductor industry was also led by foreign direct investment from the United States (especially by General Instrument and Texas Instruments, who were later followed by RCA and Zenith in the production of television sets) and Europe (especially Philips). Japanese

THE CASE OF THE SOUTH KOREAN MICROELECTRONICS INDUSTRY

companies also contributed, though in the form of joint ventures (Kuo and Wang 2001).

8. Several companies invested actively in Korea with 100 per cent share of foreign ownership. Among these were Fairchild and Singnetics (in 1966), Motorola (in 1967), AMI (in 1970), and Toko (in 1970 and 1971) (Frank, Kim and Westphal 1975).
9. In 1980, Samsung acquired Korea Telecommunication Co. and then Korea Semiconductor Co. to become Samsung Semiconductor and Telecommunications Co. In 1984, it took the name Samsung Electronics Co. Samsung's earlier successes in the trading and agricultural commodities businesses was critical for its entry into electronics.
10. Chang (2006, p.145–74) argued that the 'advantages enjoyed by the East Asian countries in terms of initial conditions are nowhere as great as they are commonly assumed to be'. He showed, for instance, that the East Asians did not enjoy a better base of human resources than existed in the Latin American economies. Neither, to refer to physical and social infrastructure, did they enjoy better telephone or railway densities. Even with regard to foreign aid, he stressed that Hong Kong and Singapore did not receive high levels (even though, the two countries relied heavily on foreign investment).
11. GNP (gross national product) is used here owing to the time during which the measure is calculated (the 1970s). At that time (1970s–1980s), the United States used GNP as a primary measure of total economic activity. Only in the 1990s did it began to use GDP. This applies to South Korea as well. South Korea did not have any significant production capacities abroad at the time.
12. Government loan guarantees came under the Law Guaranteeing Repayment of Loans in 1960 and the Law Governing the Importation of Capital Goods on a Long-Term Repayment Basis in 1962, and then the Foreign Capital Inducement Law of 1966.
13. The generous guarantees provided by the South Korean government have constituted the ground for foreign banks to adopt aggressive lending strategies, making good profits at an estimated 26.8 per cent on paid-in capital (Chung 2007).
14. Deyo (1987b) placed this argument within a dependency framework in which the United States, Japan, and South Korea and Taiwan were, respectively, located at the core, semi-periphery and periphery in the world system. In our analysis, we do not accept dependency theory (or indeed post-dependency theory). Although the role played by the United States and Japan has been critical in the development of the Asian latecomers (this is reflected extensively throughout our analysis), the relationships between latecomers and forerunners has been characterised as technological in a new sense. The South Koreans, for instance, have become world leaders in many product segments and have broken into various top-ten lists. This is not predicted within a dependency-theory framework.
15. In September 1985, under US pressure, the Japanese government agreed to support a rise in the yen relative to the dollar as part of the Plaza Accord. The yen appreciated by almost 50 per cent over the period 1985–88, creating serious economic problems for Japanese corporations. Hence South Korean exports were, initially, able to take advantage of the appreciation of the yen to increase their own sales in the US market. While the yen was rising relative to the dollar, the South Korean government 'engineered' a decline in the value of

the won relative to the dollar, allowing it to rise again by 16 per cent in 1988 and another 3 per cent in the first half of 1989 (Hart-Landsberg et al. 2007b).
16. Samsung imported the design, process and assembly technology of 64K and 256K DRAM from the US company Micron Technology (Byun 1994). It set up an R&D outpost in Silicon Valley in 1983 and hired five Korean–Americans with Ph.D.s in electronic engineering and who together brought previous experience of working for IBM, Honeywell, Zilog, Intel and National Semiconductors (Kim 1997b).
17. Gold Star licensed the 4M and 16M DRAMs from Hitachi of Japan; Hyundai also relied on licensing from Japanese firms (Hobday 1995).
18. Growing demand and short supply kept pushing up the prices – from $2 in 1986 to $5 in 1988 for 256K chips – allowing the South Korean producers much needed breathing space during their early development (Kim 1997a).
19. S.R. Kim (1998, p.296) notes that the role of the South Korean state has been 'only supplementary' in the early establishment of the DRAM. Others, like Yoon (1992, p.256), went even further, arguing that 'unlike Japan, the government role in the development of the Korean semiconductor industry was not important'. According to Chang (1994), the state played a minimal role in the success story of the South Korean semiconductor industry.
20. Sanyal and Yu (1989) discuss some heated debates between businesses and the government; some argued that Korea was not yet ready to be involved in the chip market and compete head on with economic giants like the United States and Japan. Samsung, however, saw the potential for gaining a foothold.
21. As part of the fourth Five-Year Plan (1977–81), the government arranged foreign loans of about $221.6 million. It also set up the Korea Institute of Electronics Technology to assist the semiconductor and computer industries. Later, in 1985, KIET's tasks were taken over by the Electronics and Telecommunication Research Institute (ETRI), which was to play a critical role in the technological development of memory chips (Hobday 1995).
22. By the mid-1980s, the chaebols, following Samsung's initiative, issued commercial paper totalling $285 million through various foreign financial markets with a view to investing in the semiconductor business. Samsung came to the forefront in raising funds abroad *without* state repayment guarantees, amounting to $190 million in 1984 alone (Hong 1997, p.103).
23. Samsung, which followed an intensive in-house development strategy, were unwilling to share knowledge.
24. Government-sponsored training and education has also played a pivotal role. In 1972, the government set up a new graduate school of engineering and applied sciences, the Korea Advanced Institute of Science (KAIS), later renamed KAIST (Korea Advanced Institute of Science and Technology). For an evaluation, see Lee (2009b).
25. In discussing profitability as a measure of enterprise performance there are important limitations. It is difficult to decide which measure of profitability should be used. Different measures give different, sometime, misleading results. Should net profits be used? Operating profits? Or should returns on assets be deployed as an appropriate measure of enterprise performance? These issues are critically assessed in Chang (2006, p.284). Chang, for instance, observes that South Korea has one of the lowest rates of corporate profitability in the world if the rate-on-assets criterion is employed. In our analysis, we rely on operating profits, that is, profits before paying financial expenses such as interest payments

THE CASE OF THE SOUTH KOREAN MICROELECTRONICS INDUSTRY 143

and foreign exchange losses (or gains). The objective is merely illustrative. We wish to demonstrate the general tendency of comparative corporate performances. In practical terms, with most corporate firms today following similar accounting and auditing standards, an index of operating profits is one of the most readily available measures.

26. In 2007, *iSuppli* reported that for the first time a fabless firm, Qualcomm, had made it into the top-10 list (see also Table 5.5).
27. By 2006, Samsung had established an extensive design network: Global Corporate Design Centre (Seoul); Samsung Design Europe (London); Samsung Design Milan (Milan); Samsung Design China (Shanghai); Samsung Design Japan (Tokyo); Samsung Design America (San Francisco); Samsung LA Lab (Los Angeles) (Samsung Electronics Annual Report 2007). Each of these centres analyses local culture, lifestyles and industry trends. This information becomes a critical input for the Corporate Design Centre.
28. By 2001, of Interbrand's top 50 most valued brands in the world, only four were from Asia. Three were Japanese – Sony, Toyota, and Honda. The fourth was Korea's Samsung; it was ranked 42nd (Interbrand, http://www.interbrand.com2001).
29. Recently, Samsung has invested $19 billion over five years (1998–2003) in new microchip facilities (Samsung Electronics, 'Annual Report 2004', http://www.samsung.com/uk/aboutsamsung/corporateprofile/ourperformance/annualreports.html).
30. Wafer size contributes most significantly to manufacturing costs, as also does cost of equipment, raw materials and cleanliness of the manufacturing environment – wafer fabrication takes place in a highly controlled, clean environment – to minimise dust and other quality-limiting contaminants. In addition, semiconductor production requires reliable and uninterrupted power supplies, vast quantities of pure water, and wastewater treatment facilities.
31. Samsung also licenses the chip design of its SDRAM, DDR DRAM, and RDRAM from a technology provider, Rambus Inc. of the United States. The case of Samsung's adoption of the RDRAM is particularly illustrative. Chip makers, including Samsung, were increasing their knowledge on the earlier chips – SDRAMs and DDR SDRAM. However, once RDRAM came along – actually pushed forward by Intel, Rambus' partner – learning efforts were diverted towards understanding the new design technology. Learning was suspended on other tracks. Samsung had to ramp up the implementation work and manufacture the new chip on a large scale and at high speed.
32. Something similar, if rather more obvious, has taken place in the car industry. The split within the industry (in the mid-1980s), at the global stage, between assembly lines and component suppliers resulted in a systematic *suspension* of learning at assembly lines. No matter how many cars are coming out of the assembly line, technological learning and development are taking place (at least at the more intensive and critical levels) elsewhere – at the parts and components manufacturing sites. In view of this, adjusting to the new industrial structure is not proving an easy task for the South Korean automobile industry.
33. Both American and Japanese firms have participated in (and effectively founded) standards-setting organisations such as SEMI. From their positions at SEMI they led the technological development of the industry on two defining fronts; chip design, and the design of manufacturing equipment.

34. Only in packaging and assembly have South Korean companies managed to push forward, developing the ability to make wafer handlers and positioners (KSIA, http://www.ksia.or.kr/eng/main/).
35. The RCA index of country *i* for product *j* is measured by the product's share of the country's exports in relation to the product's share of world total exports:

$$RCA_{ij} = (X_{ij} / X_{it}) / (X_{wj} / X_{wt})$$

where *w* is the world and *t* means total. If the RCA index for country *i*'s product *j* exceeds 1, that country is said to have a revealed comparative advantage in the product. Similarly, if the value is less than 1, the country has a revealed comparative disadvantage in the product. It must be noted however, that the World Bank statistics do not indicate the technological content of each component. The index also does not take into consideration that many parts and components can enter into the production of other products and hence do not appear in the list of exports.
36. Such claims, though they may be supported by various kinds of evidence, do not touch upon the fundamental issues (see Chang 2006 for a critical assessment).
37. See Fine (1999) for a general review on the demise of the developmental state.
38. Many scholars have argued that the heavy and chemical industry (HCI) promotion policy was found to be a failure with regard to the electronics industry as a whole and to semiconductors in particular (Choi 1995, p.75). According to Soh (1997, p.228), the electronics industry was originally intended to account for 12.9 per cent of overall HCI funding, the equivalent of $1.19 billion. Instead, by 1979, the amount had reached only $421 million, representing about 4.9 per cent. The share of the electronics industry in total HCI support stood at just 7 per cent in 1976 and 6 per cent in 1977. Kim (1997a, p.152) explains that whole businesses preferred to concentrate on consumer electronics (and later on semiconductors), whilst the government's focus was on defence.
39. In South Korea, KIET (then ETRI, the Electronics and Telecommunications Research Institute) contributed significantly in the technological development process for semiconductors until the early 1980s. In addition to its direct role in R&D projects, KIET has played other important roles, including providing training for engineers and organising coordinated research activities (Lee 2005). However, the role of ETRI in developing the DRAM industry had almost ceased after the late 1980s. Later in the 1990s, ETRI promoted the adoption of CDMA network system technology and, accordingly, participated actively in the development of the telecommunication and networks business.
40. In response to various analyses suggesting the government's involvement in industrial practices as the prime cause of the 1997 crisis, Chang (2006, p.188) is famous for arguing that '[i]t was actually the demise of industrial policy, rather than its continuation, which was mainly responsible for the 1997 crisis in Korea'.
41. One researcher from KIST explains that, as government research institutes receive much of their funding from the private sector, they become secondary to corporate research and merely following their lead (interview by Cyhn 2002, p.131).
42. For instance, while the South Korean government was gradually withdrawing from its active engagement in industrial development, it suddenly stepped in,

adopted the new CDMA technology, and took a leading role in promoting it. This would not have been possible if the United States and its native company Qualcomm had not pushed for multiple telecommunications standards. CDMA would give the United States a means of escape from the European-based global system for mobiles (GSM).

43. On 23 August 1999, Compaq announced it was to discontinue participation in the development of Windows NT and moved to replace it with Alpha systems of its own. A week later, Microsoft announced in return that there would be no release of Windows 2000 for Alpha (Microprocessor Forum 1999, at http://www.electronicsweekly.com).

44. Ironically, the phasing out of Alpha was not necessarily due to its inferior technology. The two fastest computers in 2002 in the United States (made by Hewlett-Packard) both used Alpha processors (ASCI Q-AlphaServer SC45, 1.25) (Top500 Supercomputer Sites, 2002, http://www.top500.org).

45. Compaq, in phasing out Alpha, was giving way to the IA-64 architecture that was co-developed by Intel and Hewlett-Packard. The new chips came along under the name Itanium (Microprocessor Forum 1999, in electronicsweekly.com).

6
Globalisation and the Decline of the Developmental State

Iain Pirie

6.1 INTRODUCTION

Social scientists eager to critique the thesis that globalisation is creating pressures towards convergence upon a neoliberal model of economic governance have over the last two decades rushed to emphasise the resilience of national models of capitalism (see Boyer and Drache 1996; Palan, Abbott and Deans 1996; Vogel 1996; Weiss 1998, 2003a; Miller 2005). Indeed, with the possible exception of economics, the dominant understanding of the impact of globalisation across the social sciences has stressed the limits of any convergence upon a universal neoliberal model. The alleged heterodox challenge to dominant theories of convergence in fact represents the prevailing orthodoxy. As the title of this chapter suggests, we argue that the developmental state model is no longer viable in the contemporary global economy. The constraints that global structural change impose on national capitalist strategies are more serious than scholars who stress the continued importance of nationally embedded models frequently suggest. This is not necessarily to say that we are witnessing a clear convergence around an abstract neoliberal model. Movement away from 'developmental' policy regimes does not automatically lead to the construction of functioning neoliberal regimes. Any attempt to categorise states such as Korea or Taiwan as 'neoliberal' or 'developmental' ideal types is more likely to lead to opacity than to analytical clarity. What we are seeking to do in highlighting how the developmental state has been undermined by globalisation is not to advance any grand thesis of universal convergence, but simply to illustrate how policy space has effectively been narrowed.

The lack of clear convergence around a neoliberal model has provided a key source of evidence for the supporters of the developmental state thesis who argue that the model remains viable (see particularly Weiss 2003b; Thurbon and Weiss 2006). In this analysis the developmental state ceases to take the role of an analytical ideal type and becomes a residual category. If we read much of the work on the 'flexible' developmental state it is difficult to escape the conclusion that the developmental state becomes any state form that is neither entirely dysfunctional nor conforms perfectly to an abstract neoliberal model. Obviously, this is an unsustainable definition and effectively allows us to label as developmental any state towards whose policies we are sympathetic. Given that the United Kingdom and the United States both invest heavily in supporting private research and development (R&D) and have used public power to secure their respective positions within the global financial industry we might argue that these states are developmental. Indeed, Weiss's most recent work has sought to highlight the 'developmental' aspects of the contemporary US state (Weiss 2008). Within this chapter we argue that a meaningful definition of the developmental state as an alternative to neoliberalism must be based upon the practices of the 'classical' North-East Asian developmental states. At the heart of the definition lies the developmental state's commitment to achieving some degree of self-sufficiency in key industrial sectors through dirigiste means. When we abandon this definition there is an inevitable conceptual slippage whereby any evidence of policies that seek to leverage maximum benefits from foreign investments or support industrial innovation is taken as proof that the developmental state remains a relevant concept and model for emulation.

The central argument of this chapter is that structural changes in the global political economy have effectively rendered the developmental state obsolete. More precisely, we would argue that increasing barriers to entry in key industries related to the increasing dominance of multinational corporations and the costs of technology have rendered quixotic any aspiration, on the part of developing states, to develop an autonomous industrial base. This is not to say that controls on capital or strategic industrial policies are necessarily destabilising and counterproductive, simply that the form these policies must now take is radically different from that taken within the classical developmental state model.

In order to advance the arguments set out above, this chapter is divided into three main sections. In the first section we review the various definitions of the 'developmental state' offered within the literature and examine the thesis that the classical North-East developmental states (we focus on Korea for reasons of brevity) retain a distinctive mode of governance that remains viable under conditions of globalisation. Against this context, the second section focuses on the structural changes in the global economy that have rendered the capitalist developmental state obsolete. The final section of the chapter suggests the outline of a progressive alternative to the developmental state model.

6.2 THE DEVELOPMENTAL STATE: FROM AN IMPOSSIBLY ILLUSIVE TO A WORKABLE CONCEPT

The existing literature on the developmental state is vast and the task of understanding the key arguments it articulates is complicated by a lack of consistency in how the developmental state is defined.[1] As Fine (2009a) suggests, there exists a division between those scholars who are concerned with understanding the institutional relationships that underpin development (the political school) and scholars focused on the policies necessary to achieve development (the economic school). The division is not absolute. The political school touches upon policy questions and institutional arrangements that are not entirely neglected by the economic school. Nevertheless, it is remarkable how reluctant large sections of the political school are to discuss policy (Johnson 1982; Evans 1995; Weiss 1998; Waldner 1999; Kohli 2004). Equally, the economic school is frequently concerned with institutional design, in terms of recognising the need for 'pilot agencies' staffed with autonomous and competent bureaucrats, but it never engages in any detailed analysis of the social conditions supporting the creation of these institutions (Amsden 1989; Wade 1990; Chang 1994; Hsueh, Hsu and Perkins 2001).[2]

A serious problem with the political school's relative lack of concern with policy is that it becomes rather easy to employ the concept of the developmental state in an overly flexible manner. Any state that demonstrates a capacity to intervene effectively in the economic process can, in practice, be considered developmental. Whether the author chooses to do so ultimately depends more upon personal preference than on any strict analytical criteria. In her analysis, Weiss (1998) is very careful to contrast the United Kingdom as a weak liberal state with more effective developmental states. She argues that rather than leading economic restructuring, the British state passively allowed the market to restructure as it saw fit. This may be true with regard to certain sectors. However, it is very difficult to see how British financial policy fits into such a model. Instead, when we look at the reform of systems of financial regulation since the 1980s, we see a state that has committed itself, relatively successfully, to securing London's position as a major global financial centre (Moran 1991). In so doing, the state has demonstrated not simply a clear vision, but a willingness to act against the interest of certain established domestic financial firms which have been undermined by exposure to global competition. While Weiss acknowledges the influence of finance on British policy, she effectively understands this as an anti-industrial policy that seeks to maintain the illusion of global great power status at the expense of the national economy. There are certain rather obvious problems related to Britain's economic dependency on its role as a nodal point in the global financial system, most notably the inherent volatility of the industry. Nevertheless, Weiss's analysis needs to acknowledge that the financial sector is a large source of employment in the United Kingdom and that Britain, or more particularly south-east England, has derived real material benefits from its position as a financial centre. There is no obvious reason why we should not regard the British state's promotion of the City of London as a form of 'industrial policy', as an attempt actively to manage the restructuring of a critical sector of the economy.

Equally, if we turn our attention to the United States we may ask ourselves why a state divorcing itself from questions of industrial competitiveness has for a sustained period of time funded over a quarter of total R&D expenditure and has directly funded between 10 and 15 per cent of total corporate R&D (United States National Science Foundation 2010a, pp.5–6). Even allowing for the impact of the inflated military sector, this remains relatively high by international standards and demonstrates a commitment to supporting US firms in maintaining competitiveness in key high-technology sectors. Indeed, in her most recent work, Weiss (2008) acknowledges that the US state has certain key 'developmental aspects'. This is logical given Weiss's own framework for analysing the developmental state, but reinforces the argument that her definition is so broad as to be practically useless – all major national political economies may effectively be defined as developmental. We need a stronger definition of the developmental state, in terms of policy, if the concept is to be analytically useful.

Given the lack of any set of policies against which to judge the claims of any particular state to be developmental, it becomes relatively simple for the political school to argue that, despite the 1997 economic crisis, the East Asian developmental states retain their essential character (see Vogel 1996; Weiss 2003a). Provided that we accept the basic premise that a set of 'developmental' relationships lies at the heart of the state, we may interpret the pursuit of policies little different from those that we find in actually existing neoliberal states as 'developmental'. What matters is the unquantifiable essence of the state. Weiss, for example, argues that Korea remains a developmental state because of its support for small high-tech firms and the state's management of FDI. The problem with Weiss's arguments regarding the promotion of high-tech firms lies in her failure to explain adequately how these forms of support differ fundamentally from the forms of support provided by other states which she does not regard as developmental (Weiss 2003b; Thurbon and Weiss 2006). A feature of the majority of states in the core capitalist area is that industrial policy is increasingly defined as innovation policy (Wren 2001; Beath 2002). Weiss's argument concerning the continuation of a distinctive set of policies in Korea would have been greatly strengthened if she had focused on the existence of a wider array of subsidies rather than on directed support for selected high-tech start-ups. If we analyse the use of credit guarantees for small firms these subsidies do exist, but serve more of a social than a strategic economic purpose in sustaining non-viable firms (OECD 2008).

The evidence that Weiss provides to support her arguments concerning the management of FDI is equally unconvincing. She argues that the Korean state consistently favoured FDI in technologically intensive sectors, used FDI to promote the restructuring of the domestic economy and sought to control foreign banks (Weiss 2003b; Thurbon and Weiss 2006). In truth, however, all major states clearly favour some forms of foreign investment over others. When states subsidise the construction of science parks and use financial incentives to promote linkages between public research universities and MNCs, they are not seeking to promote FDI in some generic sense. Rather, they are seeking to promote investments in high-tech high-value-added activities. Again, we return to the point that if this alone continues to make Korea developmental then what major state is not?

The arguments that Weiss makes regarding the control of the banking system also lack any real creditability. Weiss discusses the implementation of measures to control the expansion of foreign banks, but, in 2007, foreign financial institutions held 72.2 per cent of equity within nationwide banks in Korea (Moon 2009). If the state did intend to limit foreign influence within the system, it clearly failed. Equally, the existence of informal pressures, which are difficult to prove or quantify, on these institutions to appoint Koreans to senior positions can hardly be seen as a credible attempt to re-establish some form of strategic national control over the system.

A stronger argument to support Weiss's position could perhaps be made by focusing on the telecommunications sector. The state has used its control over technical standards in this sector to create a captive market for highly successful domestic manufacturers. Furthermore, restrictions on foreign investments remain in place, no fully independent regulator exists, and facilities-based providers must pay a tax of between 0.5 and 0.75 per cent of total sales revenue to support R&D (Pirie 2008, p.121). But evidence from one sector, or even from a limited range of sectors, cannot be used to support the continued existence of a developmental state. A balanced comprehensive analysis of the contemporary Korean political economy reveals that Korea does not comfortably fit the ideal type of either a neoliberal or a developmental state.

Kalinowski takes Weiss's arguments that equate any form of effective state with the 'developmental' state to a (possibly illogical) conclusion by arguing that Korea remains a form of remodelled developmental state partly because of an increase in the overall size of the state since 1997. General public spending (this includes local government expenditure) rose from 28.8 per cent of GDP in 1996 to 35.6 per cent in 2006 (Kalinowski 2008, p.458). Furthermore, massive government guarantees played a pivotal role in restoring some form of stability to the financial system in the wake of the 1997 crisis. Given that almost all western European states spend in excess of 35.6 per cent of GDP and have intervened to support the financial sector during the current financial crisis these states must all presumably be regarded as 'developmental'.

A focus on policy does not guarantee descriptive clarity and prevent unsustainable stretching of the concept of the developmental state. Amsden and Chu (2003), for example, argue that Taiwan remains a developmental state because of the role the state plays in funding R&D. This argument fails to engage with, or even recognise, that the government's share of R&D expenditure is less in Taiwan than in the European Union and approximately the same as in the United States (United States National Science Foundation 2007). Nevertheless, a policy-based definition at least offers the possibility of clarity. Furthermore, if the concept of the developmental state is to possess a degree of continuity over time and descriptive value than we must define it in relation to the practices of those states, Korea and Taiwan, that are commonly understood as exemplars of the developmental state model. If we are to make meaningful judgements about the continued viability of developmental state strategies in the contemporary world economy we must highlight the key policies and concrete objectives that have historically defined this model. In the absence of a definition rooted in historical practice we move towards a position that sees any form of effective state intervention as evidence of the existence of a developmental state.

We are fortunate in that two members of the economic school, Alice Amsden (1989) and Robert Wade (1990), produced magisterial accounts of policy in Korea and Taiwan respectively from the 1960s through to the 1980s. Using these texts we can define a core set of the policies that lay at the heart of the developmental state project. In both these cases we witnessed the consistent use of protectionism, restrictions of foreign capital, and state controlled financial systems to promote the development of indigenous capacity in key global industries. As Wade is careful to highlight, there were highly significant differences between the policies that Taiwan and Korea pursued. Most notably, foreign direct investment (FDI) played a far more substantive role in the Taiwanese development project than in the Korean (or for that matter the Japanese). The goals of Taiwanese state managers were fundamentally different from their Korean and Japanese counterparts. In the latter cases, state elites sought to promote the development of internationally competitive nationally owned firms in a full range of major global industries. In both these cases the achievement of a high degree of industrial self-sufficiency can be considered to have been an important objective. Leaving aside any other political or economic considerations, Taiwan's relatively small population alone made this objective unrealistic. Instead, the Taiwanese state adopted more flexible and sectorally sensitive policies towards FDI than either Korea or Japan. Efforts to promote domestic capacity were combined with the selective promotion of FDI. In a number of sectors, the state accepted a dominant role for foreign firms, but sought actively to manage their participation in the economy. There was a conscious strategy to ensure that foreign firms built strong linkages with domestic suppliers and exported an agreed proportion of their total output. Equally, from the 1970s onwards there was a clear policy of not seeking simply to attract FDI, but rather to attract particular forms of it that improved Taiwan's position in global commodity chains, such as investments in technologically intensive economic activities (Wade 1990).

The key consideration that structured the sectoral-level policy towards FDI was an assessment of the opportunities to develop domestic capacity in particular sectors. While Taiwan did not seek to construct nationally owned firms in a full range of major global industries it sought to construct capacity in key selected strategic industries. Within these industries high export requirements and other restrictions were frequently used to protect domestic firms from multinational competition. One of the central insights that Wade (1990, p.364) draws from the Taiwanese experience is that multinational firms must be prevented from dominating the domestic market, so that 'government efforts to promote restructuring do not have to go through multinational firms, whose objectives will not wholly coincide with the development of national capacity'. At the same time as firms in selected sectors were afforded a degree of protection from foreign competition, the state intervened through its control of the financial system and through a large nationalised sector to promote the growth of indigenous industrial capacity. The banking system was state owned, and private investors in priority areas enjoyed enhanced access to cheap loans, provided they met performance targets. Equally significantly, between 1951 and 1980 public firms accounted for well in excess of 30 per cent of gross capital formation (p.177). These firms developed in what economic planners regarded as key capital-intensive industries.

Policy in Taiwan towards foreign firms was sensitive to the material conditions that existed in particular sectors. However, the diversity of policies the state applied should not disguise the coherence of the state's objectives. Taiwan was committed to promoting the development of indigenous firms and ensuring that such firms remained at the core of the economy. Furthermore, the relationship between foreign and domestic capital within particular sectors has shifted over time. While new industries tended to be dominated by foreign capital in their initial stages of development, the state promoted progressive indigenisation of these industries (Amsden and Chu 2003).

In addition to different attitudes towards FDI a key difference between the Korean and Taiwanese political economies can also be found in the relative prevalence of own brand manufacturing (OBM), own design manufacturing (ODM) and original equipment manufacturing (OEM). Whereas in Korea OEM/ODM tended to be understood as learning processes from which firms should seek to graduate, a large OEM/ODM sector remains a feature of the contemporary Taiwanese economy (ibid.). In certain major sectors (semiconductors) Taiwanese firms act as major independent producers. In other industries (laptop computers), however, firms act as manufacturers for major global flagship firms. According to Hobson (2003, p.300) leading Taiwanese firms:

> could be most accurately described as 'hybrid' firms, containing features of leadership in some product areas (e.g. advanced R&D), 'followership' in other areas (i.e. having R&D capability but following others quickly into markets) and basic latecomer activities in still other areas.

The relationship between Taiwanese OEM/ODM firms and their customers is complex. Large suppliers will themselves engage in research and development activities and will frequently provide customers with component design and product engineering services. Amsden and Chu (2003) suggest that approximately 15 per cent of the total workforce in major Taiwanese computer suppliers is involved in design engineering. In extreme cases (ODM), suppliers may actually be asked to take the lead in designing products. In the apparel and bicycle industries OEM/ODM proved to be a precursor to OBM. However, there is no real evidence that any shift towards OBM is taking place with respect to finished computer products – although a shift is taking place in the motherboard industry. Importantly, economic and financial liberalisation in the 1980s and particularly the 1990s has limited the capacity of the state to enforce a shift effectively.

The prevalence of OEM/ODM arrangements in the notebook industry might be seen as demonstrating the limits of the Taiwanese developmental state project. While Taiwan has developed considerable indigenous industrial capacity, its achievements in this area have been more limited than those of Korea. This does not, however, necessarily undermine the prospects for future growth. Major OEM/ODM firms have successfully maintained competitiveness by shifting most labour-intensive aspects of manufacturing to mainland China while maintaining high-value activities in Taiwan (ibid.).

Taiwan differed from Korea not simply in terms of its greater openness to foreign capital. Wade has suggested, and we see no reason to question him, that controls on private capital were far less pervasive in Taiwan than in Korea. The differences in the regulation of the private sector reflects the fact that in Korea large private firms were the central mechanism through which the state sought to promote the development of key industrial sectors, whereas within the Taiwanese political economy state-owned firms provided an alternative mechanism.

The key distinctive feature of the developmental states lay in their systematic commitment to developing relatively autonomous exporting capacity in key global industries through dirigiste means. In the Taiwanese case, this meant the development of capacity in selected industries. The most important high-tech domestic manufacturing firms are concentrated in the semiconductor and computer hardware industries, not across the full range of modern industries. Furthermore, a greater proportion of Taiwanese firms continue to display a degree of technological dependence on leading global MNCs. Nevertheless, the Taiwanese effort was still significant. This is what renders the developmental state project distinct from contemporary neoliberally oriented projects. In the latter we may well see a host of interventions to secure the competitiveness of the space, to assist local firms in technological upgrading, or to try to maximise the benefits that can be derived from FDI. However, policy will not be centred upon systematic attempts to develop independent exporting capacity, through measures that go far beyond support for R&D, in a significant range of major global industries. Only when we see such an objective being prioritised does the use of the concept of the 'developmental state' yield analytical value.

The definition of the developmental state advanced above forces us to focus our attention on how structural changes in the global political economy have affected the ability of underdeveloped states to construct independent industrial capacity in key industries. If we conclude that the impact of such changes has been minimal, then the experiences of the North-East Asian developmental states remain, at least theoretically, replicable. On the other hand, if the impact of these changes has been more pronounced, then the developmental state must be regarded as little more than a historical relic. It is to the evolution of the structural constraints on the capacity of underdeveloped states to develop relatively autonomous industrial capacity through dirigiste means that we now turn.

6.3 STATE-LED DEVELOPMENT AND CONTEMPORARY CAPITALISM

When assessing the prospects for contemporary underdeveloped states to construct internationally competitive firms in key global industries, we need to focus upon both the structures of these industries and the key institutions of global economic governance. In many respects this division is a false one. Global governance structures have clearly developed in relation to changing material conditions in key industries, and a dynamic relationship exists between political and economic structures. A central argument that drives the work of the most important advocates of state-led capitalist development is that the creation of the WTO and related agreements has led to a closure of policy space (Chang 2002, 2007; Wade 2003). Wade (2003) argues persuasively that WTO agreements limit the capacity of states to access technologies and regulate market access in order to implement a coherent strategic development policy. The point is not simply that the (selectively) highly restrictive policies that the East Asian developmental states pursued cease to be viable. Rather, it is that policies that seek to impose performance requirements (in terms of technology transfer or exporting) also become problematic. The contemporary key argument is less about whether these policies are viable than about the reform of the systems of global governance necessary to make them so. This is a reasonable position. However, it presents the question of how we ought to understand the development of supra-national systems of governance. Scholars such as Chang (2002, 2007) and Wade (2003) essentially advance a neocolonial understanding of global governance structures. Developed states use their control over international economic institutions to promote a self-interested agenda based upon market access that is detrimental to the developing world. We do not dispute that there is a great deal of truth in this explanation but, nevertheless, feel that it lacks analytical depth.

While there is little agreement among radical scholars on the nature of contemporary imperialism (or even on whether the concept of imperialism retains analytical value) there exists a broad consensus that the way in which international relations are organised reflects changing material realities in core capitalist states.[3] Critical scholars of imperialism have never understood imperialist domination as simply reflecting political choices. Phases and crises of imperialism must instead be related to the development of the tendencies of capitalism itself. While there exists a number of highly divergent arguments concerning what the defining characteristics of contemporary 'imperialism' are, it is widely agreed that important changes in the organisation of the global system have taken place since the 1970s and that these changes have been shaped by profitability pressures in the core capitalist area (Harvey 2003; Wood 2003; Petras and Veltmeyer 2003; Panitch and Leys 2004). This consensus on the role that changing conditions of accumulation have played in reshaping imperialism is striking given the lack of agreement on other important issues.

The issue of whether the creation of the WTO framework was simply a political choice or reflected deeper changes in the structure of capitalism is not simply an academic one. If we accept the former understanding of contemporary global governance systems, the solution to the inadequacies of the system is relatively simple. Concerned global citizens must, in alliance with developing states, force core capitalist elites to be more reasonable and to construct a more equitable system. However, if we accept the idea that systems of supra-national governance are a reflection of deeper structural logics, then a challenge to these systems must be linked to a far more developed critique of the entire basis of accumulation in the contemporary global economy.

The primary problem, however, with the developmental statists' analysis of the continued viability of dirigiste development strategies relates to their understanding of the role that MNCs play in the global economy and the barriers to entry that exist in key global industries. In relatively technologically mature industrial sectors (e.g. steel) there may be considerable potential for certain third world states to develop internationally competitive domestically-owned firms. However, the promotion of indigenous firms is simply not viable in key, technologically dynamic, rapidly growing sectors. Two related points can be made in this regard. First, we have moved from a world clearly dominated by nationally-owned firms to a far more complex situation. In the 1980s global FDI stock grew at four times the speed of global GDP. This expansion was modest, however, when compared to the increase in the global stock of FDI from $1,942 to $15,696 billion that took place between 1990 and 2007 (UNCTAD 2009, p.217). In 2007 the world's 100 largest firms held 57 per cent of their total assets outside of their home states, (ibid: 19). Equally significantly, 40 per cent of total world trade is internal trade within the affiliates of MNCs (Kegley and Raymond 2009, p.298).

While these statistics are striking they ignore the significance of non-equity linkages. An accurate assessment of the power of MNCs in the contemporary global economy would have to take into account their effective control of nominally independent subcontractors. Admittedly it is difficult to define control; but in situations where there are massive power asymmetries between a host of relatively small firms providing standardised products who are dependent on one major consumer, the concept of clear boundaries between firms makes little sense. If we define the boundaries of a firm in terms of effective control rather than ownership we may conclude that the majority of world trade is in fact intra-firm trade.

The second closely related issue with the continued viability of policies that seek to develop globally competitive indigenous firms lies with how barriers to entry have developed in key global industries. One of the key justifications for dirigiste industrial policies in the global periphery has been the difficulties faced by firms from relatively underdeveloped states in mobilising the levels of capital necessary to compete in key global markets. This argument remains valid; but the levels of capital now necessary to compete in key industries has grown to such a point that it is unrealistic to expect the vast majority of states outside the core capitalist world to act as viable sources of capital. The role of technology in the production process has changed significantly over the last five decades. Non-federal R&D spending in the United States has grown from 0.6 per cent of GDP in 1952 to 2.06 per cent in 2008. Levels of non-federal R&D spending as a proportion of GDP have doubled since the 1970s (United States National Science Foundation 2010a; 45–6). These statistics are made all the more remarkable by the growing weight of the service sector, which engages in limited R&D, within the core capitalist area. In 2007 Korea itself spent the highest proportion of GDP on R&D (3.6 per cent) of any major economy and Taiwan's (2.6 per cent) was higher than that of the United States (United States National Science Foundation 2010a: 48).

We are witnessing a massive consolidation in important industries as fewer firms are able to support independent R&D efforts. Technological barriers to entry are particularly high in those sectors that the North-East Asian developmental states successfully prioritised during their drive to industrial maturity. This is significant because these sectors (car manufacturing, chemicals and electronics) were not simply the most important manufacturing industries at the time, but remain so today. According to WTO figures, chemicals, automobiles, and office and telecommunications equipment accounted for 28.6 per cent of world merchandise trade in 2008, whereas total trade in all other manufactured goods accounted for 37.9 per cent of world merchandise trade (WTO 2009, p.41).

Obviously, some of the categories that the WTO employs are very broad and these three sectors will include relatively low-tech firms.

Clearly not all forms of chemical or electronic device manufacture require large-scale investments in R&D. However, what is clear is that involvement in potentially higher-value-added products, or more precisely higher-value-added elements of the production process, do require these investments. So the production of basic calculators may not require great expertise, but sustaining competitiveness in the semiconductor industry clearly does. The success of the North-East Asian developmental states in substantially closing income gaps with established capitalist economies lay in their capacity to move effectively into these higher-value-added activities. In order to assess the potential for such a strategy to be replicated it is necessary to examine the barriers to achieving competitiveness in the higher-value-added activities in the car, electronics and chemicals industries.

Ten independent producers effectively dominate the global car industry. The consistent trend since the late 1980s in the car industry has been towards consolidation as formerly independent firms merge (Sturgeon, van Biesebroeck and Gereffi 2008). It is plausible that we shall see a further reduction in the number of lead firms within the industry should the current global downturn prove more severe than is currently expected. One major factor driving long-term processes of consolidation relates to the escalating costs of developing new technological platforms. The lead firms that remain have themselves been forced to scale down radically the number of basic technological platforms they produce. Volkswagen have reduced the number of basic platforms supporting their Audi, Seat, Skoda and VW models from 16 to four, the primary differences between these models being in their surface features (Dicken 2003, p.285). The costs associated with developing a small number of competitive platforms is illustrated by the fact that VW invested over £5.7 billion in research and development in the 2007/8 financial year (Department for Business Innovation and Skills 2008). Realistically, the production of a range of cars that are competitive in major international markets is likely to require sustained investment running into the tens of billions. It is difficult to see how the experiences of Korea and Japan in car manufacturing can be effectively replicated. The structural conditions within the industry have created far stronger barriers to new entrants.

A sceptic might suggest that our analysis of the car industry is negated by the fact that China is currently the world's leading car producer. However, even scholars who are optimistic concerning the prospects for the Chinese economy admit that Chinese cars are vastly inferior and not technologically comparable to those produced by the major transnational global manufacturers. In 2009 over 97 per cent of Chinese cars were sold on the protected domestic market. Furthermore, the major export markets for Chinese firms were almost exclusively outside the OECD area and the models exported were cheap inferior substitute products. Given the very low margins in this sub-market, the significance of China's exporting cars rather than traditional low-cost products is primarily symbolic. Equally significantly, the leading five car manufactures within China are joint ventures producing foreign-designed cars. Of course the North-East Asian developmental states employed joint ventures during the early growth of their own car industries. However, WTO commitments make it much harder for the Chinese government effectively to manage these relationships in order to ensure technology transfers and to establish the basis for later autonomous production. The contemporary Chinese car industry may bear certain similarities to the Korean industry in the early 1980s. However, there are reasons, related to increased barriers to entry, to believe that the industry is unlikely to follow the same course.

Despite the volume of their production the question remains whether Chinese car firms can become internationally competitive. Even if they are able to do so the wider significance of this is clearly questionable given the unique size of the domestic market and the funding platform they enjoy. Very few other states are in a position to offer firms a lengthy 'learning' period in a protected market with guaranteed sales in excess of 10 million units a year. The experience of the one other developing state with a comparable market, India, is similar to China: India's exports to other, almost exclusively non-OECD, economies accounts for less than 3 per cent of the leading domestic firms' total passenger car sales (Tata Motors, 'Tata Motors Annual Report 2009', www.tatamotors.com)

Evidence from the electronics industry is no more encouraging for the advocates of the developmental state model. At the heart of the industry is the production of the critical basic component semiconductors that allows the entire digital world to function. The global semiconductor industry accounts for well in excess of $200 billion of sales a year.[4] From the 1970s both the Korean and Taiwanese states (following the lead of Japan) invested heavily in developing expertise in this strategically important industry. These efforts have proved successful; Korean and Taiwanese firms feature prominently amongst the leading producers in this sector. Again, however, the prevailing conditions in the contemporary industry are very different from those which existed when nascent Korean firms first entered the marketplace. Modern semiconductor foundries costs in excess of $3 billion. By contrast in the late 1960s a modern foundry cost approximately $2 million (Dicken 2003, p.364). In addition to the rising fixed capital costs, R&D requirements are formidable. Intel, the market leader, invested just under £4 billion in chip development in the 2007/8 financial year (Department for Business Innovation and Skills 2009). Samsung Electronics invested considerably more, but in this case it is difficult to delineate clearly between spending in chip- and non-chip-related investments.

In addition to the barriers to entry in the semiconductor market, the R&D costs associated with the wider high-value-added electronics market are formidable. If we focus on mobile communications, we see that in addition to the large-scale investments necessary to construct and maintain brand image, the market leader in mobile communications, Nokia, invests almost £5 billion a year in R&D. Other major firms in the sector, such as Ericsson, routinely invest almost £2 billion a year (Department for Business Innovation and Skills 2009). Looking at software development, we see the dominant firm, Microsoft, investing over £6 billion a year in R&D. Obviously there are areas within the broader electronics industry in which technological barriers to entry are less formidable. However, a strategy focused upon these products would have very different implications from the one historically pursued by the North-East Asian developmental state of seeking to develop long-term competitiveness in major high-value-added products.

While they are not as dramatic, it is also important to recognise the changes that have taken place in the chemicals industry (an important component of the Korean industrialisation strategy). While barriers to entry may not be prohibitive with regard to basic chemical products, movement into the major global growth areas of specialist and 'life sciences' chemicals (including genetically engineered products) has become increasingly difficult since the early 1980s. On average, the major global chemical firms have invested over 40 per cent of their total operating profits in R&D. While industry giants have very high budgets, it is possible for smaller highly specialised firms to occupy market niches profitably. However, for this strategy based upon the supply of highly specialist products to function, such firms need to be embedded within, rather than protected from, the major global networks that are dominated by MNCs. It is also worth pointing out that major chemical firms are also far more internationalised (in terms of the distribution of assets) than their counterparts in the car or the electronics sectors (UNCTAD 2002, p.98).

The focus on particular sectors is necessary if we are to present concrete evidence regarding barriers to upgrading. However, it unavoidably presents us with an incomplete analysis of the constraints and opportunities that exist for contemporary underdeveloped states. Sectoral analysis can be useful if complemented by a more overarching analysis of the 'success' of capitalist development projects in the contemporary underdeveloped world in promoting the growth of relatively autonomous indigenous industrial capacity in major global industries. Even a cursory glance at the most economically dynamic underdeveloped states reveals how limited the development of autonomous economic capacity has in fact been. If we turn to China, what is striking is how both the neoliberal *Economist* magazine and radical political economists have highlighted the fundamental differences in the relationship between domestic and foreign firms in Korea and Taiwan in the 1960 and 1970s on the one hand and contemporary China on the other (Halevi and Kriesler 2007). While China has attempted to promote the development of globally competitive domestic firms in key areas, it also allowed the entry of MNCs at a far earlier stage in development. When we analyse the development of high-tech production in China, we see that foreign firms, which retain control over key technologies, are increasing their share of high-tech production in both domestic and export markets. According to the Chinese government's own figures, in 2002 82.1 per cent of total high-tech exports were produced by foreign firms. By 2005 88 per cent of total technological exports were built by foreign firms (Hart-Landsberg 2010). Whereas in Korea and Taiwan there was a gradual move towards greater indigenous high-value-added activities, in China the opposite is occurring. The US National Science Foundation has highlighted how limited China's technological achievements have been. According to a 2010 report, 'China's share of patents remained in the 1 per cent range in all major technology areas. Indigenous inventive activity, a focus of government policy, appears elusive, at least as indicated by patents filed in a major Western market' (United States National Science Foundation 2010b: 14). The problem is not the lack of funds, but the lack of a sophisticated innovation infrastructure. Of course one could make the point that Taiwan and Korea too lacked such an infrastructure at a similar stage in their development. However, the world's leading systems, which China must seek to emulate, are immensely more elaborate than the systems that were in place during the early stages of Korean and Taiwanese industrialisation. In a sense, rising levels of R&D expenditure are indicative of the development of a more intractable set of structural constraints. Clearly there are issues regarding the coherence of industrial upgrading policy in China, given inter-regional competition. Questions relating to state agency should not be ignored. Nevertheless, we would suggest that the generalised failure of upgrading is a product of increasing barriers to upgrading in key sectors. These barriers make it impossible for an underdeveloped state to replicate the Korean experience and develop independent capacity across a range of major global industries. Taiwan's achievements in developing market-leading firms in the semiconductor industry are equally unlikely to be emulated. The difficulties that contemporary underdeveloped states face in promoting the development of indigenous firms capable of acting as first-tier suppliers to leading MNCs should not be underestimated. The development of large multinational OEM/ODM manufactures presents a barrier to the capacity of indigenous firms to upgrade in key industries. Major Taiwanese, North American and European OEM/ODM firms themselves are major MNCs in their own right. Major Taiwanese laptop manufacturers, such as Wistron and Quanta, organise their activities on a transnational basis, enjoy revenues of several billion pounds a year (approximately £8 billion in Wistron's case) and invest heavily in continuously upgrading design and integration technologies. In short, the idea that contemporary underdeveloped states can construct genuinely autonomous indigenous capacity in major global industries is simply quixotic, and the development of first-tier suppliers is likely to prove a considerable challenge.

What we have sought to do in this section is outline the contemporary limitations of the forms of industrial policy that the North-East Asian developmental states pursued. The window of opportunity that these states were able to take advantage of is largely closed. In doing so, we have not suggested a more appropriate role for industrial policy or outlined any form of alternative development model. It is to this task that we turn in the next section of the chapter.

6.4 AFTER THE DEVELOPMENTAL STATE

The argument that global changes have undermined the potential for underdeveloped states to repeat the success of the North-East Asian developmental states does not automatically support the conclusion that industrial policy is irrelevant. Many of the advocates of state-led capitalist development, particularly those from the economic school, suggest, at least implicitly, that policies derived from the North-East Asian developmental states are generally applicable to other national social formations with very different economic, social and cultural histories (Amsden 1989; Wade 1990; Chang 2006). However, the desirability of any policy option can only be assessed in particular national circumstances, relative to the alternatives. For example, Fine (2009d) has argued that neoliberalism in South Africa is leading to systematic capital flight and pathetic rates of investment. Clearly in this situation a recognition of the limitations of industrial policy in generating capacity in key global industries does not automatically lead to the conclusion that some form of activist industrial policy has no role to play in raising investment levels.

Industrial policy may be more successful if applied to developing domestic capacity in technologically mature industries (steel, shipbuilding, etc.). Furthermore, there is an important role for the state to play in managing FDI so as to maximise the social and economic benefits of such investment. Within the process of managing FDI it is reasonable for states to support local firms embedded within MNC-dominated production networks in enhancing their production and innovation capacities. A problem that cannot be ignored with policies focused on the development of greater capacity in the more technologically mature industries when employed by large or multiple underdeveloped states is that they will ultimately create strong deflationary pressures in these sectors. Where the state clearly retains a critical universal role is in the provision of infrastructure and the promotion of linkages between MNCs and the domestic economy. While industrial policy may remain relevant, one conclusion that is difficult to avoid is that the inability of third world states to develop autonomous capacity in more dynamic global industries necessitates reasonably open policies towards MNCs.

A successful industrial policy may seek to emulate certain key policies that the Taiwanese developmental state pursued, in terms of seeking to promote the development of indigenous firms as first-tier suppliers to multinationals. However, the significance of these policies is transformed when they are isolated from the parallel policy of supporting the creation of independent, nationally owned technological firms in other sectors. When a focus on advancing the position of domestic firms within foreign MNC-led networks becomes the sole focus of policy, this can, we would suggest, be said to represent a pragmatic form of neoliberalism rather than a challenge to the neoliberal project.

A common feature of the bulk of the heterodox capitalist analysis of the developmental process has been an intense focus on industrial policy (Amsden 1989; Wade 1990; Chang 1994, 2006). States such as Korea have often been presented as models worthy of emulation, or at least examples to draw from selectively, because of the success of these policies. Questions relating to political freedoms or social justice have effectively been relegated to second place. We would argue that this order of prioritisation needs to be reversed. Industrial policy, so far as it can facilitate the development of productive capacity and the avoidance of macroeconomic crisis, may be useful in supporting broader processes of social development. However, it must be understood as a support for a set of core objectives related to the decommodification of key aspects of social life, not as the central focus for progressive reform. Furthermore, in the long term, progressive reform that seeks to decommodify key aspects of social life is likely to undermine the conditions for growth based upon a capitalist model.

The starting point for any progressive project to reform capitalism should not be any particular model of industrial policy, but a focus on redrawing the lines of commodification. There are key necessities of life whose commodification is not fully accepted by large sections of the global population. For example, in the United Kingdom the majority of the population clearly does not believe that health care ought to be regarded as a commodity to be exchanged on the marketplace. This initial recognition invites a wider challenge to systems of drug production and the global regulation of access to medicines. Equally, the legitimacy of fully commodifying food systems, the provision of utilities, and access to housing is clearly contested on a global scale. Progressive national-level projects should seek to promote non-market-based democratic systems of provision within these areas.

There are objective limits to what reform can achieve when pursued within individual states within a global capitalist economy, but these limits can only be discovered in the process of pursuing reform. The important point is that the impact of changes in global economic structures on the scope for progressive social policy is more ambiguous than their impact on the ambitious forms of industrial policy that leading advocates of the developmental state promote. The impact of expanding barriers to entry in key global industries on the capacity of the state to provide reasonable quality water as a social right is far less obvious than on the capacity of third world states to promote competitive domestically-owned car industries.

Linked to this reconceptualisation of key goods within different national contexts we need to pursue parallel reform at a global level. In particular we would stress the importance of redefining the institutions that address the problems of global provision of 'basic needs' goods. Responsibility for global management of these systems ought to rest with specialists in particular issue areas rather than the global financial and trade institutions. For example, responsibility for regulating trade in medicines and promoting the development of systems of health care in the third world ought to rest primarily with the World Health Organisation (WHO) rather than with the World Bank and the WTO. The point is not that this institution lacks its own flaws or that this change is in anyway revolutionary; clearly it is not. Rather, it is that we would expect institutions primarily staffed by non-economists to possess a set of primary concerns different from those of the neoliberal financial institutions and to be more open to alternative ways of conceiving issues. Indeed, the WHO has frequently employed Cuba as a model for primary health-care provision (World Health Organisation 2008). The management of this organisation seems to be primarily concerned with measurable health outcomes rather than with promoting the role of markets in delivery.

Reforms will be difficult to achieve because movements towards greater commodification since the 1970s have reflected not simply political choices but the structural logics of capitalism in crisis. However, even though reform is limited by the basic logics of capitalism, it is still important to pursue such reform. Even unsuccessful reform efforts have the potential to expose the inadequacies of the system and to provide a basis for more radical action. This global reform agenda is, we would suggest, more positive than the global governance agenda frequently advanced by advocates of the developmental state, based upon a fairly uncritical defence of state sovereignty. In its extreme form, as adopted by Chang (2002, 2007), the entire approach to the reform of global governance structures ultimately amounts to little more than a call to enhance the autonomy of third world state elites, allowing them to behave as they please. Given the manifest failings of many post-colonial states, this position is neither politically nor morally tenable.

The national and international reform agendas set out above, based upon selective decommodification, provides a firmer basis for building a more radical project, seeking to break from capitalism by progressively extending the scope of decommodification, than developmental statist projects that focus on building competitiveness. If non-market, democratically organised supply of essential goods succeeds, this may open up space to challenge market-based provision in other arenas and to construct a socialist global system within which market-based, international economic interactions are subordinate to altruistic cooperation. The reform agenda that we outline above, in sharp contrast to that advanced by the developmentalists, does not seek to create a better capitalism, but rather to construct the foundations for an alternative society.

6.5 CONCLUSION

This chapter has sought to advance three central arguments. The first of these is that any definition of the developmental state must focus as much on policy as on relationships. The problem with definitions of developmental states based primarily on the concept of a component bureaucracy with a set of functional relationships with, but autonomous from, private capital is that it is overly flexible. We can find evidence of these relationships in all functioning capitalist states. If the developmental state is to remain an analytically useful category we must seek to define it in terms of the central policies that Korea, Japan and Taiwan pursued during key stages of their industrialisation. The defining feature of these political economies was the centrality of the conscious use of state power to develop internationally-competitive firms in key global industries within their overall economic strategies. This leads us to our second key argument, namely, that structural changes in key global industries, relating to technological barriers to entry and the growing significance of MNCs, have rendered this strategy redundant. In seeking to construct an alternative to the dominant neoliberal development model we should not obsess on the issue of industrial policy, as the advocates of the developmental state have traditionally tended to. Rather than simply seek to promote international competitiveness in a more effective manner, our primary focus should be on promoting processes through which the key necessities of life (food, water, health care, housing, education, etc.) are redefined as social rights rather than commodities to be exchanged on the marketplace.

NOTES

1. This chapter is not concerned with radical class-based critiques of the developmental state (Hart-Landsberg 1993; D.-O. Chang 2009). Rather, we

confine ourselves to engaging with the dominant statist literature, whose primary objective is to argue for the potential efficiency of the activist, dirigiste state in achieving industrialisation.
2. Wade (1990) perhaps comes closest to providing an integrated analysis.
3. A key debate concerns how we understand the differences and continuities between earlier periods of direct imperialist control and the contemporary era, in which formal independence is the norm and the use of overt physical coercion is more spasmodic – and invariably counterproductive (Kiely 2007).
4. Figures ascertained from the Semiconductor Industry Association's website (http://www.sia-online.org/).

7
The IT Industry and Interventionist Policy in India

Jyoti Saraswati

7.1 BACKGROUND AND CONTEXT

Between 1960 and 1990 the economies of Japan, South Korea, Taiwan and Singapore grew more rapidly than those of the United States, Western Europe, the Communist Bloc and other developing countries outside of East Asia. While these countries were championed as exemplars of free-market capitalist dynamism during the Cold War, by the mid-1990s it had become widely accepted that state intervention, rather than neoliberal policies, had been integral to East Asia's spectacular economic development. It was foreseeable, therefore, that, following the collapse of the Soviet Union, literature in favour of industrial policy and the transformative potential of state intervention would overwhelmingly focus on East Asia. While the attraction to the East Asian experience for scholars critical of the anti-statist Washington Consensus was understandable, an unfortunate consequence of this geographical preoccupation has been that the practical and theoretical issues surrounding effective industrial policy over the past 15 years have been almost entirely influenced by the examples of these few countries, as discussed in Chapter 1.[1] Furthermore, the emphasis on East Asia has given rise to an underlying perception of a regional dichotomy between effective and ineffective industrial policy: effective industrial policy in East Asia; ineffective industrial policy everywhere else in the developing world. An inevitable outcome of this has been a woeful neglect of successful state intervention outside of East Asia (as well as of failed industrial policy in East Asia).

This chapter addresses the above deficiency by examining the Indian state's interventions in the IT industry. While widely portrayed as the product of neoliberal globalisation in the 1990s, the Indian IT industry is in reality the outcome of a wide range of highly interventionist policies dating back to the 1970s.

Moreover, as this chapter subsequently illustrates, each of these interventions played an integral role in the development of what is now the largest and most technically advanced software industry in Asia. The current prevalence of software vis-à-vis hardware in the Indian IT industry, the domination of local IT firms in the software industry, and their advanced capabilities vis-à-vis such firms in other developing countries can only be accounted for by incorporating into the explanation the cumulative impact of interventions in the 1970s, 1980s and 1990s. What is particularly striking is that these development-inducing state interventions did not conform to the developmental state paradigm (DSP), despite various attempts at identifying the presence of a developmental state (see Evans 1995; Pingle 1999). They were not solely comprised of intelligently designed, effectively implemented policies that induced developmental outcomes in the manner expected. For example, one intervention was poorly designed, failing to fully capitalise on the commercial opportunities available. Another intervention was justified on the grounds of stimulating competitiveness in the industry, but was implemented in a manner which privileged only a narrow set of interests. Moreover, its implementation directly undermined the capabilities in one sub-sector of the Indian IT industry while, inadvertently, opening up the possibility of explosive growth in another.

7.2 APPROACH AND STRUCTURE

In view of the complexity of the relationship between interventions and outcomes, the chapter adopts an identical analytical approach to industrial policy and structural change to that put forward by Lee in this book (Chapter 3), which connects the political economy of state interventions with the structural transformation of sectors and industries. The analytical starting point is neither the state nor its policies, but the identification of the underlying economic interests within the particular industry under examination. It is assumed that the primary imperative of such interests lie in sustaining capital accumulation. Given that industries are highly complex and almost certainly embroiled in the global economy, it is highly likely that (a) there are a variety of economic interests within any given industry; and (b) they are unlikely to have a uniform preference over what type of policy should be pursued. To understand the various pressures shaping industrial policy it is necessary to be familiar with the underlying interests attached to a specific industry.

For the Indian IT industry, the key private economic interests have been local hardware capital and local software capital. However, given the importance of computers in the wider economy, the vested interests with a stake in Indian IT policy include those of India's largest corporations and, increasingly, foreign capital.

As the opportunity, pattern and pace of such accumulation is heavily determined by and reflected in state policy, the focal point of analysis lies in examining how these interests are revealed in the shaping of state policy. Certain interests are better able to exert political influence than others, and the extent of their influence is dependent on a myriad of factors subject to change over time. The DSP, by seeking state autonomy, has tended to exclude such interests from its sphere of analysis, deeming them as absent in cases of development success. In the minority of DSP works that have incorporated these private economic interests into their analyses, they have been confined to the role of providers of industrial policy advice; that is, as consultants fine-tuning state policy rather than as vested interests exercising a significant degree of influence in the formulation of policy. In contrast, the approach taken in this chapter perceives the political relations and configurations of these economic interests as *integral* to the direction and form industrial policy takes. Such policy is deemed to be an outcome of the conflict, cooperation and, ultimately, compromise between the various economic and political interests with a stake in policy. This approach is particularly relevant to Indian state interventions, where the influence of classes and fractions of capital are widely acknowledged and claims of state autonomy are likely to be met with derision.

A further element of the analysis is the impact of industrial policy on industry outcomes. All too often the success or failure of a policy is attributed to exports or total revenues, or to production figures. However, this chapter deems such metrics not only as insufficient in assessing the effects of industrial policy, but as potentially misleading. For example, the growth in the Indian software industry can be at least partially attributed to the increase in the global software market, which the Indian state's interventions have played no part in creating. Thus a better assessment of the direct outcomes of industrial policy would be to examine what effect, if any, policy has had on the underlying economic relations of the industry. That is, to examine whether policy has engendered a structural transformation of the industry and a new pattern of capital accumulation. Rather than success or failure, judgement should be directed towards whether the new pattern is more productive or developmental than its predecessor, and who the primary beneficiaries of the changes have been. The key economic relations underpinning the Indian IT industry are those between local computer hardware and software capital, each fraction's relations with foreign capital, and the competitive structure of the hardware industry. Any structural transformation of the Indian IT industry needs to be understood within the context of changes across these economic relations. Given the linkages between relations, it is essential to appreciate that a state-induced change in one relation can and often does impact on the other inter-industry relations.

In short, the analytical approach adopted in this chapter conceives of industrial policy as a dynamic, four-stage cycle. The first stage is the presence or formation of economic interests within a system of accumulation. The second stage is the manifestation of these interests within the state apparatus, conceived of as a terrain of contestation between various economic and political interests. The design and implementation of industrial policy through conflict, cooperation and compromise in industrial policy represents the third stage. The fourth stage is the change in the economic relations of the industry and the emergence of a new system of accumulation. The new system of accumulation, once established, alters the accumulative imperatives of the economic interests and, relatedly, the power relations between them, leading to different demands and pressures on the state to facilitate new patterns of capital accumulation in accordance with the emerging economic interests. As a result, the industrial policy cycle continues.

The chapter is structured accordingly. One section is devoted to each of the three key policy phases in the Indian IT industry between 1970 and 2000. Moreover, each section first identifies the economic and political vested interests at play in the phase, then presents in detail the various interventions, and finally examines how the industry was restructured and what type of system of accumulation was engendered. Thus the next section (7.3) examines the first intervention, aimed at fostering an indigenous computer hardware industry, but with significant implications for local software capital's relations with foreign capital. Section 7.4 examines the subsequent intervention in the competitive structure of the hardware industry, initiating regulated competition via the 1978 Minicomputer Policy which, inadvertently, reshaped relations between local hardware and local software. Section 7.5 examines the state's interventions in restructuring the relationship between local software capital and foreign capital. The concluding section discusses the key lessons that can be drawn from the case of the Indian software industry regarding state intervention.

7.3 PHASE ONE: BUILDING AN INDIAN COMPUTER INDUSTRY

7.3.1 Vested Interests

Despite the grandiose rhetoric of India's first prime minister, Jawaharlal Nehru, regarding the Indian state's commitment to scientific and technological progress, it was only in the early 1960s that national capacity in electronics and in particular IT began to be mooted in the corridors of power (Grieco 1982, p.76). The initiator of this emergent discourse was the Sino-Indian conflict in 1962, in which the Chinese military commanded formidable technical superiority over their Indian adversaries, attributed to the Chinese army's access to more advanced electronic equipment and IT support systems (Pingle 1999, p.123). New Delhi's concerns over the lack of access to advanced electronics would be compounded after the 1965 Indo-Pakistan war, when the United States had issued an arms embargo on India. National security, in light of issues of technical backwardness and dependency in electronics, prompted the establishment of the Electronics Committee, which immediately conducted an investigation into electronics in India, published as the Bhabha Report (Agarwal 1985, p.283).

The Bhabha Report focused on three core issues: (1) the nation's requirements in electronic components and equipment; (2) existing and potential sources of supply for such components and equipment; and (3) policies which could rapidly establish national self-sufficiency in such components and equipment. To achieve self-sufficiency in computers, it was recommended that wholly-owned Indian firms should emerge to satisfy the bulk of the nation's computer requirements. Up until that point there was no genuine Indian computer industry: the country was dependent on importing expensive computers from the United States, Europe and the USSR (Grieco 1982). Thus the recommendation to develop an indigenous computer industry through Indian firms was strikingly bold. In 1970 Prime Minister Indira Gandhi established the Department of Electronics (DoE), a central government agency with the remit to formulate and implement IT policy. This establishment of an institutional foundation was a critical step in translating the Bhabha Report's recommendations into concrete policies in general, and in building an indigenous computer industry in particular.

However, to understand why Indira Gandhi felt suitably emboldened to pursue indigenisation requires an appreciation of the facilitative political economy in the early 1970s. Until the middle of the 1960s, India's largest conglomerates, commonly referred to as 'business houses', had exerted a powerful influence over the Indian state's macro-economic, industrial, and science and technology policies. Being the key users of computers in India, they opposed the granting of a near monopoly to, and tariff protection for, a national computer company (or companies), as this would adversely affect (at least in the short term) access to relatively low-cost computers from overseas. Moreover, being the major users of IBM computers in India and reliant on IBM for maintenance and services, they opposed any actions curbing the use of IBM computers or IBM operations in India. The breakthrough for those pushing for indigenisation came when the business houses were usurped from political influence in the late 1960s by the rise of a socially reactionary and economically conservative fraction of petty producers and traders referred to by Prem Shankhar Jha (1990) as an 'intermediate class'. It is one of the many ironies that litter the history of the Indian IT industry that a conservative, reactionary class, by usurping the business houses' political influence, should have indirectly paved the way for the state to develop a high-technology industry with socially modernising tendencies.

7.3.2 State Interventions

Within this wider political and economic context of technical dependency, security imperatives and the neutering of business-house influences, the first intervention by the Indian state in the IT industry was formulated and implemented. In 1972 the DoE convened the Minicomputer Panel to decide on an appropriate IT policy in light of the Bhabha Report's recommendations. The Panel's report, published the following year, was upbeat on the potential for breaking India's dependence on foreign computers and achieving self-sufficiency in computer production via wholly-owned Indian enterprises, alongside the dilution of the equity stake of foreign computer firms operating in India.[2]

Electronics Corporation of India Limited (ECIL), a state-owned enterprise producing telecommunications and instrumentation equipment, was selected by the DoE to be India's 'national champion' in computer production. In addition, foreign computer firms such as ICL and Burroughs agreed to equity dilution in order to maintain or establish a presence in the Indian computer market. However,

IBM refused to dilute. Its subsequent departure as a result of this decision meant that breaking India's computer dependency would, in the main, be spearheaded by ECIL rather than by joint ventures. This would have major implications for the inter-capital competition structure of the Indian hardware industry, the relationship between the local hardware and local software industries, and also that between local software capital and foreign capital.

In terms of intra-industry competition, ECIL was granted a near monopoly in local production of computers (alongside Burroughs and ICL) and a full monopoly at the higher end of the computer market. Although this decision has been criticised (Athreye 2005), it rested on a clear rationale. It was believed that the monopoly would provide ECIL with the time to master the technical side of computer production without having to concern itself with competition from foreign or local computer companies. Moreover, the monopoly over production, combined with high tariffs on imported computers, ensured that ECIL would enjoy preferable access to the Indian domestic market, a prerequisite in developing its productive capacities. And, finally, the monopoly ensured that scarce resources (skilled labour and foreign exchange) could be channelled into developing ECIL's computer production.

The prioritisation of ECIL also impacted on the relationship between the local hardware and software industries. While there was a nascent Indian software industry by the late 1960s, it consisted primarily of small management consultancies leasing programmers to business houses to develop specific software services on business houses' mainframe computers. By undertaking domestic computer production, ECIL afforded the opportunity for closer relations between the local software industry and the local computer hardware industry. For example, there was in theory the opportunity for local software firms to provide packages for ECIL computers. However, this was foreclosed by the DoE's decision to bundle software with hardware (Pingle 1999, p.134). The rationale behind this decision was a fear that leaving ECIL computers open to various software solutions would lead to a lack of standardisation and a variety of computer systems being used in India. This in turn might exacerbate foreign-exchange shortage (through importation of various software packages) as well as making maintenance of the country's installed computer hardware base more complex.

The issue of foreign exchange also prompted another state intervention, establishing a relationship between local software capital and foreign capital. Given that it would take time to develop a local production complex of peripherals and components, in the short term ECIL would have to rely on imports. In order to generate the foreign exchange needed for ECIL, the DoE decided to establish an export-oriented software industry. Thus, by 1974, the Software Export Scheme was being implemented. Essentially the scheme set out to harness the energies of software firms and guide them towards the export market. Firms signing up to the scheme were allowed to import computers at significantly lower duties and were provided with 100 per cent loans for their purchases. To direct the firms towards the international market, loans had to be repaid in the foreign exchange generated by exports. However, to further ensure that the firms' energies were directed towards exports, they were prohibited from providing services to the domestically installed hardware base.

7.3.3 Industrial Restructuring and the System of Accumulation

The system of capital accumulation produced by these interventions failed to deliver the developmental outcomes expected. The manner of the implementation of each of the policies was poor. Despite its monopoly, ECIL failed to produce computers at the rate and price expected. This was in part due to its delinking from foreign capital. While the Bhabha Report had argued for self-sufficiency based on selective delinking, the DoE had taken this to an extreme, undermining any form of technology transfers under misplaced optimism about what could be achieved via delinking. The Software Export Scheme also failed to generate the export revenues expected. This was in part due to the logistical problems of exporting software, which would require a process referred to as body-shopping. Software programmers from Indian software firms would have to travel to foreign clients' headquarters to write the majority of the software. This would entail travel, accommodation and living costs, cutting deeply into profit margins. The scheme had failed to appreciate such logistical problems. Indian software firms were locked into a low-value-added relationship with foreign capital, which gave them limited opportunity to reinvest profits into upgrading. This was compounded by the foreclosing of domestic software services provision, which might have served as a springboard to export success. After all, the domestic market provided an opportunity for firms to learn and build up technical and commercial capabilities, as well as capacity. Thus the objective of generating foreign exchange as quickly as possible actually impeded the development of the software industry over the longer term.[3]

Nevertheless it would be wrong to characterise these interventions as unmitigated failures. During this period, Indian software firms established relations with foreign capital, albeit fragile and dependent ones. More importantly, these linkages were established before most developing countries had even considered harnessing their technical workforce in the export of software. Furthermore, despite the obstacles encountered and the mistakes made in establishing a domestic computer hardware industry, by the mid-1970s a genuine indigenous hardware industry had been created. After initial teething problems, ECIL's rates of computer production began to increase rapidly, with twice as many computers produced in 1977 as in 1976 (Subramanian 1992, p.185). Moreover, the DoE secretary, Menon, had drawn up a draft policy for the production of minicomputers under regulated competition and, to support it, the development of an indigenous peripherals and components industry. Ten Indian companies engaged in manufacturing calculators had been granted licences to diversify into computer peripherals manufacture (Subramanian 1992, p.24). Given these developments, alongside the closing down of IBM's operations in India after its rejection of equity dilution, the system of accumulation in the Indian IT industry by 1977 appeared highly conducive to rapid growth. As the next section illustrates, a change in the configuration of political and economic power in India in the late 1970s would undermine this system.

7.4 PHASE TWO: ESTABLISHING A VEILED COMPUTER IMPORT SYSTEM

7.4.1 Vested Interests

The IT policies implemented in the early 1970s were reliant for their longevity on the continued political domination of the 'intermediate class'. Its political power kept business-house influence over state policy at bay. If the intermediate class's domination ended, the business houses could be expected to fill the breach and re-exert their traditionally heavy influence over the Indian state, re-establishing their own interests as government priorities. One of these priorities would no doubt be to ensure easy access to cheap and reliable computers. In 1977, this is exactly what happened.

The 1977 general election has been widely portrayed as a revolt by the electorate against the intermediate class and Indira Gandhi's dissolution of parliament and turn to authoritarianism for two years (commonly referred to as 'the Emergency').[4] However, while the Janata Party may have come to power on the votes of the masses, the raft of policy measures it enacted almost immediately afterwards provided a clear indication of where the locus of power lay. The internal liberalisation and deregulation of state controls carried out by the new government primarily favoured the business houses. IT policy, too, was not exempt from business-house influence.

7.4.2 State Interventions

The weeks following the election of the Janata Party saw fundamental changes made in the regulatory regime across a whole range of industries and sectors. A committee, chaired by the respected parliamentarian M.L. Sondhi, was charged with evaluating IT policy and making recommendations for the improvement of the local IT industry. It took as its basis a Minicomputer Policy drafted a few months prior to the general election by the DoE, which suggested a movement to selective licensing for the manufacture of minicomputers while preserving a monopoly for ECIL in mainframe and higher-end minicomputers. The draft policy also included the promotion of an indigenous components and peripherals industry and, therefore, an IT complex. The committee recommended the implementation of the draft policy and, in 1978, the Minicomputer Policy was officially introduced.

As noted, the stated focus of the policy was to establish regulated competition in the domestic manufacture of minicomputers via selective licensing. The monopoly granted to ECIL was in part blamed for its poorer-than-expected performance. Competition, it was argued, would promote efficiency, while selective licensing would ensure that scarce resources would not be spread too thinly. The ability of the state to revoke a licence if a company was not performing to the levels set would be a further big stick to ensure cheaper, better-quality computers. The rhetoric surrounding the new policy evoked the emulation of Taiwan, encouraging the state to guide or, as Wade (1990) would later refer to it, 'govern' the market. The policy would, it was also proclaimed, play an integral role in the computerisation of the nation.

However, while the statements were grandiose, the claims developmental, and the arguments for the policy shift compelling, the implementation was poor. Selective licensing was a necessity in order both to harness scarce human and capital resources and to ensure firms a market share through which they might achieve economies of scale. However, within the first two years more than

40 licences to manufacture computers were issued to companies, clearly breaching the entire point of selective licences as stated above. Economies of scale were impossible due to over-competition in the marketplace, hindering the potential for reinvestment. Moreover, the indigenous production of peripherals never materialised. There was no effort outside of the pages of the policy document to establish an indigenous components and peripherals industry. Peripherals and components would continue to be imported from abroad. The state's direct interventions were confined to the provision of numerous licences for the manufacture of minicomputers

7.4.3 Industrial Restructuring and the System of Accumulation

It would be easy to attribute such a ramshackle implementation of sound policy to buffoonish bureaucrats. Indeed, many such interventions in India and elsewhere have been attributed to the incompetence or naivety of policymakers. However, more often than not, what may appear superficially as incompetence of the highest order can, upon closer examination, be reinterpreted as a deliberate, premeditated decision to benefit certain specific interests – that is, as a failure by design rather than by accident. An examination of the new system of accumulation ushered in by the Minicomputer Policy strongly suggests that the intervention's shortcomings were deliberate and intentional.

Most compelling of all is the fact that, despite all of its deficiencies, the Minicomputer Policy's poor implementation provided business houses with immediate access to (relatively) low-cost computers, i.e. it met their primary objective in IT policy. Moreover, it did not lead to the wider computerisation of the country, since the inefficiencies of small-scale production meant that the costs remained prohibitively high for smaller firms and individual users. Other regulatory oversights would appear to confirm that the DoE was no longer interested in either developing India's IT industry or enhancing the country's computer usage. For example, the DoE did not reprimand ICIM, the firm established by the dilution of ICL's India operations, when it stopped producing computers in India and reverted to importing them from ICL in the United Kingdom (Subramanian 1992, p.185). Given that a few years earlier the DoE had engaged in lengthy negotiations with ICL to ensure production of computers in India, the change in priority is striking. Similarly, while the DoE's energies had initially been spent on ensuring the funds for ECIL's foray into computer production and maintaining a market for its products, following the policy shift the DoE overlooked the importation of powerful computers into the higher-end computer market that had, on paper at least, been reserved for ECIL. This further encroached on ECIL's market, severely undermining its growth. It did, however, ensure that business houses had available all the computers they desired.

Unsurprisingly, if we consider the wider restructuring brought about by the intervention in the local hardware industry, via an examination of the economic relations of the Indian IT industry, we see a fundamentally different system of accumulation emerging. The shift to licensing had occurred without any support being given to establishing a local peripherals and components industry. This undermined the conditions upon which a genuine local sub-assembly system might develop. Instead, a dependent, low-value-added relationship emerged between local hardware capital and foreign computer firms, particularly those from Taiwan. This involved local computer enterprises importing what are known as SKDs (simple knock-down kits) or CKDs (complete knock-down kits) from much larger East Asian computer firms. The local firms would subsequently assemble these kits into computers in small factories, in a process known as screwdriver assembly. The firm's logo would then be attached and the assembled computer passed off as Indian. There was little added value in such a system. The Indian computer industry, in terms of computers 'manufactured' in India, looked impressive on paper, but was a facade.

However, while the Minicomputer Policy undermined the indigenous capabilities of the Indian computer hardware industry and, in its place, established a relationship between the local computer industry and foreign computer hardware capital that was dependent and added little value, it also played a significant if inadvertent and underappreciated role in the evolution of the Indian software industry. The knock-down kits did not come with software. As the Indian computer firms were primarily engaged in small-volume production based on screwdriver operations, they did not develop their own software to bundle with their computers. After all, it would only make financial sense for a firm to invest in the development of its own software and bundle this with its computers if the firm was engaged in mass production of computers. As a result, the Indian software companies which had been established by the 1972 Software Export Scheme, and had recently (and for separate reasons) been allowed to provide services domestically, were able to provide the software services required. Given such facilitative conditions, revenues accruing to the Indian software services industry from domestic service provision increased more than 30-fold between 1981 and 1985, in contrast to export revenues, which increased just sevenfold (Pingle 1999, p.121).

To conclude, the system of accumulation engendered had both positive and negative aspects. The direct intervention of the Minicomputer Policy served to undermine indigenous capabilities built up in the preceding years and failed to deliver its promise of replicating the Taiwanese model of an IT production complex based on indigenous production of components and peripherals, alongside a sub-assembly system. Moreover, while the screwdriver assembly system ensured the immediate availability of computers for India's business houses, it impeded wider computerisation of the country. At the same time, it indirectly catalysed the Indian software services industry. The fragmented local computer industry, which lacked the financial motivation to bundle software with their hardware, provided a large and rapidly growing software services market which the local software firms were able to meet. The second great irony in the evolution of the IT industry is that despite its projection as one of India's least corrupt industries, it has been significantly shaped by one of the country's most corrupt and deceitful policies.

7.5 PHASE THREE: PROMOTING SOFTWARE EXPORTS

7.5.1 Vested Interests

The growth of the Indian IT industry following the Minicomputer Policy (including both Indian hardware and software firms) spawned an industry-wide association in 1983. The Manufacturers' Association of Information Technology (MAIT) was set up primarily to give a 'coherent voice to hardware interests' (Sridharan 1996, p.180). However, software firms had also joined, as it provided a platform for them to articulate their own interests. Moreover, given that the wider the membership the greater the leverage, hardware firms welcomed the entry of software firms. The greatest imperative for both hardware and software firms would be to enhance the Indian IT industry's influence in the corridors of power and its leverage over the state.

However, by 1987 the software firms had left MAIT and set up the National Association for Software and Service Companies (NASSCOM). This split was partly due to the growing recognition that the interests of software and hardware firms had diverged too far to justify a unified association. For example, by the mid-1980s hardware firms were focused on resisting the state's initiatives on reducing trade protection in the Indian computer market. The assassination of Indira Gandhi in 1984 and the subsequent election of her son Rajiv Gandhi as prime minister had further boosted moves to liberalise the Indian economy generally and the computer industry in particular.[5] As a result, in the mid-1980s MAIT was engaged in defensive action to prevent or at least limit trade liberalisation in the computer industry (Pingle 1999). In contrast, the Indian software firms' primary interest was not in defending privileges, but in securing government support for expansion. Given that most software firms continued to be active in the global software services market as well as in the domestic market, they were aware of the growth opportunities afforded by the advances in telecommunications technology of the mid-1980s. These advances would allow Indian software firms in theory to develop a greater proportion of their software in India and export it via satellite technology and optic fibres. If the necessary telecommunications infrastructure could be made available to Indian software firms, body-shopping would be confined to the beginning and end of the software project, massively reducing costs and enhancing competitiveness. However, for firms to access this technology, the Indian state's support was necessary.

Thus, NASSCOM's primary objective was to influence the state to provide the domestic telecommunications support that would facilitate the export of software. The wider political economy of India in the 1980s was particularly favourable for NASSCOM. The ongoing liberalisation of the Indian economy had brought to the fore the issue of generating foreign exchange. Sectors that could deliver on this could expect to have the ear of the Ministry of Finance. Crucially, while Indian software firms remained small vis-à-vis India's largest business houses, they were already prominent amongst Indian firms with an export presence. Moreover, the establishment of a Texas Instruments (TI) subsidiary in Bangalore, where software would be written by Indian employees and relayed back to TI's headquarters in Houston via satellite technology, provided evidence that the new telecommunications technologies could be harnessed for transnational software provision. The case that NASSCOM brought to the state was convincing. Should the state intervene in providing the necessary telecommunications infrastructure, revenues from the export of software might be expected to increase exponentially. That the global software market was undergoing rapid expansion further underlined the potential of establishing India as a major software exporter.

7.5.2 State Interventions

Given the wider political economy conditions in India during the mid-1980s, alongside an awareness of the genuine export potential of the software industry, the Indian state intervened, with remarkable haste, to establish the International Packet Switching Service (IPSS) in India. It allowed Indian software companies to connect to an international network via a domestic Packet Switch Stream (PSS) line, by which they could connect to the online databases and mainframe systems used by their clients and transmit data to them. By 1989 the IPSS network became operational and Indian software companies could write and transmit most of their software from their own offices to their clients abroad. Such facilities were a massive boost to the software export capabilities of Indian firms. Partly to facilitate international connections, Software Technology Parks (STPs) were established a few years afterwards. Technically these parks eliminated the need to use telephone lines by providing direct satellite links for international telecommunications. In addition, larger software firms were granted the title of 'Individual STPs' which meant that they did not need to relocate to the STPs to access the advanced telecommunications (Vittal and Mahalingham 2001, p.371).

However, to facilitate the expected export expansion, a number of other policy measures were also implemented by the Indian state, which was eager to capitalise on the potential for massive foreign-exchange generation from the export of software. In addition to providing access to satellite telecommunications, STPs would also provide subsidies, specialised conditions for the duty-free import of computers, and various tax holidays and credit initiatives. For example, 100 per cent export-oriented firms would be provided a tax-free status for five years within the first eight years of operation. Such promotional mechanisms were already in place via Economic Processing Zones (EPZs), but the STPs brought these within one policy space and under the sole jurisdiction of the DoE. Throughout the 1990s the number of STPs rapidly increased, all offering a standardised system of tax, import and credit incentives for exporters, alongside various electricity and water subsidies.

7.5.3 Industrial Restructuring and the System of Accumulation

The focus of intervention was to facilitate closer relations between local software firms and their foreign clients. By this measure, the telecommunications infrastructure interventions, first via IPSS and then through the more holistic STP scheme, have been a resounding success. Software exports increased exponentially after the telecommunications infrastructure was provided (Heeks 1996). Moreover, the infrastructure allowed software firms to increase their export competitiveness and profits rapidly, in turn driving their expansion. Not only did software firms become more closely integrated with foreign capital but the major Indian software firms also expanded their number of clients significantly during this period. Furthermore, the telecommunications infrastructure allowed software firms to move more rapidly up the services ladder to high-value-added sectors such as IT consulting.

However, other relations have been adversely affected. Most prominently, the relations between the installed computer hardware base and local software firms, pivotal to the earlier system of accumulation, have substantially weakened. This was at first a gradual process, with software export revenues only exceeding domestic software services revenues in 1998 (Parthasarathi and Joseph 2004, p.88). However, since then, the trend towards exports and away from domestic software services provision has quickened. As such, by the turn of the century, the interests of Indian software firms lay firmly outside of India. Moreover, the competition structure and foreign linkages of the computer hardware industry have also changed. Seeing that the future of the Indian IT industry lay in software rather than hardware, the larger Indian computer firms such as Wipro and HCL successfully shifted their energies to software services provision. This has left the domestic computer industry more fragmented and also more reliant on imports of peripherals and components.

To conclude, by 1999 the system of accumulation outlined above was set up perfectly for the export of software. From this narrow perspective, it can be considered a great success. However, a survey of the IT industry as a whole reveals a number of deficiencies. The local hardware industry has become more fragmented than ever, with little interest from the state in rectifying it. And yet an indigenous computer hardware industry, producing cheap computers designed for the needs of the rural and urban poor, is integral to the wider computerisation of the country. Moreover, the absence of wider computerisation could jeopardise the future development of the Indian software industry. This system has demonstrated that, despite all the praise for the DoE, the state's interventions were based on the power configurations of economic interests rather than on any broader and longer-term developmental objectives.

7.6 CONCLUDING REMARKS

The chapter has explained how economic and political interests have consistently shaped Indian interventionism in the IT industry from 1970 to 2000, albeit in different ways, at different times, and with different effects, some more developmental than others. This has imparted a number of important lessons regarding the role of the state in development. First, it provides yet another example of the importance of state interventionism in fostering and guiding successful development. The state's importance in the development of the Indian software industry is particularly evocative given that the latter is regularly portrayed as the avatar of free-market globalisation. Second, it has demonstrated that effective intervention is not dependent on the state's autonomy from societal forces. The national milieu in which these interventions took place is particularly significant in ascertaining this point. India, with a vibrant, chaotic democracy set within a heterogeneous, pluralistic society, is the precise opposite of the autocratic states and homogeneous societies of East Asia. If the state is able to intervene effectively in India, the prescriptions of autonomy and the assumptions about a dichotomy between East Asia and the rest of the developing world are difficult to justify. Third, the chapter has emphasised the importance of a political-economy approach in understanding the dynamics of state intervention. In particular, it has demonstrated the necessity of linking economic and political interests with a stake in policy and the structural changes such policy induces. It has thus shown that effective and ineffective interventions are more likely to be located within economies than between economies, a fact which the DSP has unfortunately tended to obfuscate.

NOTES

1. Over the past five years an increasing number of works have applied the DSP to non-East Asian countries, including Botswana and Ireland. However, the theoretical approach and analytical assumptions remain grounded in the DSP's examination of East Asian industrialisation.
2. While foreign computer firms were operating in India, they were primarily engaged in trade and servicing rather than manufacture. IBM, for example, would import second-hand and outdated computers from the West and then loan

them to firms on a pay-per-day contract. The only manufacturing they carried out in India was that of printing machines.
3. By the late 1970s, the problems were widely acknowledged, and the policy was changed to allow firms which had signed up to the scheme to provide domestic services.
4. 'The Emergency' refers to the period between 1975 and 1977 when Gandhi dissolved parliament.
5. Rajiv Gandhi was nicknamed 'the computer kid' by the Indian media, owing to the emphasis he gave computerisation in his political speeches.

8
Lessons for Nigeria from Developmental States: The Role of Agriculture in Structural Transformation

Eka Ikpe

8.1 INTRODUCTION

The interpretation of the role of the state in East Asian development success has been dominated by the developmental state paradigm (DSP) that perceives the state as a core facilitator of development. This has given rise to a narrowly focused attention on industrialisation and the rapid economic growth that has resulted in these countries. The DSP has been slow to react to examining sectors of the economy that contribute to the industrial process outside of the industrial sector itself, let alone concern with the non-industrial itself in its own right.

More generally, the DSP has drawn attention away from the examination of other stages of development in terms of the broader economic and social transformation of the structure of the economy, including the role of agriculture. As a result, the interaction between the agricultural and industrial sectors and the critical role this plays in development, even within the developmental states, is little considered within the framework.

The analytical impact of this has been one of self-limitation, not only of topic, with attention being given to industry, but also geographically and chronologically, with a bias also towards success in case studies. This confines the DSP by excluding non-industrial, largely agrarian, developing economies. In particular, Africa offers a challenge for the DSP, given the dominance of the agricultural sector, with the end result that the continent is largely overlooked, being considered as non-developmental in outcome and statehood, with fleeting exceptions such as Botswana and Mauritius. In short, the DSP is potentially broad in scope and principle (development and the state) but, with its exclusive focus on successful latecomer industrialisation, has been extraordinarily narrow in practice. This suggests close examination of the degree to which its analytical framework is capable of extended application to incorporate other aspects and phases in development (and the corresponding role of the state) and other contexts, especially where there has not been industrial development.

This chapter pursues such an extension in the proposed 'enhanced developmental state paradigm' (EDSP) for application in the case study of Nigeria: a non-industrial developing economy. The idea of refining and extending the DSP can be contentious, particularly on account of its basis in the state–market dichotomy. But the DSP has the capacity to be comprehensive, as it is essentially the conceptualisation of the role of the state in development. To pursue its extended use it is necessary to explore the level to which it can encompass cases where industrial development is yet to occur as well as overcome its basis in the state–market dichotomy.

In this chapter we pursue paradigm extension by basing the EDSP on the empirical experiences of the first-tier developmental states of Japan, Taiwan and South Korea and the second-tier developmental state of Indonesia. We focus particularly on the interaction between agriculture and the process of structural transformation, using classical development economics concepts on constraints to industrialisation with reference to the first-tier developmental states. The Indonesian case study is used to address the reality within economies with diversified primary sectors, in agricultural and mineral resources, where structural transformation has also been characterised by particular intra-primary sector linkages as part of the process. The EDSP also emphasises the underlying economic, political and social factors that influence these dynamics in a rejection of the state–market dichotomy. From this we distil a conceptual framework to understand the role of the state in enabling the contribution of agriculture to industrialisation. The result is the extension of the DSP to the EDSP for application in non-industrial developing economies, such as our country case, Nigeria.

The chapter begins with a presentation of the principal component of the EDSP in Section 8.2, focusing on the empirical experiences of the first-tier developmental states and the concept of inter-sectoral resource transfers between the agricultural and industrial sectors. Section 8.3 puts forward the secondary component of the EDSP, drawing on the empirical experience of the second-tier developmental state, Indonesia, and the facilitation of linkages between the oil and agricultural sectors to enable industrialisation. In section 8.4 we apply the EDSP to the Nigerian case in two stages, beginning with the secondary component and ending with the principal component. The final section concludes the chapter and finds that the EDSP is a useful extension of the DSP, since it enables analysis of non-industrial economies using knowledge from the valuable experiences of the developmental states.

8.2 PRESENTING THE PRINCIPAL COMPONENT OF THE EDSP: LESSONS FROM THE FIRST-TIER DEVELOPMENTAL STATES

For the principal component of the EDSP, we rely on the empirical experiences of the developmental states of Japan, South Korea and Taiwan for comprehending the workings of inter-sectoral resource transfers between the agricultural and industrial sectors in the process of structural transformation. In particular we draw on their approaches to addressing the stylised constraints to industrialisation, namely, savings, marketed surplus, demand and labour.

In summary, we find that developmental states managed savings constraints by extensively taxing the agricultural sector and manipulating foreign-exchange rates in relation to agricultural trade. They also addressed marketed surplus constraints by appropriating food from producers at low prices; obliging producers to pay for land, inputs and credit in rice; widespread public investments to improve agricultural output; and pursuing protectionist policies in relation to the agricultural sector. They dealt with demand constraints by protecting the domestic industrial sector from competition and making efforts to improve agricultural incomes. They mitigated labour constraints by locating industrial activity in rural areas and investing in rural infrastructure and social services to enable pluriactivity, as well as prioritising land- and labour-saving technology to facilitate the outflow of labour from agriculture.

This principal component of the EDSP addresses the fundamental role played together by the state and agriculture in the process of structural transformation, as put forward in classical developmental economics. As Byres (2006, p.238) has acknowledged, this role has been a 'critical part of all major historical instances of capitalist development'. Karshenas (1995) utilises the notion of resource flows for his investigation into the value of prioritising intra-sectoral resource allocation vis-à-vis inter-sectoral resource flows. His approach provides a useful conceptual basis which we adopt to categorise inter-sectoral resource flows as generalised requirements in the processes of economic transition.

The generalised requirements of an economic transition are succinctly captured in the assessment of the dominant constraints to the industrialisation process, namely, in savings constraints; marketed surplus constraints; demand constraints; and labour constraints (Karshenas 1995). In addition, Francks, Boestel and Kim (1999) implicitly utilise the 'constraints' as markers for examining the mechanisms through which the agricultural sector contributes to the process of structural transformation, as experienced in Japan, South Korea and Taiwan. The handling of these constraints within the first-tier developmental states is the principal element of the analytical framework of the EDSP.

8.2.1 The Japanese Developmental State: Agriculture and Structural Transformation

For Japan, Ohkawa and Rosovsky (1973) show that at the initial stages of Japanese industrialisation domestic demand played a significant role in addressing the *demand constraint*. The early manufactured goods were basic, given the rudimentary nature of the industrial sector.[1,2] This category of manufactured products greatly influenced the significance of domestic demand in structural transformation.

Rural agricultural incomes are significant for determining the capacity of the agricultural sector to address the demand constraint. At some level, the Japanese state's investment in improving agricultural output drove agricultural income increases. Ishikawa (1988) reports that prior to the First World War non-farm wages accruing to rural households resulted in up to ten times the value of rents paid to landlords by rural households. Hence, state support for pluriactivity, through investment in social services and capital saving technology, was significant in raising rural incomes as well as ensuring the local supply of consumer manufactures.

On the *savings constraint*, Francks, Boestel and Kim (1999) note that the Japanese state, from the Tokoguwa and Meiji eras, viewed 'industrialisation as the key to national strength and survival'. The implication of this was the heavy taxation of the agricultural sector. According to Mody, Mundle and Raj (1985), at its peak the savings transferred out of the agricultural sector have been cautiously estimated to have reached 20–30 per cent of non-agricultural investment in the 1900s and in the 1920s.[3]

On *marketed surplus constraints*, the role of the agricultural sector has been mostly understood in terms of the supply of food to the industrialising classes. Anderson (1983) has reported that the Japanese state successfully pursued a regime of protection in the pre-war period, in order to address the prevalent food market conditions of supply constraints, by raising output levels in rice production domestically (and in the colonies) and thus ensuring price stability and self-sufficiency. The state made substantial efforts to drive productivity increases in terms of both land and labour. This included the extensive dissemination through producer associations of improved input varieties, methods and capital inputs, including irrigation (Francks, Boestel and Kim 1999).

Agricultural labour played a major role in addressing the *labour constraint* in the movement of labour from the agricultural sector to the industrial sector. Ohkawa and Shinohara (1979) show that the labour outflow from agriculture rose from 705,000 to 2,950,000 in the period 1900–20, against an increase in the number of workers in the non-agricultural sector over the same period from 1,118,000 to 3,566,000. The Japanese case presents a pattern of labour contribution from the agricultural sector (at least initially) that was enabled by heightened levels of pluriactivity. This reflects the significance of adequate levels of formal education in rural areas. Industrialisation was thus greatly facilitated by the decentralised industrial activity that arose, allowing dual roles for farm households, in both agriculture and industry, with gendered characteristics.[4]

The discussion thus far has referenced the broader context of the Japanese state's engagement with the agricultural sector for the purpose of structural transformation. Now we focus briefly on key factors within this context that influenced the process of inter-sectoral resource transfer from agriculture to industry.

Public investments that were intended to strengthen the agricultural sector targeted the crucial constituency of small-scale producers, particularly through the producer associations.[5] Although attempts were made to raise output levels using large-scale agricultural techniques, these were abandoned when they failed to advance the predominantly small-scale agricultural system. In returning to the policy of sustaining small-scale agricultural systems, Francks, Boestel and Kim (1999) report that the Ministry of Agriculture and Commerce relied on experienced farmers as experts and instructors alongside indigenously developed technologies funded by government subsidies. Also, the Japanese state strongly engaged producer associations, for policy dissemination and ensuring broad access to agricultural investment, while the latter in turn influenced agricultural policy.

The Japanese state utilised agriculture to address the noted constraints to industrialisation, as has been discussed; however, the agricultural constituency (producer associations) was influential in the process. As such the agricultural sector was in a position to robustly address three of the four noted constraints: demand; marketed surplus; and labour.

8.2.2 The Taiwanese Developmental State: Agriculture and Structural Transformation

In Taiwan, the agricultural sector was pivotal in mitigating the *savings constraint* in structural transformation. At the inception of import-substitution industrialisation in the 1950s, agriculture provided the bulk of Taiwanese exports and the majority of foreign exchange earnings until the 1960s (Francks, Boestel and Kim 1999). This was therefore a significant source for resources aimed at reinvestment into industry. A critical source for savings transfers out of the agricultural sector was agricultural taxes. Following the 1930s, agricultural taxes were dominated by forced rice sales and high fertiliser prices exacted by the government (Karshenas 1995).

Rice was also central to the state's efforts at mitigating the *marketed surplus constraint* as it related to the availability of food for industrial workers. As a staple food, the state sought to ensure its supply and price stability in order to guarantee the availability of food. Beyond tax payments in rice, the Taiwanese state sourced rice from the producers by legally obliging rice production on designated land; requesting payments in rice for land acquired under the land reform programme; requesting repayments of government credit in rice; and requesting payments for fertiliser in rice (Francks, Boestel and Kim 1999).[6] The result is that the Taiwanese state is estimated to have secured over half of all the rice marketed in the 1950s (Moore 1985).

In spite of the substantial tax burden on agriculture, the sector was expected to support structural transformation by addressing possible *demand constraints* to industrialisation. To this end the domestic manufacturing sector was initially effectively protected from foreign competition (Francks, Boestel and Kim 1999). The conditions for the agricultural sector to contribute to industrial demand were improved by state investments towards increased agricultural output. For instance, the land reform process saw substantial wealth redistribution to farmers, including small-scale producers, which led to growth in rural incomes through the 1950s and the 1960s and made the agricultural sector the principal source of demand for industrial goods (Thorbecke 1979; Park and Johnston 1995).

In Taiwan, the agricultural sector made a vital contribution to addressing the *labour constraint* to industrialisation. A pertinent factor that characterised labour supply in the Taiwanese structural transformation process is the efficacy of a pattern of transfer that did not necessitate rural–urban migration. This is reflected in estimates of net labour outflows from the rural areas, from 0.9 per cent per annum between the early 1950s and the mid-1960s, rising to 2.1 per cent between the mid-1960s and the mid-1970s (Thorbecke 1979).[7] Rather, industrial work was undertaken in rural areas, pointing to the significance of rural infrastructural and social services investments. Ho (1979) observes that 46 per cent of new employees within the manufacturing sector, in the decade 1956–66, were based in rural areas, reflecting the location of 50 per cent of manufacturing jobs outside of the main cities by the early 1970s. Hence, this pattern of transfer was also highly linked to the emergent structure of the industrial sector.

This contribution of rural labour to the industrial sector has been associated with the adoption of labour- and land-saving techniques in agricultural activity. The release of agricultural labour for industrial activity was tied to the increasing labour productivity brought about by the use of technology as enforced by the Taiwanese government (Lee 1971). Karshenas (1995) highlights complementary efforts in land-augmenting technologies that were specifically targeted at small-scale production systems also in the 1950s and 1960s.[8]

In examining the context within which the Taiwanese state pursued agricultural extraction to support structural transformation, we reflect on significant factors that influenced the inter-sectoral resource transfers from agriculture to industry. First, the support to the agricultural sector was focused predominantly on small-scale producers. The case for support to the agricultural sector was strengthened by the need for the Taiwanese state to solicit rural political backing to check the political clout of the landlord class (Francks, Boestel and Kim 1999). This was also reinforced by the state's engagement with producer associations.[9]

Second, the support to the agricultural sector was on the back of broader assistance to agriculture from colonial investment and foreign aid. Kikuchi and Hayami (1985) state that the success of agriculture was enabled by previous investment in communications, roads, irrigation and other agricultural infrastructure in rural Taiwan as part of Japan's colonial policy. Also Thorbecke (1979) suggests that the USA financed agriculture extensively, making up about 60 per cent of its capital formation between 1951 and 1965.

The Taiwanese state managed all four of the noted constraints to industrialisation from its robust agricultural base. The context within which this occurred influenced the process and outcome. As with Japan, support to agriculture targeted the most significant small-scale production systems, though linked to different political factors. The participation of the key constituency of associations was central to the success of surplus extraction.

8.2.3 The South Korean Developmental State: Agriculture and Structural Transformation

The contribution of the South Korean agricultural sector in the post-war era was less significant than in its fellow developmental states, Japan and Taiwan. Nonetheless, the following review is useful as part of a full empirical examination of the role of the agricultural sector in developmental states, in order to provide lessons for the EDSP.

Agriculture did not contribute extensively to addressing the *savings constraint* for structural transformation. Savings were generated within the industrial sector by phenomenal levels of industrial export growth, which was supported and promoted by the state from the 1950s in the form of credit allocation and trade barriers to protect domestic industry (Mason et al. 1980).[10] Thus South Korea is seen as having followed the classic industrialisation path suggested by Lewis. Against limited extraction from the agricultural sector there was extensive public investment in the agricultural sector, e.g. in irrigation, transport facilities, including roads, and electricity infrastructure (Teranishi 1997).

The extent to which investment by the South Korean state enabled agriculture to address the *marketed surplus constraints* has been limited. As has been mentioned, there was widespread public investment in the agricultural sector. Substantial rice deficits implied that these efforts did not address domestic demand (including for industrial workers) during the process of structural transformation. This is confirmed by the substantial growth in rice imports over the period 1966–77, which reached 907,000 tonnes in 1971 (Francks, Boestel and Kim 1999).

The role of the agricultural sector in addressing the *demand constraint* was also limited. Moon and Kang (1991) find that through the 1960s agricultural incomes grew at only 3.5 per cent per annum, while urban wages grew at 14.6 per cent per annum. The substantial income differentials between the agricultural and industrial sectors suggest that demand constraints were largely mitigated by the industrial sector.

Agriculture played its most significant role in industrialisation in South Korea by addressing the *labour constraints* to structural transformation. The sector's share of employment is shown as decreasing from 79 per cent in 1960 to 34 per cent in 1980, alongside the increase of the urban population from 27.9 per cent to 57.3 per cent and the decrease of the rural population from 72 per cent to 42.7 per cent in the same period (Francks, Boestel and Kim 1999).[11] This out-migration of labour from agriculture and the rural areas to the cities has been directly linked to structural transformation. According to Sloboda (1981) the urban location of industrial activity influenced by the South Korean state is a substantial factor that drove migration to the urban-based industrial sector.

In reviewing the context within which the South Korean state utilised (or did not utilise) the agricultural sector for structural transformation, we consider three factors that shaped inter-sectoral resource flows between agriculture and industry. First, the contribution of Korean agriculture was hampered on account of unfavourable initial conditions. Notably, Japanese colonial investment in Korea favoured industrial activity vis-à-vis agricultural activity, in contrast with Taiwan (Moore 1985). Second, the smaller role of agriculture in South Korea can be attributed to a less significant power base within the agricultural constituency. It has been argued that prior to the 1960s the South Korean state, unlike pre- and post-war Japan and post-war Taiwan, did not require rural support (Moon and Kang 1991; Moore 1985). Third, the political elite leaned towards treating agriculture with 'kid gloves', owing to rural affiliations. Park Chung-hee's government is reported as having treated agriculture more delicately than his predecessors on account of his rural background (Haggard, Kim and Moon 1991).

In South Korea, the contribution of the agricultural sector to the process of structural transformation was limited in comparison to Taiwan and Japan. The sector was most significant in addressing only one of the noted constraints, that of labour outflows to the industrial sector.

8.3 LESSONS FROM INTRA-PRIMARY SECTOR LINKAGES IN INDONESIA: THE SECONDARY COMPONENT OF THE EDSP

The secondary component of the EDSP relies on the empirical experiences of the second-tier developmental state of Indonesia, in order to address the role of the state in the use of oil resources to strengthen the agricultural sector for its contribution to structural transformation. On this, we find that the developmental state ensured *fiscal linkages* between agriculture and oil by enabling fiscal transfers to the former through the provision of subsidised inputs and access to credit to producers alongside rural infrastructural developments. This secondary component of the EDSP is important, since analyses of many developing economies might benefit from an EDSP that engages agriculture in the context of a buoyant mineral economy.

The situation of the Indonesian case within the EDSP is based on three factors: Indonesia's status as a developmental state (albeit a second-tier one); its shared experience with the first-tier developmental states of a strong role for agriculture within industrialisation that is driven by the state, as will be seen later in the section; and the state's use of oil resources to enable this role for the agricultural sector.

The empirical experience of Indonesia lends support to the stance that sees as significant the linkages between oil and agricultural sectors in its industrialisation trajectory as well as the central role that the state has played in related processes. This role for linkages can be seen as resonating with the principal component of the EDSP, since the management of production,[12] consumption and fiscal linkages effectively represent the management of the marketed surplus, demand and savings constraints especially.[13]

The Indonesian state pursued structural transformation with its dedicated agenda of industrialisation programmes, including import-substitution and export-orientation strategies, through the 1970s (Soehoed 1988). During this period of structural transformation, the economy was characterised by the archetypal dualistic primary sector. Through the 1970s and 1980s, oil and gas exports gained much significance through the global oil-price boom period.[14]

The economy was also essentially agrarian. In 1970 agriculture accounted for 47.2 per cent of GDP as against manufacturing at 9.3 per cent of GDP (Booth 2007). Although industrialisation was directly supported by the oil economy, it was strongly led by the agricultural sector.[15] This continued significance of the role of the agricultural sector in structural transformation highlights the importance of comprehending the linkages between agriculture and oil in the Indonesian state's pursuit of industrialisation.

Resource transfer from the oil sector to the agricultural sector has been most pronounced through *fiscal linkages*. For instance, in the period 1978–83, proceeds from the oil economy consistently constituted over half of total government revenues. Booth (1989) has shown that corporate taxes from the oil sector contributed to 54.1 per cent of total government domestic revenues in 1978/9 rising to 65.9 per cent in 1983/4. However it is important to note that government revenue accruing from the oil economy has been in decline since 1988, quickly falling below the 50 per cent mark (Booth 1994).[16]

With this revenue base the Indonesian state made substantial investments in the economy. Over the 1978–83 period, gross total investment as a proportion of GDP averaged 23 per cent, 44.3 per cent of which was financed by the Indonesian state (Booth 1989). In turn, public expenditure on agriculture was substantial as a proportion of the total government spend. In the Repelita II (1974–79) and III (1979–84) development plan budgets the allocated spend to the agricultural sector stood at 19.1 per cent and 14 per cent respectively (Booth 1989). From the data it appears that a strengthened agriculture sector emerged on the basis of fiscal transfers that gave rise to widespread public investment.

In the state support to the agricultural sector, Glassburner (1988) highlighted the significance of the BIMAS[17] and INMAS[18] rural agricultural programmes alongside targeting small-scale producers, through strengthening village cooperatives, with increases in fertiliser use that led to the eventual coverage of 72 per cent of the harvested area in 1984 (up from 31 per cent in 1974).[19] This resulted in improved agricultural output growth. Pinto (1987) highlights the consistent growth of rice production, with yields increasing between 1968 and 1978 at the rate of 4.2 per cent per annum, and after the oil boom at 6.7 per cent per annum until 1984.

Underlying political and class factors have been significant drivers in the Indonesian state's pattern of support to agriculture. Frederick and Worden (1993) and Hart (1986, p.198) have argued that investments in agriculture were tied to the state's need to secure the support of the rural landowning elite, as well as ensure that the agricultural constituency was recompensed, as this was deemed necessary for political stability.

The agricultural investment patterns and dedicated interaction with producer associations and small-scale production systems by the Indonesian state strongly resonate with the principal component of the EDSP. Furthermore, the political influence of a powerful agricultural constituency on state activity is an added element of similarity with the analyses of the first-tier developmental states. On this account the Indonesian experience reveals the state's preparation of agriculture for extraction in a manner that is in sequence with the principal component of the EDSP. It therefore enables the consideration of these diverse experiences as component parts of the EDSP.

8.4 APPLYING THE EDSP: THE CASE OF NIGERIA

The application of the EDSP is carried out at two levels. First, we apply the secondary component of the EDSP, examining fiscal linkages between oil and agriculture. Second, we apply the principal component of the EDSP, considering inter-sectoral resource transfers between the agricultural and industrial sectors alongside the noted constraints to industrialisation – savings, marketed surplus, demand and labour.

Both stages of the EDSP are carried out in the distinct policy regime periods in Nigeria. Emphasis is placed on the period covering the first, second, third and fourth national development plans, given the dominance of development planning and the shared characteristics with the developmental states during this period.[20] We rely on indicators of public spending on agriculture alongside government policy, to establish the commitment of the state to enabling transfers from the oil to the agricultural sector.[21] We then draw upon data on savings and investments, fiscal transfers from the agricultural sector, the rice economy and rural–urban migration drawn from databanks and literature to assess agriculture's contribution to the process of structural transformation.

The application of the EDSP will reference the agricultural sector as a whole, with focus on the rice sub-sector for its significance within the developmental states as well as its pivotal social, economic and political roles in Nigerian agriculture and the broader national economy.[22]

8.4.1 From Oil to Agriculture for Development in Nigeria: The First Phase of Deploying the EDSP

The most significant means of inter-sectoral resource transfer between the oil and agricultural sectors are fiscal transfers. This is the reality in Nigeria, where upstream activities have dominated the oil economy (Odularu 2008; Ogunbodede, Ilesanmi and Olurankinse 2010). As such, the state control of the oil sector and therefore financial control of the economy has been central to the transfer of resources to other sectors within the economy, including agriculture.

We consider the fiscal transfers from the oil sector starting from the 1970s as it is at this juncture that the contribution of the oil sector to government revenue began its exponential upward trend. Assessing net resource transfers between the oil and agricultural sectors through public expenditure in Nigeria is challenging, not least because of the problematic data on the two sectors.[23] Nonetheless, to obtain an indication of net resource transfer patterns we account for the contribution of the agricultural sector to government revenue using customs and excise duties.

Between 1970 and 1985 there is a direct relationship between total government revenue and total oil revenue (as a proportion of government revenue) (see Table 8.1). The growth of customs and excise duties as a component of government revenue is dwarfed by the increases in oil-revenue receipts. This discrepancy between government revenue from the oil and agricultural sectors can be explained by the reduced significance of non-oil exports in this period, and thus tax receipts, particularly from agriculture.

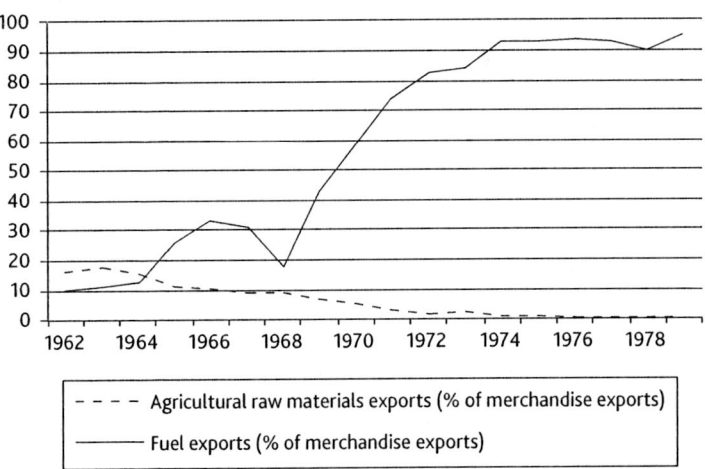

Figure 8.1 Agricultural Exports as a Proportion of Merchandise Exports in Nigeria (1962–79)

Source: World Bank Africa Development Indicators 2007

Table 8.1 Public Expenditure on Agriculture in Relation to Government Revenue in Nigeria (1962–85) (₦m)

Development plans	Total planned expenditure	Total actual expenditure	Total planned expenditure on agriculture	Percentage of total planned expenditure on agriculture	Total actual expenditure on agriculture	Percentage of total actual expenditure	Government revenue from customs and excise duties	Government revenue from oil revenue	Total government revenue
First development plan (1962–68)	1,352.3	1,073.4	183.5	13.6	105.0	9.8	–	–	–
Second development plan (1970–74)	3,350.2	2,237.7	331.7	9.9	218.6	9.7	2,357.0	6,181.0	9,402.0
Third development plan (1975–80)	43,313.5	29,433.9	3,042.7	7.0	2,107.1	7.0	6,205.0	30,980.0	41,257.3
Fourth development plan – reviewed after oil price shocks (1981–85)	42,200.0	17,334.4	5,400.0	12.7	3,147.0	18.2	12,534.0	51,390.0	73,843.8

Sources: Central Bank of Nigeria Statistical Bulletin 2005, vol.16; First, Second, Third and Fourth National Development Plans

The decade of the 1970s saw the marked decline of agricultural exports (see Figure 8.1). The decline in agricultural exports began in 1966 and can arguably be linked to the disruption of agricultural production, particularly in the south-east, as a result of the 3-year civil war from 1967. The downward trend of agricultural exports, as a proportion of total exports, was consolidated as fuel exports began to rise exponentially in 1968, a pattern that remains unchanged to date. This trend in agricultural exports evidences the drop in customs and excise taxes related to exports, thus reflecting the reduced contribution from agriculture to the public purse.

From the 1970s, fiscal transfers to agriculture have been reliant on the sustained increases in oil revenue accruing to the government. However, the pattern of fiscal transfer to the agricultural sector does not match the increase in government revenue from massive increases in oil revenue. In the period 1962–85, planned government expenditure on agriculture only ever reaches 13.6 per cent of total planned expenditure during the First Development Plan, significantly before the oil boom (Table 8.1). Planned actual expenditure interestingly, given the oil price shocks, fares best in the Fourth Developmental Plan, at 18.2 per cent of total actual government expenditure. This is a marked improvement on actual expenditure on agriculture of 9.8 per cent of total actual expenditure in the First Development Plan period.

Investment in the agricultural sector was extensive in infrastructure, particularly heavy capital investments. In spite of the dip in public agricultural expenditure in the Third Development Plan, this period saw extensive investment in irrigation infrastructure to the tune of ₦975.6 million, constituting 31 per cent of the total actual expenditure on agriculture (FGN 1970). For the rice sub-sector, investment was considerably biased towards large-scale cultivation systems, despite the dominance of small-scale producers.

Of the total irrigation capacity of 159,517 hectares, developed under the extensive River Basin Development Authorities from the 1970s, only 55,000 hectares represent the Fadama (small-scale irrigation) system (FAO 2005). This is despite the fact that the performance rate of the non-Fadama irrigation capacity of 154,517 hectares has been recorded as being 20 per cent on average as compared with 100 per cent of the Fadama irrigation capacity of 55,000 hectares for rice production (FAO 2005).

Beyond infrastructural investment, public expenditure in agriculture included providing access to inputs such as seeds and fertiliser, as well as training in extension services. This was the mainstay of a host of programmes in the 1970s and into the early 1980s, such as Integrated Rural Development Projects (IRDPs) and Agricultural Development Projects (ADPs). Additionally, institutions were established to provide credit to producers, including the Rural Banking Scheme, whereby the Central Bank mandated all commercial banks to establish a rural presence and to make 30 per cent of their credit facilities availed to rural-based activities, the creation of the National Agricultural and Cooperative Bank in 1973, and the Agricultural Credit Guarantee Scheme Fund, which guaranteed loans for commercial farmers, i.e. large-scale producers (Osinubi, 2003; Mogues et al., 2008: 49–51).

In spite of the transfers between the agricultural and oil sectors, the performance of the former suffered, with agricultural exports as a proportion of total exports falling from 36 per cent in 1970 to 4 per cent in 1980 and agricultural sectoral growth averaging 0.5 per cent for the same period.[24] A key theme regarding this failure has been the support for large-scale agriculture at the expense of small-scale producers, despite the dominance of the latter in the production system and arguably antithetically to the experiences of the developmental states. Furthermore, the efficiency of the dominant small-scale production system was clear; examples range from its critical role in the provision of public revenue in the immediate post-independence period to the improved performance of irrigation systems noted earlier.

The bias against small-scale producers was further enabled by the 1978 Land Use Decree that followed the Land Tenure Law inherited from the colonial period and saw the 'vesting of the ownership of all land in the state's Governor and giving him/her the rights to grant statutory rights of occupancy to any person' (LFN 1990). This allowed the state to allocate land to 'capitalist' large-scale farmers at the expense of the smaller-scale producers.[25]

From 1986 development planning was effectively ousted in line with the increasingly dominant policy directions of the Washington Consensus. A structural adjustment programme (SAP), conceived by the international financial institutions (IFIs), pronounced the superiority of market-led processes and the primacy of the price mechanism, especially emphasised by the devaluation of the Naira. Nigeria's SAP was initially instated from 1986 until 1988, although this was extended until 1993. This period was characterised by the objective of an undermined role for the state, including in the agricultural sector. The negative impact of the SAP on Nigerian agriculture is well documented (Nwosu 1991; Alaofin 1999; Gibbon and Olukoshi 1996; Mustapha 1993).

The shabby treatment of the rural agricultural sector speaks to the political weakness of the sector as a whole with the advent of a dominant petroleum sector. Abdu and Marshall (1990) make the point that in the development planning period the agricultural policy regime simply failed to engage the realities of the rural population. A rural–agricultural aristocracy that might have bargained on behalf of the agricultural sector seems to have been absent. In fact, Hill (1982, ch.16) argues that historically the failure of the Nigerian state to establish an agrarian hierarchy challenged the progression of the sector.

8.4.2 Fulfilling the Savings Constraint: The Role of Nigerian Agriculture in Development

To what extent did agriculture contribute to savings, and therefore investment, particularly in the development planning period? As we have seen, taxation was an important means of surplus extraction from the agricultural sector within the EDSP. Export and producer taxes were levied on producers and accompanied by widespread marketing board surpluses (Ladipo 1990). Through the 1960s duties on export crops, including cocoa, groundnuts, rubber, cotton and palm oil, ranged from 5 per cent to 60 per cent (Oyejide 1986, p.25). Between 1961 and 1965, the fiscal extraction from agriculture was so extensive that producers' losses, per tonne of produce sold, averaged at 30.5 per cent for cocoa, 8 per cent for groundnuts, 2.6 per cent for cotton, 10 per cent for palm kernels, 17.2 per cent for palm oil, and 19.6 per cent for rubber (Ladipo 1990).

Although it is difficult to establish the direct contribution of agriculture to total government revenue during the First Development Plan period of 1962–68, the dominance of the sector is evident in its contribution of ₦10,200 million to a total GDP of ₦17,586 million (FGN 1970). Furthermore, the fact that total actual expenditure on agriculture stood at ₦105 million within the Plan, with public expenditure on trade and industry, electricity, transport and communications totalling ₦498.7 million, is indicative of its contribution to the process of structural transformation (see Table 8.1; FGN 1970).

For the Second Development Plan, total expenditure on the Plan stood at ₦2,237.7 million of which expenditure on manufacturing and industry stood at ₦85.5 million against government revenue of ₦9,402 million, with trade taxes totalling ₦2,357 million and oil revenue totalling ₦6,181 million (see Tables 8.1 and 8.2). From these data it is clear that trade taxes, and therefore agriculture, played a substantially reduced role in the execution of the Plan in the context of the increasing dominance of oil revenue.

From 1970 to 1974, although GDP from agriculture increased from ₦10,200 million to ₦16,946 million, as a proportion of a much higher total GDP of ₦60,159.3 million, it decreased to 28 per cent from 58 per cent (Table 8.2). This is explained also by the exponential increase in the GDP generated from the mining sector, which stood at ₦25,203 million in the period 1970–74, against ₦707 million in 1962–68 (FGN 1970).

With the Third and Fourth Development Plans, both the contribution of trade taxes to total public revenue and the proportion of GDP generated from agriculture continued on a downward trend vis-à-vis government expenditure on industry. Table 8.1 shows the poor performance of trade taxes as a proportion of government revenue during the period of the Second, Third and Fourth Development Plans.

Table 8.2 shows GDP from agriculture improving dramatically from the Second to the Third Development Plan periods, from ₦16,946 million to ₦36,846.4 million. However, as a proportion of total GDP this represents a fall from 28 per cent to 23 per cent. This is significant in comparison with the exponential increase in manufacturing expenditure to ₦2,569.7 million, 30 per cent of public expenditure. By the Fourth Development Plan, GDP from agriculture fell, both as a proportion of total GDP to 19 per cent and in absolute terms to ₦19,786 million. This, alongside the fall in trade taxes corroborates the declining contribution of the agricultural sector to government revenue and therefore to addressing the savings constraint.

Towards the end of the post-development plan period and afterwards, the state's engagement with the agricultural sector changed irrevocably. By 1982 the agricultural taxation that had characterised the state's drive for surplus extraction had largely been displaced by subsidies (Oyejide 1986). Thus, the agricultural sector initially contributed substantially to savings for the industrialisation project from the 1960s to the mid-1970s, but progressively less so since then. In the post-independence period it can be argued that the state's support to agriculture for savings extraction has been limited.

The progressive centralisation of the Nigerian state has been a critical influence on the deterioration of agriculture's contribution to addressing the savings constraint. The post-independence

Table 8.2 Agricultural Output, Public Revenue and Public Expenditure in the Manufacturing/Industrial Sector (1970–84) (₦m)

Development plans	Total gross domestic product from agriculture for development plan period	Total gross domestic product from mining for development plan period	Total gross domestic product for development plan period	Expenditure on manufacturing/industry
Second development plan (1970–74)	16,946.0	25,203.0	60,159.3	85.5
Third development plan (1975–80)	36,848.4	37,058.8	156,647.0	2,569.7
Fourth development plan (1980–84)	19,786.0	26,613.5	142,489.9	861.9

Source: Central Bank of Nigeria Statistical Bulletin, 2005, vol.16; First, Second, Third and Fourth National Development Plans

state adopted a federal system of government and the immediate post-independence relationship between surplus extraction and agriculture was reliant on the regional production systems and market structures that prevailed. Following this period, the centralisation of state power has been financially driven by state control of oil production and politically achieved through military rule and the declining significance of the regionally based agricultural economy and political system.

8.4.3 Agriculture and the Marketed Surplus Constraint in Nigeria: A Surer Role for Agriculture in Development?

Within the EDSP, addressing marketed surplus constraints has principally implied ensuring food supply to industrial workers. In focusing on the key staple food, rice, it is possible to grasp the contribution of the agricultural sector to the process of structural transformation. In Nigeria, domestic demand for rice increased exponentially from 1973. From this time production has lagged behind consumption, with imports filling the gap (see Figure 8.2). The growing demand for rice from the 1970s, particularly in the urban areas that constituted a base for industrial workers, has meant the significant engagement of the state with the rice sub-sector. To some extent, this is highlighted in the public expenditure and investment in agriculture noted earlier.

As with the developmental states, low and stable rice prices for urban consumers were maintained by the Nigerian state in two main ways. The first was the direct purchase of rice from producers by the state. The second was direct state control of imports, in order to absorb marketing costs as well as to increase the rice supply to the market (from stocks) and thus manipulate prices.[26]

Figure 8.2 shows, on the one hand, a negative relationship between rice imports and production.[27] On the other hand, imports steadily mirror consumption throughout the period, apart from the pronounced rise in consumption alongside a dip in imports in 2002/3.[28]

Given the volume of rice imports, in Nigeria domestic agriculture does not seem to have been exploited as a source of food for industrial workers. Rather, as with South Korea, this marketed surplus constraint was mainly addressed through imports. It seems that even where domestically produced rice might have mitigated the food supply gap for urban consumers, the competition from imported varieties prevented this. Developmental states are presented as having targeted gains in domestic food supply through

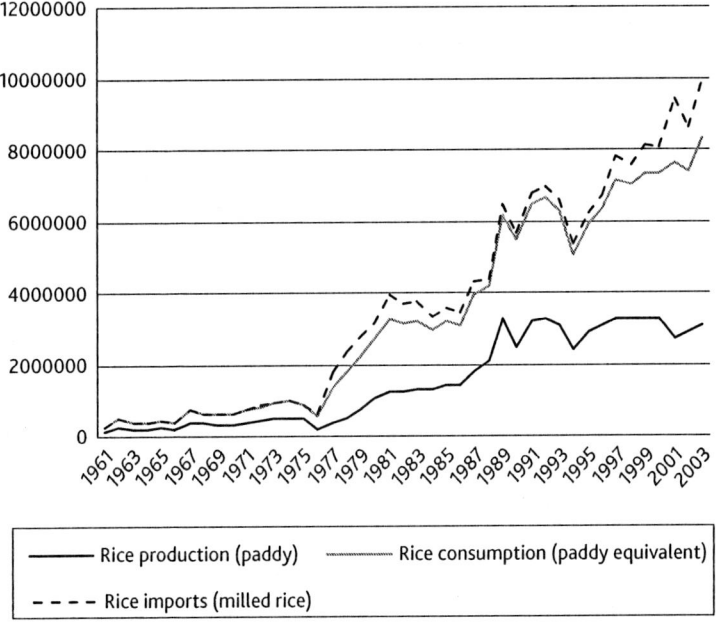

Figure 8.2 Rice Production, Consumption and Imports in Nigeria (1961–2003) (tonnes)

Source: FAOSTAT, 2007, http://www.fao.org/economic/ess/en/

support to small-scale producers. However for Nigeria, the majority of small-scale producers faced immense challenges as a result of public investment that targeted large-scale 'capitalist' producers in the 1970s.

We earlier referred to the loss of political clout of the agricultural constituency in the power consolidation process of the Nigerian state from the 1970s to the 1980s. On the return to democracy in 1999, agriculture began to rise in the list of policy priorities (at least nominally); the period saw the pursuit of major presidential initiatives on key crops including the Presidential Initiative on Rice. The president at the time, President Obasanjo, was himself a politician farmer; a product of the 1970s drive to create capitalist farmers. This connection is significant and calls to mind Park Chung-hee's championing of Korean agriculture on the basis of his rural background. On the other hand, the power base of the agricultural elite is radically checked by the lobby for rice imports. Access to rice import licenses in eras of protection have been notoriously subject to negotiated access by the political elite.[29]

8.4.4 Industrial Demand and the Agricultural Sector in Nigeria: A Relevant Constituency?

The EDSP has highlighted the significance of a healthy rural economy for supporting domestic industrial demand; with the developmental states this was evident in the higher level of incomes that resulted from substantial agricultural output levels. Williams (1965) made the point of the anticipated role of agriculture as the key market for domestically produced industrial goods in post-independence Nigeria.

Bevan, Collier and Gunning (1999) have stated that throughout the 1970s, high wages drew agricultural workers to the manufacturing sector as demand grew in the urban industrial sector. Eicher and Baker (1982) assert that the mass exodus of agricultural labour led to the poor performance of the sector, notably in deteriorating levels of production.

Andrae and Beckman (1985, p.4) also argue that the outflow of agricultural labour led to increased wages and production costs for commercial agricultural production. Oyejide (1986, p.41) shows that real rural wage rates increased threefold alongside the real rural wage rate index increase from 100 in 1970 to 232 in 1982.[30] In addition, the SAP exacerbated this decline of the agricultural sector through the 1980s. Nwosu (1991) finds that the use of wage labour fell due to rising labour costs, resulting in reduced output levels.[31] He considers that it was this increase in wages, rather than increased levels of consumption, that decimated the agricultural sector.

These higher wages and production costs suggest that the agricultural sector had a limited impact on industrial demand. Furthermore, the focus of state support on the minority of large-scale producers and its failure to address the outflow of agricultural labour have undoubtedly contributed to the incapacity of the agricultural sector to address the demand constraint.

8.4.5 Structural Transformation in Nigeria and the Labour-strapped Agricultural Sector

In Nigeria, the most significant outflow of labour from agriculture to industry occurred during the period following the oil boom of the 1970s. For the period 1970–85, Table 8.3 shows a 9 per cent increase in the urban population as a percentage of the total population, against a 9.1 per cent decrease in the rural population as a percentage of the total population. Furthermore with the exception of the immediate post-independence period, 1975–80 had the highest annual urban population growth rate.

Table 8.3 Selected Demographic Statistics for Nigeria

Year	Proportion of the total population that is urban based (%)	Proportion of the total population that is rural based (%)	Year intervals	Urban annual growth rate (%)
1960	16.2	83.8	1960–65	6.71
1965	20.1	79.9	1965–70	4.86
1970	22.7	77.3	1970–75	4.93
1975	25.5	74.5	1975–80	5.26
1980	28.6	71.4	1980–85	4.92
1985	31.8	68.2	1985–90	4.98
1990	35.3	64.7	1990–95	4.80
1995	38.9	61.1	1995–2000	4.49
2000	42.5	57.5	2000–05	4.15
2005	46.2	53.8	2005–10	3.78

Source: Population Division of the Department of Economic and Social Affairs of the United Nations Secretariat, World Population Prospects: The 2006 Revision and World Urbanization Prospects: The 2007 Revision

According to the EDSP, the labour outflow from agriculture needed to have fed industry to constitute a contribution to industrialisation as with South Korea. For Nigeria, this was indeed the case. Udeh (1989) and Andrae and Beckman (1985, p.5) have argued that agricultural workers were pulled into the unskilled labour markets as demand grew for industrial labour.[32] The movement of agricultural labour to industry followed the expansion of manufacturing and the industrial sector alongside heavy state investment, particularly in the period of the Third Development Plan of 1975–80.

The role of the Nigerian state in the emergent pattern of labour transfer is not explicit, but one may reflect on how its engagement with the agricultural and industrial sectors impacted on outcomes. In the period 1975–80, public agricultural expenditure actually dropped in proportional terms (see Table 8.1). This compares with the 29-fold increase in public expenditure on manufacturing and industry, from ₦85.5 million to ₦2,569.7 million in the same period (see Table 8.2).

The success of the labour contribution from the agricultural sector was arguably called into question as manufacturing GDP growth declined from a height of 25 per cent in 1970 to 4 per cent in 1980 (CBN 1999; World Bank 2008; WTO 2008). Unlike in South Korea, where the manufacturing sector was powered by the savings in the industrial sector, in Nigeria savings were initially drawn from a declining agricultural sector and subsequently from the volatile petroleum economy. On this basis, rather like Japan, employment in manufacturing could not be viewed as certain in Nigeria. Thus in Japan (and unlike Nigeria) labour transfer was based on pluriactivity, since manufacturing and industrial sites were located in the rural areas.

The contribution of the agricultural labour to the industrial sector in Nigeria effectively backfired with the crisis of the 1980s. The EDSP draws on the experiences of Taiwan and Japan to put forward public investment in rural areas for industrial activity in order to enable pluriactivity and the gradual movement of labour out of agriculture. In the absence of pluriactivity, the anomalous South Korean experience underlines the strength of an industrial sector that is capable of retaining its labour influx. Thus, without this capacity, the EDSP necessarily pronounces the Nigerian state as having failed to enable agriculture to effectively address the labour constraint to industrialisation.

8.5 CONCLUSION

For Nigeria, the analysis of the EDSP makes advances vis-à-vis the DSP in two ways. First, the milieu for the analysis of developmental state status is the more relevant agricultural sector, with reference to its contribution to alleviating the noted constraints to industrialisation. Second, economic, social and political factors are treated as intrinsic to the policies that are pursued by the state to enable the contribution of agriculture to the process of structural transformation.

In the deployment of the secondary component of the EDSP, the Nigerian state enabled linkages between oil and agriculture via fiscal transfers from the 1970s in a manner that resonated with the Indonesian experience. However, in Nigeria these programmes did not principally target the majority smallholder agricultural producer constituency, as they did in Indonesia. Furthermore, the agricultural support that was provided was eventually stifled by policy changes that advocated a decreased role for the state in the economy.

From the principal component of the EDSP, the Nigerian state attempted to address the savings constraint through the extensive taxation of the agricultural sector as well as the manipulation of producer prices in the 1960s. However, this role of agriculture has steadily declined from the early 1970s to the present time, with the increasing dominance of oil revenue as a proportion of government revenue alongside the free fall in agricultural export levels in absolute and relative terms. The Nigerian state pursued stability in food supply to manage marketed surplus constraints predominantly through food imports, seemingly at the expense of the domestic sector, as evidenced by the trends in rice imports and production through the 1970s and beyond. The poor performance of the domestic agricultural sector undermined its possible role in alleviating the industrial demand constraint. The Nigerian state bears some responsibility for this outcome as a result of public policies that led to the decline of agricultural performance and therefore of incomes. The agricultural sector made immense contributions to relieving labour constraints, predominantly through the large-scale exodus of agricultural workers to urban industrial centres. This development also contributed to the sector's problems due to the coincidence of labour outflow without adequate commensurate labour and land productivity improvements.

In this case study of Nigeria, the EDSP has ensured reflection on the underlying economic, political and class factors in the review of the state's support to agriculture and its possible contribution to the process of structural transformation. These are dominated by the progressive centralisation of economic and political power within the state through the 1970s and by a largely absent rural agricultural elite to influence agricultural policy on behalf of the broad base of agricultural producers.

With this in mind, the pronouncement of the EDSP on the developmental status of the Nigerian state is damning. From the first stage of the EDSP deployment, although fiscal transfers from the oil sector into agriculture were considerable, they substantially abstracted from the broad base of agricultural producers and the lifeblood of the sector. The result of this was an agricultural sector in a precarious position for providing support to an intended industrialisation process; the sector has been increasingly characterised as labour constrained, investment maligned (small-scale) and poorly performing. This was evident in the incapacity of agriculture to meaningfully mitigate any of the noted constraints to industrialisation in the critical development planning period.

As we are considering Nigeria within the EDSP as a case of failure, it is necessary to reflect on the case of South Korea, where agriculture played a less than satisfactory role in the industrialisation process. Two factors that stand out in the South Korean case are the large-scale exodus of agricultural labour to urban industrial centres and the reliance on rice imports to address food supply needs. However the critical differences between the two country cases, in development process and outcome, are clear. For South Korea, with regard to process, the constraints that agriculture failed to address were ameliorated by the industrial sector as directed by the state; with regard to outcome, the end of industrialisation has arguably absolved the South Korean state's failings on agriculture. In Nigeria, the oil sector was unable to ameliorate the constraints that agriculture failed to address; the case of Indonesia is the lesson to learn from here. On outcomes, the absence of industrialisation is the ultimate penalising point.

NOTES

1. There are, however, difficulties in measuring the transfer from the agricultural to the industrial sector, given the dynamic complementarity between the two sectors. Francks, Boestel and Kim (1999, p.56) contend that the ambiguity in the direction of the transfer speaks to the challenge of measuring inter-sectoral resource transfers, due to the high level of integration between the sectors. There is generally an iterative relationship between the sectors; for example, the increase in know-how and technological knowledge in the industrial sector also impacts on the agricultural sector in the introduction of new inputs and methods. In addition, the 'constraints' do not function in isolation from one another. For instance, Lewis (1954) focuses on the savings and labour constraints in his analysis of the role of the traditional sector in modernisation.
2. Hanley (1986) shows that prior to the Second World War, domestic demand for manufactures was dominated by basic consumption goods, including improved quality foods, clothing and home improvements.
3. However Francks, Boestel and Kim (1999) suggest that the savings surplus transfer from agriculture was a small element of the total capital base that served industrialisation, and thus the industrial and commercial sector provided the bulk of the resources for structural transformation – much in the manner postulated by Lewis.
4. Francks, Boestel and Kim (1999) note that it was only from the period of the First World War that this pattern became clearer, as industrialisation took a different form in factory-based heavy manufacturing.
5. Francks, Boestel and Kim (1999, p.70) note that these associations were dominated by landlords, but simultaneously served as pressure groups by exerting influence at the level of the state in the interest of producers.
6. To maintain low rice prices, the government is reported to have released its stocks on to the market when necessary.

7. It is notable that Huang (1993) estimates 2.4 per cent through the 1960s; this is still quite a low figure.
8. The demand for agricultural producer goods is put forward as having increased from 23 per cent in 1911–15 to 43 per cent in 1956–60, with more than 90 per cent of the goods constituting land-augmenting technologies that were applicable to small-scale production systems (Karshenas 1995). In addition, bearing in mind the shortcomings of total factor productivity measurements, Karshenas suggests that the estimated 60 per cent output growth in the period 1911–60 is indicative of productivity improvements in the Taiwanese agricultural sector as a result of technology use.
9. The associations were self-financing organisations that were also responsible to government institutions (Stavis 1982; Francks, Boestel and Kim 1999).
10. Agricultural taxes between the 1950s and the 1970s are reported as having peaked at 7 per cent of tax revenue in 1963, with the contribution from farm household income to total taxes not exceeding 3 per cent in the 1960s (Ban, Moon and Perkins 1982; Francks, Boestel and Kim 1999).
11. They also note that this labour outflow was a core contributory factor to the poor performance of agricultural output and to deficiencies in food supply.
12. Here, reference to production linkages is to forward linkages between the agricultural and manufacturing sectors as opposed to backward linkages.
13. Although for the secondary component of the EDSP the linkages service the agricultural and oil sectors and for the primary component of the EDSP the constraints address the interaction between the agricultural and industrial sectors.
14. The sector was controlled by the state through the National Oil and Natural Gas Mining Company (Pertamina) and dominated the wider economy, constituting 82 per cent of export revenue and 73 per cent of government revenue by 1981 (MacIntyre 1994).
15. Beyond the intra-primary sector linkages, the agricultural sector is shown to be pivotal to structural transformation in Indonesia. Uphoff (1999) has argued that for 30 years, agriculture motivated the industrial sector in consumption and production linkages. The consumption linkage in the demand generated by the agricultural sector has been singled out as especially important for Indonesia's industrialisation. Bautista, Robinson and El-Said (1999) make the point of agricultural demand of manufactures in Indonesia as a powerful inter-sectoral resource flow mechanism in being the source of the highest increases in real GDP on the basis of domestic demand. Daryanto (1999) expands on this point by tying the realities of the benefits of agriculture investments to the smallholder farmers who, as a result of improved output levels, increased their demand for locally produced industrial goods and labour-intensive goods and services. An additional factor of importance to this development is the role of non-farm rural incomes. James, Naya and Meier (1989, p.159) have argued that technological improvements to agricultural performance contributed to higher levels of non-farm agricultural occupation and therefore higher rural (non-farm) incomes.
16. This outcome has been the deliberate policy direction of the Indonesian state to reduce its dependence on the oil sector.
17. Bimbingan Massal (Mass Guidance) and later Bimas National (National Guidance).
18. Intensifikasi Massal (Mass Intensification).

19. The extensive impact of agricultural investment is emphasised by Martin and Warr (1993) who note that the development of the agricultural sector saw the highest rates of technical change in all sectors of the economy.
20. For Nigeria, the development planning period between 1962 and 1985 is significant. It represents the period that largely preceded neoliberal dominance in economic development policy as led by the international finance institutions (IFIs). In this period Young (2004) has described states in Africa as post-independence, and subsequently post-colonial, on account of their pursuit of policies aimed at socio-economic transformation, among other factors.
21. We proceed with the deployment cognisant of the problems of the incompleteness and inaccuracy of secondary macro-economic data on Nigeria. Data on agricultural spending is particularly notorious in this regard. Beyond the development planning period, data on agricultural public expenditure is limited to national budget allocations (until 2002). Alpuerto et al. (2009) note inconsistencies in data from different sources, such as the Central Bank of Nigeria (CBN), the primary data source, vis-à-vis the IMF Statistical Index for Nigeria, as well as the conjunction of missing data at the state level and complete data at the composite federal level. As much as possible, in order to minimise errors we rely on data from the CBN, as it is the principal data source even for the IMF.
22. For instance, the discussion on the savings and labour constraints as well as transfers between the oil and agricultural sectors largely draw on the broader agriculture economy. This is because fiscal transfers from agriculture to the state and between oil and agriculture as well as labour movements are not disaggregated on a crop basis in any reliable data sources.
23. Relating government revenue to profits and revenue in the petroleum sector presents challenges. These include the reported lack of transparency on the accounting of oil revenue proceeds on the part of the Nigerian state and the multinational oil corporations and the paucity of adequate data management mechanisms. It is on the basis of these challenges of addressing the link between public expenditure and oil revenue that the Nigerian Extractive Industries Transparency Initiative (NEITI) was initiated by the Nigerian government in 2004, as an attempt to increase data transparency on revenue in the petroleum sector amongst others. There are also problems with relying on public expenditure on agriculture for assessing state commitment to the agriculture sector. Fundamentally, there is a paucity of accurate data on agriculture in Nigeria. This is the result of weak data management systems within the public institutions that have the responsibility for reporting public expenditure in agriculture. This point is underscored in a 2008 report by the International Food Policy Research Institute (IFPRI) in which the authors find 'poor systems of recording, verifying and reporting data on public expenditure in agriculture' – see IFPRI (2008).
24. World Bank (2006).
25. More broadly it does appear that customary land use rights remain dominant in agricultural production, although challenges emerge when land is considered more valuable, such as in urban areas and mineral-producing areas. Aluko (2004) puts forward the case of the Niger Delta, where the state's access to oil-rich land and environmental degradation from oil production have negative impacts on land availability for agricultural production.
26. Direct rice purchases from producers as well as controlling supply was the mandate of the Nigeria Grains Board from its inception in 1977 to the start of

the SAP in 1986 (Ogundele and Akpokodje 2004). In addition, rice imports were almost entirely state controlled over the same period. Between 1977 and 1986 about 80 per cent of rice imports were directly managed by the state via the Nigerian National Supply Company (Ogundele and Akpokodje 2004). The argument is also made that the state's involvement in rice imports was driven by elements of the political elite who exploited the domestic market by unofficially reselling officially acquired imports (Williams 1988).

27. A drought between 1972 and 1974 had a drastic impact on agricultural output in Nigeria (Teal 1983).
28. In drawing conclusions from the data on the relationship between rice imports, production and consumption one must be cognisant of the impact of rice smuggling.
29. This is reflected in the ceding of sole rice import rights to the Dangote Group under the Obasanjo regime between 1999 and 2003, given the affiliation of its chairman, Aliko Dangote, to the ruling political party, the People's Democratic Party (PDP) and his donation of ₦1 billion to the 2003 PDP presidential election campaign (Dike 2003). In 2004 a budding venture capital firm, GNOBU Rice Limited, reported attempts to establish local operations by building a local mill and processing the rice paddy purchased from the farmers at market prices. GNOBU claimed that as a result of the influence of a powerful group of rice importers, the local government thwarted the firm's efforts.
30. Caution should be applied in the use of these wage rates as there are no official time series data on wages in Nigeria; Oyejide (1986) constructs these data from scattered point estimates.
31. It is important to note also that although agricultural output prices were shown to have been on the increase from 1985 to 1988, the period of the SAP, costs of production were also on the increase, including the cost of fuel following the removal of petroleum subsidies in 1988, thus undermining any perceived gains from price rises (Nwosu 1991).
32. There was also movement into the non-enumerated urban sector, usually to service the manufacturing sector workers; this included small producers of goods and services, traders and contractors, as well as migration for education opportunities (Andrae and Beckman 1985).

9
Finance and the Developmental State: The Case of Argentina

Daniela Tavasci

9.1 INTRODUCTION

This volume addresses a number of weaknesses of the developmental state paradigm (DSP), and of the way in which industrial policy and the role of the state in general have been conceptualised in the literature. The present chapter contributes to this critique by addressing the literature on the evolution of the Argentinean external debt throughout the 1990s up to the crisis of 2001 and by providing evidence for an alternative interpretation of the Argentinean political economy, shifting away from the predefined theoretical rigidities of the radical political-economy literature inspired by the DSP framework.

The issue of the role of the state in Argentina became widely debated after its 2001 sovereign default, still the largest ever recorded. A profound economic and social crisis was associated with this event: unemployment surged to over 20 per cent; GNP dropped by more than 4 per cent in 2001 and by almost 11 per cent in 2002; barter became widespread; and 36 per cent of the Argentinean people lived below the poverty line. The crisis came a decade after swift privatisation and liberalisation processes.

In what follows, the radical political-economy literature on Argentina is criticised for its use of the predefined notions of state autonomy interlinked with the relatively new concept of financialisation. Augmenting the critiques presented in the previous chapters of this volume, this chapter addresses the instrumental use of financialisation to explain, ex post, the loss of state autonomy which, allegedly, led to the crisis: taken together, these chapters explain successes (or failures) as the result of state autonomy (or its absence). Hence the 2001 crisis needed an account of how the Argentinean state was captured by particular interests. The rise of finance was then incorporated into the picture and assigned the role of villain.

The chapter shows that this view, as far as the Argentinean crisis is concerned, is theoretically unsound and empirically flawed.

The chapter is organised as follows: Section 9.2 gives some background and reviews the DSP literature on the Argentinean external debt; Section 9.3 gives an alternative account of the evolution of the Argentinean political economy in the 1990s; the concluding section sketches some critical considerations and concludes that, given the integrated investment strategies of financial and real (as well as foreign and domestic) capitals, their interests are difficult to disentangle and, for this reason, it would be more appropriate to talk about linkages between real and financial capitals rather than about relations.

9.2 FROM THE PERONIST DEVELOPMENTAL STATE TO THE RISE OF FINANCE

After the 2001 Argentinean crisis, the economic literature tended to concentrate on the technicalities of the sovereign default, neglecting a historical analysis of the origins and evolution of the external debt during the 1990s. The international financial institutions (IFIs) also demonstrated a certain lack of originality in commenting on the Argentinean crisis: within the IMF, fiscal policy and excessive government spending were blamed (Krueger 2002, Mussa 2002).

Alternatively, within the political-economy tradition, the UNESCO institution Facultad Latino Americana de Ciencias Sociales (FLACSO) in Buenos Aires[1] developed an alternative account of the evolution of the Argentinean political economy that had led to the 2001 crisis. This school made extensive use of the DSP and, in particular, of its pivotal concept of autonomy (see Chapter 1). Like the accounts of the development of the NICs (Amsden 1989, Wade 1990), this school provided an inestimable empirical account of the role of the state in Argentina in the 1990s (Basualdo, Nahón and Nochteff 2005; Kulfas and Schorr 2003a, 2003b), the liberalisation process (Azpiazu 1999), and the privatisation processes (Azpiazu 2002).

The evolution of the concept of the developmental state and the ancillary notions of autonomy and embeddedness are discussed in Chapters 1 and 6 of this volume. However, it is worth noting here that, within the DSP, the empirical literature became problematic when it attempted to ascribe economic successes to the state's capacity to adopt successful developmental policies. This capacity, in the theoretical scaffolding of the DSP, depended on the state's autonomy from interests arising from society.

First, in the empirical literature, the dichotomy autonomous state–successful policy versus non-autonomous state–failing policy was difficult to prove across various countries and was resolved by progressively including additional conditions for the state to be considered as developmental (see Chapter 1): for example, in discussions of state interventions in Latin America where the state was not sufficiently autonomous, it was assumed that it needed to be strong, possibly authoritarian, to face the popular demands of wage increases and state expenditure (Silva 1996). On the one hand, it was argued, these demands could lead to macroeconomic instability and hyperinflation. On the other hand, they could undermine state autonomy and lead to brutal authoritarian regimes supported by an oligarchy whose profitability was endangered by the rise in wages (Basualdo 2001).

Second, if the autonomy of the state and the conditions for it to be developmental created a conceptual problem in the explanation of diverse experiences in cross-country comparisons, it created an even more prominent problem when it had to explain autonomy, and other conditions for the state to act developmentally, in the historical accounts of a single country (Chapter 6).[2] In the case of Argentina, the autonomous character of the state, and therefore its developmental nature, has appeared and disappeared; and this has been used ex post to explain, respectively, both periods of high growth and those of unsuccessful economic policies.

Third, statists have also been criticised on specific grounds, especially in terms of the relations between the state and businesses, for having neglected the effects of the international insertion of developing countries on the state (Schneider 1998). These questions have been addressed, with respect to Argentina, in two ways: first, an argument was developed around the idea that the 1990s opening up of the capital account, and the consequent entrance of foreign capital, shifted the power relations in favour of foreign business and investors (Bonnet 2006). On the one hand, this thesis developed within a theoretical framework that sees capital as accumulating on a global scale, but attacking labour nationally, as the conditions of the interaction between labour and capital are domestically determined (Bonefeld, Brown and Burnham 1995). On the other hand, since foreign capital is, by definition, outside the embeddedness network, it undermines one of the conditions for the state to act developmentally (Chapters 1 and 6).[3]

A second tendency has been to merge the statist approach centred on embedded autonomy with elements of the Gramscian tradition, such as *transformismo*,[4] and the concept of financial valorisation.[5] Accordingly, during the 1990s, the Argentinean political economy was seen as evolving around a shift in the accumulation strategy of the domestic conglomerates, allied with foreign capital, towards finance. In this view, the Argentinean state, captured by the power of large capital, played the fundamental role of keeping the financial sector exceptionally profitable thanks to the fixed exchange rate and by increasing its public debt in order to guarantee high interest rate spreads, and hence high returns, on financial assets (Basualdo 2006; Kulfas and Schorr 2003a).[6]

In spite of an extensive empirical analysis, however, this account presents a number of shortcomings. First is the idea that successes (or failures) are associated with state embedded autonomy (or the lack thereof). However, a convincing account of where these state characteristics were derived from and how they vanished during the recent history of Argentina has been left aside. For example, during the import-substitution era, embeddedness played an important role in the DSP narrative: the state could guarantee more peaceful relations between domestic manufacturing capital and the working class, thanks to the Peronist Party.[7] According to the DSP, this functioned as social glue by representing the demands of the working class while simultaneously mediating with domestic capital. The Peronist Party could then ensure the two-way relationship between state and society, working class and domestic capital. On the contrary, in more recent periods, the relations between state and society have been interpreted differently: the state's weakness, or lack of autonomy, was associated with the government's inability to implement *transformismo* and keep its autonomy from the conflicting interests of manufacturing and financial (now allied with foreign) capitals.

Second, the assumption that large capital was divided into two fractions, identified with the financial and the real spheres respectively, worked instrumentally to explain the alleged hegemonic power of finance, which, it was argued, by capturing the state, had provoked the 2001 social, political and economic collapse. To explain the rise of finance, FLACSO scholars have used the concept of financialisation.[8] Nevertheless, this alleged shift towards finance has to be considered with caution: on the one hand, its empirical justification is based on the rise of the ratio of financial assets to real assets. The next section will discuss how this was only temporary.[9]

On the other hand, by separating capital into two fractions, the Argentinean DSP has neglected its high degree of integration and diversification during the 1990s.

Third, this interpretation of the Argentinean crisis as a result of an intra-capital conflict neglects the relation between capital and labour and is conceptually unsound and empirically unjustified: it assumes that the Argentinean large capital had a certain degree of self-consciousness, a capacity to act collectively and to foresee events.

The next section first discusses the role of the state in the accumulation strategies of the Argentinean conglomerates during the 1990s, through privatisation and transformation of the credit and the labour markets: large (domestic and foreign) firms operating within Argentinean boundaries managed to invest in the financial and in the real sectors, to accumulate assets and liabilities in both currencies, in tradable and non-tradable sectors, both within and outside the country. As a consequence, the identification of which sectors the various conglomerates operated in was far from clear-cut. In short, to put it bluntly, it was impossible to delimit the interests of real sector firms such as Pérez Companc, Soldati and Techint without considering those of Citibank, Bank Boston or J.P. Morgan, given the internationalisation strategy of the local conglomerates and the degree of integration of real and financial capital. The section illustrates the centralisation of the Argentinean capital, and, finally, it discusses the role of the state in the internationalisation of the Argentinean conglomerates, financed through the sale of privatised companies and the accumulation of (cheaply provided and state financed) external debt.

9.3 BEYOND THE ARGENTINEAN DEVELOPMENTAL STATE

This section gives an account of the evolution of the Argentinean political economy during the 1990s. It sheds new light on the role of the state in the accumulation strategy of the domestic conglomerates. First, contrary to the idea of policy formation of the DSP (Chapters 1 and 7), the notion underpinning this chapter is that a policy may be resisted by current configurations of economic and political interests; this resistance may be overcome by economic and political means and through negotiation. The way in which privatisation was adopted and enforced at the beginning of the 1990s, discussed in the next subsection, provides support to this idea.[10]

Second, privatisation also initiated a new cycle of indebtedness, and both privatisation and the transformation of the credit system reshaped the linkages between the real and the financial sides of the economy. Section 3.2 gives an account of these phenomena and highlights how, far from being only a matter of intra-capital conflict and autonomy from capital's interests, the Argentinean state supported a profound restructuring of the privatised companies by expelling significant amounts of labour.

Third, this restructuring increased profitability and market values of the ex-state companies, which were then sold to realise significant capital gains. The proceeds were invested in the financial sector only temporarily and in relatively small amounts. As a result, this account disproves the hypothesis of financialisation: the idea of a separation of the Argentinean capital into two fractions and the takeover of the state by the financial fraction. Rather, it further confirms the degree of integration of both domestic and foreign capital operating in the country in the 1990s.

Fourth, the section illustrates how the transformation of the credit system initiated a process of centralisation of Argentinean capital. Overall figures can give an idea of the scale of this phenomenon: the sale of privatised companies and the acquisitions resulting from the process of centralisation led to 900 changes of ownership during the decade. Nevertheless, a change occurred in the accumulation strategies of the conglomerates: firms (especially privatised ones) were increasingly perceived as collections of assets to buy and sell in order to extract value, rather than as instruments of value creation and employment generation. Overall, then, it can be said that what was privatised was both the right to shed and discipline labour and the right to accrue returns through the financial markets, with these two processes being mutually supportive.

9.3.1 Dismantling Public Ownership

In 1989, emergency regulations sanctioned privatisation and liberalisation of large sectors of the economy in order to solve, it was argued, the country's external debt inherited from the military dictatorship (1976–83).[11] Previous attempts to sell state assets to pay back the country's external debt were strongly contested: a programme of swift liberalisation and privatisation was going to be opposed because of its profound implications on the accumulation strategies of large conglomerates. Trade unions and a number of political parties were also resisting it. Over the previous four decades, the industrial policy measures and the system of accumulation gravitating around the main state companies had consolidated important backward and forward linkages, mainly thanks to overpriced supplies to, or underpriced inputs from, those companies.[12] For example, during the 1980s, the largest company in the country, the state-owned oil producer Yacimientos Petrolíferos Fiscales (YPF), used to spend half its revenues on the purchase of (overpriced) inputs from domestic steel and petrochemical conglomerates such as Techint and Pérez Companc (Etchemendy 2001). Unsurprisingly, then, the privatisation process was strongly opposed by these businesses because of their concerns not to lose their special privileges with state companies.

In 1978, large firms which were suppliers to state companies, trade unions and the military opposed the first privatisation plan. In 1985, in a context of growing public external debt, President Alfonsín made a new attempt to privatise but, again, had to face the reactions of trade unions, the association of industrialists, the military and the managers of state companies. There was evidence that the conglomerates in business with state companies helped trade unions to organise massive strikes to oppose privatisation (Corrales 1996).

However, at the end of the 1980s, a shift occurred in the perception about state ownership of productive activities, and the diverse front that had opposed privatisation in the previous decade started to crack. This shift was primarily triggered by a concatenation of events, starting with the hyperinflation crisis in 1989. The first democratic government since the end of the 1976–83 military dictatorship ended with a de facto debt moratorium on the public external debt in 1988.[13] Commercial banks that held this debt set in motion a currency flight that prompted a hyperinflation crisis, with annual rates of up to 3,000 per cent in 1989 (World Bank 2010). These banks were themselves under the pressure of the Basel I Committee, which required the cleaning of junk debt from their balance sheets.[14] At the time, the market value of the Argentine bonds was estimated at around 15–20 per cent of their nominal value (Wierzba and Golla 2005). The four-digit inflation caused riots and roadblocks as the Argentine peso was losing value by the minute. In these circumstances, the call for general elections, with the early departure of President Alfonsín, was the only viable option to avoid further social unrest.

Because of the widespread resistance, for liberalisation and privatisation of state companies to be feasible, the conglomerates' opposition had to be overcome; similarly, resistance from trade unions had to be tackled and endless parliamentary debates over privatisation had to be avoided.

Various mechanisms worked in diluting this opposition. First, liberalisation and privatisation were presented as the only possible remedies for hyperinflation: the only way out of hyperinflation, it was argued, was to sell state assets to pay back the banks and sort out the long-lasting external debt problem:

> In the face of such a distressing situation, urgent reforms were considered necessary if the scourge of hyperinflation was to be overcome and economic stability and growth were to be resumed. As a result, the Reform of the State Act (23.696) and the Economic Emergency Act (23.697) were considered necessary and urgent. (Menem 2009, author's translation)

However, second, international circumstances also played a role in shaping the conditions favourable for privatisation. The opportunity to negotiate a resolution to the problem of external debt by selling state assets came with the change in the US administration.[15] A new attempt to resolve the issue of Latin American external debt was launched with the design of a programme named after the new US Secretary of Treasury, Nicholas Brady.[16] It is commonly reported that this US-led debt-restructuring initiative was proposed on condition that developing countries reformed their economies according to the principles embodied in the Washington Consensus. These conditions included the privatisation of state companies (Cavallo 2004).

Third, the legitimacy (or the acceptability) of privatisation and liberalisation was argued for on two interlinked fronts: on the economic front, these measures were an open invitation to foreign direct investment and to the repatriation of local capital eager to expand its business opportunities in the country. Between 1992 and 1998, foreign direct investment linked to privatisation reached US$ 6,019 million, 15 per cent of the total foreign direct investments for the period, and US$ 3,506 million was registered as portfolio investment (Kulfas 2001). Firms that had not operated in Argentina before acquired state companies for a total of about US$ 9,500 million. During the 1990s, out of about US$ 126 billion in total investment realised by foreign companies, 13 per cent of this amount was spent to acquire state companies (CEP 2000). Net inflows were about US$ 35 billion, even though portfolio investment left the country as a result of the emerging market crises from 1994. Despite international financial instability during the 1990s, the sum of all the inflows was about half of GDP produced during the period (about US$ 72 billion) and about 84 per cent of the sum of gross capital formation of the decade (World Bank 2010). The involvement of capital that had not traditionally operated in Argentina meant that the negative balance of the financial account in 1989 (US$ −8,083 million) quickly turned into a positive US$ 7,579 million in 1992. Local capital that had left the country during the 1970s and 1980s eventually began to repatriate (Basualdo 2006). These inflows not only supported the resumption of growth, they also guaranteed the fixed exchange rate as a nominal anchor against inflation, resolving the traumatic hyperinflation crisis of the end of the 1980s.[17] On the political front, the Economic Emergency Act was also supposed to protect labour with ad hoc measures that would guarantee employment in the privatised sectors. However, the deregulation of collective contracts with the employees of the ex-state companies turned labourers into freelance service suppliers, a catastrophe for the labour force (Damill and Frenkel 2005).

Fourth, the opposition from the conglomerates was also softened: privatisation was not only an open invitation to capital inflows and an opportunity to clean the balance sheets of creditor commercial banks, it was also a chance to diversify or take on important market shares in core businesses for the Argentinean conglomerates. Privatised companies were transferred free of debt: as a result, deficits of state-owned companies, amounting to 5.5 per cent of GDP in 1989 (Corrales 1996), could be considered as a net transfer to those who acquired state companies. These were newly formed consortia, the so-called *asociaciones*, composed of transnational corporations, Argentinean conglomerates, and commercial banks holding public external debt. Interestingly, more than half of the privatisation revenues between 1990 and 1995 came from those very conglomerates that had furiously opposed previous privatisation programmes. In acquiring state companies, the expansionary strategies implemented by the Argentinean conglomerates were diverse: some tended to pursue either vertical or horizontal integration in expanding their core businesses, as in the case of Pérez Companc and Techint in the oil and steel sectors, respectively. Many became heavily involved in the public utility sectors. Table 9.1 shows the involvement of the Argentinean conglomerates in the privatisation process irrespectively of their core sectors.

Finally, to soften the political opposition, liberalisation and privatisation reforms were adopted in 1989 by emergency regulations: Law 23.696, commonly known as the Reform of the State Act, and Law 23.697, known as the Economic Emergency Act. These measures suspended all subsidies and regimes of industrial promotion, including funds that had been constituted with specific industrial policy aims. At the legislative level, the use of emergency regulations allowed the government to bypass parliamentary discussion.

Interestingly, these measures were only partially and selectively enforced, even though they seem to have been inspired by neoclassical economic theory (linkages between conglomerates and large state-companies were to be dismantled and the opening of the economy had to guarantee the entrance of abundant credit, efficient producers and technological upgrading). Privatisation was often, in fact, a transfer of *public* monopoly to the *private* sector. Moreover, measures of industrial policy in the traditional forms of subsidies, restrictive entry, protection, and selective liberalisations continued, even though this kind of state interventions was made illegal by the 1989 emergency regulations. Overall, far from being truly reformists, the liberalising measures represented an element of continuity: the very same interests that were served during the operation of state companies and restrictive trade policy were now served through liberalisation and privatisation. A few examples may clarify this point.

Entel. Entel and Aerolíneas Argentinas were two of the five biggest state companies and the first to undergo privatisation. In accordance with the Brady Plan, the stakes in Entel were paid for by the exchange of titles of the external debt. As an immediate consequence, its creditor commercial banks were in an advantageous position to buy its assets. The state monopoly was divided into two, one in the south owned by Telefónica de España (acquired by the steel industry giant Techint and Citibank), and one in the north owned by Stet-France (acquired by Telecom, the oil industry giant Pérez Companc and J.P. Morgan) ('Corporate Actions in Argentina', 2010, http://www.bloomberg.com).

The expected advantage of privatisation in terms of increased competition and lower tariffs did not materialise, as tariffs were doubled just before the public utility companies were privatised (Kulfas 2001). Also, in the attempt to minimise the possibility of an opposition to privatisation, the suppliers of Entel, thanks to a negotiation with the sector's trade union, became part of the acquiring consortia and received a 10 per cent stake in the two new companies. Nevertheless, substantial reductions in the number of employees were carried out in the next two years (see below). Both the staff reductions and the tariff surge dramatically increased the profitability of the two companies, paving the way for a substantial rise in both their external debts and their market values.

YPF. Oil and steel were the sectors in which, traditionally, state intervention was most pervasive; these sectors had been subjected to a prolonged industrial policy since the 1930s. Until the 1989 emergency regulations, the state company YPF used to regulate prices both upstream and downstream, from extraction to the final consumer. Within this sector, most of the industrial policy was carried out by subcontracts. Prices paid to contractors in the upstream sectors were always many times higher than international prices. Among the contractors in the extraction phase, Pérez Companc, a powerful conglomerate, had operated in Argentina since the Onganía dictatorship in the late 1960s. It was involved mainly in the extraction phase, with YPF remaining formally the owner of the crude. At the beginning of the 1990s, the reform simply granted the ownership of the extracted oil to Pérez Companc, by transforming the old subcontracts into concessions. Moreover, the administrative framework to award new concessions was repeatedly changed until all the competitors of Pérez Companc dropped out of the bidding (Gerchunoff and Torre 1996). As a result, Pérez Companc increased its assets and displaced Amoco as the largest private producer in the country (see Table 9.2). Before the reform, more than 70 per cent of oil was extracted under regulatory regimes.

As a result, the increased asset ownership and market share by Pérez Companc worked as collateral and positively affected its capacity to take on new debt. This argument will be taken up in the next subsection.

Somisa. By the beginning of the 1990s, the steel industry had experienced a long tradition of linkages with the oil industry as an energy consumer and as a supplier of oil pipes. The second-largest state company, Somisa, and two large private companies, Acindar and Techint, dominated the sector. Exports increased during the 1980s, but the overvalued exchange rate in the 1990s and the abolition of various pro-export policy instruments inevitably had an adverse effect on this trend. Nevertheless, during privatisation, in this case too, extensive proof is available to show that the competitors Iritecnia and Thyssen decided to abandon the bidding because of the lack of clarity in the conditions of sale (Bisang and Chidiak 1995). Somisa was eventually sold to a large public debt

Table 9.1 Presence of Main Conglomerates in the Privatisation Process

	Electricity	Gas	Oil	Railways	Telecommuni-cations	Manufacturing	Others
PÉREZ COMPANC	Costanera Central Transener Edesur	Gas del Sur Metrogás	Puesto Hernández Santa Cruz II 11 secondary areas Port Terminales Marít. Patagónicas Oil pipelines del Valle	Ferroexpreso Pampeano	Telecom Argentina Telefónica de Argentina	Oil refinery San Lorenzo Oil refinery Campo Durán	
TECHINT	Edelap	Gas del Norte	Area Tordillo Area Aguaragüe 10 secondary areas Terminales Marít. Patagónicas Oil pipelines del Valle	Ferroexpreso Pampeano	Telefónica de Argentina	SOMISA (siderur.)	National motorways
SOLDATI	Guemes Central	Metrogás Gas del Norte	Interpetrol Palmar Largo Santa Cruz I Aguaragüe	Ferroexpreso Pampeano Ramal Delta-Borges	Telefónica de Argentina	Oil refinery Dock Sud Oil refinery San Lorenzo	Water – Obras San Nación Television Canal 11
MACRI			9 secondary areas			Oil refinery Campo Durán	National motorways Cable Red Acceso

Source: Data from Kulfas (2001), Bloomberg (2010) and various company websites

Table 9.2 Petroleum Extraction by Company under Different Regimes, 1987–88 (Pre-Reform), and 1993–94 (Post-Reform)

Company	1987–88		1993–94	
	($m^3 \times 1000$)	(%)	($m^3 \times 1000$)	(%)
YPF	16,501	64.73	14,886	40.58
Pérez Companc	2,156	8.46	5,341	14.56
P. San Jorge	126	0.50	1,770	4.83
Astra Capsa	600	2.36	1,836	5.01
Bridas	745	2.92	1,688	4.60
Pluspetrol	428	1.68	1,090	2.97
Tecpetrol	0	0.00	1,068	2.91
Amoco	2,413	9.47	2,688	7.33
Cities Service	1,489	5.84	0	0.00
Total Austral	0	0.00	2,300	6.27
Other (50 smaller companies)	1,033	4.05	4,011	10.93
Total	25,494	100.00	36,680	100.00

Source: Etchemendy (2001)

holder, Techint, and paid for by public debt titles. As a result, as for Pérez Companc with YPF, the market share of Techint increased dramatically in every sub-sector (Etchemendy 2001).

The automotive sector. The automotive sector provides further proof of continuity with the previous period. The sector was able to retain the instruments of industrial policy it had inherited from the golden age of the 1930s (and, exceptionally, even the state apparatus for industrial policy), despite the declaration of their illegitimacy. The Committee of Reconversion of the Auto Industry was created in 1990, consisting of representatives of the government, the trade unions and the business associations. Substantial measures of trade policy were retained: while the average tariff in Argentina was about 10 per cent for manufacturing products, the automobile sector's special regime enjoyed 30 per cent tariffs (Schvarzer 1994). Import quotas were established for 10 per cent of domestic production. The only element of discontinuity was the ending of special credit to the sector (FIEL 1996).

The domestic market increased dramatically in the period after the reform, clearly also as a result of the resumption of growth, going from a production of 156,000 units in 1991 to 508,000 in

1994 (Etchemendy 2001). Nevertheless, imports grew faster than domestic production, possibly thanks to the overvalued exchange rate, which compensated for the tariff barriers of the sector. So, while in 1991 83 per cent of the cars purchased in the country were produced locally, this share was reduced to 70 per cent in 1994. Nevertheless, exports improved from just 5,000 units in 1991 to over 228,000 in 1998. As a result of the augmented production, the automobile industry was the only sector that increased the numbers of employees during these first years of the 1990s, from 17,000 workers in 1990 to 26,000 in 1996 (Adefa 2007). Nevertheless, Smata (the sector union) negotiated new and more flexible contracts for the new workers employed by the multinational corporations attracted in Argentina by the Mercosur agreement (Adefa 2001).

The above examples show how a number of the measures adopted in the 1990s allowed the consolidation and the expansion of the very same interests that had prevailed in the previous period. However, a number of transformations did occur. First, the balance sheets of large conglomerates looked dramatically different: government bonds valued at 20 per cent of their nominal value at the end of the 1980s were now exchanged at their full nominal value for highly profitable privatised assets (see below).

Second, the privatisation process did not sort out the public external debt problems: state companies were all sold free of debt. On the one hand, this meant that public external debt was no longer in the hands of commercial banks. Creditors now consisted of a myriad of small investors who could buy Argentinean bonds issued in US dollars on the international market; US$30 billion was transferred from commercial banks (which acquired stakes in privatised companies in exchange) to the public (World Bank 2010), with important implications for the 2001 sovereign default. This is discussed in the concluding section. On the other hand, state intervention had subsidised the cleaning of the balance sheets of the privatised companies. This favoured the start of a new cycle of indebtedness; thanks to the pegged exchange rate, US dollars could be acquired cheaply.

Finally, the state was no longer financing any productive activity *directly*, neither via the ownership of productive assets nor by providing credit internally. Also, the apparatus that had supported the formation of industrial policy in the previous decades, including ministerial departments and research institutes, was dismantled, and the national development bank was closed down; the only exception was the retention of an automobile industry committee (Azpiazu 1999, 2002; Corrales 1996).

9.3.2 Centralisation, Internationalisation of Argentinean Conglomerates and Linkages between Real and Financial Spheres

The privatisation of state companies initiated a new cycle of indebtedness since free-of-debt privatised assets could be used as collateral. At the same time, the transformation of the credit system, driven by the Basel Accords and the privatisation of the pension funds, by penalising small and medium firms, contributed to the centralisation of Argentinean capital.[18] This is discussed in the next subsection; the subsection after that discusses the large number of acquisitions associated with privatisation and the centralisation process.

9.3.2.1 *The Transformation of the Credit System*

The transfer of the pension funds to the private sector released a considerable number of funds to be managed privately, contributing to the financial sector's growth and diversification. The portion of total savings collected by the banking system went down from 92 per cent of the total savings in 1991 to 70 per cent in 2000 and the private pension system grew dramatically.

With the privatisation of the pension funds, contributions from employers collapsed and public finances were hit dramatically: the public deficit increased by US$5 billion on average between 1994 and 1998 (Gaggero and Sabbaini 2002). Moreover, this measure was a net transfer to local business and, more specifically, to large companies: small companies tended to avoid registering their employees and paying employer contributions to the social security system anyway. Nevertheless, the intended function of this measure as a fiscal stimulus faded away, since the proportion of non-registered employees grew from 28 per cent in 1994 to 37 per cent in 1998 (Ministerio de Trabajo 2003).

Also, the Argentinean financial system was re-regulated under the aegis of the Basel I committee and in response to the 1994 Mexican crisis, which made capital flows towards emerging markets more scarce. However, the liberalisation process and the subsequent regulation activated during the 1990s further encouraged the use of new instruments to ease access to foreign credit in different forms, especially in facilitating investment from aboard and easing the transfer of financial instruments outside the country. This reform also increased the number of debt instruments that were commonly used, widening the choice between different sources of financing, which, allegedly, helped to smooth out the difficult times of the Mexican crisis (Wierzba and Golla 2005).

On the one hand, and as a result of the Mexican crisis, firms' debt further increased, even though banks became an even more important source of financing for non-financial firms (Figure 9.1). On the other hand, the increased capitalisation targets established by Basel plus largely favoured the concentration of the financial sector: the new regulations required an important capitalisation effort, which many banks could not cope with. As a result, many of them had to face liquidation or acquisition by larger banks (Blejer and Rozenwurcel 2000).

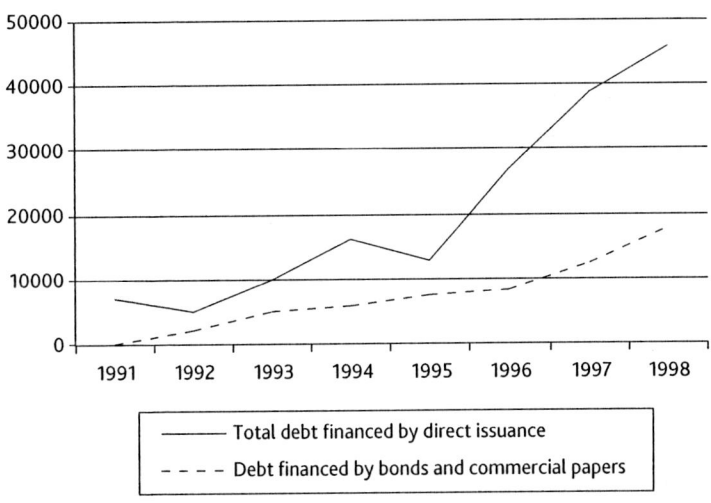

Figure 9.1 Non-Financial Firms' External Debt per Year, Issuance vs. Direct Credit (US$m)

Source: FLACSO (2002)

As a result, the financial system underwent a fundamental transformation. The ten largest banks went from holding 59 per cent of deposits in 1995 to holding 74 per cent of them in 2001. The five biggest pension funds went from 61 per cent of the market in 1995 to 80 per cent of it in 2001. A similar tendency was experienced by the 10 biggest investment funds: 74 per cent of the segment in 1995, 87 per cent in 2001 (Wierzba and Golla 2005).

The concentration in the supply of credit was associated with a bifurcation of the market: access to credit was increasingly difficult for small and medium firms.[19] By the end of the decade, a small or medium enterprise was subject to a rate of interest, on average, 1.9 times higher than the rate that a big enterprise could pay in the local financial market, 3.5 times what a big firm had to pay on a negotiable obligation, and 5.2 times the Libor rate (BCRA 2011). Moreover, measures that had worked for decades of industrial policy, such as negative interest rates by tax agencies at national as well as at local levels, were no longer available (FIEL 1996). For bigger firms, this transformation meant the replacement of traditional sources of financing with bank credit, which increased continuously throughout the decade. Figure 9.1 shows how, after a reduction in bank debt from 1992, non-financial private firms increasingly used bank credit rather than other forms of debt during the decade, the only exception being the year of the Mexican crisis.

The painful effects of the credit market bifurcation were even more impressive if compared to real economy figures: small and medium size companies achieved only 20 per cent of the financing possibilities, even though they generated 2,500,000 jobs, about 62 per cent of the total employment (Blejer and Rozenwurcel 2000).

9.3.2.2 Big Fish Eat Little Fish, or 'the Ruin of Many Small Capitalists'[20]

Unsurprisingly, as a consequence of this transformation in the credit market the economy experienced a process of centralisation through an enormous wave of mergers and acquisitions (M&As). In analysing these corporate actions, two distinct tendencies can be teased out: the increasing involvement of the transnational corporations within the Argentinean economy (mainly addressed in this subsection), and the internationalisation strategy of the Argentinean conglomerates (mainly addressed in the next subsection).

Overall, between 1992 and 1999 centralisation and the sale of privatised companies translated into 900 changes in ownership; foreign companies made 88 per cent of the acquisitions for a total sum of more than US$ 55 billion. This means that the entrance of foreign companies should not be underestimated from a macroeconomic point of view: capital inflows associated with acquisitions showed an upward trend for the entire decade, peaking in 1997, when 308 acquisitions were completed for a total of US$ 15,110 million. Technically, these inflows guaranteed the sustainability of monetary stability, lending legitimacy to a government that was able to end hyperinflation by anchoring the exchange rate to the US dollar. It is important to remind the reader that memories of the 1989 hyperinflation and the frustrating queues to exchange pesos for dollars were still vivid.

The main targets of this huge number of acquisitions were the stakes in ex-state companies, which were sold to the private sector at prices lower than their market values and were free of debt at the beginning of 1990s (Azpiazu 1998, 2002). These were now delivering a profitability higher than similar activities elsewhere: for example, in the United States, the United Kingdom and France a normal rate of profit on net assets for water and sewage service providers was considered to be between 6 and 7 per cent. The average rate of profit in the same sector in Argentina was about 16 per cent (Rodríguez-Boetsch 2005). In the case of telephone services, Telecom Argentina generated an average rate of profit three times larger than its parent companies, France Telecom and Telecom Italia, while Telefónica Argentina was twice as profitable as Telefónica de España (Abeles, Forcinito and Schorr 2001). Another telling example comes from the two companies in charge of natural gas transportation, whose average rate of return was 40 per cent; a reasonable rate of return for this sector would have been between 10 and 20 per cent (Azpiazu 2003). These assets were acquired by non-financial as well as by financial firms: paradigmatic is the example of Exel investment fund (founded by a former executive of City Corporation), which acquired shopping malls and property developments across the country (http://www.bloomberg.com, 2011).

Even within the Argentinean economy, privatised firms showed higher returns on sales compared with other firms (Table 9.3).

Table 9.3   Return on Sales of Privatised and Non-Privatised Companies, 1991–97

Return on sales (top 200 private firms)	1991–95	1995–97	1991–97
Privatised firms	10.6	12.0	11.0
Non-privatised firms	3.1	3.0	2.9
Firms holding shares in privatised	6.5	8.5	7.1
Firms not holding shares in privatised	2.4	1.5	1.9

Source: Kulfas (2001, p. 50)

This high profitability had a number of sources: the lax regulatory framework in which privatisation was carried out increased concentration and market power in the privatised sectors (Azpiazu 1998, 2003; Basualdo 2006; Schorr 2006). Also, even though the stabilisation measure had ruled out any automatic inflation indexation, providers of public services and utilities were allowed to increase tariffs even above domestic inflation, in line with the US inflation rate. The reason for this, it was argued, was that they had to import inputs from the USA (Azpiazu 1998). However, an important source of increased profitability was the profound process of restructuring allowed by the new labour regulations. A few examples may clarify the magnitude of this phenomenon: within four years after privatisation, the steel sector went from 32,000 to 16,000 employees; formal jobs at YPF went from 37,000 to 9,350 (about one third of employees continued to be employed as freelance service providers); in Entel half of the employees were laid off: out of 45,000, 80 per cent of these lost their formal jobs and 20,000 of them became freelance personnel (Etchemendy 2001; Schvarzer 2001).

The above examples show how the 1990s were not only a matter of intra-capital conflict. Also these examples have to be read in conjunction with the fact that, increasingly, Argentinean conglomerates were more concerned with capturing value by buying, restructuring and selling companies than with productive activities: companies were increasingly perceived as bundles of assets to be assembled and exchanged rather than as instruments of value creation.

Accordingly, the sales of such increasingly profitable firms provided important capital gains to the sellers (banks and conglomerates that had acquired them in the context of the Brady Plan). Paradigmatic were the cases of Entel, the state telephone company, divided into Telefónica de Argentina (bought by Telefónica de España and Citicorp Equity Investment) and Telecom Argentina (acquired by France Telecom and Stet/Telecom Italia). The conglomerates Soldati, Techint, Pérez Companc and the bank J.P. Morgan invested about US$ 300 million to buy their stakes at the beginning of the decade and realised around US$ 1,400 million in total when they sold them: the annual return on these investments has been calculated as 20.9 per cent for Soldati (Sociedad Commercial del Plata), 34.8 per cent for Techint (Catalina), 20.8 per cent Grupo Pérez Companc (Inter Río Holding) and up to 54.8 per cent for J.P. Morgan (Abeles, Forcinito and Schorr 2002).

Given the integrated investment strategies of domestic and foreign firms operating in Argentina in both the real and the financial spheres, we cannot talk about relations between financial and real capitals. Rather, it is more accurate to describe these connections in terms of linkages.[21] The fact that during the 1990s firms traditionally operating in the real sector were realising gains in financial activities and firms traditionally operating in the financial sector were expanding towards commercial and productive activities makes this exploration much more complex: the distinction between real and financial becomes more blurred and increasingly difficult to analyse. The approach taken by the present chapter is to consider the buying of firms, their restructuring and their subsequent sales as genuine financial activities which contributed to the repositioning of the capital operating in Argentina (of both domestic and foreign origins) in different real sectors.

The next section focuses on how the funds realised by these sales were used by the Argentinean conglomerates in their international expansion.

9.3.2.3 'Where Did the Money Go'?

In Michelangelo Antonioni's film *The Eclipse*, Monica Vitti meets her stockbroker lover after a catastrophic day of tumbling crisis on the bourse. 'Millions were lost', he says, distraught. 'Where did the money go?' she asked' (Chick 1987, p.124). In Chick's paper the question refers to the speculative activity of the financial markets, where, of course, no real money was involved. In this case, however, the same question refers to the investment of the realised funds from the sale of ex-state companies and the increased external debt.

As discussed in the previous section, the radical literature of FLACSO reports that the Argentinean conglomerates mainly invested in financial assets, especially government bonds, whose yields were kept high by the increasing public external debt. This justifies, empirically, the process of financialisation and the subsequent intra-capital conflict which *transformismo* was unable to negotiate. As discussed, according to the DSP, this inability led the financial fraction to capture the state and eventually provoked the crisis.

In reality, it is necessary to highlight, first, that the Argentinean conglomerates did not pursue a homogenous investment strategy. Some conglomerates abandoned their core productive activities and acquired financial assets. For example, the group Astra sold its oil company to acquire an investment fund. However, this was not a widespread strategy: Techint adopted a strategy of consolidation and expansion in its core sectors by acquiring the second-largest company in the country, the state-owned Somisa. A third strategy was based on diversification: some groups, in anticipation of a likely devaluation, pursued an intense diversification towards the tradable sector and invested in agribusiness. This was the case with the Pérez Companc Family Group (which bought stakes in the biggest food-processing company, Molinos de Río), the Gruneissen family, and the Macri Group. The Mastellone and Bunge-Born families abandoned their manufacturing activities to concentrate on the production and trading of agricultural products, and bought conspicuous amounts of land. Land acquisition was engaged in by a number of relatively small groups, such as Loma Negra, Bemberg, Werthein and Ledesma. These groups, together with the Bunge-Born Group, became the owners of about 17 per cent of the total arable land in the province of Buenos Aires (Basualdo 2006).

Second, the Argentinean conglomerates were not exclusively interested in investing in financial assets to exploit interest-rate differentials kept high by public debt. Evidence suggests that they finally invested their resources abroad in real assets, mainly by buying privatised companies and government concessions, not only in the rest of Latin America, but also in Europe and North America. The ratio between financial and real assets, mentioned by the FLACSO literature as a proof of financialisation, increased to 32 per cent in 1996 and decreased to less than 29 per cent (the 1980s average) in 1999. This can be interpreted in terms rather of precautionary motives than of a structural change towards a new system of accumulation based on finance: to illustrate this point, it is necessary to explain that, with the exchange rate established at parity with the dollar, Argentineans could buy assets in pesos (which carried both country and currency risk), in *argendolares* (i.e. dollar-denominated assets and cash kept within the country, which carried country risk but not currency risk), or in dollars outside the country (which carried neither of the two risks). In periods of financial turmoil, Argentineans turned from pesos to *argendolares* and from these to dollars. Since cash and financial instruments were easily moved out of the country, a temporary increase of financial assets relative to real assets was to be expected. Once these were moved out of the country, the sale of ex-state companies and the returns on financial investments could be fully realised. However, the transfer of these resources abroad also served to finance the internationalisation of the Argentinean conglomerates and to allow them to take the opportunity to invest in other countries' privatisation processes.

Third, and in relation to the previous point, funds could be shifted abroad in cash or in financial assets: a number of new financial instruments and regulatory arrangements facilitated capital outflows.[22] Government bonds were ideal instruments that could be used to buy other assets abroad, thus avoiding the restrictions of the central bank. The enforcement of stricter regulation, it was argued, would reduce the depth of the bond market (Wierzba and Golla 2005). As a result, Argentinean conglomerates did not invest in domestic government bonds only because of their high yields. Additionally, investors also used the stock market to shift funds out of Argentina, mainly to the United States. This was accomplished by purchasing Argentinean shares listed in the United States and traded as American depositary receipts (ADRs). Shares were converted into ADRs and sold in the USA. While ADRs and underlying share prices typically trade in a very narrow range, during the time when ADR conversions were permitted in Argentina, a large premium existed on share prices in Argentina compared with ADR prices. This premium reflected the capital loss expected on peso investments in Argentina and the value of capital control avoidance (Melvin 2003; Comisión Especial Investigadora de la Cámara de Diputados 2005). This practice was made illegal only after the 2001 crisis. Also, within the Mercosur area, private banking operations could be carried out only up to a limit of US$2 million.

Further proof that conglomerates invested in real assets abroad is shown by the fact that financial assets increased in absolute terms, but remained a relatively low proportion of the total assets that Argentinean residents held abroad. During the 1990s, investment of financial-sector firms outside the country increased fourfold, while funds invested abroad by the non-financial sector doubled. Nevertheless, at the end of the 1990s about 90 per cent of the total assets kept abroad by Argentineans belonged to non-financial firms: outward foreign direct investments increased threefold during the period (Table 9.4).

Similarly to their operating strategy in Argentina, Argentinean conglomerates formed consortia with local or multinational companies in the rest of Latin America to acquire privatised assets or government concessions to run public services. This, of course, raises the question of how various national states compete to attract foreign capital, not only by providing high spreads appealing to international capital markets and tax incentives for FDIs, but also by more or less openly inviting foreign companies to acquire attractive state assets.

Techint, for example, formed a joint venture with the second-largest steel producer in Japan, and signed agreements with the Canadian Algoma Steel and the Brazilian Confab with the aim of exploiting

Table 9.4 Capital Outflow from Argentinean Residents by Destination during the Period 1992–98 (US$m)

	1992	1993	1994	1995	1996	1997	1998
Financial sector	4,300	6,065	6,563	7,469	11,377	17,362	16,546
Direct investments	921	921	1,106	1,261	1,466	1,494	1,451
Indirect investments (equity and bonds)	27	64	78	146	845	1,291	930
Liquid assets	2,473	4,032	3,980	3,640	5,770	8,283	6,443
Loans and other credits	879	1,048	1,399	2,422	3,296	6,294	7,722
Non-financial sector	54,154	56,500	62,706	75,277	82,073	91,075	96,983
Direct investments	4,871	5,575	6,402	7,770	9,140	12,282	14,298
Real estate	2,984	3,197	3,456	3,668	3,821	3,956	4,084
Others	1,887	2,378	2,946	4,102	5,319	8,326	10,214
Deposits	15,304	14,612	15,912	19,002	20,566	21,154	21,333
Other assets	29,108	30,738	33,990	40,735	43,227	45,357	47,054
Total	58,454	62,565	69,269	82,746	93,450	108,437	113,529

Source: INDEC (2010)

corresponding markets (Kulfas 2001). Pérez Companc was very active in various privatisation processes across Latin America, especially in its core business.[23]

All the large Argentinean conglomerates, including Macri, Pérez Companc, Arcor, Bunge and Born, IMPSA and Bemberg, installed new subsidies and production lines in Mercosur countries. For example, by 1997 Sideco Americana (Macri Group) was conducting its waste management businesses in Brazil in a joint venture with a subsidiary of Waste Management Inc., the world's leading company in the sector. The Macri group also moved part of its automobile production to Brazil in order to exploit export incentives significantly more advantageous than those in Argentina during the period (Leipziger et al. 1997). However, the group underwent a major repositioning towards the Brazilian public services and food industries as well. Roggio was also involved in Brazil in infrastructure projects. Other conglomerates invested heavily in state assets in the rest of Latin America, outside the Mercosur countries. For example, in the oil sector, Pérez Companc and Soldati invested in the privatisation of energy in Venezuela, Peru, Bolivia, Brazil, Ecuador and other Central American countries. The largest Argentinean conglomerate, Pérez Companc, pursued an important internationalisation strategy by selling stakes in its Argentinean non-core business, such as Telefonica, and by acquiring privatised energy companies in its core business across Latin America, in Bolivia (1998), Venezuela (1994), Peru (1996) and Ecuador (2000) (Figure 9.2).

Some conglomerates expanded their activities beyond neighbouring countries. For example, Bridas had interests in Turkmenistan and IMPSA reached the Philippines. Techint, given its owner's Italian origins, combined investments in Latin America and in the rest of the world, especially in Italy, not only expanding existing business, but also branching out in very different directions. In 1994 it bought the Veracruz mill in Mexico and acquired the privatised Venezuelan Siderúrgica del Orinoco (SIDOR) and the privatised Dalmine seamless pipe mill in Italy. Many operations were undertaken in participation with other international firms and banks. For example, in 1996, as part of an investor group that included Ansaldo (a unit of the privatised former Finmeccanica), Sondel (a unit of Falck), Ruhrkohle, and Destec Energy (a unit of Dow Chemical), Techint acquired Carbosulcis from the Italian state-owned Ente Nazionale Idrocarburi (ENI). In 1996, an investor group consisting of Mannesmann, Techint and Fiatimpresit (a unit of the Italian government-subsidised Fiat), planned to acquire a

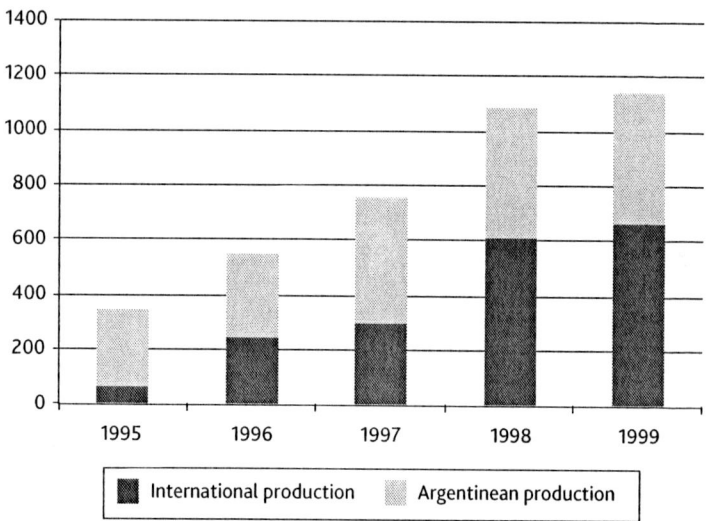

Figure 9.2 Internationalisation of Pérez Companc (average daily production, thousand barrels of oil equivalent)

Source: Pérez Companc Financial Information, various years

majority interest in the Italian state-owned Innocenti Sant'Eustachio. It also acquired an interest in the newly privatised operations in Venezuela, Bolivia, Brazil, Ecuador, Mexico, Peru and Colombia. However, Techint also diversified away from its core business by acquiring Humanitas Hospital in Milan (Italy), and in 2000 the Gavazzeni Hospital, Bergamo, both government-paid services. Furthermore, in 2000, an investor group led by Interbanca and Techint invested in the privatised telecommunications cable-laying service provider, Telecom Italia SPA. The acquisition of these highly diversified investments evolved mainly around the provision of inputs for state-owned companies or the acquisition of state assets in various countries. By the beginning of 2000, the group had 40 per cent of its assets outside Argentina.

In summary, this analysis suggests that each conglomerate had a diverse strategy as a result of a number of factors, including the advantages of exploiting other state interventions across the rest of the region. So Argentinean large capital cannot be lumped together under the same flag as domestic capital, other than as a collection of diverse agents in economic restructuring.

Finally, in aggregate terms, some figures may give an idea of the importance of the hard-currency flight which, in 2001 alone, amounted to US$18 billion, US$14 billion for companies and almost US$4 billion for individuals, many of whom were members of the conglomerate families (Comisión Especial de la Camera de Diputados 2005). However, the amount reported from the currency flight official documentation reflects only what was registered by the central bank. There are various estimates of capital flight towards various currencies in the region of US$130–140 billion (Gaggero, Casparrino and Libman 2007). However, it is interesting to know that, by the end of the decade, the very same conglomerates that had accumulated external debt were taking hard currency abroad, especially from March 2001.

The public sector financed this flight by keeping the fixed exchange rate: the current account was in deficit during the decade and consistently compensated for by the capital account. During the first part of the decade, this compensation was assured by capital inflows aimed at the acquisition of privatised firms. On the contrary, at the end of the decade the reversal of capital inflows endangered the fixed exchange rate, which became sustained by public external debt alone (an annual average of more than US$8 billion) (BCRA 2010). Public external debt made up about 86 per cent of total external debt at the beginning of the decade. This declined to 63 per cent in 2001. By the end of the decade, about half of private debt was concentrated in the top 20 non-financial companies (ENGE 1999).

9.4 CONCLUSIONS

The account presented in this chapter has implications in terms of the role of the state in shaping the part played by finance during the evolution of the Argentinean external debt and its sovereign default. Rather than being a state captured by the power of finance at the expense of industrial development, the Argentinean state continued to support the accumulation strategies of the conglomerates, whose interests had been served by state companies during the previous decades.

More specifically, first, this empirical account has shown how certain policies may be opposed or supported depending on how they interact with existing interests: so, for example, privatisation was resisted for a long time in Argentina until it was eventually adopted in very particular conditions. Second, the transformation of the credit system supported a specific pattern of accumulation based on centralisation. Third, the chapter has also shown how the separation between finance and real capital was an artificial categorisation that was instrumentally used by the Argentinean DSP in order to blame, as the cause of the 2001 crisis, the lack of state autonomy due to the rise of finance. In reality, Argentinean capital became increasingly involved in various sectors of the economy, both domestically and abroad. The Argentinean conglomerates had a wide range of financing and investment opportunities, both inside and outside Argentina, in the tradable and in the non-tradable sectors, and in the real as well as in the financial sectors. Very often their interests were reshaped across different sectors during the decade. There is sufficient evidence to suggest that it would be impossible to disentangle the interests of financial and real, or domestic and foreign capitals, so intermingled were they.

NOTES

1. The members of this school are leading intellectuals in Latin America, though they are less well-known in the English language tradition. The authors of studies included in the bibliography who belong to this school are M. Arceo, D. Azpiazu, E. Basualdo, M. Kulfas, C. Lozano, C. Nahón, H. Nochteff, J. Nun and M. Schorr.
2. In the literature on the East Asian countries, this question has been resolved by assuming a self-termination of the developmental state once its developmental outcome has been achieved (Fine and Rustomjee 1996).
3. The notion of embedded autonomy represented the basis for a redefinition of the developmental state in the work of Evans, where autonomy is central to the state's effectiveness. Embedded autonomy depends on 'an apparently contradictory combination of Weberian bureaucratic insulation with intense immersion in the surrounding social structure' (Evans 1989, p.574). Embeddedness and autonomy would not work in isolation: 'a state that was only autonomous would lack both sources of intelligence and the ability to rely on decentralised private implementation', while a state that is only embedded is subject to capture and dismembering (Schneider 1998): 'Only when embeddedness and autonomy are joined together can a state be called developmental' (p.12).
4. *Trasformismo* has its origins in Italy in 1876. It had negative connotations, inasmuch as it served to describe a way to 'buy' political consensus through corruption and, more generally co-optation. Gramsci re-elaborated the concept. *Trasformismo* was not a sort of 'original sin' of the Italian political system owing to the polarisation of the latter; it was, rather, an accurately studied, specific strategy, implemented by dominant classes to absorb and accommodate the elites of other political forces in order to annihilate their political representation. In this respect, Basualdo affirms that, thanks to the Argentine *trasformismo*, the dominant classes replaced the physical annihilation of the dictatorship with the decapitation of the organised movements of the working class (Basualdo 2006, p.58). This process has then shaped the relation between the working class and the dominant classes in a way that has been fundamentally different

to the experience of other democracies that are based on the alternation of two political parties.
5. Financial valorisation can be defined as the 'collocation by big firms of surplus in various financial assets (titles, bonds, deposits) in both the domestic and the international markets' (Schorr 2006, p.17). Basualdo (2006) defines 'financial valorisation' in Argentina as a new social system of accumulation that started with military rule and was completed during the 1990s. Its determinants were the high spreads maintained by high levels of public debt. The existence of financial valorisation is said to be demonstrated by the increase in the ratio of financial assets to physical assets registered on the balance sheets of the manufacturing companies.
6. Furthermore, the fixed exchange rate could guarantee the return of the financial assets in dollars (rather than in 'unsafe' pesos).
7. Founded by Domingo Peron in 1947, the party was identified with Argentinean populism. It ruled the country for most of its democratic life (with the exclusion of the years of military regimes). It was the party of both Menem, who implemented privatisation and liberalisation in the 1990s, and Kirchner, who is currently renationalising state companies.
8. Financialisation was taken from the heterodox economic literature to explain the changing role of the financial sector (see Stockhammer 2000, for example, for a theoretical approach).
9. This division of capital, it was argued, had considerable implications even for monetary policy and the management of the 2001 financial crisis: the two fractions of capital supported devaluation, which had to boost primary commodity export, and dollarisation, which had to guarantee financial asset returns in dollars, respectively (Basualdo 2001, 2006).
10. Privatisation and liberalisation were adopted during a hyperinflationary crisis.
11. In 2001, an Argentinean federal court declared a large part of the Argentinean external debt as illegal, because it was an odious debt (see Krakowiak 2005 for a definition).
12. For a detailed exposition related to various sectors, see Etchemendy (2001) and Kulfas (2001).
13. Payments of service and principal were suspended without a formal moratorium declaration (Kulfas and Schorr 2003a).
14. Basel I is the 1988 Basel Accord which primarily focused on credit risk. Assets of banks were classified into five categories according to credit risk. Asset risk was represented by a weight ranging from 0 (no risk) to 100. Banks with international business had a capital requirement of 8 per cent of the risk-weighted assets.
15. In 1989 George H.W. Bush became president of the USA and promoted a new relationship between his country and Argentina, supporting Argentina's policies even in the face of IMF opposition – for example, with respect to the Convertibility Law. For an account of the new attitude of the US government towards Argentina within the post-Berlin Wall context and the influence of the US government on the relations between the IMF and Argentina, see Cavallo (2004).
16. The programme's general mechanism was based on the fact that banks agreed to restructure their claims in return for guarantees. To qualify, the plan stipulated that debtor countries should undertake policies aimed at increasing domestic

saving and foreign investment and promoting the return of flight capital (Sachs 2001). Secretary Brady proposed

> a series of individual market-based transactions [with the creation of a secondary market in which Brady Bonds could be traded] in which (i) creditors would be invited to participate voluntarily, (ii) debt relief would be tied into the conversion of loans into collateralised bonds, (iii) debtor nations would be permitted to repurchase their own discounted debt on the secondary market and (iv) debt-equity schemes would be promoted ... [This was seen as] a strong call for the development of capital-market-based solutions, and an official acceptance that some debt forgiveness was essential. (Buckley 1997, p.1804)

The Argentinean debt resulted from the absorption of a considerable proportion of the private foreign debt. This explains, to a great extent, the jump in the participation of the public sector in total debt. 'It should also be stressed that no haircut provided relief to the public debt in the early eighties default situation: this would only come late and in homeopathic doses with the Brady agreement in 1992–93' (Damill and Frenkel 2005, p.14). Out of its US$6 billion in interest arrears, Argentinean debt reduction was of only US$2 billion (Damill and Frenkel 2005).

17. The Convertibility Law was the core of the stabilisation measures adopted at the beginning of the decade. It sanctioned the hard peg with the US dollar and froze the automatic inflation indexation of salaries and tariffs.
18. Centralisation of capital and the role of credit in this is described in Marx (1990, p.393).
19. Small and medium firms are those not listed in the top 500 companies by turnover (ENGE 1993–97).
20. Marx (1990, p.777).
21. Within development economics, the term was made famous by Hirschman (1958, for example). Fine (1992) follows the definition of linkages as the effects of an economic activity on another and argues that Hirschman neglected both an analysis of the agents who bring linkages about and of the relation between agents and linkages (for example, whether agents are forced or willing to bring linkages about).
22. Of course, these were in addition to traditional instruments used to take capital abroad, such as sub-invoicing and over-invoicing of imports and exports, respectively.
23. Pérez Companc website, accessed on 10 February 2011.

10
Systems of Accumulation and the Evolving South African MEC

Sam Ashman, Ben Fine and Susan Newman

10.1 INTRODUCTION

The limitations of the developmental state paradigm (DSP) were discussed in the introductory chapter to this volume. This chapter offers an alternative approach to the DSP, using the notion of systems of (capital) accumulation, and with specific application to South Africa's evolving political economy, which, following Fine and Rustomjee (1996), we characterise as the 'minerals–energy complex' (MEC).[1] Using this notion we reveal what a systems-of-accumulation approach can achieve relative to what the DSP cannot. The argument is focused on South Africa, but relates also to more general theoretical questions about the relationship between the general tendencies of capitalist development, how to specify capitalist formations, the role of 'middle-range theory', and how to account for ongoing differentiation within global capitalism. We seek to marry abstract laws and tendencies of capitalist development with the analysis of specific class relations, social formations, and their many concrete determinations. Whilst capital has powerful tendencies which universalise features of development, these never settle nor are they reproduced in exactly the same way in concrete social formations. Analysis needs therefore to trace the particular historical development and articulation of capitalist relations. In particular, we argue that through an emphasis on class relations and dynamics situated in the context of the world economy, it is possible to integrate the analyses of:

1. different spatial scales, in a manner which recognises that national capital relations are conditioned by global capital relations, but that they also contribute to and are constitutive of the global whole;

2. economics and politics (including the state), through emphasis on evolving class relations and conflicts and the ways in which these are reflected in patterns of accumulation and economic and social reproduction;
3. the role played by finance and its impact on class formation;
4. labour, through foregrounding understanding of capital as a social relation.

In South Africa itself, the term 'MEC' has gained some currency, and has been employed (and extended) in a number of recent analyses (e.g. Bond and Ndlovu 2010; Hallowes 2010; Marais 2011; Mbeki 2009). The term has even been used casually by members of the South African Chamber of Mines – though on the assumption that the domination of the economy by mining and energy is a good thing. Rigorous understanding of this notion in the sense in which it is employed here needs it to be tied firmly both to its 'parent' notion of a system of accumulation and to a broader theoretical understanding of the abstract tendencies and dynamics of capitalism on a world scale. The separation of different dimensions of analysis is a general limitation of institutionalist economics, especially given the predilection of the latter for 'methodological nationalism', and its insistence upon the importance of institutions without adequately tying them to an underlying political economy of capitalism. Emphasis on institutions, or on corresponding middle-range theory more generally, is also a limitation of some forms of Marxist political economy, such as the Regulation School or the Social Structures of Accumulation approach. To develop concrete historical analyses, Marxist political economy best proceeds by linking together the abstract and the concrete in a unified framework or dialectic of mediations.

In many respects, this is exactly the opposite of what has been attempted by the immediately mentioned approaches when they have been applied to South Africa. For the Regulation school, as represented by Gelb (1991), the notion of Fordism was hijacked and forcibly married with apartheid to produce the notion of racial Fordism. Thus, one indisputable empirical characteristic, institution even, was analytically imposed upon Fordism, irrespective of the theoretical and empirical merits of the latter.[2] This soon gave birth to its 'flexible specialisation', post-Fordist version (ISP 1995), an even more blatantly superimposed and alien analytical construct on South African realities (Fine 1995).

Otherwise, Heintz (2002, 2010) has sought to incorporate South Africa into the Social Structures of Accumulation approach. In its construction, this is more attuned to South African realities than the Regulation approaches, but draws more or less arbitrarily and judiciously upon empirically observed characteristics of the South African formation to frame the structures of accumulation. But why is one characteristic chosen rather than another, and how are we to identify the causal factors that underpin these characteristics and their interaction, especially when accumulation is punctured by crises of the social structures (such as the demise of apartheid)?

In short, such approaches suffer from some combination of imposing 'foreign' frameworks on South Africa and deploying more or less casual empirical observation as a theoretical factor that, inevitably, is found to be both justified on its terrain of application and suspended from deeper, systemic explanation. But is the MEC (as the South African system of accumulation) open to the same criticism of being middle-range or empiricist? Significantly, the MEC was first proposed in the context of a specific rejection of the DSP (although lessons were drawn from the South Korean experience) (Fine and Rustomjee 1996). This was because of the judgement that the state–market dichotomy as analytical prime mover is particularly inapplicable to South Africa, where class relations and interests have been formed through both the state and market according to the interests acting upon and through them. And, unlike J.K. Galbraith's military–industrial complex, with which it shares at most a partial nomenclature, the MEC is not formed simply out of a coincidence of given interests. Rather, the MEC is the historically derived dynamic of capitalist accumulation peculiar to South Africa's political economy.

Our discussion of South Africa, therefore, relies, however implicitly, on a general theoretical argument, as well as providing a close analysis of the most industrialised society in Africa, where discussion of the notion of the 'developmental state' (DS) has most recently been particularly intense (see Ashman, Fine and Newman 2010a; Edigheji 2010).[3] We have argued previously that, despite the self-pronounced desire to become a DS, South Africa is particularly *unlike* one as that is understood in the literature on East Asia or, more broadly, one where high rates of growth were the product of high levels of investment in strategic industries, creating a pattern of production and investment which would not have arisen without state intervention and, famously, without 'getting prices wrong' in pursuit of domestic industrialisation (Amsden 1989). South Africa instead has, since the defeat of apartheid in 1994, been in key respects the antithesis of a DS. The government explicitly adopted a neoliberal macroeconomic framework from 1996 onwards with the Growth, Employment and Redistribution (GEAR) programme. Despite its name, GEAR was neither employment-centred nor redistributive. The results of the deregulation of financial markets, tariff reduction and trade liberalisation have been capital flight and deindustrialisation combined with (sectoral) corporate concentration and the relative absence of strategic industrial policy.[4]

As a consequence, South Africa's pattern of economic and industrial development remains heavily skewed towards the industries around which racial segregation and apartheid grew, highly dependent on world commodity prices and vulnerable to currency crises when commodity prices collapse, and lacking in secondary industrialisation and employment, while financialisation and capital export have contributed to widening inequality, jobless growth and lack of investment. Indeed calls for South Africa to become a DS gained momentum in response to growing anger and frustration with the lack of post-apartheid change and achievement, and the ANC announced its intention that South Africa should become a DS in a discussion document (ANC 2005) which criticises Washington Consensus policies, despite the country having implemented them itself, for failing to bring about economic development. The notion of a DS has, then, become politically contested, uniquely so and beyond the realms of academia, in terms of disputing its substantive content: for some, it is a platform around which to mobilise for greater state intervention and reform in the interests of the majority; but for others it is the ideological form taken by neoliberal business as usual. This is indicative of a tension within the South African state between the discursive shift in using the DS to create a 'New Growth Path' (EDD 2010) and the substantial continuities which remain in policies and outcomes that have prompted that shift.

This chapter, then, makes some arguments about South Africa but is also theoretically self-aware. For a critical question for Marxist political economy is how to move from abstract categories of value and capital to an understanding of concrete forms of class society in time and space – ascending from the simple or the abstract to the complex and combined (the concrete being the unity of many determinations) – a movement which also goes from the concrete to the abstract in a two-way process (Marx 1973; Ilyenkov 1982). How do we integrate theory, history and empirical analysis without collapsing into empiricism? How do we move from capital to capitalism and then to understanding the differences which exist within capitalism? How do we operationalise Marxist theory in a historical and dynamic context, uniting abstract tendencies and concepts to the empirical analysis of the concrete within a unified framework? This requires the close examination of the specific way in which capitalist value relations – including the state form that expresses and mediates class relations – are constructed, organised, reproduced and also influenced by the class struggle itself. And, whilst capital relations are conditioned by global capital relations, they also contribute to, and are constitutive of, the global whole.

These are questions beyond our scope here, but we suggest that the notion of a system of accumulation, conceived in a particular way, can be extremely helpful in moving from abstract concepts to diverse concrete realities. But such 'middle-range' concepts, whilst necessary and revealing to a greater or lesser degree however they are composed, are not a substitute for general, systemic theory, which, if we confine ourselves to Merton's (1968) exposition of middle-range theory, remains at best implicit and at worst fudged. Accordingly, a system of accumulation (not necessarily a national entity) can be seen in broad or narrow terms. Narrowly, it can, for example, be specified as a core set of industrial sectors, with strong linkages with one another and relatively weaker linkages with other sectors, as demonstrated through input–output tables. This is important empirically, as we shall see, though it is compatible with a technicist conceptualisation that we reject. For such core sectors need to be located in relation to the state, finance, class relations and value creation, and the impact of these across society as a whole. As will be discussed in greater depth, South Africa is dominated by the MEC, which incorporates core sectors, but this dominance needs to be understood in conjunction with (not at the expense of) broader considerations (Fine and Rustomjee 1996). As a result of the particular articulation of class relations in South Africa, manufacturing has been confined to a limited number of industries around primary production and has remained weak in the capital- and intermediate-goods sectors. Both apartheid and post-apartheid economies have failed to diversify out of the core base within the MEC, and this structure of production remains critical to understanding South Africa's enduring levels of mass unemployment and its large reserve army of labour (Ceruti 2010). We argue that the MEC has changed over time in the light of both domestic and international developments, which have combined to produce, through the actions of both state and capital, the financialisation of the South African economy alongside its continuing concentration on core MEC sectors. These interactions – the domestic and the global – combine to reproduce the specific contemporary form of the MEC as an evolving system of accumulation.

In this light, we proceed in the next section by specifying the system of accumulation specific to South Africa and the distinctiveness of the MEC analysis as developed by Fine and Rustomjee. In Section 10.3 we look at the historical development of the MEC, placing emphasis on the evolution of class relations, before considering, in Section 10.4, the MEC since 1994 under the impact of neoliberalism and financialisation. In Section 10.5 we review the shifting DS debate in South Africa, arguing that this needs to be situated in terms of the reaction against the neoliberal policies of GEAR. In the concluding section, we comment upon how the DSP has dovetailed with recent political and policy developments within South Africa.

10.2 AN ABBREVIATED HISTORY OF THE MEC AS A SYSTEM OF ACCUMULATION

So what then is the MEC? It is the specifically South African system of accumulation, centred on core sectors around mining and energy, which has evolved with a character and dynamic of its own that has shifted over time. This system of accumulation has determined the economic trajectory of South Africa from the discovery of diamonds and gold in the second half of the nineteenth century to the present day. Since the emergence of capitalist relations in mining, South African economic development has been shaped by an array of interdependencies between fractions of capital, industrial sectors and the state.

The conglomerate structure of the South African economy has its origins in mining. Capitalist relations were first established on the diamond fields of the Northern Cape. 'Diggers' democracy' initially prevailed in the diamond fields of the Northern Cape, where the 'individual small digger was paramount' and legislation curtailed the number of claims per (white) miner (Innes 1984, p.23). But this was transformed in the space of 35 years, from 1867, into a monopolistic structure centred on De Beers Consolidated, with a corresponding reform of legal and political relationships, governed by the need to minimise costs by ensuring large quantities of cheap labour (Innes 1984). The goldfields were first proclaimed in 1886, and a process of capital restructuring parallel to that on the diamond fields took place, and far more rapidly. Involvement of the diamond magnates in gold mining accelerated this process of consolidation, and monopoly institutions such as the joint-stock company or mining finance houses and groups reflected the character of British capitalism of the time. Labour control was intensified through formal labour stratification established in the Gold Law of 1886, whereby the owners of the means of production were to be exclusively white, and 'non-whites' were only tolerated on the fields if they were in the service of white men (Innes 1984).

By the time of the formation of the Pact Government in 1924, consolidation across mining and industry had taken place, with the Anglo American Corporation (AAC), under the control of the Oppenheimer family, at the centre of economic power. Consolidation in this period strengthened monopoly control and brought new areas under the dominance of mining capital. But as Innes argues (1984, pp.111–12)

> Consolidation was not carried through without the eruption of severe economic crises in both branches of the industry; without an intensification of open class conflict through the launching of savage onslaughts against workers in gold (in 1922) and diamonds (during the depression); and without the development of considerable internecine strife and restructuring (especially in diamonds).

Industrial development and diversification up to this point were confined to the development of industries to which mining was backwardly linked, most notably explosives for blasting. By 1911, the chemicals industry was the largest sub-sector of manufacturing, with explosives making up the largest share.

With the rise of Afrikaner nationalism, attempts were made by the state to create and support its own Afrikaner capital, giving rise to a disjuncture between economic power, in the hands of 'English' mining capital, and the political power deployed by the state.[5] The success of this was, however, conditioned by the generation of a surplus in mining and the extent to which part of this surplus could be deployed in subsidising Afrikaner capital. In reality the state was far from monolithic, and industrial development during the interwar period inevitably reflected an uneasy compromise between English mining capital and Afrikaner capital, with a mutual interest in generating and sharing the surplus out of mining as well as in the exploitation of black (migrant) labour in mines, farms and more generally. In the interwar and immediate post-war period, then, core MEC sectors drove the economy, furnishing a surplus for the protection and growth of Afrikaner capital.[6] The establishment of state corporations in electricity, steel and transport (to reduce the cost of industrial inputs) constituted a major step in this accommodation between the economic power of the mining conglomerates and the political power of the Afrikaners – an uneasy compromise of evolving fractions of classes and their interests forged through both the state *and* the market. The repressive labour system was a common bond across all capitals and against labour. But this acted to strengthen core MEC activity rather than to bring about diversification into related sectors, leading to a vacuum in intermediate and capital goods and a failure to accrue economies of scale and scope other than within core MEC sectors. Whilst Afrikaner capital remained weak and small-scale, it could not be promoted on the basis of a broader policy for industrialisation; but nor could mining capital be deployed for the same purpose without the danger of an unacceptable political backlash (and the risk of appropriation of state-supported, diversifying mining conglomerates). The corresponding failure to diversify out of the MEC is signalled in part by the absence of coherent state policy, both for broad aggregate industrial sectors of the economy and for certain sub-sectors of manufacturing, as a consequence of the disjuncture between economic and political power (Fine and Rustomjee 1996).

Towards the end of the interwar period it was increasingly recognised that if Afrikaner capital was to be able to compete with English capital, it could do so only on the basis of larger scale and greater state support. The Afrikaner Economic Movement was initiated in 1934 and was shaped at the first Economiese Volkskongres (People's Economic Congress) in 1939. Initially, it was primarily based upon Afrikaner populism, small-scale enterprise and farming. But with the formation of Anglovaal in the early 1930s a notable accumulation and consolidation of Afrikaner capital did take place in the mining sector, albeit with no direct state assistance. In contrast to the European financing utilised in the rest of the mining sector, Anglovaal grew through indigenous equity financing. Increasingly, though, small-scale capital, whilst still heavily supported by tariff protection and subsidies, was losing out to larger-scale capital in terms of influence. But, despite the increasing significance of larger-scale capital, the weight of Afrikaner capital in national economic activity was not rising, and became the target of concerted action.

Accordingly, the National Finance Corporation (NFC) was created in 1949, not long after the National Party came into power in 1948. The NFC provided an instrument for the channelling of short-term funds into the hands of government bodies. For the first time, there was a major institution in the financial sector that allowed for deposits to be invested in treasury bills and mining debentures rather than having short-term funds re-deposited in London. This development marked a major step in changing the interplay between English capital and the state. Rather than relying solely upon private capital, or finance from Britain, Anglo American Corporation was able to access NFC financing for the development of the Orange Free State Goldfields. The success of the development of the Goldfields in turn channelled financing to the state, which benefited from the 'spread' between deposits and investment through the NFC. This deepened the interdependency between the state and English capital and provided the conditions for the further erosion of the disjuncture between English and Afrikaner capital (Fine and Rustomjee 1996).

These processes of consolidating Afrikaner capital and integrating it with English capital continued into the 1950s with state intervention in industry focused on large-scale investments in electricity[7] and the establishment of Sasol in the fuel and chemicals industry through the involvement of the Industrial Development Corporation (IDC). These sectors were both heavily dependent on demand from the mining sector, and their development contributed to the growth of the MEC core. The 1950s thus saw the growing presence of Afrikaner capital in finance as well as its increasing penetration into core MEC sectors and the strengthening of several important groups including Volskas, Sanlam and Rembrant.[8] These groups were highly centralised and involved in a number of diverse and overlapping activities and, together with Anglovaal and AAC, were able to exert their influence across most sectors of the economy.

The 1960s saw increasing interaction between Afrikaner and English capital and the consolidation of the conglomerate structure, which accelerated with the Sharpeville massacre and the consequent withdrawal of foreign capital, with ownership passing instead to domestic conglomerates. This trend continued into the 1970s with the increased penetration between English and Afrikaner capital and between different factions of Afrikaner capital. By the 1980s, the 'six axes' of private capital which had come to dominate all sectors of the economy, including finance, increased in strength and cohesion through extensive concentration across most of the productive sectors. These six conglomerates – Anglo American Corporation, Sanlam, SA Mutual, Rembrant, Anglovaal and Liberty Life – controlled 84.3 per cent of the Johannesburg Stock Exchange in 1985 (Fine and Rustomjee 1996).

The disjuncture between English and Afrikaner capital had eroded sufficiently to allow coordinated industrial policies to be effective and for diversification out of MEC core activities to be possible. But, with the collapse of both the post-war boom and the Bretton Woods system based on gold at $35 per ounce, and the sharp rise in oil and energy prices, a huge premium attached to expanding the production of both gold and energy. As a result, an industrial strategy for diversification was scarcely considered, let alone adopted. Instead, the 1970s witnessed an extraordinary state-led expansion of gold and energy production, including huge growth in Eskom power generation and the construction of the Sasol II and III plants to convert coal to oil (as a defence against sanctions). In addition to coalmining, electricity and chemicals, the 1970s also saw the expansion of several other manufacturing industries within the MEC core, including aluminium, titanium and platinum smelting. During this period, the apartheid state resembled a DS more closely than at any time in South Africa's history, with its expanded role in large-scale investment in targeted sectors and the coordination of its operations with private capital (Freund 2011).

Into the 1980s, the burgeoning crisis of apartheid also precluded both state and private strategies for industrial promotion. But, whilst the core MEC industries remained central to the economy, capital controls and economic sanctions meant that profits generated internally that were not illegally transferred abroad were confined to accumulation within the South African economy. This gave rise both to further conglomeration across the economy and to the expansion of a huge and sophisticated financial system. Paradoxically, the development of the financial sector saw reductions in the share of investment in long-term physical assets (particularly in the non-MEC sectors) as financial conglomerates reoriented themselves towards short-term and speculative investments, reflecting broader shifts in finance and banking at the global level as well as a shift towards monetarism as economic orthodoxy. MEC conglomerates representing both English and Afrikaner capital shifted increasingly towards outward orientation from the 1970s, exemplified by high levels of illegal capital flight between 1980 and the debt memorandum of 1985, which saw a strengthening of capital controls (Mohamed and Finnof 2005). Towards the end of the 1980s, with the anticipation of political transition, physical investment by the private sector became focused on high-capital-intensity projects that were dependent on export marketing, as a strategy for keeping their assets out of reach of the post-apartheid state to as great an extent as possible (Fine and Rustomjee 1996).

10.3 THE CONTINUING CENTRALITY OF THE MEC

At the sectoral level, the MEC provides an analytical description of historical industrial development in South Africa as skewed in favour of mining and related industries, and of the failure of the emergence of a diversified industrial base. Industrial development in South Africa has been centred on a core set of industrial sectors organised around mining and related activities, which exhibit very strong input–output linkages amongst themselves, and relatively weaker linkages with other sectors.[9] Table 10.1 shows the identification of the MEC core sectors based on input–output tables published by Quantec for 2010. The core MEC sectors remain the same as

Table 10.1 Interdependence of MEC Input–Output Linkages, 2010

MEC subsector	Share of inputs from MEC sectors (% of total)	Share of output to MEC sectors (% of total)
Coal mining	26	90
Gold and uranium ore mining	55	5
Other mining*	23	77
Coke and refined petroleum products	88	18
Basic chemicals	77	60
Other chemicals and man-made fibres	67	37
Plastic products	68	30
Non-metallic minerals	73	8
Basic iron and steel	82	59
Basic non-ferrous metals	91	59
Metal products, excluding machinery	70	41
Machinery and equipment	63	53
Electricity gas and steam	53	47
Non-MEC manufacturing	23	6

* The category other mining includes: extraction of crude petroleum and natural gas; service activities incidental to oil and gas extraction (excluding surveying); mining of iron ore; mining of non-ferrous metal ores, except gold and uranium; stone quarrying, clay and sandpits, mining of diamonds (including alluvial diamonds); mining of chemical and fertiliser minerals; extraction and evaporation of salt; mining of precious and semi-precious stones (except diamonds), asbestos, and other minerals and materials; service activities incidental to mining of minerals.

Source: Quantec, input–output tables, 2011, www.quantec.co.za

those identified by Fine and Rustomjee (1996) based on input–output figures for 1988; 64.4 per cent of productive inputs into the MEC sectors come from the MEC core itself and 53.0 per cent of output from MEC sectors goes back into the MEC core as inputs. The weakness of linkages between the MEC core and non-MEC manufacturing – non-MEC manufacturing sectors draws 23 per cent of its inputs from the MEC core and provides just 6 per cent of inputs into the MEC sectors as a whole – in part explains the extent to which the development of the MEC sectors has occurred at the expense of other manufacturing activities.

This descriptive identification of the MEC reveals the historical importance of the MEC core sectors as a site of accumulation within the South African economy in and of itself. In 1924 the relative contribution of the MEC sectors to GDP stood at around 20 per cent. With a share of 16 per cent of GDP, mining made up the bulk of activities at this time. Between 1924 and 1960 the contribution to GDP of the MEC core fluctuated between 17 per cent and 26 per cent, albeit with a decline in the share of GDP from mining from over 20 per cent in 1933 to just 7 per cent in 1971. The MEC's contribution to GDP fell in the 1960s from 22 per cent to about 17 per cent but rose to a high of 32 per cent in 1980.[10] Between 1994 and 2010, the share of MEC sector output to GDP continues to be significant, fluctuating between 21 per cent and 23 per cent, even though shifting in composition (Figure 10.2).[11] MEC sectors continue to be important earners of foreign exchange, making up just below 60 per cent of total exports. Moreover, mining has increased its share of total exports since 2007, largely because of the rise in gold prices following the onset of the global financial crisis (Figure 10.3). By contrast, non-MEC manufacturing was stagnant between 1960 and 1990, fluctuating within a narrow band of 15–17 per cent of GDP (Fine and Rustomjee 1996, p.81). Non-MEC manufacturing has declined since the 1990s from 22 per cent in 1990 to under 15 per cent in 2010 (Figure 10.1).

A key correlate of the persistence of such a sectoral bias in the industrial composition of output in South Africa is the chronic level of structural unemployment. The unemployment rate, together with inequality, has increased since the end of apartheid; unemployment stood at 25 per cent in the first quarter of 2011.[12] Productive activity within the MEC core tends to be highly capital intensive and the weakness of linkages between the MEC core and other productive sectors means that its expansion has few multiplier effects across

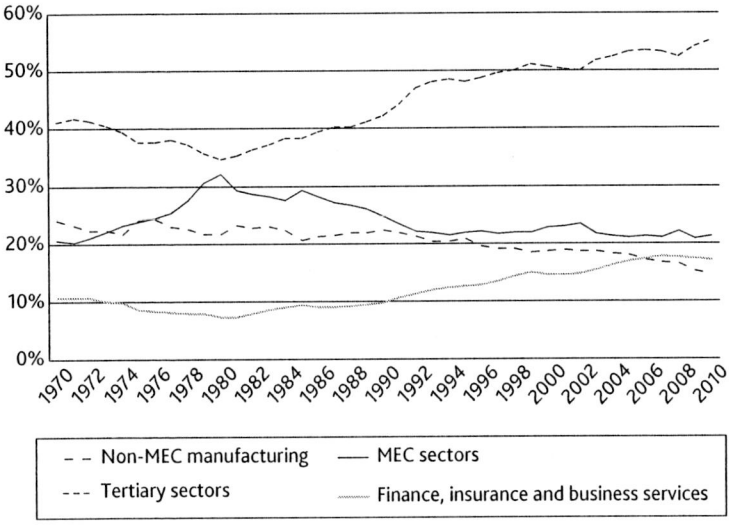

Figure 10.1 GDP Contribution of the MEC, 1970–2010

Source: Authors' calculations, based on data from Quantec, 2011

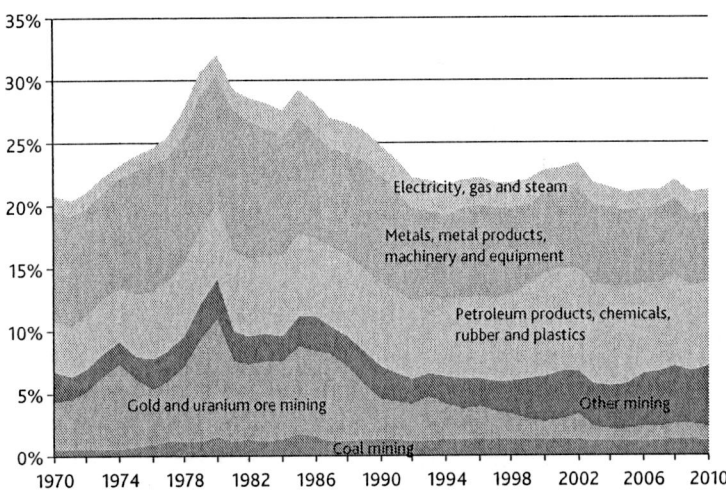

Figure 10.2 GDP Contribution of MEC sectors

Source: Authors' calculations, based on data from Quantec, 2011

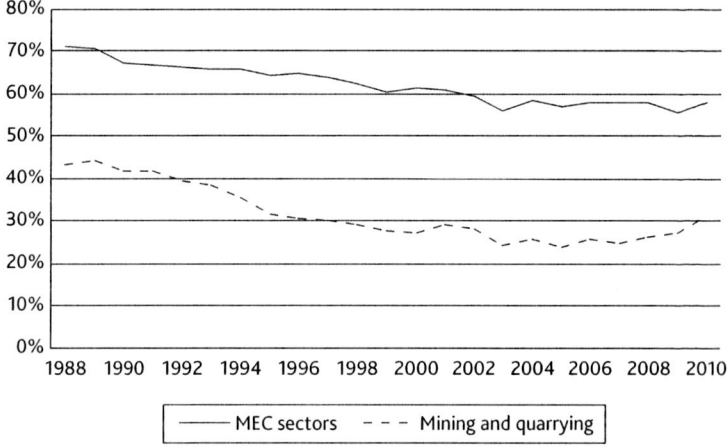

Figure 10.3 MEC Exports as a Percentage of Total Export Value

Source: Authors' calculations, based on data from Quantec, 2011

the economy as a whole. Figure 10.4 shows the sectoral shares of total employment. Employment within the MEC core has been in decline since the late 1980s, decreasing from 1.4 million in 1987 to 1.1 million in 2010 (employment numbers within the MEC were at their lowest point since 1994 at just under 0.9 million in 2001). The share of total employment of the MEC core has fallen below that of non-MEC manufacturing, despite the relatively small and declining weight of the latter.

Over the past decade, the services sector has seen dramatic expansion in terms of its share of GDP and employment, and has been regarded as central to solving the unemployment problem, at least in the short term (ANC 2006; Tregenna 2008). Much of this expansion has taken place in finance and business services, along with wholesale and retail. Employment in these sectors has been highly casualised and precarious (Mohamed 2009; Tregenna 2008). In addition, much of the employment in retail and wholesale, and other personal services, has resulted from debt-driven consumption that came with an expansion of credit in the decade or so prior to the global financial crisis and is, thus, highly susceptible to sudden changes in economic conditions (Mohamed 2009).

Tables 10.2 and 10.3 show the share of fixed capital stock and changes in capital stock, respectively, across economic sectors between 1970 and 2009. The relative shares of capital stock across

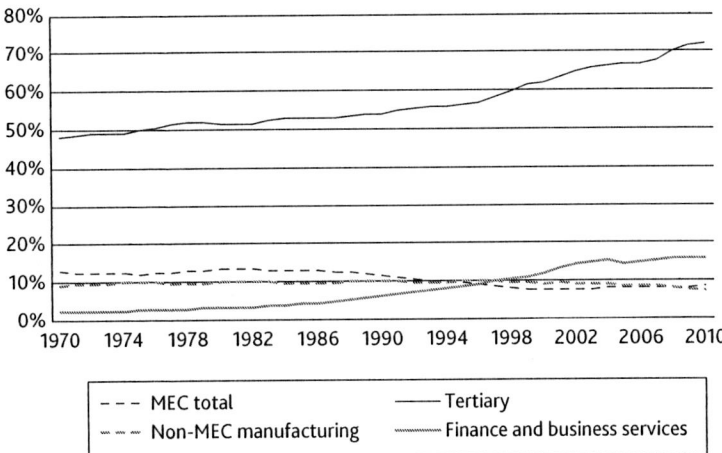

Figure 10.4 Sectoral Shares of Total Employment

Source: Authors' calculations, based on data from Quantec, 2011

economic sectors have remained remarkably unchanged since 1970. The 1970s and 1980s saw enormous physical investment in MEC sectors and, despite a decline in physical investment in the 1990s, the noughties has seen an increase in investment across MEC sectors, and especially in mining, while manufacturing sectors in general and non-MEC manufacturing in particular have experienced an absolute decline in capital stock (Ashman, Fine and Newman 2010b).

Table 10.2 Fixed Capital Stock as a Percentage of Total Fixed Capital Stock in the Economy

	1970	1980	1990	2000	2009
Mining total	6.11%	6.32%	8.59%	7.90%	8.02%
MEC sectors total	15.12%	19.91%	23.30%	22.20%	21.26%
Manufacturing total	8.94%	12.00%	12.10%	13.94%	12.33%
Non-MEC manufacturing	4.03%	3.56%	3.55%	4.05%	4.10%
Non-MEC manufacturing (excluding cars)	3.65%	3.20%	3.13%	3.45%	3.44%
Tertiary sectors	67.94%	66.20%	65.19%	67.07%	68.45%
Finance, insurance and business services	22.55%	20.40%	21.89%	22.57%	22.42%

Source: Authors' calculations, based on data from Quantec, input–output tables, 2011, www.quantec.co.za

Table 10.3 Change in Capital Stock (R billion, at 2005 Prices)

	1970–79	1980–89	1990–99	2000–09
Mining total	43.47	79,549	0.372	60,703
MEC sectors	177.56	162.34	28.72	127.07
Manufacturing total	104.86	46.42	76.87	44.87
Non-MEC manufacturing	17.85	15.17	20.97	30.78
Non-MEC manufacturing (excluding cars)	16.56	12.22	16.71	24.48
Tertiary sectors	494.17	279.63	187.09	527.25
Finance, insurance and business services	130.95	127.92	65.69	156.69

Source: Authors' calculations, based on data from Quantec, input–output tables, 2011, www.quantec.co.za

10.4 THE MEC TODAY

In short, post-apartheid economic development has been marked by the persistence of the MEC as the dominant system of accumulation, although in a different form in view of the evolution of class relations that has taken place with, and since, political transition. The post-apartheid period has seen the strengthening of the influence of capital over the state and policy; a reduction in the concentration of capital among the six large conglomerates, through capital restructuring driven by the need to update outdated (centralised) corporate and managerial structures; increased financialisation and international expansion of the conglomerates; and the shifting structure of capital through 'black economic empowerment' (BEE) deals – the enrichment of those with political and other connections through a variety of means, but who rarely undertake productive investment as opposed to surplus appropriation. A number of commentators, even those broadly sympathetic to the MEC approach, have remarked upon the decline of the importance of the MEC in modern South Africa (Bond 2005; Chabane, Goldstein and Roberts 2006; McDonald 2009) on the grounds of the increasing sectoral share of output and employment in the tertiary sector. We argue that such a conclusion is drawn from an overly technicist reading of the MEC as limited to the sectoral structure of the economy (i.e. to the empirical outcome of the MEC in terms of composition of output alone, and possibly inter-sectoral linkages, important though these are), to the exclusion of an understanding of evolving class relations and the persistence of the MEC in increasingly globalised and financialised forms, sometimes extending beyond its traditional core. On this reading, then, the MEC has survived more or less intact over the post-apartheid period. This is not to say it has remained unchanged; quite the opposite is true, just as it has experienced significant change in the past (as with the incorporation of Afrikaner capital, the growth of financial interests tied to the MEC, and growing conglomerate ownership across the economy). In particular, the South African economy over the post-apartheid period has been driven by financialisation and globalisation. These have dominated both the low pace of domestic accumulation and the form and composition taken by the restructuring of the domestic economy. Whilst the MEC core sectors have strengthened, the fastest-growing sector in the economy over the last 20 years has been finance and related services, now taking as much as 20 per cent of GDP, although 40 per cent of the population benefit from no financial services at all. Domestic levels of investment are half those generally acknowledged to be necessary for DS status.

Financialisation has not only produced credit-based consumption based on speculation in housing markets; it has been accompanied by unprecedented levels of capital flight, much of it illegal and managed by big corporations through transfer pricing. This illegal capital flight was extensive during the apartheid period, but it has now attained new heights (Ashman, Fine and Newman 2011). Such levels of capital flight place the economy permanently on the cusp of instability, with interest rates being held high in order that volatile short-term capital inflows can compensate for long-term outflows. The exchange rate has been held at a high level, with the effect of making capital outflows worth more in foreign currency to those who benefit from them, whilst making it ever more difficult to sustain both the exchange rate and economic growth. And whilst the orthodox macroeconomic policy of GEAR was supposed to attract FDI, growth in FDI inflows between 1996 and 2002 was around 2 per cent per annum; this figure would be even lower if we removed capital inflows from South African corporations that have been relisted abroad (Cronin 2002) and the acquisition by overseas capital of shares in two of South Africa's big four banks. Moreover, though the conglomerate structure has been dismantled to a certain extent, this has only served to create sectoral monopolies, whose profitability depends upon high prices and not on productivity increases. Industrial policy has been token, with the only major exception being the automobile industry. Absent has been any commitment to securing long-term finance for investment in labour-intensive domestic production to meet domestic consumption of basic needs, thereby creating jobs, alleviating unemployment and addressing the inequalities inherited from apartheid.

10.5 THE SHIFTING DEVELOPMENTAL STATE DEBATE IN SOUTH AFRICA

The democratic transition in South Africa also saw the transition of the ANC government from its ideological roots in the Freedom Charter to the apparent wholehearted embracing of neoliberalism. By 1994, the ANC had abandoned almost all of the socially progressive policies that had been developed, notably by the ANC's Department of Economic Policy (DEP) from 1990 and the Macroeconomic Research Group (MERG) between 1991 and 1993 as the ANC prepared to take office in the first democratic election. By the time it did so, the Reconstruction and Development Programme (RDP) was the only remaining policy programme with progressive policies, juxtaposed with the neoliberal macroeconomic framework that was made explicit in the implementation of the Growth, Employment and Redistribution (GEAR) programme in 1996. The inclusion of the RDP in the ANC's 1994 election manifesto was largely driven from below by trade unions and civic organisations

> and adopted only rather more opportunistically by the core group of the ANC senior leaders ... [I]t emphasized the centrality to the planning process of both the meeting of the populace's basic needs and the active empowerment of that populace in driving its own development process. (Saul 2001, p.439)

The RDP thus appeared as an add-on to the broader developmental strategy based on trickle-down and growth through liberalisation. This is in stark contrast to the centrality of progressive social and economic policies within the strategy of 'growth through redistribution' that was envisaged in the policy documents of the DEP and the MERG.

The main protagonists in the South African DS debate have been the left within the ANC Tripartite Alliance, who have harnessed the concept in their critique of the government's adoption of neoliberal policies in general, and of the Mbeki administration in particular. The concept has been particularly important for the South African Communist Party (SACP), for whom it has been intellectually central in their understanding of the National Democratic Revolution

(SACP 2008).[13] The DS debate started to gain momentum when it became clear that GEAR had failed to deliver on almost all aspects of growth and development. In face of widespread anger and frustration at the lack of change and achievement since the demise of apartheid, the ANC projected itself as offering a prospective DS, casually referencing the US-funded Marshall Plan for reconstructing post-war Europe, the experience of the East Asian NICs, and the European Union as examples of successful economic development in the twentieth century (ANC 2005).

A flurry of academic interest immediately attached itself to the notion of the South African DS following this declaration of intent. Much of the analysis of the DS in South Africa has been couched in terms of institutional capacities (as in the DSP in general) and has assessed 'developmentalism' in light of its capacity to formulate appropriate policies, mobilise and allocate resources in line with identified policy targets, as well as monitoring and evaluating policies and their implementation. On this basis, the conclusion has been drawn that the South African state, while not powerless, is weak in terms of its capacities (Gumede 2008; Pillay 2007; Southall 2006; van Dijk and Croucamp 2007). The weakness of the state's capacities has, however, been exaggerated. There are numerous examples where both the state and the private sector exhibit high levels of capacity, with the staging of the FIFA World Cup in 2010 as just one; if only similar effort had gone into housing for the poor as went into the building of stadiums.

The DS debate marked the battlefield within the increasingly divided ANC between supporters of Mbeki and those of Jacob Zuma, then deputy president, with many commentators speaking of an inevitable split in the ANC (McGreal 2007). The South African DS became a political project of the Zuma camp, in direct opposition to Mbeki as the orchestrator of South Africa's neoliberal policies. The ANC's internal power struggle came to a head in December 2007 at the 52nd ANC Annual Conference in Polokwane, where Mbeki suffered a humiliating defeat, with Zuma taking 60 per cent of the vote. In September 2008, Mbeki was forced to step down as president before completing his second term in office.

At the ANC policy conference in June 2007, there was talk of a 'broad consensus' over the need for a DS with correspondingly more government intervention. It inspired a renewed flurry of academic activity around the DS, notably the Sanpad conference in June 2007 and the Human Sciences Research Council (HSRC) Conference on the Developmental State in South Africa in 2008 – the proceedings of which have, ultimately, been published in volumes edited by Maharaj, Desai and Bond (2010) and Edigheji (2010), respectively.[14] In this respect, as suggested in the opening chapter, the DS has indeed become a buzzword and fuzzword.

10.6 CONCLUDING REMARKS

South Africa, then, offers a relatively unusual example of the intersection between academic endeavour and immediate political manoeuvring, with the DS serving as both a conceptual and a political football. With regard to the latter, and in respect of policy, the 2006 National Industrial Policy Framework (NIPF) and the subsequent Industrial Policy Action Plans (IPAPs) of 2007 and 2010 have reflected, at least in principle, an increasingly interventionist approach to industrial policy, targeted at the generation of decent and sustainable employment. On coming into office, President Jacob Zuma undertook a dramatic reshuffling of the cabinet, with appointments of prominent figures from the left of the Tripartite Alliance in key positions relating to economic policy. Rob Davies, a member of the SACP central committee, was appointed minister of trade and industry, while prominent trade unionist Ebrahim Patel was appointed minister for economic development, heading the new Department of Economics Development.

In its purported aim of building a strong institutional structure around economic policy making and implementation, the Zuma government has sought a compromise between the right and the left in the Tripartite Alliance, incorporating the former through the appointment of Pravin Gordhan as minister of finance, alongside his predecessor Trevor Manuel as head of the new National Planning Commission, which comes under the office of the presidency. The transition from Mbeki to Zuma has also seen a change in the discourse coming from the ANC, which now talks about South Africa needing to charter a 'New Growth Path' (NGP) (on which there is apparent consensus within the ANC) rather than becoming a DS

This is evident in a number of pronouncements from the new government. Thus, 'Now is the time to lay the groundwork for stronger growth going forward, and for growth that gives rise to more jobs' (President Jacob Zuma, State of the Nation Address, 11 February 2010). And

> The negative, unintended consequences of this [old] growth path are manifold: they include large and unsustainable imbalances in the economy, continued high levels of unemployment and a large current account deficit. These weaknesses have been exacerbated by the global recession. Taken together these challenges are enormous and make it critical that we upscale our industrial policy efforts. (Rob Davies, minister of trade and industry, National Assembly statement on IPAP2, 18 February 2010)

Whilst

> in growing the wider economy, broadening participation, deepening trade and strengthening our revenue base, we have recognised that a new growth path is needed, that industrial policy has to be founded on a well-considered action plan and that we need to do more to promote a dynamic economy, capable of responding both to domestic demand and international opportunities. (Pravin Gordhan, minister of finance, Budget Vote speech, 11 May 2010)

And

> Faced with these realities and the challenges of very high inequality and deep levels of poverty, we are working on ways to improve the employment performance of the economy and create many more decent work opportunities and better social outcomes. We call this the development of a new growth path. (Ebrahim Patel, minister of economic development, debate on Budget Vote 27: Economic Development, in an extended public committee meeting of the National Assembly, 23 March 2010)

In this light, rather than simply abandoning the DS agenda as a conduit to, but not of, power, the NGP strives to serve as yet another false unifier for consensus, both departing in major part from, and yet flexibly reinventing, the DS to suit. For Minister Patel, and those on the left, a fully functioning South African DS provides the means by which the NGP is to be achieved (EDD 2010). Yet despite the apparent commitment to a progressive, redistributive agenda, Ministers Patel and Davies face serious obstacles in their ability to pursue this further, not least because of the compromises attached to the NGP–DS dualism. And we have sought to establish that these compromises derive from the evolving class nature of South

Africa as a system of accumulation, in which the MEC has played a continuing if shifting role, especially through the capital-intensive accumulation within the domestic economy that currently underpins the globalisation and financialisation of domestic conglomerates (not least through a tolerated if illegal capital flight).

Of course, in the world of scholarship, such complicity is not inevitable. The DS can be reinvented once more to be more progressive, and more inclusive both of agencies other than industrialists and of economic and social activity other than industry. But, if the DSP is to succeed in its goals, in South Africa or elsewhere, it will need to be more mindful of how it is class relations and systems of accumulation that inform the role of the state and the global market and their determinants, rather than vice-versa.[15]

NOTES

1. Fine (2010f) gives an account of the intellectual origins of the MEC.
2. The result was a theory that was essentially underconsumptionist in claiming that racially restricted consumption constrained domestic mass production.
3. In Ethiopia also the ruling party has declared itself in favour of the country becoming a DS. Prime Minister Meles Zanawi presented a paper titled 'African Development: Dead Ends and New Beginnings' at the Policy Dialogue Initiative in London in 2006 which declared neoliberalism a failure in Africa and advocated a developmental state model based on East Asia. See http://cgt.columbia.edu/files/conferences/Zenawi_Dead_Ends_and_New_Beginnings.pdf
4. Over one million workers in the formal sector lost their jobs between 1994 and 2002. In 2002 the narrow definition of unemployment was 27 per cent of the workforce, and 45 per cent of the workforce according to the broader figure which includes those no longer actively seeking work. Income inequality also increased between 1994 and 2002 and continued to be highly racialised (Cronin 2002).
5. For some classic references for what follows, see Kaplan (1974, 1977, 1979), Davies (1979), O'Meara (1983) and Davies et al. (1976).
6. See also Fine and Rustomjee (1992).
7. State intervention in the electricity sector also acted to strengthen Afrikaner capital in mining through coal contracts from Eskom. See Clark (1994).
8. Together with Anglovaal and AAC, these Afrikaner groups would constitute three of the six axes of capital that would come to dominate the South African economy throughout the apartheid period.
9. Fine and Rustomjee (1996) identified the following core MEC sectors based on the input–output linkages amongst them (and the relatively weaker input–output linkages with 'non-MEC' sectors): coal, gold, diamonds and other mining activities; electricity; non-metallic mineral products; iron and steel basic industries; non-ferrous metals basic industries; and fertilisers, pesticides, synthetic resins, plastics, other chemicals, basic chemicals and petroleum.
10. The expansion of the MEC in the 1970s was largely driven by massive state-led investment in electricity generation and petrochemicals.

11. While gold- and coalmining have been in decline, the mining share of MEC output has been maintained by the expansion of platinum mining in the 'other mining' category.
12. Inclusion of discouraged workers in the calculation for unemployment increases the rate to one third of the labour force.
13. Despite its origins in the left of the Tripartite Alliance, the DS debate has been less promoted by the Congress of South African Trade Unions (COSATU). Prior to the mainstreaming of the DS debate within the ANC from 2005, COSATU had been relatively silent on the notion. While COSATU has been generally supportive of a South African DS, its understanding of it conforms to the ANC's relatively shallow reading of the experiences of late industrialisation in East Asian economies, as effectively pursuing top-down reforms around industrial policy, with no consideration of the role of labour or broader aspects of development (Pillay 2007).
14. The HSRC project was engendered as a way of providing intellectual legitimacy for the DS as a political project. However, the intellectual content of the conference and the subsequent edited volume turned out to be highly critical of the concept of the DS in general and the notion of South Africa as a DS in particular.
15. The financial assistance of the National Research Foundation (NRF) towards this research is hereby acknowledged. Opinions expressed and conclusions arrived at are those of the author and are not necessarily to be attributed to the NRF.

References

Abdu, M.S. and R. Marshall (1990) 'Agriculture and Development Policy: A Critical Review of Nigerian Experience in the Period up to 1985', *Journal of Rural Studies*, vol.6, no.3, pp.311–23.

Abe, M. (2008) 'Kankoku Tekkōgyō no Sangyō Saihen: Sangyō Seisaku no Tenkan to Kiketsu' (Industrial Organization of the South Korean Steel Industry: Consequences of the Transformation of Industrial Policy) (in Japanese), in H. Sato (ed.) *Ajia-shokoku no Tekkōgyō: Hatten to Henyō (The Steel Industry in Asian: Development and Restructuring)*, Chiba: Institute of Developing Economies.

Abeles M., K. Forcinito and M. Schorr (2001) *El Oligopolio Telefónico Argentino frente a la Liberalización del Mercado. De la Privatización de ENTel a la Conformación de los Grupos Multimedia*, Buenos Aires: FLACSO/Editorial UNQUI/IDEP, Colección Economía Política.

————— (2002) 'El Mercado Argentino de Telecomunicaciones', FLACSO, Área de Economía y Tecnología, Buenos Aires.

Adefa (Asociación de Fábricas de Automotores) (2001, 2007) Statistics in http://www.adefa.com.ar/v2/index.php?Itemid=77.

Agarwal, S. (1985) 'Electronics in India: Past Strategies and Future Possibilities', *World Development*, vol.3, no.3, pp.273–92.

Ahearne, A., J. Fernald, P. Loungani and J. Schindler (2006) 'Flying Geese or Sitting Ducks? China's Impact on the Trading Fortunes of Other Asian Economies', International Finance Discussion Paper no.887, Board of Governors of the Federal Reserve System, Washington, DC.

Aiyede, E. (2009) 'The Political Economy of Fiscal Federalism and the Dilemma of Constructing a Developmental State in Nigeria', *International Political Science Review*, vol.30, no.3, pp.249–69.

Alaofin, V. (1999) *Structural Adjustment Program and Agricultural Tradables: The Case of Cocoa Farming in Nigeria*, European University Studies, Frankfurt: Peter Lang Publishing.

Al-Jazaeri, H. (2008) 'Interrogating Technical Change through the History of Economic Thought in the Context of Latecomers' Industrial Development: The Case of the South Korean Microelectronics, Auto and Steel Industries', University of London, unpublished Ph.D. thesis.

Alpuerto,V., X. Diao, S. Salau and M. Nwafor (2009) 'Agricultural Investment for Growth and Poverty Reduction in Nigeria', Background Paper no.NSSP 001, Nigeria Strategy Support Program (NSSP), Development Strategy and Governance Division, International Food Policy Research Institute (IFPRI) and ReSAKSS–West Africa International Institute of Tropical Agriculture (IITA).

Aluko, M.A.O. (2004) 'Sustainable Development, Environmental Degradation and the Entrenchment of Poverty in the Niger Delta of Nigeria', *Journal of Human Ecology*, vol.15, no.1, pp.63–8.

Amsden, A. (1989) *Asia's Next Giant: South Korea and Late Industrialization*, New York: Oxford University Press.

—— (2001) *The Rise of 'The Rest': Challenges to the West from Late Industrializing Economies*, New York: Oxford University Press.

—— and W.-W. Chu (2003) *Beyond Late Development: Taiwan's Upgrading Policies*, Cambridge, MA, Massachusetts Institute of Technology.

—— and T. Hikino (1994) 'Project Execution Capability, Organisational Know-How and Conglomerates: Corporate Growth in Late Industrialisation', *Industrial and Corporate Change*, vol.3, pp.111–49.

—— and L. Kim (1985) 'The Acquisition of Technological Capability in Korean Industries', World Bank, mimeo.

ANC (2005) 'Development and Underdevelopment: Discussion Document for the National General Council', March 3–June 29.

—— (2006) 'A Catalyst for Accelerated and Shared Growth–South Africa (ASGISA)', available at http://www.info.gov.za/speeches/briefings/asgibackground.pdf, accessed on 23 July 2011.

Anderson, K. (1983) 'Growth of Agricultural Protection in East Asia', *Food Policy*, vol.8, no.4, pp.327–36.

Andrae, G. and B. Beckman (1985) *The Wheat Trap: Bread and Underdevelopment*, London: Zed Press.

Aoki, M., K. Murdock and M. Okuno-Fujiwara (1997) 'Beyond the East Asian Miracle: Introducing the Market-Enhancing View', in Aoki, Kim and Okuno-Fujiwara (1997).

Aoki, M., H.-K. Kim, and M. Okuno-Fujiwara (eds) (1997) *The Role of Government in East Asian Economic Development: Comparative Institutional Analysis*, Oxford: Clarendon Press.

Arora, A. and A. Gambardella (eds) (2005) *From Underdogs to Tigers: The Rise and Growth of the Software Industry in Brazil, China, India, Ireland and Israel*, Oxford: Oxford University Press.

Ashman, S., B. Fine and S. Newman (2010a) 'The Developmental State and Post-Liberation South Africa', in N. Misra-Dexter and J. February (eds) *Testing Democracy. Which Way is South Africa Going?* The Institute for Democracy in South Africa, Cape Town: ACD Press.

—— —— —— (2010b) 'The Crisis in South Africa: Neoliberalism, Financialisation and Uneven and Combined Development', *Socialist Register*, no.47, pp.174–95.

—— —— —— (2011) 'Amnesty International? The Nature, Scale and Impact of Capital Flight from South Africa', *Journal of Southern African Studies*, vol.37, no.1, pp.7–25.

Athreye, S. (2005) 'The Indian Software Industry', in Arora and Gambardella (2005).

Azpiazu, D. (1998) 'La Concentración en la Industria Argentina a mediados de los Años Noventa', FLACSO, Buenos Aires.

—— (1999) 'La Desregulación de los Mercados. Paradigmas e Inequidades de las Políticas del Neoliberalismo', Grupo Editorial NORMA/FLACSO, Buenos Aires.

—— (2002) 'Privatizaciones y Poder Económico. La Consolidación de una Sociedad Excluyente', FLACSO/Editorial UNQUI/IDEP, Colección Economía Política Argentina, Buenos Aires.

—— (2003) 'Las Privatizaciones en la Argentina. Diagnóstico y Propuestas para una Mayor Equidad Social', Editorial Miño y Dávila/CIEPP/Fundación OSDE, Buenos Aires.

Bae, Y. and J. Sellers (2007) 'Globalization, the Developmental State and the Politics of Urban Growth in Korea: A Multilevel Analysis', *International Journal of Urban and Regional Research*, vol.31, no.3, pp.543–60.

Bailey, D., H. Lenihan and J. Arauzo-Carod (2011) 'Editorial: Industrial Policy After the Crisis', *Policy Studies* vol.32, no.4, pp.303–08.

Balassa, B. (1988) 'The Lessons of East Asian Development: An Overview', *Economic Development and Cultural Change*, vol.36, no.3 (supplement), pp.273–90.

Baldwin, C.Y. and K.B. Clark (1997) 'Managing in an Age of Modularity', *Harvard Business Review*, September–October, pp.84–93.

Baldwin, C.Y. and K.B. Clark (2000) *Design Rules: the Power of Modularity* vol.i, Cambridge, MA: MIT Press.

Ban, S.-H., P.-Y. Moon and D. Perkins (1982) *Rural Development: Studies in the Modernisation of the Republic of Korea, 1945–1975*, Cambridge, MA: Harvard University Press.

Barbara, J. (2008) 'Rethinking Neo-Liberal State Building: Building Post-Conflict Development States', *Development in Practice*, vol.18, no.3, pp.307–18.

Bardhan, P. (2010) 'The Paradigm of Capitalism under a Developmental State: Does It Fit China and India?', *Singapore Economic Review*, vol.55, no.2, pp.243–51.

Basualdo, E. (2001) *Sistema Político yMmodelo de Acumulación en la Argentina. Notas sobre el Transformismo Argentino durante la Valorización Financiera (1976–2001)*, Universidad de Buenos Aires: Quilmes Ediciones.

—— (2006) *Estudios de Historia Económica Argentina: Desde mediados del siglo XX a la actualidad*, Buenos Aires: Siglo XXI ediciones.

—— C. Nahón and H. Nochteff (2005) 'Trayectoria y Naturaleza de la Deuda Externa Privada en la Argentina. La Década del Noventa antes y después', FLACSO Área Economía y Tecnología, Buenos Aires.

Bautista, R.M., S. Robinson, and M. El-Said (1999) 'Alternative Industrial Development Paths for Indonesia', TMD Discussion Paper no.42, International Food Policy Research Institute, Washington, DC.

Bayliss, K., B. Fine and E. Van Waeyenberge (eds) (2011) *The Political Economy of Development: The World Bank, Neo-Liberalism and Development Research*, London: Pluto Press.

BCRA (Banco Central de la República Argentina) (2010) 'Estadísticas e Indicadores', Buenos Aires.

BCRA (Banco Central de la República Argentina) (2011) 'Estadísticas e Indicadores', Buenos Aires.

Beath, J. (2002) 'UK Industrial Policy: Old Tunes on New Instruments?', *Oxford Review of Economic Policy*, vol.18, no.2, pp.221–39.

Beeson, M. (2009) 'Developmental States in East Asia: A Comparison of the Japanese and Chinese Experiences', *Asian Perspective*, vol.33, no.2, pp.5–39.

Bennett, D. and K. Sharpe (1985) *Transnational Corporations Versus The State: Political Economy of the Mexican Auto Industry*, Princeton, NJ: Princeton University Press.

Berger, M.T. (2004) *The Battle for Asia: From Decolonization to Globalization*, London: Routledge Curzon.

—— and D. Ghosh (2010) 'Geopolitics and the Cold War Developmental State in Asia: From the Culture of National Development to the Development of National Culture in Independent India', *Geopolitics*, vol.15, no.3, pp.586–605.

Bernard, M. and J. Ravenhill (1995) 'Beyond Product Cycles and Flying Geese: Regionalization, Hierarchy, and the Industrialization of East Asia', *World Politics*, vol.47, no.2, January, pp.171–209.

Bevan, D., P. Collier and J. Gunning (1999) *The Political Economy of Poverty, Equity and Growth: Nigeria and Indonesia*, Oxford: Oxford University Press.

Bisang R. and M. Chidiak (1995) 'Apertura Económica, Restructuración Productiva y Medio Ambiente', Centro de Investigaciones para la Transformación, Buenos Aires.

Blecher, M. (2008) 'Into Space: The Local Developmental State, Capitalist Transition and the Political Economy of Urban Planning in Xinji', *City*, vol.12, no.2, pp.171–82.

Blejer L. and G. Rozenwurcel (2000) 'Financiamiento de la PyMEs y Cambio Estructural en la Argentina', *Desarrollo Económico*, vol.40, pp.45–71.

Bond, P. (2005) *Elite Transition: From Apartheid to Neoliberalism in South Africa*, 2nd edn, Pietermaritzburg: University of KwaZulu-Natal Press.

—— and M.M. ka Ndlovu (2010) 'Development Dilemmas of Mega-Project Electricity and Water Consumption', in Freund and Witt (2010).

Bonefeld, W. (2008) 'Global Capital, National State, and the International', *Critique*, vol.36, no.1, pp.63–72.

—— A. Brown and P. Burnham (1995) *A Major Crisis? The Politics of Economic Policy in Britain in the 1990s*, Boston, MA: Dartmouth Publishing.

Bonnet, A.R. (2006) '¡Qué se Vayan Todos! Discussing the Argentine Crisis and Insurrection', *Historical Materialism*, vol.14, no 1, pp.157–84.

Booth, A. (1989) *Repelita V and Indonesia's Medium-Term Economic Strategy*, Bulletin of Indonesian Economic Studies, vol.25, no.2, pp.3–30.

—— (1994) 'Repelita VI and the Second Long-Term Development Plan', *Bulletin of Indonesian Economic Studies*, vol.30, no.3, pp.3–39.

—— (2007) 'Colonial Legacies: Economic and Social Development in East and Southeast Asia', Honolulu: University of Hawaii Press.

Bowen, J. (2007) 'Global Production Networks, the Developmental State and the Articulation of Asia Pacific Economies in the Commercial Aircraft Industry', *Asia Pacific Viewpoint*, vol.48, no.3, pp.312–29.

Boyer, R. and D. Drache (eds) (1996) *States Against Markets: The Limits of Globalization*, London: Routledge.

Brown, C. and G. Linden (2005) 'Offshoring in the Semiconductor Industry: A Historical Perspective', Centre for Work, Technology and Society, Institute for Research on Labour and Employment, available at http://repositories.cdlib.org/iir/cwts/bdetwps/cwts-02-2005.

Buckley, R.P. (1997) 'The Facilitation of the Brady Plan: Emerging Markets Debt Trading from 1989 to 1993', *Fordham International Law Journal*, vol.21, Issue 5, Article 6.

Burkett, P. and M. Hart-Landsberg (2000) *Development, Crisis, and Class Struggle: Learning From Japan and East Asia*, New York: St Martin's Press.

Byres, T. (2006) 'Agriculture and Development: Towards a Critique of the New Neoclassical Development Economics', in Jomo and Fine (2006).

Byun, B.-M. (1994) 'Growth and Recent Development of the Korean Semiconductor Industry', *Asian Survey*, vol.34, no.8, pp.706–20.

Caldentey, E. (2008) 'The Concept and Evolution of the Developmental State', *International Journal of Political Economy*, vol.37, no.3, pp.27–53.

Cao, J. (2009) 'Developmental State, Property-Led Growth and Property Investment Risks in China', *Journal of Property Investment and Finance*, vol.27, no.2, pp.162–79.

Carney, R. (2009) 'Chinese Capitalism in the OECD Mirror', *New Political Economy*, vol.14, no.1, pp.71–99.

Cavallo, D. (2004) 'Argentina and the IMF During the Two Bush Administrations', *International Finance*, vol.7, no.1, pp.137–50.
CBN (Central Bank of Nigeria) (1999) 'Central Bank of Nigeria Annual Report and Statements of Accounts (1960–1999)', Central Bank of Nigeria, Abuja.
CEP (Centro de Estudios para Producción) (2000) 'Estudios de la Economía Real', pp.9–13.
Ceruti, C. (2010) 'One Class or Two? The Labour Reserve and "Surplus Population" in Marx and Contemporary Soweto', *South African Review of Sociology*, vol.41, no.2, pp.77–103.
Chabane, N., A. Goldstein and S. Roberts (2006) 'The Changing Face and Strategies of Big Business in South Africa: More Than A Decade of Political Democracy', *Industrial and Corporate Change*, vol.15, no.3, pp.549–77.
Chalfin, B. (2010) 'Recasting Maritime Governance in Ghana: The Neo-Developmental State and the Port of Tema', *Journal of Modern African Studies*, vol.48, no.4, pp.573–98.
Chan, S., C. Clark and D. Lam (eds) (1998) *Beyond the Developmental State: East Asia's Political Economies Reconsidered*, London: Macmillan.
Chandler, A.D. (1997) 'The United States: Engines of Economic Growth in the Capital-Intensive and Knowledge-Intensive Industries', in D.A. Chandler, F. Amatori, and T. Hikino (eds) *Big Business and the Wealth of Nations*, New York: Cambridge University Press.
—— (2001) *Inventing the Electronic Century: The Epic Story of the Consumer Electronics and Computer Science Industries*, New York: Free Press.
Chang, D.-O. (2009) *Capitalist Development in Korea: Labour, Capital and the Myth of the Developmental State*, London: Routledge.
Chang, H.-J. (1994) *The Political Economy of Industrial Policy*, New York: St. Martin Press.
—— (ed.) (2001) *Joseph Stiglitz and the World Bank: The Rebel Within*, London: Anthem Press.
—— (2002) *Kicking away the Ladder: Policies and Institutions for Development in Historical Perspective*, London: Anthem Press.
—— (2003) *Globalisation, Economic Development and the Role of the State*, London: Zed Books.
—— (2006) *The East Asian Development Experience: The Miracle, the Crisis and the Future*, London and New York: Zed Books.
—— (2007) *Bad Samaritans: Rich Nations, Poor Policies, and the Threat to the Developing World*, London: Random House.
—— (2009) 'Kim Changeun Gyosuedaehandapbyeon' (A Reply to the Research Professor Kim), *Marxism 21*, vol.4, no.2, pp.223–37.
—— and I. Grabel (2004) *Reclaiming Development: An Economic Policy Handbook for Activists and Policymakers*, London: Zed Books.
—— G. Palma and D.H. Whittaker (1998) 'The Asian Crisis: Introduction', *Cambridge Journal of Economics*, vol.22, no.6, pp.649–52.
—— and H.-J. Park (2004) 'An Alternative Perspective on Government Policy Towards the Chaebol in Korea: Industrial Policy, Financial Regulations and Political Democracy', in S.-H. Jwa and I. Lee (eds) *Competition and Corporate Governance in Korea: Reforming and Restructuring the Chaebol*, Cheltenham: Edward Elgar.

—— —— and C.-G. Yoo (1998) 'Interpreting the Korean Crisis: Financial Liberalisation, Industrial Policy and Corporate Governance', *Cambridge Journal of Economics*, vol.22, no.6, pp.735–46.

—— and J.-S. Shin (2003) *Restructuring Korea Inc.*, London: Routledge Curzon.

Chang, K.-S., B. Fine and L. Weiss (eds) (2012) *Developmental Politics in Transition: The Neoliberal Era and Beyond*, London: Routledge.

Chen, E.I. (1972) 'Formosan Political Movements under Japanese Colonial Rule, 1914–1937', *Journal of Asian Studies*, vol.31, no.3, pp.477–97.

Cherry, J. (2007) *Foreign Direct Investment in Post-Crisis Korea: European Investors and 'Mismatched Globalization'*, London: Routledge.

Chia, S. (2007) 'Whither East Asian Regionalism? An ASEAN Perspective', *Asian Economic Papers*, vol.6, no.3.

Chick, V. (1987) 'Speculation, the Rate of Interest, and the Rate of Profit', *Journal of Post Keynesian Economics*, vol.10, no.1, pp.127–40.

Cho, H.Y. (2000) 'The Structure of South Korean Developmental Regime and its Transformation- the statist mobilization and authoritarian integration in the anti-communist regimentation', *Inter-Asia Cultural Studies*, vol.1, no.3, pp.408–26.

Choi, D.-S. (1995) 'The Limits of State Strength in South Korea: The Case of the Heavy and Chemical Industrialisation Plan', *Korea Observer*, vol.24, pp.63–95.

Choi, K. and Y. Lee (1990) 'The Role of the Korean Government in Industrialization', in H.C. Lee and I. Yamazawa (eds) *The Economic Development of Japan and Korea*, Honolulu: East–West Center.

Chu, Y. (2009) 'Eclipse or Reconfigured? South Korea's Developmental State and Challenges of the Global Knowledge Economy', *Economy and Society*, vol.38, no.2, pp.278–303.

Chung, Y.-I. (2007) *South Korea in the Fast Lane: Economic Development and Capital Formation*, New York: Oxford University Press.

Clark, N. (1994) *Manufacturing Apartheid: State Corporations in South Africa*, New Haven, CT: Yale University Press,

Clarke, S. (1991) *Marx, Marginalism and Modern Sociology: From Adam Smith to Max Weber*, London: Macmillan.

Comisión Especial Investigadora de la Cámara de Disputados (2005) *Informe sobre la Fuga de Divisa de Argentina*, Buenos Aires: Siglo XXI.

Cornwall, A. and D. Eade (eds) (2010) *Deconstructing Development Discourse: Buzzwords and Fuzzwords*, Oxford: Oxfam and Rugby: Practical Action Publishing.

Corrales, J. (1996) 'Entrevista efectuada por J. Corrales el 7 de agosto de 1991, "From Market-Correctors to Market-Creators: Executive–Ruling Party Relations in the Economic Reforms of Argentina and Venezuela, 1989–1993"', Harvard University, unpublished Ph.D. thesis.

Crafts, N. (1999) 'Implications of Financial Crisis for East Asian Trend Growth', *Oxford Review of Economic Policy*, vol.15, no.3, pp.110–31.

Crandall, R. (1996) 'From Competitiveness to Competition: The Threat of Minimills to Large National Steel Companies', *Resources Policy*, vol.22, nos 1–2, pp.107–18.

Cronin, J. (2002) 'Post-Apartheid South Africa: Reply to John S. Saul', *Monthly Review*, vol.54, no.7, pp.28–42.

Cumings, B. (1987) 'The Origins and Development of the Northeast Asian Political Economy: Industrial Sectors, Product Cycle, and Political Consequences', in Deyo (1987a).

Cyhn, J.W. (2002) *Technology Transfer and International Production: The Development of the Electronics Industry in Korea*, Cheltenham: Edward Elgar.

D'Costa, A.P. (1994) 'State, Steel and Strength: Structural Competitiveness and Development in South Korea', *Journal of Development Studies*, vol.31, no.1, pp.44–81.

—— (1999) *The Global Restructuring of the Steel Industry: Innovations, Institutions and Industrial Change*, London: Routledge.

Damill, M. and R. Frenkel (2005) 'Las Cuentas Públicas y la Crisis de la Convertibilidad en Argentina', *Desarrollo Económico–Revista de Ciencias Sociales*, no.170, pp.203–30.

Daryanto, A. (1999) 'Indonesia's Crisis and the Agricultural Sector: The Relevance of Agricultural Demand-Led Industrialisation', *UNEAC Asia Papers*, vol.62, no.2, pp.61–72.

Davies, R. (1979) *Capital, State and White Labour in South Africa, 1900–1960: An Historical Materialist Analysis of Class Formation and Class Relations*, Brighton: Harvester.

—— R. Kaplan, M. Morris and D. O'Meara (1976) 'Class Struggle and the Periodisation of the State in South Africa', *Review of African Political Economy*, no.7 (September–December), pp.4–30.

Department for Business Innovation and Skills (2008) 'Research and Development Scorecard', available at http://www.innovation.gov.uk/rd_scoreboard.

—— (2009) 'Research and Development Scoreboard', available at http://www.innovation.gov.uk/rd_scoreboard.

Deyo, F.C. (1987a) (ed.) *The Political Economy of the New Asian Industrialism*, Ithaca, NY: Cornell University Press.

—— (1987b) 'State and Labour: Modes of Political Exclusion in East Asian Development', in Deyo (1987a).

—— S. Haggard and H. Koo (1987) 'Labor in the Political Economy of East Asian Industrialization', *Bulletin of Concerned Asian Scholars*, vol.19, pp.42–53.

Dijk, H.G. van and P.A. Croucamp (2007) 'The Social Origins of the Developmental State: Reflections on South Africa and its Local Sphere of Government', *Journal of Public Administration*, vol.42, no.7, pp.664–75.

Di John, J. (2010) 'The Concept, Causes and Consequences of Failed States: A Critical Review of the Literature and Agenda for Research with Specific Reference to Sub-Saharan Africa', *European Journal of Development Research*, vol.22, no.1, pp.10–30.

Dicken, P. (2003) *Global Shift: Reshaping the Global Economic Map in the 21st Century*, 4th edn, London: Sage.

Dike, V. (2003) 'Nigeria and the Politics of Unreason: Political Assassinations, Decampments, Moneybags and Public Protests', available at http://www.niger-deltacongress.com/narticles/nigeria_and_the_politics_of_unre.htm (accessed 20 November 2009).

Draibe, S. and M. Riesco (2007) 'Introduction', in M. Riesco (ed.) *Latin America: A New Developmental Welfare State Model in the Making?* Basingstoke: Palgrave.

EDD (Economic Development Department of South Africa) (2010) 'The New Growth Path: The Framework', available at http://www.info.gov.za/view/DownloadFileAction?id=135748, accessed 24 July 2011.

Edigheji, O. (ed.) (2010) *Constructing a Democratic Developmental State in South Africa: Potentials and Challenges*, Cape Town: Human Sciences Research Council Press.

Eicher, C.K. and D.C. Baker (1982) 'Research Agricultural Development in Sub-Saharan Africa: A Critical Survey', International Development Paper no.1, Michigan State University, East Lansing, MI.

Eimer, T. and S. Lütz (2010) 'Developmental States, Civil Society, and Public Health: Patent Regulation for HIV/AIDS Pharmaceuticals in India and Brazil', *Regulation and Governance*, vol.4, no.2, pp.135–53.

ENGE (1993–97) *Encuesta Nacional a Grandes Empresas*, Buenos Aires: INDEC.

—— (1999) *Encuesta Nacional a Grandes Empresas*, Buenos Aires: INDEC.

Enos, J.L. and W.-H. Park (1988) *The Adoption and Diffusion of Imported Technology*, London: Croom Helm.

Ernst, D. (2000a) 'Catching-Up and Post-Crisis Industrial Upgrading: Searching for New Sources of Growth in Korea's Electronics Industry', in F. Deyo, R. Doner, and E. Hershberg (eds) *Economic Governance and Flexible Production in East Asia*, Rowman & Littlefield Publishers.

—— (2000b) 'Placing the Networks on the Internet: Challenges and Opportunities for Managing in Developing Asia', 2nd Asia Academy of Management Conference, December 15–18, Singapore.

—— (2003) 'Pathways to Innovation in Asia's Leading Electronics Exporting Countries: Drivers and Policy Implications', Economics Study Area Working Paper no.62, East–West Center, available at http://www.eastwestcenter.org/fileadmin/stored/pdfs/ECONwp062.pdf.

—— T. Ganiatsos and L. Mytelka (1998) *Technological Capabilities and Export Success: Lessons from East Asia*, London: Routledge.

Etchemendy, S. (2001) 'Construir Coaliciones Reformistas: la Política de las Compensaciones en el Camino Argentino hacia la Liberalización Económica', *Desarrollo Económico*, vol.40, pp.675–706.

Evans, P. (1989) 'Predatory, Developmental, and Other Apparatuses: A Comparative Political Economy Perspective on the Third World State', *Sociological Forum*, vol.4, no.4, pp.561–87.

—— (1992) 'The State as Problem and Solution: Predation, Embedded Autonomy, and Structural Change', in S. Haggard and R.R. Kaufman (eds) *The Politics of Economic Adjustment*, Princeton, NJ: Princeton University Press.

—— (1995) *Embedded Autonomy: States and Industrial Transformation*, Princeton, NJ: Princeton University Press.

—— D. Rueschemeyer and T. Skocpol (eds) (1985) *Bringing the State Back In*, Cambridge: Cambridge University Press.

FAO (Food and Agriculture Organization) (2005) 'FAO AQUASTAT Survey: FAO', Rome.

Ferdinand, P. (2007) 'Russia and China: Converging Responses to Globalization', *International Affairs*, vol.83, no.4, pp.655–80.

Ferguson, C.H. (1985) 'American Microelectronics in Decline: Evidence, Analysis and Alternatives', VLSI Memo no.85–284, Massachusetts Institute of Technology, Cambridge, MA (December).

FGN (Federal Government of Nigeria) (1970) 'Second National Development Plan (1970–74)', Federal Ministry of Finance, Lagos.

FIEL (Fundación de Investigaciones Económicas Latinoamericanas) (1996) 'Las Pequeñas y Medianas Empresas en la Argentina', FIEL, Buenos Aires.

Fine, B. (1992) 'Linkage and the State: The Case of South Korea', SOAS Department of Economics Working Paper no.2, School of African and Oriental Studies, University of London.

—— (1993) 'Economic Development and Technological Change: From Linkage to Agency', SOAS Department of Economics Working Paper no.14 (March), School of African and Oriental Studies, University of London.

—— (1995) 'Flexible Production and Flexible Theory: The Case of South Africa', *Geoforum*, vol.26, no.2, pp.107–19.

—— (1997a) 'Industrial Policy and South Africa: A Strategic View', NIEP Occasional Paper Series no.5 (April), pp.1–71, National Institute for Economic Policy, Johannesburg.

—— (1997b) 'Industrial and Energy Policy', in J. Michie and V. Padayachee (eds) *The Political Economy of South Africa's Transition: Policy Perspectives in the Late 1990s*, London: Dryden Press.

—— (1999) 'The Developmental State Is Dead: Long Live Social Capital?', *Development and Change*, vol.30, no.1, pp.1–19.

—— (2001) *Social Capital versus Social Theory: Political Economy and Social Science at the Turn of the Millennium*, London: Routledge.

—— (2005) 'Beyond the Developmental State: Towards a Political Economy of Development', in C. Lapavitsas and M. Noguchi (eds) *Beyond Market-Driven Development: Drawing on the Experience of Asia and Latin America*, London: Routledge.

—— (2006) 'The Developmental State and the Political Economy of Development', in Jomo and Fine (2006).

—— (2007) 'State, Development and Inequality: The Curious Incidence of the Developmental State in the Night-Time', paper presented to Sanpad Conference, Durban, June 26–30, available at http://*www.networkideas.org/ideasact/jan09/PDF/Fine.pdf*.

—— (2008) 'Engaging the MEC: Or a Lot of My Views on a Lot of Things', paper for MEC workshop at University of KwaZulu-Natal, Durban (June), available at https://*eprints.soas.ac.uk/5813/, in shortened version as Fine (2010f)*.

—— (2009a) 'Development as Zombieconomics in the Age of Neo-Liberalism', *Third World Quarterly*, vol.30, no.5, pp.885–904.

—— (2009b) 'Social Policy and the Crisis of Neo-Liberalism', prepared for conference on 'The Crisis of Neo-Liberalism in India: Challenges and Alternatives', Tata Institute of Social Sciences, Mumbai, and International Development Economics Associates, 13–15 March, networkideas.org/ideasact/jan09/ia27_International_Conference.htm.

—— (2009c) 'Financialisation and Social Policy', prepared for conference on 'Social and Political Dimensions of the Global Crisis: Implications for Developing Countries', 12–13 November, UNRISD, Geneva, https://eprints.soas.ac.uk/7984; shortened and revised version in Utting, Razavi and Buchholz (2012).

—— (2009d) 'Submission to the COSATU Panel of Economists on "The Final Recommendations of the International Panel on Growth" (The Harvard Panel)', *Transformation: Critical Perspectives on Southern Africa*, no.69, pp.5–30.

—— (2010a) *Theories of Social Capital: Researchers Behaving Badly*, London: Pluto Press.

—— (2010b) 'The Developmental State?', in Maharaj, Desai and Bond (2010).

—— (2010c) 'Can South Africa Be a Developmental State?', in Edigheji (2010).

—— (2010d) 'Flattening Economic Geography: Locating the World Development Report for 2009', *Journal of Economic Analysis*, vol.1, no.1, pp.15–33.

—— (2010e) 'Social Capital', in A. Cornwall and D. Eade (eds) *Deconstructing Development Discourse: Buzzwords and Fuzzwords*, Oxfam and Rugby: Practical Action Publishing.

—— (2010f) 'Engaging the MEC: Or a Few of My Views on a Few Things', *Transformation: Critical Perspectives on Southern Africa*, no.71, pp.26–49.

—— (2011) 'Social Capital and Health', in Bayliss, Fine and Van Waeyenberge (2011).

—— (2012) 'Neo-Liberalism in Retrospect? It's Financialisation, Stupid', in Chang, Fine and Weiss (2012).

—— C. Lapavitsas and J. Pincus (eds) (2001) *Development Policy in the Twenty-First Century: Beyond the Post-Washington Consensus*, London: Routledge.

—— and D. Milonakis (2009) *From Economics Imperialism to Freakonomics: The Shifting Boundaries between Economics and Other Social Sciences*, London: Routledge.

—— A. Petropoulos and H. Sato (2005) 'Beyond Brenner's Investment Overhang Hypothesis: The Case of the Steel Industry', *New Political Economy*, vol.10, no.1, pp.43–64.

—— and Z. Rustomjee (1992) 'The Political Economy of South Africa in the Interwar Period', *Social Dynamics*, vol.18, no.2, pp.26–54.

—— —— (1996) *The Political Economy of South Africa: From Minerals–Energy Complex to Industrialisation*, London: Hurst.

—— and C. Stoneman (1996) 'The State and Development: An Introduction', *Journal of Southern African Studies*, vol.22, no.1, pp.5–26.

Fitzgerald, R. and Y. Kim (2004) 'Business Strategy, Government and Globalization: Policy and Miscalculation in the Korean Electronics Industry', *Asia Pacific Business Review*, vol.10, nos3–4, pp.441–62.

FLACSO (2002) 'Database of External Debt during the 1990s', FLACSO Área Economía y Tecnología, Buenos Aires.

Fleming, J. (1955) 'External Economies and the Doctrine of Balanced Growth', *Economic Journal*, vol.65, no.258, pp.241–56.

Forester, T. (1993) *Silicon Samurai: How Japan Conquered the World's IT Industry*, Oxford: Blackwell Business.

Francks, P., J. Boestel and H.C. Kim (1999) *Agriculture and Economic Development in East Asia: From Growth to Protectionism in Japan, Korea and Taiwan*, London: Routledge.

Frank, C.R., K.S. Kim, and K. Westphal (1975) *Foreign Trade Regimes and Economic Development: South Korea*, New York: Columbia University Press.

Frederick, W.H. and R.L. Worden (1993) *Indonesia: A Country Study*, Washington, DC: General Printing Office for the Library of Congress.

Freund, B. (2011) 'A Ghost from the Past: The South African Developmental State of the 1940s', mimeo.

—— and H. Witt (eds) (2010) *Development Dilemmas in Post-Apartheid South Africa*, Scottsville: University of KwaZulu–Natal Press.

Fritz, V. and A. Menocal (2007) 'Developmental States in the New Millennium: Concepts and Challenges for a New Aid Agenda', *Development Policy Review*, vol.25, no.5, pp.531–52.

Fukagawa, Y. (1989) *Kankoku: Aru Sangyō Hatten no Kiseki (South Korea: The Track of an Industrial Development)* (in Japanese), Tokyo: JETRO.

—— (1999) 'Kankoku: Keizai Kaihatsu no Sōkessan to Senshinka eno Shiren' (South Korea: Settlement of Its Economic Development and Challenges to Become an Advanced Country) (in Japanese), in Y. Hara (ed.) *Ajia Keizai*, Tokyo: NTT.

Gaggero, J.A., C. Casparrino and E. Libman (2007) 'La Fuga de Capitales, Historia, Presente y Perspectivas', Centro de Economia y Finanzas Para el Desarollo de la Argentina, Buenos Aires.

—— and J.C. Sabbaini (2002) *Argentina: Questiones Macrofiscales y Reforma Tributaria*, Buenos Aires: Fundacion OSDE/CIEPP.

Garon, S. (1987) *The State and Labor in Modern Japan*, Berkeley, CA: University of California Press.

Gelb, S. (ed.) (1991) *South Africa's Economic Crisis*, Cape Town: David Philip.

Gerchunoff, P. and J.C. Torre (1996) 'La Política de Liberalización Económica en la Administración de Menem', *Desarrollo Económico*, vol.36, pp.733–68.

Gibbon, P. and A. Olukoshi (1996) 'Structural Adjustment and Socio-Economic Change in Sub-Saharan Africa: Some Conceptual, Methodological and Research Issues', *Nordic Africa Institute Research Report*, no.102.

Glassburner, B. (1988) 'Indonesia: Windfalls in a Poor Rural Economy', in A. Gelb and associates (eds) *Oil Windfalls: Blessing or Curse?* New York: Oxford University Press.

Gomez, E. (2009) 'The Rise and Fall of Capital: Corporate Malaysia in Historical Perspective', *Journal of Contemporary Asia*, vol.39, no.3, pp.345–81.

Gopinathan, S. (2007) 'Globalisation, the Singapore Developmental State and Education Policy: A Thesis Revisited', *Globalisation, Societies and Education*, vol.5, no.1, pp.53–70.

Gordon, A. (2003) *A Modern History of Japan: From Tokugawa Times to the Present*, Oxford: Oxford University Press.

Grabel, I. (2011) 'Not Your Grandfather's IMF: Global Crisis, "Productive Incoherence" and Developmental Policy Space', *Cambridge Journal of Economics*, vol.30, no.5, pp.805–30.

Grant, W. (1982) *The Political Economy of Industrial Policy*, London: Butterworth.

Gray, K. (2008) 'The Global Uprising of Labour? The Korean Labour Movement and Neoliberal Social Corporatism', *Globalizations*, vol.5, no.3, pp.483–99.

Green, A. (1992) 'South Korea's Automobile Industry: Development and Prospects', *Asian Survey*, vol.32, no.5, pp.411–28.

—— (2007) 'Globalisation and the Changing Nature of the State in East Asia', *Globalisation, Societies and Education*, vol.5, no.1, pp.23–38.

Greene, J. (2008) *The Origins of the Developmental State in Taiwan: Science Policy and the Quest for Modernization*, Cambridge, MA: Harvard University Press.

Grieco, J. (1982) 'Between Dependence and Autonomy: India's Experience with the International Computer Industry', Cornell University, Ph.D. thesis.

Gumede, V. (2008) 'South Africa: A Developmental State?', Thought Leader, Mail and Guardian Online, available at http://www.thoughtleader.co.za/vusigumede/2008/07/09/south-africa-a-developmental-state/ , accessed 30 May 2009.

Haan, L. de (2010) 'Perspectives on African Studies and Development in Sub-Saharan Africa', *Africa Spectrum*, vol.45, no.1, pp.95–116.

Haggard, S., B.-K. Kim and C. Moon (1991) 'The Transition to Export-Led Growth in South Korea: 1954–1966', *Journal of Asian Studies*, vol.50, no.4, pp.85–73.

Halevi, J. and P. Kriesler (2007) 'The Changing Patterns of Accumulation and Realization in East Asia since the 1990s', in Hart-Landsberg, Jeong and Westra (2007a).

Hallowes, D. (2010) 'Environmental Injustice through the Lens of the Vaal Triangle: Whose Dilemma?', in Freund and Witt (2010).

Haltmaier, J., S. Ahmed, B. Coulibaly, R. Knippenberg, S. Leduc, M. Marrazi and B. Wilson (2007) 'The Role of China in Asia: Engine, Conduit, or Steamroller?', International Finance Discussion Paper no.904, Board of Governors of the Federal Reserve System.

Hanley, S. (1986) 'The Material Culture: Stability in Transition', in M. Jansen and G. Rozman (eds) (1986) *Japan in Transition: From Tokugawa to Meiji*, Princeton, NJ: Princeton University Press.

Haque, I. (2007) 'Rethinking Industrial Policy', UNCTAD Discussion Papers no.183 (April), United Nations Conference on Trade and Development, Geneva.

Harrison, S.S. and V.C. Prestowitz (1998) 'Overview, New Priorities for U.S. Asia Policy', in S.S. Harrison and V.C. Prestowitz (eds) *Asia After the 'Miracle': Redefining U.S. Economic and Security Priorities*, Washington, DC: Economic Strategy Institute.

Hart, G.P. (1986) *Power, Labour and Livelihood: Processes of Change in Rural Java*, Berkeley, CA: University of California Press.

Hart-Landsberg, M. (1993) *Rush to Development: Economic Change and Political Struggle in South Korea*, New York: Monthly Review Press.

—— (2010) 'The US Economy and China: Capitalism, Class and Crisis', *Monthly Review*, vol.61, no.9 (online edition).

—— (2011) 'The Chinese Reform Experience: A Critical Assessment', *Review of Radical Political Economics*, vol.43, no.1, pp.56–76.

—— and P. Burkett (1998) 'Contradictions of Capitalist Industrialization in East Asia: A Critique of "Flying Geese" Theories of Development', *Economic Geography*, vol.74, no.2, pp.87–110.

—— S. Jeong and R. Westra (eds) (2007a) *Marxist Perspectives on South Korea in the Global Economy*, Aldershot: Ashgate.

—— —— —— (2007b) 'Introduction: Marxist Perspectives on South Korea in the Global Economy', in Hart-Landsberg, Jeong and Westra (2007a).

Harvey, D. (2003) *The New Imperialism*, Oxford, Oxford University Press.

Hasegawa, H. (1996) *The Steel Industry in Japan: A Comparison with Britain*, London: Routledge.

Hausmann, R. and D. Rodrik (2003) 'Economic Development as Self-Discovery', *Journal of Development Economics*, vol.72, pp.603–33.

Hayashi, S. (2010) 'The Developmental State in the Era of Globalization: Beyond the Northeast Asian Model of Political Economy', *Pacific Review*, vol.23, no.1, pp.45–69.

Heeks, R (1996) *India's Software Industry: State Policy, Liberalisation and Industrial Developmentvm*, New Delhi: Sage.

Heintz, J. (2002) 'Political Conflict and the Social Structure of Accumulation: The Case of South African Apartheid', *Review of Radical Political Economics*, vol.34, no.3, pp.319–26.

—— (2010) 'The Social Structure of Accumulation in South Africa', in T. McDonough, M. Reich and D.M. Kotz (eds) *Contemporary Capitalism and its Crises*, Cambridge: Cambridge University Press.

Hill, P. (1982) *Dry Grain Farming Families: Hausaland (Nigeria) and Karnataka (India) Compared*, Cambridge: Cambridge University Press.

Hirschman, A.O. (1958) *The Strategy of Economic Development*, New Haven, CT: Yale University Press.

—— (1992) *Rival Views of Market Society and Other Recent Essays*, Cambridge, MA: Harvard University Press.

Ho, S.P.S. (1979) 'Decentralized Industrialization and Rural Development: Evidence from Taiwan', *Economic Development and Cultural Change*, vol.28, no.1, pp.77–96.

Hobday, M. (1995) *Innovation in East Asia: The Challenge to Japan*, Cheltenham: Edward Elgar.

—— (2000) 'East versus Southeast Asian Innovation Systems: Comparing OEM- and TNC-Led Growth in Electronics', in Kim and Nelson (2000).

Hobson, M. (2003) 'Innovation in Asian Industrialization: A Gerschenkronian Perspective', *Oxford Development Studies*, vol.31, no.3, pp.293–314.

Hoeven, R. van der (2008) 'Reflections: Alice Amsden', *Development and Change*, vol.39, no.6, pp.1091–9.

Hoffmann, W. (1958) *The Growth of Industrial Economics*, Manchester: Manchester University Press.

Holloway, J. (1995) 'From Scream of Refusal to Scream of Power', in W. Bonefeld, R. Gunn and J. Holloway (eds) *Open Marxism*, vol.3, London: Pluto Press.

Hong, S.G. (1992) 'Paths of Glory: Semiconductor Development in Taiwan and South Korea', *Pacific Focus*, vol.7, no.1, pp.59–88.

—— (1997) *The Political Economy of Industrial Policy in East Asia*, Northampton, MA: Edward Elgar.

Honjo, N. (2000) 'Kankoku no Keizai Jiyūka to Kigyō Katsudō Hō no Taiō' (Economic Liberalisation and Reforms in Corporate Laws in South Korea) (in Japanese), in M. Kobayashi (ed.) *Ajia Shokoku no Sijōkeizaika to Kigyō Hō (Marketisation and Corporate Laws in Asian Countries)*, Chiba: Institute of Developing Economies.

Howell, T.R., B. Bartlett and W. Davis (1992) 'Creating Advantage: Semiconductors and Government Industrial Policy in the 1990s', Cupertino, CA and Washington, DC: Semiconductor Industry Association and Dewey Ballantine.

—— et al. (1988) *Steel and the State: Government Intervention and Steel's Structural Crisis*, Boulder, CO: Westview Press.

Hsiao, H.M. (1992) 'The Labor Movement in Taiwan: A Retrospective and Prospective Look', in D.F. Simon and M.Y.M. Kau (eds) *Taiwan: Beyond the Economic Miracle*, New York: M.E. Sharpe.

Hsu, C.K. (1989) 'Corporatist Control and Labor Movement in Taiwan', paper presented at the Conference on Northeast Asia in the World Perspective (May), Taegu, Korea.

Hsueh, L.-M., C.-K. Hsu and D.H. Perkins (2001) *Industrialization and the State: The Changing Role of the Taiwan Government in the Economy*, Cambridge, MA: Harvard University Press.

Huang, S. (1993) 'Structural Change in Taiwan's Agricultural Economy', *Economic Development and Cultural Change*, vol.42, no.1, pp.43–65.

Hundt, D. (2009) *Korea's Developmental Alliance: State, Capital and the Politics of Rapid Development*, London: Routledge.

Ichikawa, H. (1974) *Nihon Tekkōgyō no Saihensei (The Reorganisation of the Japanese Iron and Steel Industry)* (in Japanese), Tokyo: Shinhyōron.

Iida, K., S. Ohashi and T. Kuroiwa (eds) (1969) *Gendai Nihon Sangyō Hattatsu Shi (IV) Tekkō (The History of Modern Japanese Industrial Development (IV) Steel)* (in Japanese), Tokyo: Kōjun Sha.

Ilyenkov, E.V. (1982) *Dialectics of the Abstract and the Concrete in Marx's Capital*, Moscow: Progress Publishers.

INDEC (2010) 'Survey of Capital Outflows 1992–1998', Instituto Nacional de Estadística y Censos, Direccion Nacional de Cuentas Internationales, Buenos Aires, http://www.mecon.gov.ar/cuentas/internacionales/series_anuales.htm.

Innace, J.J. and D. Abby (1992) *Igniting Steel: Korea's POSCO Lights the Way*, New York: Global Village Press.

Innes, D. (1984) *Anglo American and the Rise of Modern South Africa*, New York: Monthly Review Press.

IFDC (International Fertility Development Center) (2008) 'Study of the Domestic Rice Value Chains in the Niger Basin of Mali, Niger and Nigeria, West Africa' (September).

IFPRI (International Food Policy Research Institute) (2008) 'Nigeria Strategy Support Program', IFPRI Program Brief no.2.

Ishikawa, S. (1988) 'Patterns and Processes of Intersectoral Resource Flows: Comparison of Cases in Asia', in G. Ranis and T. Schultz (eds) *The State of Development Economics*, Oxford: Blackwell.

ISP (Industrial Strategy Project) (1995) *Improving Manufacturing Performance in South Africa: Report of the Industrial Strategy Project*, Cape Town: UCT Press.

Itami, H. (1997) *Nihon no Tekkōgyō: Naze imamo Sekaiichi nanoka (The Japanese Steel Industry: Why Is It Still Number One in the World?)* (in Japanese), Tokyo: NTT.

Itoh, M. (2000) *The Japanese Economy Reconsidered*, Basingstoke: Palgrave.

James, W.E., S. Naya and G.M. Meier (1989) *Asian Development: Economic Success and Policy Lessons*, Madison, WI: University of Wisconsin Press.

Jenkins, R. (1987) *Transnational Corporations and the Latin American Automobile Industry*, London: MacMillan.

—— (1995) 'The Political Economy of Industrial Policy: Automobile Manufacture in the Newly Industrialising Countries', *Cambridge Journal of Economics*, vol.19, no.5, pp.625–45.

Jerven, M. (2011) 'The Quest for the African Dummy: Explaining African Post-Colonial Economic Performance Revisited', *Journal of International Development*, vol.23, no.2, pp.288–307.

Jha, P.S. (1990) *The Political Economy of Stagnation*, Bombay: Oxford University Press.

Johnson, C. (1982) *MITI and the Japanese Miracle: The Growth of Japanese Industrial Policy 1925–1975*, Stanford, CA: Stanford University Press.

—— (ed.) (1984) *The Industrial Policy Debate*, San Francisco: Institute for Contemporary Studies.

—— (1985) 'Political Institutions and Economic Performance: The Government–Business Relationship in Japan, South Korea and Taiwan', in R.A. Scalapino, S. Sato and J. Wanandi (eds) *Asian Economic Development: Present and Future*, Berkeley, CA: University of California Press.

—— (1999) 'The Developmental State: Odyssey of a Concept', in M. Woo-Cumings (ed.) *The Developmental State*, Ithaca, NY: Cornell University.

—— (2006) 'Chalmers Johnson on Our Military Empire', Tomdispatch interview, posted 21 March, available at http://tomdispatch.com/post/70243/tomdispatch_interview_chalmers_johnson_on_our_military_empire.

Jomo, K. and B. Fine (eds) (2006) *The New Development Economics: After the Washington Consensus*, Delhi: Tulika and London: Zed Press.

Juhn, S.-I. (1990) 'Challenge of a Latecomer: The Case of the Korean Steel Industry with Specific Reference to POSCO', in E. Abe and Y. Suzuki (eds) *Changing Patterns of International Rivalry: Some Lessons from the Steel Industry*, Tokyo: University of Tokyo Press.

Jun, Y. and D. Simon (1995) 'Technological Change and Foreign Investment Behaviour: Lessons Drawn from the New Strategic Thrust of Japanese Firms in the Asia-Pacific Region', in E. Chen and P. Drysdale (eds) *Corporate Links and Foreign Direct Investment in Asia and the Pacific*, Australia: Educational Publishers.

Kalinowski, T. (2008) 'Korea's Recovery since the 1997/98 Financial Crisis: The Last Stage of the Developmental State', *New Political Economy*, vol.13, no.4, 447–62.

Kaplan, D. (1974) 'The Politics of Industrial Protection in South Africa, 1910–1939', *Journal of Southern African Studies*, vol.1, no.1, pp.70–91.

—— (1977) 'Class Conflict, Capital Accumulation and the State: An Historical Analysis of the State in Twentieth-Century South Africa', Ph.D. thesis, University of Sussex.

—— (1979) 'Relations of Production, Class Struggle and the State in South Africa in the Inter-War Period', *Review of African Political Economy*, nos 15–16, pp.135–45.

Kaplinsky, R. (2008) 'What Does the Rise of China Do for Industrialisation in Sub-Saharan Africa?', *Review of African Political Economy*, vol.35, no.115, pp.7–22.

Karshenas, M. (1995) *Industrialization and Agricultural Surplus: A Comparative Study of Economic Development in Asia*, Oxford: Oxford University Press.

Kasza, G. (2006) *One World of Welfare: Japan in Comparative Perspective*, Ithaca, NY: Cornell University Press.

Kawabata, N. (1998) 'Kōro Mēkāno Seisan Sisutemu to Kyōsō Senryaku' (Production System and Competition Strategy of the Integrated Firms) (in Japanese), in K. Sakamoto (ed.) *Nihon Kigyō no Seisan Sisutemu (Production System of Japanese Enterprises)*, Tokyo: Chūō Keizai Sha.

—— (2005) *Higashi Ajia Tekkōgyō no Kōzō to Dainamisumu (Structure and Dynamism of the Iron and Steel Industry in East Asia)* (in Japanese), Tokyo: Mineruva Shobō.

—— (2007) 'Iron and Steel Industry in Viet Nam: A New Phase and Policy Shift', Vietnam Development Forum Discussion Paper no.9.

Kawai, N. (1997) 'Kanpō Jiken' (The Hanbo Incident) (in Japanese), *Nikkan Keizai Kyōkai Kyōkai Hō* (Monthly Report of Japan–Korea Economic Association), vol.3, pp.43–55.

Kegley, C. and G. Raymond (2009) *The Global Future*, Boston, MA: Wadsworth.

Khondker, H. (2008) 'Globalization and State Autonomy in Singapore', *Asian Journal of Social Science*, vol.36, no.1, pp.35–56.

Kiely, R. (2007) *The New Political Economy of Development: Globalization, Imperialism, Hegemony*, Basingstoke: Palgrave Macmillan.

Kikuchi, M. and Y. Hayami (1985) 'Agricultural growth against a land-resource constraint: Japan, Taiwan, Korea and the Phillipines', in Ohkawa and Ranis (1985).

Kim, D.-J., and Y.-C. Kim (2006) *Newly Industrialising Economies and International Competitiveness: Market Power and Korean Electronics Multinationals*, Basingstoke and New York: Palgrave Macmillan.

Kim, L. (1991) 'Pros and Cons of International Technology Transfer: A Developing Country View', in T. Agmon and M.A. von Glinow (eds) *Technology Transfer in International Business*, New York: Oxford University Press.

—— (1993) 'National System of Industrial Innovation: Dynamics of Capability Building in Korea', in R.R. Nelson (ed.) *National Innovation Systems: A Comparative Analysis*, New York: Oxford University Press.

—— (1997a) 'The Dynamics of Samsung's Technological Learning in Semiconductors', *California Management Review*, vol.39, no.3, pp.86–100.

—— (1997b) *Imitation to Innovation: The Dynamics of Korea's Technological Learning*, Boston: Harvard Business School Press.

—— (2003) 'Crisis, Reform, and National Innovation in South Korea', in W.W. Keller and R.J. Samuels (eds) *Crisis and Innovation in Asian Technology*, New York: Cambridge University Press.

—— J.W. Lee and J.J. Lee (1987) 'Korea's Entry into the Computer Industry and Its Acquisition of Technological Capability', *Technovation*, vol.6, no.4, pp.277–93.

—— and R.R. Nelson (eds) (2000) *Technology, Learning and Innovation: Experiences of Newly Industrialised Economies*, Cambridge and New York: Cambridge University Press.

Kim, S. and B. Cho (1999) 'The South Korean Economic Crisis: Contrasting Interpretations and an Alternative for Economic Reform', *Studies in Political Economy*, vol.60, pp.7–28.

Kim, S.R. (1998) 'The Korean System of Innovation and the Semiconductor Industry: A Governance Perspective', *Industrial and Corporate Change*, vol.7, no.2, pp.275–309.

Kim, W. (2009) 'Rethinking Colonialism and the Origins of the Developmental State in East Asia', *Journal of Contemporary Asia*, vol.39, no.3, pp.382–99.

Kipping, M. (1997) 'How Unique Is East Asian Development? Comparing Steel Producers and Users in East Asia and Western Europe', *Asia Pacific Business Review*, vol.4, no.1, pp.1–23.

Kohli, A. (2004) *State-Directed Development: Political Power and Industrialisation in the Global Periphery*, Cambridge: Cambridge University Press.

Koo, H. (2000) 'The Dilemmas of Empowered Labour in Korea', *Asian Survey*, vol.40, no.2, pp.227–50.

Krakowiak, F. (2005) 'Argentina: la deuda odiosa', CADTM (Committee for the Abolition of the Third World Debt) (22 January).

Krueger, J.A. (2002) 'Crisis Prevention and Resolution: Lessons from Argentina', available at http://www.imf.org/external/np/speeches/2002/071702.htm, accessed on 6 April 2011.

Krugman, P. (1994) 'The Myth of Asia's Miracle', *Foreign Affairs*, vol.73, no.6, pp.62–78.

—— (1998) 'Saving Asia: It's Time to Get Radical', *Fortune Magazine*, vol.138, no.5, pp.74–80.

Ku, Y. and C. Finer (2007) 'Developments in East Asian Welfare Studies', *Social Policy and Administration*, vol.41, no.2, pp.115–31.

Kulfas M. (2001) *El Impacto del Proceso de Fusiones y Adquisiciones en la Argentina sobre el Mapa de Grandes Empresas. Factores Determinantes y Transformaciones en el Universo de las Grandes Empresas de Capital Local*, Buenos Aires: Economic Commission for Latin America and the Caribbean Estudios y Persepctivas.

—— and M. Schorr (2003a) 'Deuda Externa y Valorizacione Financiera en la Argentina Actual. Factores Explicativos del Crecimiento del Endeudamiento Externo y Perspectivas ante el Proceso de Renegociación', *Revista Realidad Económica*, no.198.

—— —— (2003b) 'La Deuda Externa Argentina. Diagnóstico y Lineamientos Propositivos para Su Reestructuración', CIEPP–Fundación OSDE, Buenos Aires.

Kumar, N. (2008) 'India: A Failed Democratic Developmental State?', in V. Kukreja and M. Singh (eds) *Democracy, Development and Discontent in South Asia*, New Delhi: Sage Publications.

Kun-Chin, L. (2007) 'With Strings Attached? Improving the Administration of Central State-Financed Investment Projects in the PRC', *Asian Journal of Political Science*, vol.15, no.3, pp.319–43.

Kuo, W.-J. and J.C. Wang (2001) 'The Dynamics of Taiwan's SMEs: The Case of Electronics', in P. Guerrieri, S. Iammarino and C. Pietrobelli (eds) *The Global Challenge to Industrial Districts: SMEs in Italy and Taiwan*, Cheltenham and Lyme, NH: Edward Elgar.

Kuriyan, R. and I. Ray (2009) 'Outsourcing the State? Public–Private Partnerships and Information Technologies in India', *World Development*, vol.37, no.10, pp.1663–73.

Kwon, H.-J. (ed.) (2005) *Transforming the Developmental State in East Asia*, Basingstoke: Palgrave.

—— (2009) 'Policy Learning and Transfer: The Experience of the Developmental State in East Asia', *Policy and Politics*, vol.37, no.3, pp.409–21.

—— and I. Yi (2009) 'Economic Development and Poverty Reduction in Korea: Governing Multifunctional Institutions', *Development and Change*, vol.40, no.4, pp.769–92.

Ladipo, R.O. (1990) 'Nigeria and the Ivory Coast: Commercial and Export Crops since 1960', in H.A. Amara and B. Founou-Tchuigoua (eds) *African Agriculture: The Critical Choices*, UNU Press/Zed Books, available at http://www.unu.edu/unupress/unupbooks/uu28ae/uu28ae0e.htm.

Lall, S. (2000) 'Technological Change and Industrialisation in the Asian Newly Industrialising Economies: Achievements and Challenges', in Kim and Nelson (2000).

—— (2003) 'Foreign Direct Investment, Technology Development and Competitiveness: Issues and Evidence', in S. Lall and S. Urata (eds) *Competitiveness, FDI and Technological Activity in East Asia*, Cheltenham: Edgar Elgar.

Lange, M. (2009) 'Developmental Crises: A Comparative-Historical Analysis of State-Building in Colonial Botswana and Malaysia', *Commonwealth and Comparative Politics*, vol.47, no.1, pp.1–27.

Langlois, R.N. (1992) 'External Economies and Economic Progress: The Case of the Microcomputer Industry', *Business History Review*, vol.66, no.1, pp.1–52.

—— (1997) 'Cognition and capabilities: Opportunities Seized and Missed in the History of the Computer Industry', in R. Garud, P. Nayyar, and Z. Shapira (eds) *Technological Learning, Oversights and Foresights*, New York: Cambridge University Press.

—— and L.P. Robertson (1992) 'Networks and Innovation in a Modular System: Lessons from the Microcomputer and Component Industries', *Research Policy*, vol.21, no.4, pp.297–313.

Lazonick, W. (2008) 'Entrepreneurial Ventures and the Developmental State: Lessons from Advanced Economies', UNU-WIDER Discussion Paper no.2008/1, United Nations University, World Institute for Development Economics Research, Helsinki.

Lee, K. (2005) 'Making a Technological Catch-up: Barriers and Opportunities', *Asian Journal of Technology Innovation*, vol.13, no.2, pp.97–131.

Lee, K.-S. (2009a) 'How Can Korea Be a Role Model for Catch-up Development?', UNU-WIDER, Research Paper no.2009/34, United Nations University, World Institute for Development Economics Research, Helsinki.

—— (2009b) 'A Final Flowering of the Developmental State: The IT Policy Experiment of the Korean Information Infrastructure, 1995–2005', *Government Information Quarterly*, vol.26, no.4, pp.567–76.

Lee, S. (2008) 'The Politics of Chaebol Reform in Korea: Social Cleavage and New Financial Rules', *Journal of Contemporary Asia*, vol.38, no.3, pp.439–52.

Lee, S.-B., M. Lee and M. Pecht (2004) *Korea's Electronics Industry*, College Park, MD: University of Maryland, CALCE EPSC Press.

Lee, T.-H. (1971) *Intersectoral Capital Flows in the Economic Development of Taiwan 1895–1960*, Ithaca, NY: Cornell University Press.

Lee, Y. and S. Kwak (2009) 'Neo-liberal Korea and Still Developmentalist Japan: Myth or Reality?', *Global Economic Review*, vol.38, no.3, pp.277–95.

—— and Y. Tee (2009) 'Reprising the Role of the Developmental State in Cluster Development: The Biomedical Industry in Singapore', *Singapore Journal of Tropical Geography*, vol.30, no.1, pp.86–97.

Leftwich, A. (2000) *States of Development: On the Primacy of Politics in Development*, Cambridge: Polity Press.

Leipziger, D.M., C. Frischtak, H.J. Kharas and J.F. Normand (1997) 'Mercosur: Integration and Industrial Policy', *World Economy*, vol.20, no.5.

Levy, J. (1981) 'Diffusion of Technology and Patterns of International Trade: The Case of Television Receivers', Ph.D. thesis, Yale University.

Lewis, W.A. (1954) 'Economic Development with Unlimited Supplies of Labour', *Manchester School*, vol.22, no.2, pp.139–91.

LFN (Laws of the Federation of Nigeria) (1990) 'Land Use Act', Chapter 202, Laws of the Federation of Nigeria, available at: http://www.nigeria-law.org/Land%20 Use%20Act.htm.

Lim, H. (2010) 'The Transformation of the Developmental State and Economic Reform in Korea', *Journal of Contemporary Asia*, vol.40, no.2, pp.188–210.

Lim, W. (2003) *Public Enterprise Reform and Privatization in Korea: Lessons for Developing Countries*, Seoul: Korea Development Institute.

Lin, J. (2010) 'Six Steps for Strategic Government Intervention', *Global Policy*, vol.1, no.3, pp.330–1.

—— (2011a) 'From Flying Geese to Leading Dragons: New Opportunities and Strategies for Structural Transformation in Developing Countries', WIDER Annual Lecture no.15, http://www.wider.unu.edu/publications/annual-lectures/en_GB/AL15/.

—— (2011b) 'New Structural Economics: A Framework for Rethinking Development', World Bank Policy Research Working Paper no.5197, *World Bank Research Observer*, vol.26, no.2, pp.193–221.

—— and H.-J. Chang (2009) 'Should Industrial Policy in Developing Countries Conform to Comparative Advantage or Defy It? A Debate between Justin Lin and Ha-Joon Chang', *Development Policy Review*, vol.27, no.5, pp.483–502.

—— and C. Monga (2011a) 'Growth Identification and Facilitation: The Role of the State in the Dynamics of Structural Change', *Development Policy Review*, vol.29, no.3, pp.264–90.

—— —— (2011b) 'Rejoinder', *Development Policy Review*, vol.29, no.3, pp.304–10.

Lippit, V., R. Baiman, D. Kotz, M. Larudee, M. Lee (2011) 'Introduction: China's Rise in the Global Economy', *Review of Radical Political Economics*, vol.43, no.1, pp.5–8.

Liu, L. (2008) 'Local Government and Big Business in the People's Republic of China: Case Study Evidence from Shandong Province', *Asia Pacific Business Review*, vol.14, no.4, pp.473–89.

Lo, D. (2010) 'China and World Development beyond the Crisis', mimeo.

—— and Y. Zhang (2011) 'Making Sense of China's Economic Transformation', *Review of Radical Political Economics*, vol.43, no.1, pp.33–55.

Longtau, S.R. (2003) 'Multi-Agency Partnerships in African Agriculture: A Review and Description of Rice Production Systems in Nigeria', Eco-systems Development Organisation (EDO) Report.

MacIntyre, A. (1994) *Business and Government in Industrialising Asia*, St Leonards: Allen & Unwin.

Magaziner, I. and M. Patinkin (1989) 'Fast Heat: How Korea Won the Microwave War', *Harvard Business Review* (January), vol.67, no.1, pp.83–93.

Maharaj, B., A. Desai and P. Bond (eds) (2010) *Zuma's Own Goal: Losing South Africa's 'War on Poverty'*, Trenton, NJ: Africa World Press.

Marais, H. (2011) *South Africa Pushed to the Limit: The Political Economy of Change*, Claremont, South Africa: University of Cape Town Press.

Martin, W. and P.G. Warr (1993) 'Explaining the Relative Decline of Agriculture: A Supply Side Analysis for Indonesia', *World Bank Economic Review*, vol.7, no.3, pp.381–403.

Marx, K. (1973) *Grundrisse: Foundations of the Critique of Political Economy*, London: Pelican.

—— (1990) *Capital*, vol.1, New York: Penguin.

Maseland, R. and J. Peil (2008) 'Assessing the New Washington Pluralism from the Perspective of the Malaysian Model', *Third World Quarterly*, vol.29, no.6, pp.1175–88.

Masina, P. (2010) 'Vietnam between Developmental State and Neoliberalism: The Case of the Industrial Sector', C.Met Working Paper no.7, Centro Interuniversitario di Economia Applicata alle Politiche per l'Industria lo Sviluppa Locale e l'Internationalizzazione, in Chang, Fine and Weiss (2012).

Mason, E. (1980) *The Economic and Social Modernisation of the Republic of Korea*, Cambridge, MA: Harvard University Press.

Mathews, A.J. (1995) 'High-Technology Industrialisation in East Asia: The Case of the Semiconductor Industry of Taiwan and Korea', Taipei: Chung-Hua Institution for Economic Research.

Matlosa, K. (2007) 'The State, Democracy, and Development in Southern Africa', *World Futures: The Journal of General Evolution*, vol.63, nos 5–6, pp.443–63.

Maundeni, Z. (2002) 'State Culture and Development in Botswana and Zimbabwe', *Journal of Modern African Studies*, vol.40, no.1, pp.105–32.

Mazurek, J. (1999) *Making Microchips: Policy, Globalization and Economic Restructuring in the Semiconductor Industry*, Cambridge, MA: MIT Press.

Mbeki, M. (2009) *Architects of Poverty: Why African Capitalism Needs Changing*, Johannesburg: Picador Africa.

McDonald, D.A. (ed.) (2009) *Electric Capitalism: Recolonising Africa on the Power Grid*, London and Sterling, VA: Earthscan and Cape Town: HSRC Press.

McGreal, C. (2007) 'South Africa in Turmoil as Mbeki Heads for Defeat', *The Guardian*, 15 December.

McKinnon, R. and G. Schnabl (2006) 'China's Exchange Rate and International Adjustment in Wages, Prices and Interest Rates: Japan Déjà Vu?', *CESifo Economic Studies*, vol.52, no.2, pp.276–303.

Meisenhelder, T. (1997) 'The Developmental State in Mauritius', *Journal of Modern African Studies*, vol.35, no.2, pp.279–97.

Melvin, M. (2003) 'A Stock Market Boom during a Financial Crisis? ADRs and Capital Outflows in Argentina', *Economics Letters*, vol.81, no.1, pp.129–36.

Menem, E. (2009) 'Discurso al Senado de la Ley 23.696', accessed 10 October 2011, http://www.eduardomenem.org/noticias_detalle.php?detalle_noticia=53.

Merton, R.K. (1968) *Social Theory and Social Structure*, New York: Free Press.

Mihn, K.-H. and K. Oh (1993) 'Strategic Outsourcing and Cooperative Relationship in the Korean Automotive Industry', paper presented at the Korea Institute for Industrial Economics and Trade International Seminar on the Automotive Industry, Seoul, Korea (25–26 November).

Miller, M. (ed.) (2005) *Worlds of Capitalism: Institutions, Governance and Economic Change in the Era of Globalisation*, London: Routledge.

Ministerio del Trabajo (2003) 'Encuesta Permanente de Hogares', available at http://www.trabajo.gov.ar/left/estadisticas/bel/index.asp, accessed on 6 April 2011.

Minns, J. (2001) 'Of Miracles and Models: The Rise and Decline of the Developmental State in South Korea', *Third World Quarterly*, vol.22, no.6, pp.1025–43.

—— and R. Tierney (2003) 'The Labour Movement in Taiwan', *Labour History*, no.85, pp.103–28.

Mitarai, H. (2000) '21 Seiki nimuketa Kankoku Zaibatsu Kigyō no Jigyō Kōzō to Keiei Keitai no Tenbō: Denshisangyō wo Chūshin ni' (Proposals for Twenty-First Century Business and Management Configuration for Korean Chaebol Firms: Chiefly in the Electronics Industry) (in Japanese), in Taniura (2000).

Mizuno, J. (1999) 'Tōshi Kajō to Keiei no Akka' (Overinvestment and Worsening of Management) (in Japanese), in Taniura (1999).

—— (2000) 'Shuyō Sangyō no Kōzōchōsei to Kongo no Tenbō' (Structural Reform and Prospects of Korean Key Industries) (in Japanese), in Taniura (2000).

Mkandawire, T. (2001) 'Thinking About the Developmental States in Africa', *Cambridge Journal of Economics*, vol.25, no.3, pp.289–313.

Mody, A., S. Mundle and K. Raj (1985) 'Resource Flows from Agriculture: Japan and India', in Ohkawa and Ranis (1985).

Mogues, T. et al. (2008) 'Agricultural Public Spending in Nigeria', IFPRI Discussion Paper no.789, International Food Policy Research Institute, Washington, DC.

Mohamed, S. (2009) 'Financialisation, the Minerals Energy Complex, and South African Labour', paper presented at the Fifth Global Labour University Conference, 'Financialisation of Capital: Deterioration of Working Conditions' (22–4 February), Tata Institute for Social Sciences, Mumbai.

—— and K. Finnoff (2005) 'Capital Flight from South Africa, 1980–2000', in G.A. Epstein (ed.) *Capital Flight and Capital Controls in Developing Countries*, Cheltenham and Northampton, MA: Edward Elgar.

Mok, K. (2007) 'Globalisation, New Education Governance and State Capacity in East Asia', *Globalisation, Societies and Education*, vol.5, no.1, pp.1–21.

Moon, C. (1999) 'Political Economy of East Asian Development and Pacific Economic Cooperation', *Pacific Review*, vol.12, no.2, pp.199–224.

Moon, P.-Y, and B.-S. Kang (1991) 'The Republic of Korea', in A. Krueger, M. Schiff and A. Valdes (eds) *The Political Economy of Agricultural Pricing Policy*, vol.2, Baltimore, MD: Johns Hopkins University Press/World Bank.

Moon, W. (2009) 'Foreign Ownership and Performance of Banks: The Case of Korea', discussion paper, available at https://editorialexpress.com/cgi-bin/conference/download.cgi?db_name=FEMES09&paper_id=540.

Moore, E.G. (1996) 'Intel: Memories and Microprocessors', in E. Blout (ed.) *Power of Boldness: Ten Master Builders of American Industry Tell Their Success Stories*, Washington, DC: Joseph Henry Press.

Moore, M. (1985) 'Economic Growth and the Rise of Civil Society: Agriculture in Taiwan and South Korea', in G. White and R. Wade (eds) *Developmental States in East Asia*, Brighton: Institute of Development Studies.

Moran, M. (1991) *The Politics of the Financial Services Revolution: The USA, UK and Japan*, Basingstoke: Palgrave.

Moudud, J. and K. Botchway (2007) 'Challenging the Orthodoxy: African Development in the Age of Openness', *African and Asian Studies*, vol.6, no.4, pp.457–93.

—— —— (2008) 'The Search for a New Developmental State', *International Journal of Political Economy*, vol.37, no.3, pp.5–26.

Müller, W. and C. Neusüss (1978) 'The Illusion of State Socialism and the Contradiction between Wage Labour and Capital', in J. Holloway and S. Picciotto (eds) *State and Capital: A Marxist Debate*, London: Edward Arnold.

Murphy, K., A. Shleifer and R. Vishny (1989) 'Industrialization and the Big Push', *Journal of Political Economy*, vol.97, no.5, pp.1003–26.

Mussa, M. (2002) *Argentina and the Fund: From Triumph to Tragedy*, Washington, DC: Institute for International Economics.

Mustapha, A. (1993) 'Structural Adjustment and Agrarian Change in Nigeria', in A. Olukoshi (ed.) *The Politics of Structural Adjustment in Nigeria*, London: James Currey.

Neo, H. (2007) 'Challenging the Developmental State: Nature Conservation in Singapore', *Asia Pacific Viewpoint*, vol.48, no.2, pp.186–99.

Nihon Tekkō Renmei (Japan Iron and Steel Federation) (1959) *Sengo Tekkō Shi (The History of Steel after the Second World War)* (in Japanese), Tokyo: Nihon Tekkō Renmei.

—— (1968) *Kankoku Tekkōgyō no Genjō to Syōrai (The Present Status and Future of the South Korean Steel Industry)* (in Japanese), Tokyo: Nihon Tekkō Renmei.

—— (ed.) (1969) *Tekkō Jyūnen Shi, Shōwa 33 ~ 42 (A 10-Year History of the Iron and Steel Industry, 1958–1967)* (in Japanese), Tokyo: Nihon Tekkō Renmei.

—— (ed.) (1981) *Tekkō Jyūnen Shi, Shōwa 43 ~ 52 (A 10-Year History of the Iron and Steel Industry, 1968–1977)* (in Japanese), Tokyo: Nihon Tekkō Renmei.

—— (ed.) (1988) *Tekkō Jyūnen Shi, Showa 53 ~ 62 (A 10-Year History of the Iron and Steel Industry, 1978–1987)* (in Japanese), Tokyo: Nihon Tekkō Renmei.

—— (ed.) (1999) *Tekkō Jyūnen Shi, Showa 63 – Heisei 9* (A 10-Year History of the Iron and Steel Industry, 1988–1997) (in Japanese), Tokyo: Nihon Tekkō Renmei.

—— (ed.) (2008) *Tekkō Jyūnen Shi, Heisei 10 – Heisei 19* (A 10-Year History of the Iron and Steel Industry, 1998–2007) (in Japanese), Tokyo: Nihon Tekkō Renmei.

Noble, G.W. (1998) *Collective Action in East Asia: How Ruling Parties Shape Industrial Policy*, Ithaca, NY: Cornell University Press.

Norton, R. (1986) 'Industrial Policy and American Renewal', *Journal of Economic Literature*, vol.24, no.1, pp.1–40.

Nozoe, S. (1999) 'Kanpō Tōsan ni miru Seikei Yuchaku' (Close Relationship between Political and Business Circles in the case of the Bankruptcy of the Hanbo) (in Japanese), in Taniura (1999).

Nurkse, R. (1953) *Problems of Capital Formation in Underdeveloped Countries*, Oxford: Basil Blackwell.

Nwosu, A. (1991) 'Agricultural Linkages, Structural Adjustment and Macro-Economy of Nigeria', NISER Monograph Series no.14-1991, Nigerian Institute of Social and Economic Research, Ibadan.

O, W. (1996) *Korean-Type Economic Construction: Engineering Approach*, vol.3 (in Korean), Seoul: Kia Economic Research Institute.

O'Donnell, G. (1988) *Bureaucratic Authoritarianism: Argentina 1966–1973 in Comparative Perspective*, Berkeley, CA: University of California Press.

OECD (Organisation for Economic Cooperation and Development) (1985) *The Semiconductor Industry: Trade Related Issues*, Paris: OECD.

—— (2008) 'Economic Survey of Korea', Organisation for Economic Co-operation and Development, Paris.

O'Hearn, D. (2000) 'Globalization, "New Tigers", and the End of the Developmental State? The Case of the Celtic Tiger', *Politics and Society*, vol.28, no.1, pp.67–92.

O'Meara, D. (1983) *Volkskapitalisme: Class, Capital and Ideology in the Development of Afrikaner Nationalism, 1934–1948*, Cambridge: Cambridge University Press.

Odularu, G.O. (2008) 'Crude Oil and the Nigerian Economic Performance', *Oil and Gas Business Journal*, Ufa State Petroleum, Russia.

Ogunbodede, E.F., A.O. Ilesanmi and F. Olurankinse (2010) 'Petroleum Motor Spirit (PMS) Pricing Crisis and the Nigerian Public Passenger Transportation System', *Social Sciences*, vol.5, no.2, pp.113–21.

Ogundele, O.O. and G. Akpokodje (2004) 'Rice Trade and Marketing in Nigeria', in M.E. Abo and A.S. Abdullahi (eds) *Nigeria Rice Memorabilia*, Abuja: Project Synergy.

Oh, K. and C. Cho (1997) *Development History and Growth Potential of the Korean Automotive Industry* (in Korean), Seoul: KIET.

Ohkawa, K. and G. Ranis (eds) (1985) *Japan and Developing Countries*, Oxford: Basil Blackwell.

—— and H. Rosovsky (1973) *Japanese Economic Growth: Trend Acceleration in the Twentieth Century*, Stanford, CA: Stanford University Press.

—— and A. Shinohara (1979) *Patterns of Japanese Economic Development: A Quantitative Appraisal*, New Haven, CT: Yale University Press.

Ohno, K. (2009) 'Avoiding the Middle-Income Trap: Renovating Industrial Policy Formulation in Vietnam', *ASEAN Economic Bulletin*, vol.26, no.1, pp.25–43.

Okimoto, D. (1989) 'Between MITI and the Market: Japanese Industrial Policy for High Technology', Stanford, CA: Stanford University Press.

Okuda, S. (2007) 'Kankoku: Kan Bei FTA Kōshō nimiru Kokunai Chōsei no Muzukashisa' (South Korea: Difficulties in Domestic Coordination Exemplified in the Korea–USA FTA Negotiation) (in Japanese), in S. Higashi (ed.) *FTA no Seijikeizaigaku (Political Economy of FTA)*, Chiba: Institute of Developing Economies.

Öniş, Z. (1991) 'The Logic of the Developmental State', *Comparative Politics*, vol.24, no.1, pp.109–26.

Osinubi, T.S. (2003) 'Macroeconomic Policies and Pro-Poor Growth in Nigeria: Conference on Inequality, Poverty and Human Well-Being', World Institute for Development Economics Research (WIDER), Helsinki, Finland (30–31May).

Oyejide, T.A. (1986) 'The Effects of Trade and Exchange Rate Policies on Agriculture in Nigeria', Washington, DC: International Food Policy Research Institute.

Ozawa, T. (2009) *The Rise of Asia: The 'Flying Geese' Theory of Tandem Growth and Regional Agglomeration*, Cheltenham: Edward Elgar.

Palan, R., J. Abbott, and P. Deans (1996) *State Strategies in the Global Political Economy*, London: Pinter.

Panitch, L. and C. Leys (eds) (2004) *Socialist Register 2004: The New Imperial Challenge*, London: Merlin Press.

Park, A. and B. Johnston (1995) 'Rural Development and Dynamic Externalities in Taiwan's Structural Transformation', *Economic Development and Cultural Change*, vol.44, no.1, pp.181–208.

Park, H. (2007) 'Small Business's Place in the South Korean State–Society Relations', *Asian Journal of Political Science*, vol.15, no.2, pp.195–218.

Park, J. (2008) 'For the FDI with Dignity: With Special Reference to POSCO–India Case', *ICES Working Paper*, Hosei Univeristy.

Park, K.-S. and M.-J.Tcha (2003) 'The Korean Steel Industry after the Economic Crisis: Challenges and Opportunities', in M.-J. Tcha and C.-S. Suh (eds) *The Korean Economy at the Crossroads*, London and New York: RoutledgeCurzon.

Parthasarathi, A. and K. Joseph (2004) 'Innovation Under Export Orientation', in A.P. D'Costa and E. Sridharan (eds) *India in the Global Software Industry: Innovation, Firms Strategies and Development*, Basingstoke: Palgrave MacMillan.

Pecht, M., J. Bernstein, D. Searls, M. Peckerar (1997) *The Korean Electronics Industry*, New York: CRC Press.

Pereira, A. (2008) 'Whither the Developmental State? Explaining Singapore's Continued Developmentalism', *Third World Quarterly*, vol.29, no.6, pp.1189–203.

Perez, C. and L. Soete (1988) 'Catching Up in Technology: Entry Barriers and Windows of Opportunity', in G. Dosi et al. (eds) (1988) *Technical Change and Economic Theory*, London: Pinter.

Petras, J. and H. Veltmeyer (2003) *System in Crisis: The Dynamics of Free Market Capitalism*, London: Zed Books.

Phelps, N. (2008) 'Cluster or Capture? Manufacturing Foreign Direct Investment, External Economies and Agglomeration', *Regional Studies*, vol.42, no.4, pp.457–73.

Pillay, D. (2007) 'The Stunted Growth of South Africa's Developmental State Discourse', *Africanus: Journal of Development Studies*, vol.37, no.2, pp.198–215.

Pingle, P. (1999) *Rethinking the Developmental State: India's Industry in Comparative Perspective*, New York: St Martin's Press.

Pinto, B. (1987) 'Nigeria during and after the Oil Boom: A Policy Comparison with Indonesia', *World Bank Economic Review*, vol.1, no.3, pp.419–45.

Piovani, C. and M. Li (2011) 'One Hundred Million Jobs for the Chinese Workers! Why China's Current Model of Development Is Unsustainable and How a Progressive Economic Program Can Help the Chinese Workers, the Chinese

Economy, and China's Environment', *Review of Radical Political Economics*, vol.43, no.1, pp.77–94.

Pirie, I. (2005) 'The New Korean State', *New Political Economy*, vol.10, no.1, pp.25–42.

—— (2006) 'Economic Crisis and the Construction of a Neo-Liberal Regulatory Regime in Korea', *Competition and Change*, vol.10, no.1, pp.49–71.

—— (2008) *The Korean Developmental State: From Dirigisme to Neo-Liberalism*, London: Routledge.

—— (2009) 'Ha-Joon Chang: A Critique of the Critique', mimeo.

Porter, M. and H. Takeuchi (1999) 'Fixing What Really Ails Japan', *Foreign Affairs*, vol.78, no.3, pp.66–81.

POSCO (1998) 'Thirty Years of POSCO, 1968–1998', POSCO, Seoul.

—— (2006) 'Sustainability Report: The POSCO Movement', POSCO, Seoul.

Poulantzas, N. (1969) 'The Problem of the Capitalist State', *New Left Review*, no.58, pp.67–78.

—— (1973) *Political Power and Social Classes*, London: Verso.

Radice, H. (2008) 'The Developmental State under Global Neoliberalism', *Third World Quarterly*, vol.29, no.6, pp.1153–74.

Randall, V. (2007) 'Political Parties and Democratic Developmental States', *Development Policy Review*, vol.25, no.5, pp.633–52.

Riain, S. (2000) 'The Flexible Developmental State: Globalization, Information Technology and the New "Celtic Tiger"', *Politics and Society*, vol.28, no.2, pp.157–94.

Riesco, M. (ed) (2007) *Latin America: A New Developmental Welfare State in the Making*, Basingstoke: Palgrave Macmillan.

Robinson, J. (2009) 'Botswana as a Role Model for Country Success', UNU-WIDER Research Paper no.2009/40, United Nations University, World Institute for Development Economics Research, Helsinki.

Rock, M. et al. (2009) 'A Hard Slog, not a Leap Frog: Globalization and Sustainability Transitions in Developing Asia', *Technological Forecasting and Social Change*, vol.76, no.2, pp.241–54.

Rodríguez-Boetsch, L. (2005) 'Public Service Privatisation and Crisis in Argentina', *Development in Practice*, vol.15, nos 3–4, pp.302–15.

Rosenstein-Rodan, P. (1943) 'Problems of Industrialisation of Eastern and South-Eastern Europe', *Economic Journal*, vol.53, nos210–11, pp.202–11.

Rueschemeyer, D. and P. Evans (eds) (1985) 'The State and Economic Transformation', in Evans, Rueschemeyer and Skocpol (1985).

Sachs, J. (2001) 'Faltan estrategias de innovación', *La Nación*, 29 May.

Sakong, I. (1993) *Korea in the World Economy*, Washington, DC: Institute of International Economics.

Sakuma, M. (1994) 'Nihon Tekkōgyō no Kaigai Bijinesu Tenkai no Haikei to Tokushitsu' (Backgrounds and Features of Globalisation of the Japanese Steel Industry) (in Japanese), in Waseda Daigaku Shōgakubu (ed.) *Tekkōgyō no Gurōbaru Senryaku (Global Strategy for Steel Industry in a Rapidly Changing Era)*, Tokyo: Chūō Keizai Sha.

Salter, B. (2009) 'State Strategies and the Geopolitics of the Global Knowledge Economy: China, India and the Case of Regenerative Medicine', *Geopolitics*, vol.14, no.1, pp.47–78.

Sanyal, B.C. and H.-S. Yu (1989) *Technological Development in the Microelectronics Industry and its Implications for Educational Planning in the Republic of Korea*, Paris: International Institute for Educational Planning.

Saul, J.S. (2001) 'Cry for the Beloved Country: The Post-Apartheid Denouement', *Review of African Political Economy*, vol.28, no.89, pp.429–60.

Schneider, B. (1998) 'Elusive Synergy: Business–Government Relations and Development', *Comparative Politics*, vol.31, no.1, pp.101–22.

Schorr, M. (2006) 'Cambios en la Estructura y el Funcionamiento de la Industria Argentina entre 1976 y 2004: Análisis Socio Histórico y de Economía Política de la Evolución de las Distintas Clases Sociales y Fracciones de Clase durante un Período de Profundos Cambios Estrucural', FLACSO, Buenos Aires.

Schvarzer, J. (1994) 'La Reforma Económica en la Argentina: ¿qué Fuerzas Sociales y para que Objetivos?', *Revista de Economía Política*, vol.14, no.4, pp.76–96.

—— (2001) 'Economía Argentina: Situación y Perspectivas', *La Gaceta de Económicas*, 24 June.

Scitovsky, T. (1954) 'Two Concepts of External Economies', *Journal of Political Economy*, vol.62, no.2, pp.143–57.

Shafaeddin, S. (2005) 'Towards an Alternative Perspective on Trade and Industrial Policies', *Development and Change*, vol.36, no.6, pp.1143–62.

Shapiro, H. (1994) *Engines of Growth: The State and Transantional Auto Companies in Brazil*, Cambridge: Cambridge University Press.

Shin, J.-S. (1996) *The Economics of the Latecomers: Catching-up, Technology Transfer and Institutions in Germany, Japan and South Korea*, London: Routledge.

Silva, E. (1996) *The State and Capital in Chile: Business Elites, Technocrats and Market Economics*, Boulder, CO: Westview Press.

Sindzingre, A. (2007) 'Financing the Developmental State: Tax and Revenue Issues', *Development Policy Review*, vol.25, no.5, pp.615–32.

Skocpol, T. (1985) 'Bringing the State Back In: Strategies of Analysis in Current Research', in Evans, Rueschemeyer and Skocpol (1985).

Sloboda, J. (1981) 'The Structure of Metropolitan-Centered Migration in Korea, 1960–1975', Working Paper no.8102, Centre for International Development, Korea Development Institute, Seoul.

Smith, A. (1986) *The Wealth of Nations*, London: Penguin Books.

Soehoed, A.R. (1988) 'Reflection on Industrialization and Industrial Policy in Indonesia', *Bulletin of Indonesian Economic Studies*, vol.24, no.2, pp.43–5.

Soh, C. (1997) *From Investment to Innovation? The Korean Political Economy and Changes in Industrial Competitiveness*, Seoul: Global Research Institute, Korea University.

SACP (South African Communist Party) (2008) 'The SACP and State Power: The Alliance Post Polokwane – Ready to Govern?', *Bua Komanisi: Information Bulletin of the Central Committee of the South African Communist Party*, vol.7, no.1, available at http://www.sacp.org.za/main.php?ID=2963.

Southall, R. (2006) 'Introduction: Can South Africa be a Developmental State?', in S. Buhlunga et al. (eds) (2006) *State of the Nation: South Africa 2005–2006*, Cape Town: HSRC Press.

Sridharan, E. (1996) *The Political Economy of Industrial Promotion*, London: Praeger.

Stavis, B. (1982) 'Rural Local Governance and Agricultural Development in Taiwan', in N.T. Uphoff (ed.) *Rural Development and Local Organisation in Asia*, Delhi: Macmillan.

Stern, J.J. et al. (1995) *Industrialization and the State: The Korean Heavy and Chemical Industry Drive*, Cambridge, MA: Harvard Institute for International Development.

Stockhammer, E. (2000) 'Financialization and the Slowdown of Accumulation', Vienna University of Economics and Business Administration Working Paper no.14.

Stout, D. (1979) 'De-Industrialisation and Industrial Policy', in F. Blackaby (ed.) *De-Industrialisation*, London: Heinemann Educational Books.

Stubbs, R. (2009) 'Whatever Happened to the East Asian Developmental State? The Unfolding Debate', *Pacific Review*, vol.22, no.1, pp.1–22.

Sturgeon, T., J. van Biesebroeck and G. Gereffi (2008) 'Value Chains, Networked Clusters: Reframing the Global Automotive Industry', Working Paper no.08-02, Institute for Technology, Enterprise and Competitiveness, Doshisha University, Kyoto, available at http://web.mit.edu/ipc/publications/pdf/08-002.pdf.

Suarez-Villa, L., and P.-H. Han (1990) 'The Rise of Korea's Electronics Industry: Technological Changes, Growth and Territorial Distribution', *Economic Geography*, vol.66, no.3, pp.273–92.

Subramanian, C.R. (1992) *India and the Computer: A Study of Planned Development*, New Delhi: Oxford University Press.

Suzuki, T. (2003) '21 seiki ni muketeno Tekkōgyō' (The Steel Industry towards the Twenty-First Century) (in Japanese), in Gendai Keizai Kenkyū Kai (ed.) *Nihonsangyō no Saikouchiku Senryaku (Rebuilding Strategy of the Japanese Industry)*, Tokyo: Eideru Kenkyū Sho.

Taniura, T. (ed.) (1999) *Kankoku Keizai: Kōzōkaikaku no Shomondai (The South Korean Economy: Problems with Structural Reform)*, Chiba: Institute of Developing Economies.

—— (ed.) (2000) *21 Seiki no Kankoku Keizai: Kadai to Tenbō (The South Korean Economy in the Twenty-First Century: Problems and Prospects)*, Chiba: Institute of Developing Economies.

Teal, F. (1983) 'The Supply of Agricultural Output in Nigeria, 1950–1974', *Journal of Development Studies*, vol.19, no.2, pp.191–206.

Tekkō Kaigai Sijō Chōsa Iinkai (1966) 'Tekkō Handbook: Kankoku 1966' (Iron and Steel Handbook: South Korea 1966) (in Japanese), Tokyo: Tekkō Kaigai Sijō Chōsa Iinkai.

Teranishi, J. (1997) 'Sectoral Resource Transfer, Conflict, and Macrostability in Economic Development: A Comparative Analysis', in Aoki, Kim and Okuno-Fujiwara (1997).

Thorbecke, E. (1979) 'Agricultural Development', in W. Galenson (ed.) *Economic Growth and Structural Change in Taiwan: The Postwar Experience of the Republic of China*, Ithaca, NY: Cornell University Press.

Thun, E. (2006) *Changing Lanes in China: Foreign Direct Investment, Local Governments, and Auto Sector Development*, Cambridge: Cambridge University Press.

Thurbon, E. and L. Weiss (2006) 'Investing in Openness: The Evolution of FDI Strategy in South Korea and Taiwan', *New Political Economy*, vol.11, no.1, pp.1–22.

Tregenna, F. (2008) 'The Contributions of Manufacturing and Services to Employment Creation and Growth in South Africa', *South African Journal of Economics*, vol.76, no.S2, pp.S175–S204.

Tsūshō Sangyō Shō (ed.) (1987) 'Sin Sedai no Tekkōgyō ni Mukete' (Towards the New Generation of the Steel Industry) (in Japanese), Tokyo: Tūsan Siryō Chōsa Kai.

Udeh, C. (1989) 'Rural Development in Nigeria', *Habitat International*, vol.13, no.3, pp.95–100.

UNCTAD (United Nations Conference on Trade and Development) (2002) 'World Investment Report 2002: Transnational Corporations and Export Competitiveness', United Nations, New York.

—— (2006) 'World Investment Report. FDI from Developing and Transition Economies: Implications for Development', United Nations, New York and Geneva.

—— (2009) 'World Investment Report: Transnational Corporations, Agricultural Production and Development', United Nations, New York.

United States National Science Foundation (2007) 'Asia's Rising Science and Technology Strength: Comparative Indicators for Asia, the European Union, and the United States', Special Report| NSF 07-319, available at http://www.nsf.gov/statistics/nsf07319/content.cfm?pub_id=1874&id=4.

—— (2010a) 'National Patterns of R&D Resources: 2007 Data Update', available at http://www.nsf.gov/statistics/nsf08318/.

—— (2010b) 'Science and Engineering Indicators', available at http://www.nsf.gov/statistics/seind10/c0/c0s9.htm.

Uphoff, N. (1999) 'Rural Development Strategy for Indonesian Recovery: Reconciling Contradictions and Tensions', paper presented at the International Seminar on Agricultural Sector During the Turbulence of Economic Crisis, Center for Agro-Socioeconomic Research, Bogor (17–18 February 1999).

Utting, P., S. Razavi and R. Buchholz (eds) (2012) *Global Crisis and Transformative Social Change*, London: Routledge.

Vernon, R. (1966) 'International Investment and International Trade in the Product Cycle', *Quarterly Journal of Economics*, vol.80, no.2, pp.190–207.

Vittal, N. and S. Mahalingham (2001) *Information Technology in the New Millennium: The Indian Vision*, New Delhi: Manas Publishing.

Vogel, S. (1996) *Freer Markets, More Rules: Regulatory Reform in Advanced Industrial Countries*, London: Cornell University Press.

Wade, R. (1988) 'The Role of Government in Overcoming Market Failure: Taiwan, Republic of Korea and Japan', in H. Hughes (ed.) *Achieving Industrialisation in East Asia*, Cambridge: Cambridge University Press.

—— (1990) *Governing the Market: Economic Theory and the Role of Government in Taiwan's Industrialization*, Princeton, NJ: Princeton University Press.

—— (1996) 'Japan, the World Bank, and the Art of Paradigm Maintenance: The East Asian Miracle in Political Perspective', *New Left Review*, no.217, pp.3–37.

—— (1998) 'From "Miracle" to "Cronyism": Explaining the Great Asian Slump', *Cambridge Journal of Economics*, vol.22, no.6, pp.693–706.

—— (2003) 'What Strategies are Viable for Developing Countries Today? The World Trade Organization and the Shrinking of "Developmental Space"', *Review of International Political Economy*, vol.10, no.4, pp.621–44.

—— (2010) 'After the Crisis: Industrial Policy and the Developmental State in Low-Income Countries', *Global Policy*, vol.1, no.2, pp.150–61.

—— (2011) 'Why Justin Lin's Door-Opening Argument Matters for Development Economics: A Response to "Six Steps for Strategic Government Intervention"', *Global Policy*, vol.2, no.1, pp.115–16.

Waldner, D. (1999) *State Building and Late Development*, Ithaca, NY: Cornell University Press.

Weiss, L. (1998) *The Myth of the Powerless State: Governing the Economy in a Global Era*, Cambridge: Polity Press.

—— (1999) 'State Power and the Asian Crisis', *New Political Economy*, vol.4, no.3, pp.317–42.

—— (ed.) (2003a) *States in the Global Economy: Bringing Domestic Institutions Back In*, Cambridge: Cambridge University Press.

—— (2003b) 'Guiding Globalization In East Asia: New Roles for Old Developmental States', in Weiss (2003a).

—— (2008) 'Keynote Speech', Ford Foundation, Berkeley Workshop, 'Tracking the Hidden Developmental State', University of California, Berkeley (June).

—— and J.M. Hobson (1995) *States and Economic Development: A Comparative Historical Analysis*, Cambridge: Polity Press.

White, G. (1998) 'Constructing a Democratic Developmental State', in M. Robinson and G. White (eds) *The Democratic Developmental State: Politics and Institutional Design*, Oxford: Oxford University Press.

Wierzba G. and J. Golla (2005) 'La Regulacion Bancaria en Argentina durante la Década del Noventa', Centro de Economia y Finanzas para el Desarollo de Argentina, Documento no.3.

Williams, G. (1988) 'The World Bank in Northern Nigeria Revisited', *Review of African Political Economy*, vol.15, no.43, pp.42–67.

Williams, P. (1965) 'The Industrialization of Nigeria', *Proceedings of the Oklahoma Academy of Science*, vol.45, pp.215–18.

Woo-Cumings, M. (1991) *Race to the Swift: State and Finance in Korean Industrialisation*, New York: Columbia University Press.

Wood, E.M. (2003) *Empire of Capital*, London, Verso.

World Bank (1993) 'The East Asian Miracle: Economic Growth and Public Policy. A World Bank Policy Research Report', Oxford: Oxford University Press.

—— (2006) 'World Development Indicators', Washington, DC: World Bank.

—— (2008) 'World Development Indicators', Washington, DC: World Bank.

—— (2010) 'World Development Indicators', Washington, DC: World Bank.

WHO (World Health Organisation) (2008) 'The World Health Report 2008. Primary Health Care: Now More than Ever', available at http://www.who.int/whr/2008/en/index.html.

WTO (World Trade Organisation) (2008) 'World Trade Organisation Statistics', Geneva: World Trade Organisation.

—— (2009) 'International Trade Statistics 2009', available at http://www.wto.org/english/res_e/statis_e/its2009_e/its09_toc_e.htm.

Wren, C. (2001) 'The Industrial Policy of Competitiveness: A Review of Recent Developments in the UK', *Regional Studies*, vol.33, no.9, pp.847–60.

Xia, M. (2008) *The People's Congresses and Governance in China: Toward a Network Mode of Governance*, London: Routledge.

Yazid, M. (2007) *Hegemonic Powers, Radical Politics and Developmental State: The Case of Indonesia–Malaysia Political Relations during the Cold War*, Kota Kinabalu: Penerbit Universiti Malaysia Sabah.

Yeung, H. (2009) 'Regional Development and the Competitive Dynamics of Global Production Networks: An East Asian Perspective', *Regional Studies*, vol.43, no.3, pp.325–51.

Yonekura, S. (1994) *The Japanese Iron and Steel Industry, 1850–1990: Continuity and Discontinuity*, New York: St. Martin's Press.

Yoon, C.-H. (1992) 'International Competition and Market Penetration: A Model of the Growth Strategy of the Korean Semiconductor Industry', in G.K. Helleiner (ed.) *Trade Policy, Industrialization and Development: New Perspectives*, Oxford: Clarendon Press.

Young, A. (1994) 'Lessons from the East Asian NICs: A Contrarian Review', *European Economic Review*, vol.38, nos 3–4, pp.964–73.

—— (1995) 'The Tyranny of Numbers: Confronting the Statistical Realities of the East Asian Growth Experience', *Quarterly Journal of Economics*, vol.110, no.3, pp.641–80.

Young, C. (2004) 'The End of the Post-Colonial State in Africa? Reflections on Changing African Political Dynamics', *African Affairs*, vol.103, pp.23–49.

Zebregs, H. (2004) *Intraregional Trade in Emerging Asia*, Washington, DC: IMF.

Zhu, A. and D. Kotz (2011) 'The Dependence of China's Economic Growth on Exports and Investment', *Review of Radical Political Economics*, vol.43, no.1, pp.9–32.

Zysman, J. and L. Tyson (eds) (1983) *American Industry in International Competition: Government Policies and Corporate Strategies*, Ithaca, NY: Cornell University Press.

Contributors

Humam Al-Jazaeri is a lecturer in economics and development at the Faculty of Economics, University of Damascus. He is working on public and development issues, especially in the context of emerging markets and economies in transition.

Sam Ashman is a post-doctoral research fellow at the University of Johannesburg and a visiting senior researcher at the Corporate Strategy and Industrial Development Research Programme in the School of Economics and Business Sciences at the University of the Witwatersrand, South Africa.

Dae-oup Chang is a senior lecturer in development studies at the School of Oriental and African Studies, University of London. His research interests include labour relations and social–labour movements in East Asia, the political economy of East Asian development, and critiques of the developmental state and Asian TNCs. He is currently investigating East Asia's place in global capitalist development.

Ben Fine is professor of economics at the School of Oriental and African Studies, University of London and senior research fellow attached to the South African Research Chair in Social Change, University of Johannesburg.

Eka Ikpe works with the African Leadership Centre, King's College London, where she teaches on its postgraduate degree programmes and heads the postgraduate fellowships programme. She has researched and published on a range of subjects in the fields of development economics and security and development, most recently as co-editor of *Women, Peace and Security: Translating Policy into Practice*, published in 2011 by Routledge.

Kwon-Hyung Lee is a research fellow for the Korea Institute for International Economic Policy. He is working on industrial policy and industrialisation in developing countries. His recent publications are on policy recommendations for promotion of the biotechnology industry in Incheon.

Susan Newman is lecturer in international and macroeconomics at the International Institute of Social Studies, Erasmus University of Rotterdam. Her main research interests include the political economy of post-apartheid industrial development in South Africa.

Iain Pirie is an associate professor at the University of Warwick. He is currently working on the rise of commercialised binge eating and its effects on mental health and developing a critique of heterodox capitalist development economics. He has published on the Korean state and the political economy of academic publications.

Jyoti Saraswati teaches on the Business and Political Economy Program at the Stern School of Business, New York University. He is the author of *Dot.compradors: Power and Policy in the Development of the Indian Software Industry*, published in 2012 by Pluto Press.

Hajime Sato is an associate senior research fellow at the Institute of Developing Economies (IDE-JETRO), Japan. His research interests include industrial development in Asian countries.

Daniela Tavasci is a lecturer and M.Sc. director at the School of Economics and Finance, Queen Mary, University of London. She is the co-editor of *Minsky, Crisis and Development*, published in 2010 by Palgrave.

Index

Compiled by Sue Carlton

Page numbers followed by 'n' refer to end of chapter notes

Abby, D. 44
Abdu, M.S. 203
Africa 13, 23, 187
  see also Nigeria; South Africa
Afrikaner Economic Movement 252
agriculture
  role in structural transformation 14, 187–215
  taxation of 189, 190, 192, 203–4, 211, 213n
Ahearne, A. 19–20, 32n
Aiyede, E. 23
Alfonsín, Raúl 222
Alpha microprocessor 137–8, 145n
American depositary receipts (ADRs) 237
Amsden, Alice 4–5, 6, 88, 135, 151, 152, 154
ANC (African National Congress) 248, 262–4, 267n
Anderson, K. 191
Andrae, G. 208, 209
Anglo American Corporation (AAC) 251, 253, 254, 266n
Anglovaal 252, 253, 254, 266n
Aoki, M. 39
apartheid 246, 248, 254
  end of 24, 248, 256, 263
Argentina 216–44
  automotive sector 228–9, 230
  centralisation of capital 220, 221, 230–5, 241
  conglomerates
    accumulation strategies 219, 220–1, 236
    diversification 235–6
    internationalisation 220, 235–41
    investment strategies 235–7
    mergers and acquisitions (M&As) 232–5, 239–40, 241
  debt crisis (2001) 25, 216–17, 220, 242
  evolution of political economy in 1990s 220–41
  external debt problem
    attempts to solve 221–3
    see also Brady Plan
    and internationalisation of conglomerates 235, 241, 242
    literature on evolution of 216, 217–20
  financialisation 216, 219, 221, 235, 242
    relation between finance and real capital 234–5, 236, 242
  foreign direct investment 218, 219, 223–4, 237
  hyperinflation 222, 223, 233
  oil and steel sectors 222, 224, 226–8, 237, 239
  privatisation and liberalisation 216, 220–33
  resistance to 222–3
  role of state 216, 219, 220–1, 241
  and state autonomy 217–19
  telecommunications sector 225–6, 227, 233, 234, 239, 240
  transformation of credit system 230–2, 241
Asian financial crises (1997/8) 7, 9, 10, 21, 61, 108, 149
  and South Korean car industry 70–1, 74
  and South Korean steel industry 33, 51, 54, 55

Baker, D.C. 208
Balassa, B. 57n
Barbara, J. 23, 30n
Basel Accords 222, 230, 231, 243n

basic oxygen furnaces (BOFs) 37–8, 44, 52–3, 55, 58n
Bautista, R.M. 213n
Beckman, B. 208, 209
Bevan, D. 208
Bhabha Report 173, 174, 176
BIMAS programme 197
black economic empowerment (BEE) 260
Boestel, J. 190, 191, 212n
Bond, P. 264
Booth, A. 197
Bowen, J. 21
Brady, Nicholas 223
Brady Plan 223, 225, 234, 243–4n
Brazil 239
Brown, C. 124
Byres, T. 189

capital, centralisation of 57n, 244n
　Argentina 220, 221, 230–5, 241
　Japan 41
capital relations 91, 97
　national and global 245, 249
　politicised 100, 101, 102–3, 105, 107
capitalism 27, 34, 90, 146, 155–63, 165
　global 25, 26, 27, 245, 246, 248–9
　and reform 166–7
　state monopoly 91, 93
capital–labour class relations 90–3, 94, 95
capital–labour relations 56, 86, 88, 89, 98, 103, 108
car industry 62, 143n, 166
　barriers to new entrants 159–60
　see also Argentina, automotive sector; South Korea, car industry
Carney, R. 17
central processing unit (CPU) 114
chaebol system see South Korea, chaebol system
Chalfin, B. 22
Chandler, A.D. 22, 114
Chang, H.-J. 11, 117, 136, 141n, 142n, 166
　developmental state and authoritarianism 95, 109n

and industrial policy 36, 50, 53, 57n, 136, 144n
and post-Washington Consensus 8
chemicals industry
　barriers to new entrants 161–2
　South Africa 251, 253
　see also heavy and chemical industry (HCI)
Chiang Kai-shek 89
Chick, V. 235
China 15, 16–21, 28, 162–3
China Steel 49
Cho, H.Y. 102
Chu, W.-W. 151, 154
Chu, Y. 22
civil society 5, 11, 88, 107
class 85, 89–90
　classes as social groups 90–1, 92, 93
class relations see capital–labour class relations
code division multiple access (CDMA) 124, 129, 144n, 145n
Cold War 87–8, 95–6, 101, 169
Collier, P. 208
communism 100
Compaq 137–8, 145n
complete knock-down kits (CKDs) 180
computer industry see Indian IT industry; South Korea, microelectronics industry
Congress of South African Trade Unions (COSATU) 267n
Cornwall, A. 1
Cuba, as model for health-care 166

Daewoo 70–1, 74, 79–80, 128
Davies, Rob 264, 265
D'Costa, A.P. 38, 40, 42, 45, 58n
Desai, A. 264
development
　and marginalisation of labour 94–7
　reliance on foreign direct investment 16, 17
　restricted by global governance structures 156–8
　role of agriculture 14, 187–215
　see also industrial development
developmental state
　definitions of 147, 148–52, 167
　Japanese model 38–42

developmental state *continued*
  labour history of 97–107
  omitted from development discourse 1, 8, 29
  origin of term 110
  South Korean model 9, 42–4
  viability under globalisation 146–7, 148, 155, 156
developmental state paradigm (DSP)
  alternative approaches 23–7, 57, 163–7
    see also systems of accumulation
  buzzword character of 3, 20–3, 29, 264
  dilution of 3, 29
  'flying geese' strategy 14–16, 28, 77
  focus on East Asian NICs 6–7, 13, 169, 185n
  and interests of progressive movements 26
  and Japanese steel industry 45
  limitation/self-limitation 10–14, 29, 187–8
  marginalisation of 1, 3, 29
  one-dimensional approach to state–society relations 85, 86–90
  role of state 7, 86–7, 187, 188
  two schools 3–9
    see also economic school; political school
  universal applicability of 3, 23
  see also enhanced developmental state paradigm (EDSP)
developmental welfare state 21, 30n
developmentalism 5, 6, 12, 25, 85, 94, 95, 97, 263
division of labour 3, 8, 15, 44, 49, 96, 105
DRAM (dynamic random-access memory) market 112, 119–22, 123, 129, 134, 136, 140n, 142–4n

Eade, D. 1
East Asian NICs
  and communism 100
  developmental success of 2, 3, 6–7, 13, 14, 61, 96–7, 169
  and globalisation 147–8, 149–50
  labour history 97–107
  response to crisis 21
  role of labour 94, 95

Economic Processing Zones (EPZs) 183
economic school 4–6, 9, 10, 12, 24, 31n, 36–7, 38, 59n, 148
Edigheji, O. 264
Eicher, C.K. 208
Eimer, T. 23
El-Said, M. 213n
electric arc furnace (EAF) sector 40–1, 42, 43, 44, 48–9, 50, 52–4, 55, 59n
  EAF process 58n
Electronics Corporation of India Limited (ECIL) 174–6, 177, 178, 179–80
enhanced developmental state paradigm (EDSP) 188–9, 210–12
  and Indonesian experience 196–8
  and Japanese experience 188, 189, 190–2
  principal component of 188, 189–95, 196, 198, 211
  secondary component 188–9, 196–8, 210
  and South Korean experience 188, 189, 194–5
  and Taiwanese experience 192–4
Entel 225–6, 234
Ernst, D. 132, 134
Evans, P. 87, 91, 92, 242n

financial valorisation 219, 243n
financialisation 216, 219, 221, 235, 236, 243n
Fine, B. 37, 148, 164, 244n, 245, 256, 266n
fiscal transfers 196, 197, 198–9, 201, 210, 211, 214n
FLACSO (Facultad Latino Americana de Ciencias Sociales) 217, 219, 235, 236
Fordism 246
foreign direct investment (FDI) 16–17, 26, 35, 49, 140n, 157
  Argentina 223, 237
  maximising benefits from 155, 164
  South Africa 261
  South Korea 74, 75, 115–18, 150, 152
  Taiwan 152–3
Francks, P. 190, 191, 212n

Frederick, W.H. 197
Fritz, V. 21

Gandhi, Indira 173–4, 177–8, 182, 186n
Gandhi, Rajiv 182, 186n
Gelb, S. 246
General Motors (GM) 71, 74, 75–6, 78, 80, 83n
Glassburner, B. 197
global crisis (2007) 2, 27–8, 61, 256
global governance structures 156, 157, 166
globalisation 9, 26–7, 146–68
Gomez, E. 22
Gopinathan, S. 21
Gordhan, Pravin 264, 265
Gordon, A. 100
Grant, W. 63
Green, A. 21
Growth, Employment and Redistribution (GEAR) 248, 250, 261, 262, 263
Gunning, J. 208

Haan, L. de 23, 30n
Haltmaier, J. 18–19, 20
Hanbo Iron and Steel 53, 54, 60n
Harrison, S.S. 118
Hart, G.P. 197
Hasegawa, H. 58n
Hayami, Y. 193
Hayashi, S. 26–7
health care 165, 166
heavy and chemical industry (HCI) 43, 82n, 83n, 117, 144n
see also chemicals industry
Heintz, J. 247
Hikino, T. 135
Hill, P. 203
Hirschman, A.O. 35, 82n, 244n
Ho, S.P.S 193
Hobday, M. 154
Hobson, J.M. 88
Human Sciences Research Council (HSRC) 263–4, 267n
Hynix 121, 122, 129
Hyundai Group
car industry 54, 55, 71, 74, 75–6, 79, 81
semiconductor industry 118, 121, 142n
and steel industry 43–4, 52–3, 54, 55, 59n, 60n
trade union 84n

IBM 120, 174–5, 177
in India 177, 185–6n
System 360 113, 114, 140n
imperialism 90, 97, 102, 156–7, 168n
import substitution industrialisation (ISI) 6, 42–3, 61, 105, 192, 219
Indian IT industry 22, 169–86
imports 173, 175, 176, 179–80
local software capital and foreign capital 172, 175–6
Minicomputer Policy 172, 178, 179, 180, 181
restructuring 176–7, 179–81, 183–5
software exports 181–5
software industry 171, 175–7, 180–1
and state intervention 169–70, 174–6, 178–9, 183–5
system of accumulation 172, 176–7, 179–81, 184–5
and US embargo 173
and vested interests 173–4, 177–8, 181–3
Indonesia 188, 189, 196–8, 210
industrial development
and balanced growth 63, 82n
barriers to entry in key sectors 147, 157, 158–61, 165–6, 167
barriers to upgrading in key sectors 162–3
constraints 189, 190
demand constraints 190, 192, 194–5, 196, 208, 211
labour constraints 191, 193, 195, 210, 211
marketed surplus constraints 189, 191, 192, 194, 196, 198, 206, 211
savings constraints 14, 189, 190, 192, 194, 196, 198, 204, 211
latecomer catch-up 13–16, 110–11, 139–40
and dependence on foreign technologies 128–36

and initial conditions 117
and labour exploitation 94
role of state 22, 29, 33, 37
and linkages between oil and agriculture 189, 196–8
Industrial Development Corporation (IDC) (South Africa) 253
industrial life cycle 64, 76, 77, 78
industrial policy 3, 8, 14, 15, 21, 27, 31n, 36–7, 61–3
  and economic forces 63, 64–9, 81
  and economic interests 66–9, 170–1, 172
  effect on industrial performance 63–4, 67–9, 81
  erosion of 64, 76–81
  Japan 7, 20, 39, 50
  and Japanese and South Korean steel industries 33–7, 38, 41, 42, 51, 53, 57n
  legislation 47, 48, 49, 55, 59n, 77
  liberalisation 45
  and outcomes 171–2
  public and private interests 65, 66
  and social development 165–7
  see also state intervention; steel industry (Japan and South Korea), role of state
Industrial Policy Action Plans (IPAPs) (South Africa) 264
'industry ageing' hypothesis 64, 76, 77
INMAS programme 197
Innace, J.J. 44
Innes, D. 251
Intel 114, 123–4, 125, 126, 127, 138
inter-sectoral resource transfers
  between agriculture and industry 188, 189–90, 191, 193, 195, 212n, 213n
  between oil and agriculture 196, 197, 198–9, 201, 210
International Monetary Fund (IMF) 6, 28, 54
International Packet Switched Service (IPSS) (India) 183
Ishikawa, S. 190
Itami, H. 45–6

Janata Party (India) 178

Japan
  agriculture and structural transformation 190–2
  and communism 99, 100
  economic growth 96
  industrial policy 7, 20, 39, 50
  investment in South Korean microelectronics industry 116, 118
  investment strategy in Asia–Pacific Rim 15
  labour history of developmental state 97–104
  Ministry of International Trade and Industry (MITI) 6, 39, 41, 47, 48, 76, 110
  as model of developmental state 38–42
  semiconductor industry 112–14, 131–2
  steel industry 33–57, 57–60n
    cooperation with foreign firms 49
    integrated firms 38, 40–2, 45–50, 55, 58n, 59n, 60n
    and new technologies 45
    rapid development of 37–42
    restructuring 45–51
    role of government 38–9, 41–2, 44, 45, 46–51, 56
    role of US 40
    stagnation 44
  and trade unions 98, 99
Japanese Communist Party 99
Jenkins, R. 62, 77
Jha, P.S. 174
Johnson, Chalmers 6, 39, 58n, 88, 95, 99, 101, 110
J.P. Morgan 220, 225, 234

Kalinowski, T. 151
Kang, B.-S. 194–5
Karshenas, M. 189–90, 193, 213n
Keynesianism 17, 27, 466
Kia 69, 70, 71, 74, 79–80
Kikuchi, M. 193
Kim, H.C. 190, 191, 212n
Korean War (1950) 40, 96
Krugman, Paul 30n, 135
Kuomintang (KMT) 101, 103–7
Kuriyan, R. 22

Kwangyang 44
Kwon, H.-J. 22–3

labour
  in development discourse 85–6
  labour history of developmental state 97–107
  marginalisation of 94–7
labour markets, deregulation of 50, 54
labour movement 30n, 32n, 79, 84n, 88, 98, 102, 106–7
Lall, S 134
Langlois, R.N. 114
Latin America 23, 30n, 83n, 218, 223
  import substitution industrialisation 6, 61
  privatisation 237, 239
Lazonick, W. 21
Lee, Y. 21
Leftwich, A. 88
Lewis, W.A. 194, 212n
Lin, J. 28–9, 32n
Linden, G. 124
List, Friedrich 6
Long-Term Promotion Plan for the Motor Industry (South Korea) 62
Lütz, S. 23

McKinnon, R. 20
Maharaj, B. 264
Manuel, Trevor 264
Manufacturers' Association of Information Technology (MAIT) (India) 181–2
Marshall, R. 203
Marx, K. 57n, 108n
Mbeki, Thabo 262, 263
Meiji government 97, 99, 109n
Menocal, A. 21
mergers and acquisitions (M&As) 46, 48, 50, 57n, 232
Merton, R.K. 249
Mexico crisis (1994) 230, 231
microchips 112, 113–14, 142n, 143n, 145n
  logic chips (microprocessors) 113, 114, 115, 137, 138–9, 140n
  memory chips 114, 115, 119–22, 140n, 142n
  production in South Korea 123, 126–7, 129–34, 137–8
microelectronics industry
  terms of entry for latecomers 112–15
  see also semiconductor industry; South Korea, microelectronics industry
Microsoft 114, 129, 137–8, 145n, 161
middle-range theory 245, 246, 249
mini-mill technology 52, 55, 58n
MNCs (multinational corporations) 26, 150, 155, 162, 163
  role in global economy 157–8, 161, 164, 167
Mody, A. 190
Mok, K. 21
Moon, P.-Y. 194–5
Moore, G. 113, 114
Mundle, 190
Murdock, K. 39

National Association for Software and Service Companies (NASSCOM) (India) 181–2
National Finance Corporation (NFC) (South Africa) 253
National Industrial Policy Framework (NIPF) (South Africa) 264
Nehru, Jawaharlal 173
Neo, H. 21
neoliberalism 1, 22, 25, 26, 31n, 94, 146–7, 155
  departure from 4–5
  and global crisis (2007) 2, 27, 32n
  and Indian IT industry 13, 169
  intervention and non-intervention 27–8, 46, 56
  and Japan 6, 46
  and South Africa 164, 248, 250, 262–3, 266n
  and South Korea 54, 64, 70, 151
new structural economics 28–9
Nigeria
  applying the EDSP 188–9, 198–210
  development planning 198, 200, 201, 202–3, 214n
  industrial demand and agricultural sector 208–9

investment in agricultural sector 201–2
labour outflow from agriculture 208–10
role of agriculture in development 203–7
Rural Banking Scheme 202
structural adjustment programme (SAP) 202–3, 208, 215n
Noble, G.W. 48
non-interventionism 28–9, 46, 56
Nwosu, A. 208

O'Donnell, G. 90
Ohkawa, K. 190, 191
oil sector
  resource transfer to agricultural sector 196, 197, 198–9, 201, 210
  see also fiscal transfers
Okimoto, D. 76
Okuno-Fujiwara, M. 39
open hearth furnaces (OHFs) 38, 40–1, 58n
Orange Free State Goldfields 253
original equipment manufacturing (OEM) 79, 135, 153–4, 163
own brand manufacturing (OBM) 153, 154, 163
own design manufacturing (ODM) 153–4, 163
Oyejide, T.A. 208

Park Chung-hee 88–9, 195, 207
Park, H. 21
Patel, Ebrahim 264, 265
Pérez Companc 220, 222, 224, 226–8, 234, 236, 239, 240
Peronist Party 219, 243n
Pinto, B. 197
Plaza Accord (1985) 47, 48, 51, 141n
political school 2, 4–6, 9, 11, 12–13, 23, 24, 25, 36–7, 39, 59n, 148, 149
Polokwane ANC conference (2007) 263
POSCO (steel-making company) 38, 42, 43–4, 47, 49, 51–3, 54–6, 59n
  and monopoly 52, 53, 54, 55
Poulantzas, N. 91

Poverty Reduction Strategy Paper (PRSPs) 8
Prestowitz, V.C. 118
product cycle theory 76–7
protectionism 6, 12, 26–7, 81, 152, 153, 207
  agricultural sector 189, 191, 207
  India IT industry 174, 182
  infant-industry protection 36
  Japanese steel industry 38
  South Africa 252
public–private partnerships 22, 87

Qualcomm 123, 124, 126, 129, 143n, 145n

Raj, K. 190
Randall, V. 21
Ray, I. 22
recession cartel 48, 57n
Reconstruction and Development Programme (RDP) (South Africa) 262
Repelita development plans (Indonesia) 197
resource allocation 34, 189
resource-curse thesis 14
Rhee Syng-man 103
Robinson, S. 213n
Rosovsky, H. 190
Rueschemeyer, D. 91, 92
Rustomjee, Z. 245, 250, 256, 266n

Saenara 72
Samsung
  car industry 70–1, 74, 83n
  dependence on foreign suppliers of core components 128–9
  semiconductor industry 111, 118, 119–29, 134, 136, 142–3n
  Alpha microprocessor 137–8
  profitability 123–7
  R&D 121, 123, 124–6, 143n, 161
Sanpad conference (2007) 263
Sasol 253, 254
Saul, J.S. 262
Schnabl, G. 20
self-interest 66

self-sufficiency 147, 152, 173, 174, 176, 191
semiconductor industry
  barriers to new entrants 160–1
  fabless (design only) firms 113, 114–15, 123, 124
  Japan 112–14, 131–2
  latecomers
    dependence on foreign components and designs 129–34.36
    profitability gap with leaders 123–7
    terms of entry 112–18, 132
  role in South Korean electronics industry 118–22
  and USA 131–2
  see also microchips; Samsung, semiconductor industry; South Korea, microelectronics industry
Shin, J.-S. 38, 39
Shinjin 74–5, 83n
Shinohara, A. 191
simple knock-down kits (SKDs) 180
Sindzingre, A. 21
Sino-Indian conflict (1962) 173
Skocpol, T. 91–2
Sloboda, J. 195
Smith, Adam 66
social capital 1–2, 22
Software Export Scheme (India) 176, 180
Software Technology Parks (STPs) (India) 183
Soldati 220, 234, 239
Somisa 226–8, 235
Sondhi, M.L. 178
South Africa 23–4, 245–67
  Afrikaner capital 251–4, 266n
  apartheid 24, 246, 248, 249, 254, 261, 262
  as developmental state 247–8, 254
  disjuncture between economic and political power 251–4
  expansion of services sector 258
  financialisation 261
  minerals–energy complex (MEC) 24, 245, 246, 247, 249–50
    continued centrality of 255–60
    contribution to GDP 256–7
    core sectors 255–6
    employment 258, 259
    history of 250–5
    share of capital stock 258–60
    survival over post-apartheid period 260–1
  and neoliberalism 164, 248, 250, 262–3, 266n
  and New Growth Path (NGP) 264–5
  repressive labour system 251–2
  shift in developmental state debate 262–3, 264–6
  'six axes' of private capital 253–4, 266n
  systems of accumulation 247, 249
  Tripartite Alliance 262, 264, 267n
South African Communist Party (SACP) 262–3, 264
South Korea 22
  agriculture and structural transformation 194–5
  car industry 62, 64, 69–84
    assembler–supplier relations 71–4
    in decline 79–81
    economic significance of 78
    entry regulation 69–70, 71
    ignoring local component sector 71–2
    industrial relations 79, 84n
    inter-assembler competition 69–71
    local assembler–multinationals relations 74–6, 79–80
    and low foreign direct investment (FDI) 74
    and state intervention 77, 79
    subcontracting system 72–3
  chaebol system 9, 26, 82n, 115, 121
  dependence on foreign technologies 111, 128–9
  as developmental state 9, 42–4, 151–5
  economic crisis (1979–80) 51, 69, 75, 77
  and economic liberalisation 51–2, 55, 61
  and foreign financial institutions 150–1
  and IMF programme 54, 61

impact of Korean War 96
inter-chaebol competition 80, 83n
labour history of developmental state 100, 101–7
microelectronics industry 110–39
  dependence on foreign equipment 129–34, 136
  foreign investment 115–18
  R&D expenditure 136–7
  role of semiconductor chips 118–22
  state intervention 121
  see also Samsung, semiconductor industry
role of government in development 111, 117–18, 121, 134–7, 141–2n, 150–1
state's management of FDI 150, 151
steel industry 33–8, 42–4, 51–6, 57–60n
  in crisis (1997) 53–4
  and East Asian crisis 44–5
  privatisation 54–5
  rapid development of 38, 42–4
  restructuring 51–6
  role of government 42–4, 52–6, 59n
telecommunications sector 151
see also Hyundai; Samsung Group
state
  authoritarian state 90, 95
  and autonomy 91–2, 93–4, 216, 217–19, 242n
  and capital 31, 89, 92, 97, 98, 107, 249
  and market 5, 8, 24–5, 34, 37
  mystification of 93–4
state intervention 6–7, 13, 21–2, 30n, 64–5, 76–8, 82
  identifying appropriate levels of 34, 37, 76
  Indian IT industry 169–70, 174–6, 178–9, 183–5
  and liberalisation 45
  market conforming 28, 39
  steel industry 36, 56, 57n, 59n
  see also industrial policy; protectionism
state–society relations, one dimensional approach to 85, 86–90

steel industry (Japan and South Korea) 33–57
  and developmental state paradigm (DSP) 33–4, 35–7
  linkages with other industries 35
  rapid development of 37–8
  role of state 35–7, 38–9, 41–5, 52–6
  see also Japan, steel industry; South Korea, steel industry
Stiglitz, Joe 7, 8, 28, 29
structural transformation 170
  of Indian IT industry 171–2
  and linkages between oil and agriculture 189, 196–8
  role of agriculture 14, 187–215
systems of accumulation 26, 172, 176–7, 179–81, 183–5, 245–67

Taisho democracy (Japan) 99, 109n
Taiwan 86, 96–7, 178, 181
  agriculture and structural transformation 192–4, 195, 213n
  automobile sector 62
  as developmental state 151–5, 188, 189
  and FDI 152–5
  labour history of developmental state 101, 103–7
  land reform 103, 192–3
  OEM/ODM sector 153–4, 163
  policy towards foreign firms 153
  and semiconductor industry 131, 140n, 160, 163
Techint 220, 222, 224, 226–8, 234, 235, 237–8, 239–40
Tee, Y. 21
Texas Instruments (TI) 114, 122, 124, 126, 140, 182
Thorbecke, E. 194
Tokugawa system 97
Toyota 74–5, 83n
transformismo 219, 235, 242–3n

Udeh, C. 209
United Kingdom (UK) 147, 148–9, 165
United States (US)
  aid to East Asian NICs 96
  developmental aspects of 147, 149
  finance for Taiwan agriculture 194

United States (US) *continued*
  investment in South Korean microelectronics industry 116–17, 118
  National Science Foundation 162
  R&D spending 158
  and semiconductor industry 131–2
Universal Suffrage League (Japan) 99
Uphoff, N. 213n

very-large-scale integration (VLSI) chips 118
Vietnam 30n, 56

Wade, R. 6, 29, 152, 153, 154, 156, 168n, 178
Washington Consensus 3, 7, 8, 28, 29, 169
  and China 17
  and neoliberalism 6, 15
  and Nigeria 202
  post-Washington Consensus 1, 7, 8, 10, 24, 28, 30, 32
  and privatisation in Argentina 223
  and South Africa 24, 248

Weiss, L. 88, 147, 148–51
welfare 8, 17, 20, 21, 30n, 94, 100
Williams, P. 208
Worden, R.L. 197
World Bank
  and developmental state approach 1, 2, 3, 20–1
  and South Korea 43, 133
  and state intervention 6, 7, 28
  and Washington and post-Washington Consensus 7–8, 10
World Health Organisation (WHO) 166
World Trade Organisation (WTO) 156, 157, 158, 160, 166

Yacimientos Petrolíferos Fiscales (YPF) 222, 226
Yeung, H. 22
Yi, I. 22–3
Yonekura, S. 46, 58n

zaibatsus 98, 99, 100
Zuma, Jacob 263, 264